World Christianity and Public Religion Series, Vol. 3

Series Editor: Raimundo C. Barreto

World Christianity, Urbanization, and Identity

World Christianity and Public Religion Series, Vol. 3

Series Editor: Raimundo C. Barreto

World Christianity, Urbanization, and Identity

Moses O. Biney
Kenneth N. Ngwa
Raimundo C. Barreto

FORTRESS PRESS
MINNEAPOLIS

WORLD CHRISTIANITY, URBANIZATION, AND IDENTITY

Copyright © 2021 Fortress Press, an imprint of 1517 Media. All rights reserved. Except for brief quotations in critical articles or reviews, no part of this book may be reproduced in any manner without prior written permission from the publisher. Email copyright@1517.media or write to Permissions, Fortress Press, PO Box 1209, Minneapolis, MN 55440-1209.

Cover image: © 2020 iStock; Favela in Rio de Janeiro by luoman

Cover design: Alisha Lofgren

Paperback ISBN: 978-1-5064-4847-3

eBook ISBN: 978-1-5064-4848-0

CONTENTS

The World Christianity and Public Religion Series   ix

Acknowledgments   xiii

Contributors   xv

World Christianity, Urbanization, and Identity: Introduction
Moses O. Biney, Kenneth N. Ngwa, and Raimundo C. Barreto   1

PART I — CONCEPTUALIZATIONS: INTERSECTING THEOLOGICAL, HISTORICAL, BIBLICAL, AND SOCIOLOGICAL PERSPECTIVES

1. *Deus Urbis* and the Right to the City
   Dale T. Irvin   15

2. Faith, Postcoloniality, and Subjectivity in Exile: Latin American Insights for Public Theology in a Globalized World
   Nicolas Panotto   43

3. Centralization of Religious Power in the City: An Essay Based on 1 Kings 1–11
   Maricel Mena-López   61

4. Configuring Christian Identities in Times of Information and Communication Technologies
   Ernesto Fiocchetto   81

PART II — CONTESTED AND NEGOTIATED IDENTITIES

5. Contested Spaces: Diola Christianity in Rural and Urban Sénégal
   Aliou Cissé Niang   101

6. Dangers and Possibilities of the City: Sexual Migration, Sexual and Gender Diversity, and the Parable of the Prodigal Son
   André S. Musskopf   123

7. Heterogeneity's Midwifery Role in Identity Transformation
   Sunder John Boopalan   143

PART III — CONFLUENCES: MIGRATION, URBANIZATION, AND INTERCULTURALITY

8. Polycentric World Christianity Comes to Winnipeg, Manitoba: The Responses of Euro-Canadian Congregations
   Peter Bush   161

9. Demands of Urbanisation and Rural Migration in India: A Call for Multicultural Leadership
   Atola Longkumer   179

10. "Ethiopianism Is Most Rampant in Cities"—African Christianity between Migration and Urban Settlement: South Africa around 1900
    Ciprian Burlacioiu   201

PART IV — CREATIVE TRANSFORMATIONS: AGENCY, CITIZENSHIP, AND PUBLIC RELIGION

11. Christianity and Urbanism: The Ecumenical Training and Advisory Center (CECA) and the Formation of the Popular Legal Agents
    Claudete Beise Ulrich and Nivia Ivette Núñez de la Paz   223

12. Between Individuality and Publicness: Christianity in Urban China since the 1980s
    Zhibin Xie   241

13. Catholicism and Modernization: *Acción Cultural Popular* and The Rise of a Centrist-Catholicism in Colombia, 1947–1962
    Sandra Londono-Ardila   257

General Conclusion
Moses O. Biney, Kenneth N. Ngwa, and Raimundo C. Barreto   281

Index   287

THE WORLD CHRISTIANITY AND PUBLIC RELIGION SERIES

During the latter half of the twentieth century, scholars began to pay closer attention to the polycentric and culturally diverse nature of Christianity worldwide. In particular, the rapid growth in the number of Christians living in the Global South caught the attention of Western scholars as a trend that would not be reversed in the near future.

A number of books have been written in the attempt to offer clues on how these drastic demographic changes affect the shape of World Christianity in the coming decades. Beyond the fascination with the exciting numbers, one might notice that the rapid Christian growth in the Global South and its diasporas have generated a new-world Christian consciousness that brings along profound cultural, social, and economic consequences, which demand further scholarly attention. World Christianity scholarship has demonstrated in the past few decades that Christianity can no longer be conceived as a Western religion. We have stepped into the threshold of a new era. New and creative theological insights have emerged, debunking any hegemonic understanding of World Christianity. Conversion to Christianity, especially in former Western colonies, can no longer be conceived as the result of the Westernization of converts. Instead, indigenous cultures and spiritualities that at some point were expected to disappear remain alive and strong. In fact, greater attention to the revitalization of indigenous traditions since the end of the twentieth century has informed new understandings of Christianity, particularly in non-Western contexts.

This series engages a number of the emerging voices from within a variety of indigenous Christianities around the world, paying attention not only to their histories and practices, but also to emerging theological articulations and their impact on the public sphere. While during the modern era the study of Christianity tended to be predominantly informed by Western perspectives and priorities, World Christianity in the beginning of the twenty-first century is better understood in the context of contextual experiences, multidirectional transnational networks, and Christian relationships with other surrounding religions. No religion is hermetically sealed. Mass migration, which has become an important mark of the current era, has increased the exchanges among different peoples and cultures, giving rise to a growing demand for studies that take intercultural communication, intercultural theologies, and interfaith dialogue more seriously. Likewise, interest in issues of hybridity, liminality, border thinking, and cultural interweaving—particularly in the context of formerly colonized cultures—has also increased.

Old problems, nevertheless, still linger. Scientific and technological advances have not reduced the existing injustices and power asymmetry around the world. Socioeconomic injustice remains as fiercely prevalent as when the first theologies of liberation emerged in the 1960s. According to Indian theologian Felix Wilfred, the demographic shift of World Christianity is not simply a shift "from the West to the South, but a shift of Christianity from the rich and middle classes to the poor." In other words, "those with below $500 dollars as annual income are the ones who will be, if not already, the most numerous Christian disciples in our world."[1]

In such a context of disparity and scarcity, standing in solidarity with the poor remains extremely important. Yet, the concern with economic justice is not enough. Christians living in contexts of poverty and injustice in different parts of the world have also been asking challenging and complex questions about the reasons for such inequality. The inhuman treatment many migrants, refugees, asylum seekers, and stateless persons receive when crossing borders, for instance, help increase awareness of the indivisibility of concerns with justice, requiring renewed moral commitments, and creative responses to what is amounting to a global human calamity. Likewise, unjust relations based on race, gender, and sexuality, along with important land-related disputes and environmental concerns are part of the public agenda Christians are called to engage in, both in the Global North and the Global South. The postcolonial rise of identity claims of previously silenced voices, contrasts with the fear of difference and a relentless economic insecurity, contributing to the revitalization of different forms of nationalist and xenophobic ideologies, which continue to poison societies across the world and increase the risk of violence against those who, for being perceived as different, are feared and discriminated against.

All these facts, combined with enlarged worldviews—that do not conceive of sharp separations between the sacred and the secular—informing particularly non-Western Christians in their relationships with the world,

---

[1] Felix Wilfred, "Christianity between Decline and Resurgence," in *Christianity in Crisis?*, ed. Jon Sobrino and Felix Wilfred. Concilium 2005/3 (London: SCM Press, 2005), 31.

make public reasoning more important than ever for World Christianity scholars. After all, Christians worldwide are key actors in what scholars commonly refer to as the public sphere. Their public living and thinking are an important source for new perspectives on the impact of religion on public life and on an array of approaches to related matters, such as concerns with citizenship, public witness, peace, justice, environmental relations, and contemporary migration, among others.

This series, which stems from a partnership between Princeton Theological Seminary and Faculdade Unida de Vitoria (Brazil), aims to provide a unique space for sustained dialogue on all those matters. It blends a number of methods and approaches in the emerging field of World Christianity, placing them in conversation with other fields of study, including diverse public theologies, postcolonial/decolonial theories, intercultural studies, migration studies, critical gender studies, critical race studies, queer theory, and globalization theories. The series intentionally brings religious scholars and theologians from diverse Christian traditions and parts of the world into conversation with one another. At its root are two schools related to the Reformed tradition, one in South America and the other in North America; one that is young (having existed for a little more than two decades) and another with a tradition spanning over two hundred years.

In the first half of the twentieth century, Princeton Seminary appointed John Mackay as president after he lived for years as a missionary in Latin America, an experience that deeply influenced him and impacted his ecumenical thinking. By turning ecumenics into a mandatory field of study for the church in the twentieth century, Mackay, in many ways, anticipated the rise of the field we know today as World Christianity.

> A new reality has come to birth. For the first time in the life of mankind the Community of Christ, the Christian Church, can be found, albeit in nuclear form, in the remotest frontiers of human habitation. This community has thereby become "ecumenical" in the primitive, geographical meaning of that term. History is thus confronted with a new fact.[2]

In turn, Faculdade Unida de Vitoria has a history marked by a commitment to the retrieval of a particular memory. Such memory is linked to theologians such as Richard Shaull and Rubem Alves. Shaull was a pioneer in encouraging young Latin American Christians such as Rubem Alves, Jovelino Ramos, João Dias de Araújo, Joaquim Beato, Beatriz Melano, and others to think theologically from their own social and cultural location, that is, as Latin Americans. Encouraging ecumenical solidarity, he contributed to the rise of Latin American liberation theology. Rubem Alves,

---

[2] John Mackay, *Ecumenics: The Science of the Church Universal* (Englewood Cliffs, NJ: Prentice-Hall, 1964), vii.

who studied under Shaull first in the Presbyterian Seminary of Campinas, Brazil, and later in Princeton, wrote the first book-length treatise on liberation theology,[3] while living in the United States. He was one of the most creative thinkers of his days, having also contributed to the rising interest in other subfields such as theopoetics.

This series is, therefore, deeply rooted in a long tradition, which continues to be renewed to respond to the challenges and circumstances of a new era. It fosters a dialogue that places priority on voices from the Global South, but which also invites participants from Europe and North America to engage with their peers from other parts of the world.

The series is published in English and Portuguese. Its bilingual nature garners an inclusionary approach. A number of texts originally produced in Portuguese (some also in Spanish), which otherwise wouldn't be available to a broader English readership, are through this series made more visible and accessible for Anglophone scholars, seminarians, and religious leaders interested in this kind of conversation. Similarly, the work of authors known in the English-speaking world who remained, nevertheless, largely unknown in Latin America are through this series made available for Latin American scholars, especially those who can read Portuguese. Above all, this series seeks to show that it is possible to advance transnational and transcultural scholarly dialogues without placing priority on one particular language as the *lingua franca*.

The series has six planned volumes. The first one, published in Brazil in 2016 and in the United States in 2017, approaches World Christianity as a form of public religion, identifying areas for possible intercultural engagement. Each of the other five volumes focuses on more specific topics of concern for a public agenda for World Christianity in the twenty-first century. Volume two, published in English in 2019 and expected to appear in Portuguese in 2020, addresses migration as an important concern in World Christianity's public discourses. Volume three discusses current approaches to urbanization and identity in World Christianity. Volume four focuses on World Christianity and interfaith relations. Volume five brings attention to pressing environmental concerns in World Christianity scholarship. Finally, volume six presents a variety of perspectives on race, ethnicity, gender, and sexuality in World Christianity research.

It is our hope that this series can become a platform for intercultural and intergenerational dialogue, creating opportunities for greater interaction between seasoned and emerging scholars from all parts of the world.

Raimundo C. Barreto

---

[3] Rubem Alves, "Towards a Theology of Liberation: An Exploration of the Encounter between the Languages of Humanistic Messianism and Messianic Humanism" (PhD diss., Princeton Theological Seminary, 1968).

ACKNOWLEDGMENTS

A work like this is the product of the efforts of many individuals. Most of all, we are grateful to each author whose work appears in the following pages and to all who in different roles made it possible for this volume to be published. As a bilingual effort, some chapters in this volume were originally written in Portuguese or Spanish and translated into English. The editors of this volume are particularly grateful to Stephen DiTrolio and Caio César da Silva Barreto for the tedious and important work of translation. Stephen also offered significant assistance proofreading the manuscript. Princeton Theological Seminary, in the person of Dean Jacqueline Lapsley, has once again provided funds for both the translation of the chapters mentioned above into English and the translation of the chapters originally written in English into Portuguese. Sun Yong Lee played a crucial role in the editing process, taking responsibility for the initial reading of all received chapters, and also preparing the index. Like in the previous volumes of this series, we have received constant support and guidance from Fortress Press and its editorial team, among whom we highlight the assistance provided by our acquiring editor, Jesudas Athyal. To all those who directly or indirectly contributed to the planning and execution of this volume, our most sincere gratitude.

Moses O. Biney
Kenneth N. Ngwa
Raimundo C. Barreto

CONTRIBUTORS

EDITORS

Moses O. Biney holds a PhD from Princeton Theological Seminary. He is Associate Professor of Religion and Society and African Diaspora Studies at New York Theological Seminary. He is also the former Research Director for the Center for the Study and Practice of Urban Religion (CSPUR) at New York Theological Seminary. He is an ordained Presbyterian Minister and currently serves as pastor of Bethel Presbyterian Reformed Church, Brooklyn, New York. Dr. Biney's research and teaching interests include the religions of Africa and the African Diaspora, religion and transnationalism, religion and culture, urban ministry, and congregational studies. He is the author of *From Africa to America: Religion and Adaptation among Ghanaian Immigrants in New York* (New York University Press, 2011) and several other essays including "Building and Expanding Communities: African Immigrant Congregations and the Challenge of Diversity (2013); "Ghanaian Presbyterians in the United America: Why Some Join American Denominations and Others Don't" (2015); "Transnational Religious Networks: From Africa to America and back to Africa" (2015); "African Christianity and Transnational Religious Networks: From Africa to America and back to Africa" (2016); Spirituality From the Margins: West African Spirituality and Aesthetics"(2019).

Kenneth N. Ngwa holds a ThM (2000) and a PhD (2005) from Princeton Theological Seminary; and a Masters of Divinity (1995) from the Faculty of Protestant Theology in Cameroon. He teaches introductory and advanced courses on the Hebrew Bible, as well as on "Africana Studies and Religion." His teaching and scholarship combines biblical exegesis, postcolonial and cultural approaches to the Hebrew Bible, with particular interest in identity construction, memory, reception theory, and narrative ethics. An ordained minister with the Presbyterian Church in Cameroon; the Director of the Religion and Global Health Forum (RGHF) at Drew Theological School, and a co-chair of the African Biblical Hermeneutics session of the Society of Biblical Literature (SBL), he is a board member of the African Renaissance Ambassador (www.araforchange. com)—a non-profit organization providing medical, financial (micro loans), and educational support to rural communities, women, and young people in Cameroon. His scholarship includes *The Hermeneutics of the 'Happy' Ending in Job 42:7-17* (2005); co-editor of Navigating African Biblical Hermeneutics: Trends and Themes from Our Pots and Our Calabashes (Newcastle, UK: Cambridge Scholars Publishing, 2018), several essays and articles, including "Did Job Suffer for Nothing? The Ethics of Piety, Presumption and the Reception of Disaster in the Prologue of Job" (2009); "The Making of Gershom's Story: A Cameroonian Postwar Hermeneutics Reading of Exodus 2," *Journal of Biblical Literature* 134/4 (2015). He is currently working on a book-long project on Exodus, titled: *Let My People Live: Towards an Africana Reading of Exodus* (Westminster John Knox Press).

Raimundo C. Barreto is associate professor of World Christianity at Princeton Theological Seminary. He earned degrees from the Seminário Teológico do Norte do Brasil, Escola Superior de Teologia, and McAfee School of Theology. He has a PhD degree in Religion and Society from Princeton Theological Seminary. His publications include *Evangélicos e Pobreza no Brazil: Encontros e Respostas Éticas*, 2nd ed, Revised and Expanded (Editora Recriar/Editora Unida, 2019) and the co-edited volumes, *Engaging the Jubilee: Freedom and Justice Papers of the Baptist World Alliance [2010-2015]* (2015), *World Christianity as Public Religion* (2017), *Migration and Public Discourse in World Christianity* (2019), and *Decolonial Christianities: Latin American and Latinx Perspectives* (2019). He is also the general editor of the World Christianity and Public Religion series and one of the three conveners of the Princeton Theological Seminary's World Christianity Conference.

Authors

Aliou Cissé Niang is Associate Professor of New Testament at Union Theological Seminary in New York. Niang has a PhD in Biblical Interpretation–New Testament from Brite Divinity School (TCU) in Fort Worth, TX; MA Th. from Logsdon School of Theology (HSU) in Abilene, TX, and; BA in Religious Studies with a minor in history at Williams Baptist College in Walnut Ridge, Arkansas. Niang is the author of *Faith and Freedom in Galatia and Senegal* (2009); co-author of *Text, Image, and Christians in the Graeco-Roman World* (2012); *A Poetics of Postcolonial Biblical Criticism: God, Human-Nature Relationship, and Negritude* (Cascade Books, 2019); "Catholic Epistles," *Anselm Companion to the New Testament* (Anselm Academic, 2014); "Catholic Epistles," *Anselm Companion to the Bible* (Anselm Academic, 2014); "Space and Human Agency in the Making of the Story of Gershom through a Senegalese Christian Lens," *Forum-Journal of Biblical Literature* (2015); "Islandedness, Translation, and Creolization," in *Islands, Islanders, and Bible: Ruminations* (Atlanta, GA: SBL, 2015); "Christianity in Senegal" in Lamport and Jenkins, *Encyclopedia of Christianity in the Global South* (Rowman & Littlefield Publishers, 2018); "Diola Religion" in Lamport and Jenkins, *Encyclopedia of Christianity in the Global South* (Rowman & Littlefield Publishers, 2018); "Négritude and Minoritized Criticism: A Senegalese Perspective," in Fernando Segovia and Tat-Siong Benny Liew, *Reading the Bible in These Times* (forthcoming book essay); "Messenger as Agent of Transformation in the Bible and Diola Faith Traditions: A Postcolonial Perspective," in Fernando Segovia and Jeremy Punt (forthcoming book essay).

André S. Musskopf is a Professor at the Department of Science of Religion at the Universidade Federal de Juiz de Fora, Brazil, responsible for issues of Religion, Gender and Education. Prior to this he has been at Faculdades EST, Brazil, as a student, earning his Bachelor's, Master's and Doctorate degrees in Systematic Theology, studying and researching on issues of gender and sexual diversity, queer studies and Theology, and finally as part of the Coordination of the Gender and Religion Program and Gender and Theology Chair at the Graduate Program. He has been involved with grassroots groups and social movements, published extensively, and lectured on several topics related to his research interests in different parts of the world and with different types of organizations and institutions.

Atola Longkumer, a Baptist from Nagaland, is a visiting faculty at SAIACS, Bangalore, India. Her recent publications include "Faith and Culture" in *Edinburgh Companions to Global Christianity: Christianity in South and Central Asia* (Edinburgh University Press, 2019), and "Economy, Greed and Liberation Theology: A Critique from a Border Location in India" in *Contextual Theology: Skills and Practices of Liberating Faith*, edited by Sigurd Bergmann and Mika Vähäkangas (Routledge, forthcoming). Longkumer is also the book review editor of Mission Studies (Brill).

Ciprian Burlacioiu is lecturer in Church History and World Christianity at the University of Munich, Germany. He earned his PhD in 2007 at the Faculty for Orthodox Theology in Bucharest, Romania and ever since, he has been working in the Department for Protestant Theology in Munich. His past work engaged with questions of religious transatlantic links between US and Africa in the early twentieth century and the emergence of missionary independent churches in South and East Africa. Currently, he works on issues related to historical processes of migration with a focus on religion of migrant workers in the context of colonial industrial expansion around 1900 in southern Africa and beyond.

Claudete Beise Ulrich is currently working on her postdoctoral research in education at the Federal University of Espírito Santo (UFES). She has also done postdoctoral work in history at the Federal University of Santa Catarina (UFSC). She has a Doctor of Theology with concentration in religion and education from Colleges EST, Brazil, and a Master's degree in practical theology, also from EST. Prior to that, she graduated in theology (EST Colleges) and qualified in pedagogy, with concentration on early childhood education (Santa Catarina State University). She teaches undergraduate and graduate students in the sciences of religion at Faculdade Unida de Vitória (FUV), where she also serves as Coordinator of the undergraduate program in sciences of religion, Coordinator of the Research Group Religion, Gender, Violence: Human Rights, and occupies the Reverend John Dias de Araújo Chair on Public Theology and Religious Studies. She is also an invited scholar on the Cultures, Partnership, Education in the Field Research Group at UFES.

Contributors

Dale T. Irvin is the former president and professor of World Christianity at New York Theological Seminary. He serves as an adjunct instructor at Georgetown University in the Department of Theology and is the Chair of the Ecclesiological Investigations International Research Network.

Ernesto Fiocchetto is a Sociologist of Religion formerly based at Universidad Nacional de Cuyo, Mendoza, Argentina. In 2017, he moved to the US to start his studies at Florida International University (FIU). In 2019, he earned a Master's degree in Religious Studies. Currently, he is a PhD student in International Relations at FIU. He works for the Miami-Florida Jean Monnet European Center of Excellence and is the secretary at the Latin American and Caribbean Interdisciplinary Initiative on Religion (LACIIR). His research interests center on the social process of religious identities configuration. In different periods, he has tackled the intersections between religious identities and sexualities, young adults (millennials), women and politics in South America, and gender studies. In the US, his research interest revolves around two topics: the intersection of religious identities and new information and communication technologies, and the intersection of religion, migration, and human rights, particularly among LGBTIQ and refugees. He has published in both Spanish and English and has presented his research at prestigious academic conferences in the US like AAR, LASA, and SSSR annual meetings.

Maricel Mena-López has done post-doctoral studies in feminist hermeneutics with a scholarship from the Amparo Foundation for Research in the State of Rio Grande do Sul, Brazil. She has a PhD in the Sciences of Religion from the Methodist University of Sao Paulo, a Master in Theology from the Methodist University of Sao Paulo, and a Science of Religions Bachelor's degree from the Javeriana University. She currently teaches Bible at the Faculty of Theology of the Santo Tomas University, having more than thirty years of experience in popular and community reading of the Bible. Her research and teaching interests include biblical exegesis, feminist studies, gender theories, black hermeneutics, and African-American and intercultural studies. She has served as consultant-advisor on issues of gender, race/ethnicity to vulnerable communities and human rights agencies. Her scholarship includes the books, *Bible and City: Pedagogies of Good Living in Urban Contexts*, and *Latin*

American Theology: Diagnosis and Epistemological Synthesis, both published in 2017. She has published a large number of articles in academic journals and other important scholarly contributions.

Nicolas Panotto is an Argentinian theologian with a PhD in social sciences and Master's degree in social and political Anthropology from the Latin American College of Social Sciences (FLACSO Argentina). He is the Director of the Multidisciplinary Study Group on Religion and Public Advocacy (GEMRIP-www.gemrip.org), a member of the board of the Latin American Theological Fellowship (FTL), and an associate researcher in the International Relations Study Center of the Arturo Prat University (Chile). Among his many publications, Panotto has authored the books *Descolonizar el Saber Teológico* (Decolonizing Theological Knowledge, Mexico: CTM-CTE 2018), *Religión y Estado Laico en América Latina* (Religion and Lay State in Latin America. Bogotá: REDLAD, 2017), *Religión, Política y Poscolonialidad en América Latina* (Religion, Politics and Postcoloniality in Latin America. Buenos Aires: Miño and Davila, 2016), *Teología y lo Publico* (Theology and the Public. Buenos Aires: GEMRIP, 2015), and *Hacia una Teología del Sujeto Politico* (Towards a Theology of the Political Subject. San José: UNA, 2013).

Nivia Ivette Núñez de la Paz received PhD (2008) and Master's (2004) degrees in theology from Faculdades EST, São Leopoldo (RS). She has a Bachelor's degree in theology (2001) from the Seminário Evangélico de Teologia, Matanzas, Cuba and BA in philosophy from SINAL-Faculdade de Ciências Humanas e Sociais, Rio Branco, Acre. Her postdoctoral project in Systematic Theology (2015–2017) at EST, São Leopoldo (RS) was titled "In Defense of Life: From Gender Violence to Humanized Relations," funded by a PNPD / CAPES research grant. She teaches education in the graduate program at International Ibero-American University–UNINI (https://www.unini.org), where she also advises PhD dissertations, at Universidad Europea del Atlantico or UNEATLANTICO (https://www.uneatlantico.es), and at the Center for Anglican Studies–CEA. She is also part of the directing board of the Centro Ecumênico de Capacitação e Assessoria–CECA, and is a member of the Religion, Gender and Violence Research Group of Faculdade Unida de Vitória (REGEVI) and of the Research and Training Group on

Interculturality and Innovation in Education at UNINI-Mexico. Her research areas include feminisms, feminist theology, violence against women, popular education, interculturality, ethics, and human rights.

Peter Bush is the Teaching Elder at St. Andrew's Presbyterian Church, Fergus, Ontario. He has served congregations in Manitoba and rural Ontario. Peter was the Cross-Cultural Liaison for the Presbytery of Winnipeg, seeking to interpret Canadian Presbyterianism to communities of Christians newly arrived in Canada and trying to ease the path for the newly arrived communities of Christians seeking to have connections with Canadian Presbyterianism. He has written extensively about The Presbyterian Church in Canada's involvement in Indian residential schools and was a contract researcher with the Truth and Reconciliation Commission on Indian Residential Schools. Peter is married to Debbie; they have one son.

Sandra Londono-Ardila is a History PhD candidate at Florida International University. Sandra's work focuses on the relationship between Catholicism and political culture in Latin America. In 2017, Sandra co-authored the book *El Discurso de una ética Catolica modernizada: El caso del Programa Accion Cultural Popular 1947–1958*. Currently a member of the Latin American Interdisciplinary Initiative on Religion-LACIIR at FIU, Sandra is active as Secretary of DARLAC-The Digital Archive of Religion in Latin America. Her current dissertation research examines the intellectual, theological, and political mobilization of the Latin American progressive-Catholic student youth in a time frame of the Cold War.

Sunder John Boopalan completed his PhD in Religion and Society at Princeton Theological Seminary. His book, *Memory, Grief, and Agency: A Political Theological Account of Wrongs and Rites* (Palgrave Macmillan, 2017), is the outcome of his tenure at the Episcopal Divinity School, Cambridge, where he served as Postdoctoral Fellow. Located broadly in the field of constructive theology, John's interdisciplinary research addresses themes and concerns in political theologies and theological ethics. With strengths in the area of Dalit Christianity and interests in redressing structural wrongs, Boopalan draws from anthropological and ethnographic data particularly pertaining to caste and race. His forthcoming essay in the *Journal* of *World Christianity* is entitled "Saving the World through Ethnography." Boopalan is an ordained minister in the progressive Baptist tradition and is part of the Collective of Dalit Ecumenical Christian Scholars (CODECS) and has recently signed a contract with Fortress Press for a co-authored book project, *Dalit Theology: A Global Introduction*.

Zhibin Xie received his PhD from the University of Hong Kong. He is professor of philosophy at Tongji University, Shanghai, P. R. China. He is a research fellow of Institute of Sino-Christian Studies in Hong Kong and a member at the Center of Theological Inquiry in Princeton. He has been a visiting scholar at Princeton Theological Seminary and at Fuller Theological Seminary. His research interests include Christian philosophy and ethics, public theology, and religion and politics in China. His major publications include *Religious Diversity and Public Religion in China* (in English, Ashgate, 2006), *Public Theology and Globalization: A Study in Max Stackhouse's Christian Ethics* (in Chinese, 2008), and *Why Public? How Theological? An Overview and Prospect for Sino-Christian Public Theology* (in Chinese, 2016). His articles appear in *Political Theology, International Journal of Public Theology, Asia Journal of Theology, Studies in Interreligious Dialogue,* and *Logos & Pneuma: Chinese Journal of Theology,* etc.

WORLD CHRISTIANITY, URBANIZATION, AND IDENTITY: INTRODUCTION

Moses O. Biney, Kenneth N. Ngwa, and Raimundo C. Barreto

> Where cross the crowded ways of life,
> where sound the cries of race and clan,
> above the noise of selfish strife,
> we hear your voice, O Son of Man.[1]

Frank Mason North's popular hymn, "Where Cross the Crowded Ways of Life," quoted above, partly captures the spirit of this book. Composed with New York City as a backdrop, North captures the attractions as well as special needs of urban life. The picture it paints of urban life with its "crowded ways," "race and clan," (diverse cultures) are as vivid today as they were for him a century ago. Whether the backdrop for the study of urbanization is a North American city or a megacity from sub-Saharan Africa, Latin America, Southeast Asia or Europe, North's poetic formulation of the spatial construction and social character and identity of the city accentuates a necessary intersectionality between the cosmopolitanism of the city as a material and social site, and its multivocal linguistic and epistemological character. Within the dense and boisterous city life, one can hear the voice of God; or, perhaps, one should say the voices of God as they take shape at the intersections of urban cultures, their languages and belief systems, and economic life. For religious thinkers and Christians in particular, these broad formulations raise particular questions and propel specific claims about the relation between the voices in/of the city and the voices of the divine in the city. For example, what theologies and methodologies provide avenues for understanding the character of the divine in the urban space? What sorts of divine beings live in the city, and how do such beings relate to rural sites and their forms of life?

---

[1] Frank Mason North, "Where Cross the Crowded Ways of Life," in *United Methodist Hymnal*, 1903, 380 (Source: Carl Abbott, *Where Sound the Cries of Race and Clan*, pg. 137).

The growth and development of urban settlements around the world is increasing rapidly. Large segments of the populations of many nations live in urban areas that are growing faster than the world's overall population. The United Nations estimate that more than 60 percent of all humanity will be urban dwellers by the middle of the century.[2] Much of this increase is fueled by migration—both in-country migrations from rural to urban centers and international migration.

Examining these changes from a religious standpoint is at the core of this volume. Christianity at its inception rapidly spread as an urban religion. Over time, urban spaces and structures have accommodated and shaped Christianity's mission and ministries. While urbanization shaped Christianity, Christianity also shaped urban areas. The convergence of urbanization and its attendant process of globalization have both positive and negative implications for urban life, rural life, and religious practice within the landscape of World Christianity. Consider, for example, the rise and impact of mega churches and emergent churches in urban communities. Also, worth noting is the fact that as part of the global migration from South to North, different brands and streams of Christian and other faith traditions have crossed over from Africa, Asia, and Latin America into many cities in North America and Europe thus changing the shape and form of the religious ecologies in those places.

Theoreticians of urbanization have addressed this reality from multiple perspectives, providing insightful analyses. Some have historicized the material and demographic shifts that have accompanied the greater focus on urbanization. The year 2008 is recognized as the year when, for the first time in world history, more than half of the world's population resided in cities. The implications of this demographic shift—beyond the significance of 2008 as a tipping point in a longer historical movement—is that "the shrinking half of the planet that lives in rural areas will be more heavily depended upon for supplying the food and other resources required to support this growing urban population."[3] The issue here is attending to the implications of the emergence of the urban space—and its construction—out of the rural space: Is such a model of urban life sustainable, and at what costs? The themes of overpopulation and a concentration of multiple identities and voices in the urban space or city have informed

---

[2] See "68% of the World Population Projected to Live in Urban Areas by 2050, Says UN," United Nations Department of Economic and Social Affairs (UN DESA), accessed May 16, 2018, https://www.un.org/development/desa/en/news/population/2018-revision-of-world-urbanization-prospects.html.

[3] Gregory M. Fulkerson and Alexander R. Thomas, "Urbanization, Urbanormativity, and Place-Structuration," in Gregory M. Fulkerson et al., eds., *Studies in Urbanormativity: Rural Community in Urban Society* (Lanham, MD: Lexington Books, 2014), 8.

theories about the character and nature of the city in correlative, if not causative, relation to the rise of the Industrial Revolution and the political infrastructure of the nation-state. The urban space signals and represents a transition from the agrarian economy to an industrial economy built on manufacturing, technology, and the infrastructure of travel.

Along with historical analyses, there is scholarship from urban geography, which has itself moved away from understanding urban areas as social and cultural spaces that gradually expand into suburbia and the rural spaces. In contrast to such ripple effect and flow from the urban center to the rural peripheries, studies in urban geography around mega cities also point to urbanization as a movement that "no longer spreads *outwards* from the central city toward the suburbs like the ripples created after a single stone is dropped into the middle of a pond. Instead, urban development seems to spread *inwards* simultaneously from several suburban and exurban centers like multiple ripples emanating from stones scattered throughout a pond."[4] This spatial character of urban theorizing can be stretched even further to consider the "global" dimension of urbanization not only as a space, but also as a particular form of discourse about the world's capacity to exist and function beyond existing boundaries of time and space. The added power of rapid technological change—its ability to simultaneously shrink space-time and stretch it beyond physical boundaries—and of media (both print and non-print) has also greatly increased scholarly appreciation of urbanization as a vibrant material and even textual space-time of identity formation and negotiation that requires breakdown of sharp distinctions or divides between urban and rural belonging; and between the cosmopolitan and perhaps even the "world" or "global" citizen and the local citizen. Both are often at work not just in sequential terms, but also in concurrent fashion. The urbanized Christian not only hears the voices of fellow citizens in the city of current residence, but also the voices from sending cities (across nations and continents), and perhaps even the voices from traditional ancestral and rural settings, which resurge in the larger urban centers in unanticipated ways.

From a sociolinguistic perspective, urbanization assumes and fosters multilingualism that develops from a clustering of persons originating from multiple rural linguistic groups who must learn other languages in order to navigate the economic and political infrastructure of the urban space. On the other hand, the intensity of the urban space as a site of linguistic multivocality also accentuates introverted notions of identity and belonging in the city, as language code patterns continuously seek to establish liaisons with its more stable histories and "homogenous" origins.

---

[4] Andrew E. G. Jonas, *Urban Geography: A Critical Introduction* (Chicester: John Wiley & Sons, 2013), 55. Italics original.

Thus, alongside other major categories of sociological and anthropological analyses—such as age, sex, gender, education, economic status, etc.—language also plays an important role in theorizing and interpreting urbanization.[5]

Drawing from these major theoretical frameworks—historical, spatial, and linguistic—this volume accentuates the intersectionality between those frameworks and ongoing discourse about urbanization and its productions of identity in World Christianity. More precisely, the essays presented here by eminent scholars engage several questions related to the role of religion, and specifically World Christianity in identity formation in urban centers, and diasporic communities, using multiple approaches—historical, sociological, anthropological, theological, and biblical.

This book, "World Christianity, Urbanization, and Identity," which is part of a six-volume series titled *World Christianity and Public Religion*, published by Fortress Press, is an interdisciplinary, intercultural, and intercontinental effort to map out the contours and intersections of urban change, religious formation and practice, and identity formation. Similarly, we intend to draw attention to the power of religion both in terms of its practice and institutions in urban centers.

This trend toward urbanization is often discussed in economic and political terms, with very little recognition given to the critical role religion plays in the complex processes and flows involved in it. Among other things, for better or for worse, religious institutions have often shaped the social and cultural attitudes as well as public policies in urban centers and have been equally shaped by them. The conflation of time and space provoked by processes of globalization, mass migration, and rapid urbanization create uncharted situations of both friction and hybridization as an increasing number of individuals and communities find themselves in liminal spaces, living in between-and-betwixt. In these porous spaces, faith is often relocated and reinvented, and religious theory and praxis is challenged to go beyond furnishing language that justifies exclusivist claims to contribute to open new horizons for creative conviviality. Coming from different continents and cultural and religious backgrounds, the authors of this volume offer a variety of perspectives and methods to engage and illuminate these and other pressing issues at hand.

Structure of the book

In his brilliant book, *African Cities: Alternative Visions of Urban Theory and Practice*, Garth Myers describes a theory of urban studies that departs from Western "rational planning" to alternative rationalities at

---

[5] Bengt Nordberg, *The Sociolinguistics of Urbanization: The Case of the Nordic Countries* (New York: De Bruyter, 2011), 3–4.

work in intersections around five themes: *postcolonialism, informality, governance, violence,* and *cosmopolitanism*.⁶ Informed by these themes and more, our volume examines the intersections of scholarship, theory, and practice in the fields of World Christianity, Urbanization, and Identity. Our working theory is that these broad categories may be organized and engaged around four concurrent themes: Conceptualizations, Contestations, Confluences, and Creative Transformations. Such broad categories underscore how the notions and realities of World Christianity, Urbanization, and Identity are not static, but continuously conceptualized, contested, convergent, and creatively transformed into theories and modes of human and divine existence intimately affiliated with place and time. As disciplinary foci transition to interdisciplinary work, enlightenment modes of interpretation are reframed for a larger global conversation in which World Christianity, Urbanization, and Identity are intersecting topics. The ancient city is placed alongside the modern city for conceptual analyses; and engagement with the Christian text, the Bible, draws from a variety of hermeneutics—from ancient rabbinic and patristic "four senses" (literal, allegorical, moral, and anagogic) of Scripture to postcolonial interpretation—that illumine issues of space and identity. These four themes of Conceptualizations, Contestations, Confluences, and Creative Transformations also provide the narrative structure for this volume, comprised of thirteen chapters.

Part I titled "Conceptualizations: Intersecting Theological, Historical Biblical, and Sociological Perspectives" comprises of four essays that provide various frameworks— theological, historical, biblical, and sociological—for understanding the city and urbanization in general. In the opening chapter, Dale Irvin reflects on the city through historical, sociological, and theological lenses. Irvin portrays the city as a constructed space that shapes the sacred and is shaped in turn by the sacred. Moving from Augustine's understanding of the two cities to Henri Lefebvre's view of the city as emerging from all urban dwellers' "right to the city" and "power to create," and finally to Edward Soja's notion of *third space*— "those related concepts that compose and comprise the inherent spatiality of human life: place, location, locality, landscape, environment, home, city, region, territory, and geography"⁷—Irvin sets the backdrop against which one can read all the succeeding chapters. He places "the expansion of the right to the city on the part not just of the poor, but of sinners, the ritually impure, and those who generally were relegated to the margins of society or outside the gates" at the center of Jesus's ministry, setting the

---

⁶ Garth Myers, *African Cities: Alternative Visions of Urban Theory and Practice* (London: Zed Books, 2011), 15, 16.

⁷ Edward Soja, *Thirdspace: Journeys to Los Angeles and other Real-and-Imagined Places* (Cambridge, MA: Blackwell, 1996), 1. Italics original.

scene for a conversation that, taking into consideration a variety of local, national, and transnational experiences, emphasizes the need for inclusion of all indwellers, but, in particular, "the poor, the marginalized, the down-trodden, and the dispossessed" as subjects of rights and as agents of creation in the life of the city.

Nicolas Panotto, in chapter 2, assesses the impact of globalization on multicultural relations, underscoring a certain ambiguity in the understanding of contemporary global dynamics. If, on the one hand, globalization can be seen as a phenomenon that enables the enrichment of processes of mutual knowledge through exchanges and possibilities of encounters with a diversity of subjects and cultures, on the other hand, it also represents a power dynamics where relationships and interconnections are often asymmetric, thus reasserting the dominance of hegemonic powers. Speaking from Latin America, Panotto argues that the global dynamics we currently experience must be understood as symptoms of the colonial imprint of the West, where stigmas and preconceptions of the different and the stranger tend to be presented as threats. He claims, therefore, that a process of deconstruction of meanings and new practices of intercultural relations and translation is crucial to help rethink public and international policies. Such a process calls for a theological vision based on a God-Completely-Other that can move us toward a commitment to and solidarity toward the excluded, expanding our horizons beyond imposed borders, toward fresh meanings and imaginaries.

In chapter 3, Maricel Mena-López explores the relationships between centralizing practices and monotheism in ancient Israel, looking particularly at the Solomonic regime in relation to two Canaanite cities described in the biblical narrative of 1 Kings 1–11: Jerusalem (of the Jebusites) and Gibeon (of the Amorites). By doing that, she uses a literary and sociocultural rhetorical approach to address complex and vexing questions of urbanization and city life in the Hebrew Bible. Informed by a postcolonial theoretical perspective and its critical assessment of empire and power, Mena-López explores the relationships between centralization, monotheism in Ancient Israel, and the emergence of cities, contending that, at the apex of Solomon's political, religious, literary, and economic power, the city that housed his rule was constituted on the basis of an "epistemic theft" of ancestral traditions and wisdom at the periphery. In other words, Solomon built his kingdom based on commercial alliances, marriages with foreigners, forced labor, imposition of taxes, and epistemic colonization.

Finally, in chapter 4, Ernesto Fiocchetto draws attention to the digitalization of urban life and its impact on performed religious identities, highlighting the reformulation of the idea of time and space in the digital era,

Introduction

which challenges the notion of urban spaces defined only on geographic basis. This digital era has produced new subjectivities that are critical to understand contemporary Western Christian religious identities.

Part 2, "Contested and Negotiated Identities," is comprised of stories and conversations on the subjects of difference, friction, and contestation in the context of inward and outward movements and influences that shape and reshape identity formation in both urban spaces and their rural counterparts.

In chapter 5, Aliou Cissé Niang analyzes the formation of Diola Christianity in West Africa through the lens of religious transmutation. Niang interrogates how the combination of missionary work and the introduction of French colonial policies in the Casamance, one of the regions of Senegal heavily populated by the Diola people, engendered religious mutation in Diola village residents who practiced an expression of African Traditional Religion. His use of the image of shifting tectonic plates to describe how lived traditional experiences of the Diola began to gradually change is particularly illuminating. This chapter evinces, in particular, how the Diola encounter of missionaries and the economic policies introduced by French colonial officials gave rise to seasonal migration from Senegalese villages to cities and how the Christianity introduced by the Holy Ghost Fathers was gradually contextualized to assume key traditional elements of Diola traditional religion.

André S. Musskopf, in chapter 6, shifts the focus back to Latin America. This chapter draws attention to how the experience of the Popular Reading of the Bible has contributed to denounce and dismantle the sexism and misogyny characteristic of patriarchalism, heterosexism, and other forms of LGBTQ phobia. Musskopf reads the Parable of the Prodigal Son in conversation with the story of Henrique, a young man who is forced to leave his rural town because of his sexual orientation, thus finding help in the biblical text to address the often-overlooked issue of sexual migration, broadly understood as that reality experienced by those who have to move from one place to another because of their sexual orientation and/or gender identity. This chapter underlines that gender and sexuality are often neglected as factors (or even as the main possible reason) informing certain experiences of migration, which, in many cases, are less a matter of choice than a survival strategy, some of which resulting from violent events.

Sunder John Boopalan, in chapter 7, examines the challenges that the relocation of new waves of migrants bring to urban contexts as they add a layer of heterogeneity to already-existing racial/ethnic identity formations. Among other things, he highlights the multiple expressions of

Christianity these migrants add to already religiously diverse urban centers. Looking at those experiences and encounters as opportunities for the reconceptualization of both religious and racial/ethnic identities, this chapter examines the challenges that accompany the process of reconceptualizing and reforming religious and racial/ethnic identities in urban contexts.

Part 3, "Confluences: Migration, Urbanization, and Interculturality," focuses on the interplay between migration, indigeneity, and cultural interchanges in Christian communities in multicultural urban spaces.

In chapter 8, Peter Bush, studying an urban context in Canada, draws attention to the responses of Euro-Canadian Christian communities in the city of Winnipeg to the innovations carried to those spaces by newly arrived Christians. Bush, therefore, identifies and discusses different models of engagement of existing local churches and denominations in Winnipeg in response to the growing presence of a polycentric World Christianity in the city.

In chapter 9, Atola Longkumer examines the impact of internal migration flows in identity formation in Indian urbanized centers such as Bangalore, Delhi, and Chennai. This chapter explores migration flows from rural, agriculture-based economies, to the urbanized, highly technologized metropolitan centers where a myriad of cultures converge. Longkumer argues that such convergences do not erase the particularities of cultural identities and their lived expressions among migrant groups, underscoring the struggle Indian rural migrants face to maintain cultural, religious, and linguistic traditions in urbanized centers. Among other things, Longkumer highlights the role and nature of religious leadership and the need for it to be attentive to the challenges and opportunities of multicultural convergences at the intersection of multiple cultures, religions, and social classes.

Finally, in chapter 10, Ciprian Burlacioiu links the phenomena of industrialization and urbanization in South Africa around 1900 to the emergence of the African Independent Churches, highlighting how the fast-growing number of South African migrant workers contributed to rapid urbanization and the formation of a new missionary frontier. At the same time, he argues, missionary hesitance to act in those urbanizing areas and the absence of consistent missionary activities among migrant workers influenced by Christianity radically changed the religious landscape of South Africa.

The fourth and last part of this book, "Creative Transformations: Agency, Citizenship, and Public Religion," examines three examples of

Introduction

Christian mobilization and public agency in contested urban spaces, where faith has inspired overt and covert political actions.

In chapter 11, Claudete Beise Ulrich and Nivia Ivette Nunez de la Paz explore the experience of popular legal agents in the state of Rio Grande do Sul, in Brazil, with a focus on the work of the Centro Ecumênico de Evangelização, Capacitação e Assessoria (CECA), and its emphases on ecumenism, gender, and human rights. The institution's key mission remains the development of citizenship based on a faith that articulates itself through a sense of ecumenicity and interreligious dialogue. This chapter reflects on the action of CECA in the formation of impoverished Brazilian women as Popular Legal Agents, showing how the performance of this ecumenical organization has been fundamental to confronting and overcoming violence against women in the southern part of Brazil.

Zhibin Xie outlines in chapter 12 the tension between individuality and publicness in contemporary urban Christianity in China. Xie argues that the search for meaning on the part of urban Christians in China and the transformation of their values has generated an increased interest in engaging discourses on constitutionalism and human rights. Xie offers a theological analysis of this emerging dynamic in urban Chinese Christianity by examining both its historical context and the contemporary political-social situation in the country. The chapter argues that the public turn in urban Chinese Christianity has theological rather than political-social motifs.

Finally, in chapter 13, Sandra Londono devotes attention to examining the case of the Catholic organization *Acción Cultural Popular* (ACPO) in Colombia during the period 1947–1962, a time in which the Catholic Church was at the center of social, political, cultural, and epistemological transformations happening in Colombian society.

The combination of themes, approaches, disciplines, localities, and perspectives presented in this collection of essays exemplifies the variety and significance of mounting scholarship on the historically and theologically relevant theme of "the city" and how it shapes and is shaped by religion. Furthermore, it also evinces the interweaving of local, diasporic, and global approaches to important issues of public interest that one can no longer expect to properly tackle from the perspective of static understandings of location. The city is above all a place of movement, flows, encounters, and conflicts. It is in the midst of its complex webs that various notions of the divine are shaped and become operative. Given the increasing revitalization of the sacred in the city, and the powerful ways it impacts the daily lives of local and trans-local citizens, the quest informing the various chapters of this book is more urgent than ever. Its

World Christianity, Urbanization, and Identity

value transcends historical and theological interest, being also a matter of increasing ethical concern. The recent revitalization of popular nationalisms around the world and the extent to which religious discourses have been used to legitimize political overturns and exclusionist and xenophobic public policies[8] are only two examples of the urgency of the task at hand: (1) Unmask the manipulation of religious discourses that legitimate walls of separation, and outright discrimination and violence; and alternatively (2) point to more inclusive, just, and harmonic possibilities of life emerging in the city, which can be learned through the processes of intercultural encounters and other concurrent centripetal and centrifugal movements related to the city.

The book ends with a general conclusion that, beyond being an attempt to summarize and wrap up the achievements of the volume, offers a final reflection by the editors about its nature, drawing from Lynn White Jr.'s theorizing on the current ecological crisis to situate the conversations in this book and point to the challenges ahead—some of which will be taken up in the following volumes of this series.

---

[8] For a reflection on the binary xenophobia versus xenophilia, see Luis Rivera-Pagan's chapter in Afe Adogame, Raimundo Barreto, and Wanderley Pereira da Rosa, *Migration and Public Discourse in World Christianity* (Minneapolis, MN: Fortress Press, 2019).

BIBLIOGRAPHY

Adogame, Afe, Raimundo Barreto, and Wanderley Pereira da Rosa. *Migration and Public Discourse in World Christianity.* Minneapolis, MN: Fortress Press, 2019.

Fulkerson, Gregory M., and Alexander R. Thomas. "Urbanization, Urbanormativity, and Place-Structuration." In *Studies in Urbanormativity: Rural Community in Urban Society,* edited by Gregory M. Fulkerson and Alexander R. Thomas. Lanham, MD: Lexington Books, 2013.

Jonas, Andrew E. G., *Urban Geography: A Critical Introduction.* Chicester: John Wiley & Sons, 2013.

Myers, Garth. *African Cities: Alternative Visions of Urban Theory and Practice.* London: Zed Books, 2011.

Nordberg, Bengt. *The Sociolinguistics of Urbanization: The Case of the Nordic Countries.* New York: De Bruyter, 2011.

Soja, Edward W. *Thirdspace: Journeys to Los Angeles and Other Real-and-Imagined Places.* Cambridge, MA: Blackwell, 1996.

PART I

CONCEPTUALIZATIONS: INTERSECTING THEOLOGICAL, HISTORICAL, BIBLICAL, AND SOCIOLOGICAL PERSPECTIVES

1

DEUS URBIS AND THE RIGHT TO THE CITY

Dale T. Irvin[1]

> For he looked forward to the city that has foundations, whose architect and builder is God. (Hebrews 11:10)

We are living in an increasingly urbanized and urbanizing world. According to a recent United Nations Human Settlements Programme report (UN-Habitat),[2] more than half of the world's population lives in human built environments with a density of at least 1,500 persons per square kilometer, or cities.[3] By the middle of this century, the percent-

---

[1] I wish to thank my faculty colleagues at New York Theological Seminary for their stimulating feedback and helpful suggestions for improvement when I presented this paper at one of our monthly Faculty Forums.

[2] "United Nations Human Settlements Programme (UN-Habitat)," *World Cities Report 2016, Urbanization and Development: Emerging Futures* (Nairobi: United Nations Human Settlements Programme, 2016).

[3] A word about the meaning of the various terms used in this chapter is needed. The Latin word "urbs," from which the English word "urban" is derived, referred to a bounded spatial entity with a built environment, a population exercising socially variegated roles, and some form of human administrative structure of governance. The Latin word "civitas," from which the English words "city," "citizen," "civil," and "civic" are derived, referred to what went on among residents in that bounded space. The distinction was similar to that of "astu" and "polis" in Greek. In contemporary usage in English, the distinctions have become reversed. The word "urban" typically serves as an adjective to describe a particular way of life while the word "city" usually refers to a specific bounded geographical area, a distinction also found in Spanish with the words "urbano" and "ciudad." "Urbanization" generally names the social process of agglomeration and differentiation that resulted in the formation of cities and eventually megalopolises, while "urban area" refers to several administratively distinct cities that function together as a combined metropolitan district. See Allen J. Scott and Michael Storper, "The Nature of Cities: The Scope and Limits of Urban Theory," *International Journal of Urban and Regional Research* 38, no. 4 (2014): 1–15.

age of the population that resides in urban areas is expected to rise to more than 70 percent. There are now more than 1,000 cities on earth with more than 500,000 inhabitants.[4] According to the 2016 report of the UN-Habitat, across the globe there were forty-four large cities, which the report defined as having between five and ten million inhabitants, and twenty-nine megacities, which it defined as having ten million or more inhabitants and are often metropolitan regions encompassing several administrative districts or cities. The number of megacities by 2018 had already risen to thirty-one and is expected to reach forty-three by the middle of the century.[5]

Megacities can now be found on five continents (Asia, Africa, South America, Europe, and North America). According to the United Nations report, China has six megacities (Shanghai, Beijing, Chongqing, Guangzhou, Tianjin, and Shenzhen). A World Economic Forum report in 2016 stated the actual number in China to be fifteen (the difference is in how a particular urban region is defined).[6] According to the United Nations, the largest megacity on earth remains Greater Tokyo (or the National Capital Region) in Japan, which includes Tokyo, Chiba, Kawasaki, Sagamihara, Saitama, and Yokohama and has a combined total population of more than thirty-eight million inhabitants. The largest megacity in both the Southern and Western hemisphere is São Paulo, Brazil, whose population numbers approximately thirty-three million, while Lagos, Nigeria, with a population of twenty-one million is the largest city on the African continent.

Numbers alone don't tell the full story of the phenomenon of global urbanization. Cities accounted for 54 percent of the world's population in 2016, but they generated more than 80 percent of the GDP.[7] They also accounted for 80 percent of the world's energy consumption and nearly that amount of the world's greenhouse gas emissions.[8] The role that a few

---

[4] "United Nations, Department of Economic and Social Affairs, Population Division," *The World's Cities in 2016—Data Booklet* (Geneva: United Nations, 2016), ii.

[5] "World Urbanization Prospects 2018—More Megacities in the Future," *United Nations Department of Economic and Social Affairs*, accessed October 10, 2018, https://www.un.org/development/desa/publications/graphic/world-urbanization-prospects-2018-more-megacities-in-the-future.

[6] Joe Myers, "You Knew China's Cities Were Growing. But the Real Numbers Are Stunning," *World Economic Forum*, June 20, 2016, accessed October 10, 2018, https://www.weforum.org/agenda/2016/06/china-cities-growing-numbers-are-stunning/.

[7] United Nations Human Settlements Programme, *World Cities Report 2016*, 7.

[8] United Nations Human Settlements Programme, *World Cities Report 2016*, 4.

"global cities" play in organizing and running the global economy has been explored by social theorists in considerable depth.[9]

Cities have, from the ancient world, played a critical role in the history of human migration.[10] That role has accelerated in the contemporary global context.[11] From ancient times, cities have played a major role in facilitating the spread of infectious diseases among human beings.[12] The recent global spread of diseases such as Ebola and SARS is but the latest chapter in this long history.[13] At the time of writing this essay, the global COVID-19 pandemic had not emerged yet. But, the virus and the disease associated with it have moved quickly in the past few months, severely impacting in particular urban areas.

Drawing connections between a contemporary megalopolis and the first human cities that appeared 10,000 years ago assumes that a degree of historical continuity can be found across what amount to enormous ruptures in urban form and identity across centuries of time and place. Henri Lefebvre's broad historical outlines of the history of the city are helpful in making these connections. Recognizing the transformations that had taken place over time, Lefebvre nevertheless posited a meaningful overall history of cities. The formations of political capitals and their surrounding supporting cities in the ancient world gave way in the early modern period to commercial and colonial cities driven by the expanding energies of capitalism and colonialism. Commercial and colonial cities in turn were succeeded by industrial cities, post-industrial cities, and then global

---

[9] Saskia Sassen, *The Global City: New York, London, Tokyo*, 2nd ed. (Princeton, NJ: Princeton University Press, 2001).

[10] See Dale T. Irvin, "Migration and Cities: Theological Reflections," in *Contemporary Issues of Migration and Theology* eds., Elaine Padilla and Peter C. Phan (New York: Palgrave MacMillan, 2013), 73–93.

[11] See International Organization for Migration (IOM), *World Migration Report 2015, Migrants and Cities: New Partnerships to Manage Mobility* (Geneva: IOM, 2015).

[12] William H. McNeill writes, "Only in communities of several thousand persons, where encounters with others attain sufficient frequency to allow infection to spread unceasingly from one individual to another can such diseases [as measles, mumps, or smallpox] persist. These communities are what we call civilized: large, complexly organized, densely populated, without exception directed and dominated by cities. Infectious bacterial and viral diseases that pass directly from human to human with no intermediate hosts are therefore the diseases of civilization par excellence: the peculiar hallmark and epidemiological burden of cities and of countryside in contact with cities." William H. McNeill, *Plagues and Peoples* (New York: Anchor Books, 1976), 69.

[13] United Nations Human Settlements Programme, *World Cities Report 2016*, 21–22.

cities.[14] Such a typology barely begins to do justice to the fuller complexity of the "dense, internally variegated webs" of urban realities and urbanization, of course. Edward J. Soja, for instance, offers six different discourses or analytical frameworks for understanding the complexities of contemporary urban spaces and experiences, provocatively titled "Flexcity," "Cosmopolis," "Exopolis," "Metropolarities," "Carceral Archipelagos," and "Simcities."[15] For both Lefebvre and Soja, despite the enormous changes and transformations that appear in the history of cities, it is still a continuous history. That means there are meaningful connections to be made between ancient cities and the cities of today.

A number of urban theorists argue that the key element that defines the urbanization process is not just agglomeration, but social differentiation. Allen J. Scott and Michael Storper, for instance, argue that "the urbanization process resides in the twofold status of cities as clusters of productive activity and human life that then unfold into dense, internally variegated webs of interacting land uses, locations, and allied institutional/political arrangements."[16] Cities are social formations that diversify internally along lines of skills, wealth, and political power. They do not only experience difference along their borders with what is outside of them. They foster difference from within.

Soja traces this experience of differentiation and variegation to the very origins of cities in human history. What set the first cities apart from the forms of human settlement that preceded them, he argues, was synekism (or synoecism, from the Greek word "synoikismos," meaning literally "to dwell together in the same house"). In ancient Greece, the term denoted the process in which several human settlements came together in a political union under a single form of governance.[17] Synekism, Soja has often said, was "the stimulus of urban agglomeration."[18] The act of members of several different settlements coming together to live in close proximity with each other under a common form of governance created the conditions for new forms of social innovation. Cities continue to be places that stimulate new ideas, Soja argues.

---

[14] Henri Lefebvre, *La révolution urbaine* (Paris: Gallimard, 1970); *The Urban Revolution*, trans. Robert Bononno (Minneapolis, MN: University of Minnesota Press, 2003).

[15] Edward J. Soja, *Postmetropolis: Critical Studies of Cities and Regions* (Malden, MA: Wiley-Blackwell, 2000), Part II, 145–348.

[16] Scott and Storper, "The Nature of Cities," 10.

[17] Soja, *Postmetropolis*, 13. See 19–51 for the full discussion of synekism.

[18] See for instance Edward W. Soja, "Writing the City Spatially," in *City: Analysis of Urban Trends, Culture, Theory, Policy, Action* 7, no. 3 (2003): 269; and Edward W. Soja, "Cities and States in Geohistory," *Theory and Society* 39, no. 3/4 (2010): 361.

Cities are spaces in which all aspects of human life and experience are enhanced and amplified. They have played a critical role in fostering the development of writing, commerce, and the arts over the past 10,000 years of human history, and they continue to do so today. Richard Sennett argues that cities are spaces where human beings hone their ethical skills, build systems for exercising justice, and learn how to live with strangers. Saskia Sassen says that they are places where those who are without social power find space to create it. She writes,

> A city is a complex but incomplete system . . .. In this mix of complexity and incompleteness lies the possibility for those without power to assert "we are here" and "this is also our city". Or, as the legendary statement by the fighting poor in Latin American cities puts it, *"Estamos presentes"*: we are present, we are not asking for money, we are just letting you know that this is also our city.[19]

In the words of the United Nations Human Settlement Programme's report from 2005, cities are places "where new things are created and from which they spread across the world."[20] In short, they help us as human beings to become more human on a global scale.[21]

Cities are not without their negative aspects and dimensions.[22] They are places of great inequalities in wealth and power as they simultaneously foster both.[23] They foster violence, suffering, and oppression alongside cooperation, healing, and freedom. They promote patriarchy even as they create space for gender differences and greater gender freedom to emerge.[24] They expand all dimensions of human experience, including the human propensities toward both good and evil. As Sennett says, "The city

---

[19] Saskia Sassen, "Who Owns Our Cities—and Why This Urban Takeover Should Concern Us All," *The Guardian*, November 24, 2015, accessed December 21, 2017, https://www.theguardian.com/cities/2015/nov/24/who-owns-our-cities-and-why-this-urban-takeover-should-concern-us-all.

[20] United Nations Human Settlements Programme, *The State of the World's Cities 2004/2005: Globalization and Urban Culture* (London and Sterling, VA: Earthscan / UN-Habitat, 2004), 10.

[21] Richard Sennett, "The Civitas of Seeing," *Places* 5, no. 4 (1989): 84.

[22] See Edward D. Banfield, *Unheavenly City: The Nature and the Future of Our Urban Crisis* (Boston: Little, Brown & Co., 1979); Edward D. Banfield, *The Unheavenly City Revisited* (Prospect Heights, IL: Waveland Press, 1990).

[23] See Mike Davis, *Planet of Slums* (New York: Verso, 2006).

[24] See for instance, Jo Little, Linda Peake, and Pat Richardson, eds., *Women in Cities: Gender and the Urban Environment* (London: Macmillan Education, 1988); Helen Jarvis, Jonathan Cloke, and Paula Kantor, *Cities and Gender* (New York: Routledge, 2009).

is a complex place, which means it is full of contradictions and ambiguities. Complexity enriches experience; clarity thins it."[25]

The ambiguity of cities is a central trope in Augustine's classic text, *The City of God against the Pagans (De civitate Dei contra paganos)*. In its opening pages, Augustine announces that he is writing the book to defend Christians against the charge that their abandonment of the Roman gods caused these gods to withdraw their protection, thereby allowing the "Eternal City" to be sacked by a Visigoth army in 410 C.E. Christians have actually made Rome a better place, Augustine argues. But more importantly, he goes on, neither Rome nor any other city on earth is where Christian citizenship ultimately resides.

Augustine posits two cities as types that have a sustained existence through human history. On the one hand, there is the city of God (*civitatem Dei*), which in the latter part of the book he also calls the heavenly city (*caelestis civitatis*), while the other is what he consistently calls the earthly city (*civitatis terrenae*). The foundations of the two cities lay "in the difference that arose among the angels" at the beginning of creation, he argues in Book 11, Chapter 1.[26] The founder of the first can nevertheless be said to be God and it is populated by those who love God, both angels and humans; while the founder of the latter can be said to be the devil and those angels and human beings that follow him in rebellion and disobedience, he says in Book 11, Chapter 13.[27] The human beings in the latter category are all those born of Adam who are not subsequently grafted onto Christ, he asserts in the opening chapter of Book 15.[28] Augustine summarizes his argument in Book 14, Chapter 28.

> Accordingly, two cities have been formed by two loves: the earthly by the love of self, even to the contempt of God; the heavenly by the love of God, even to the contempt of self. The former, in a word, glories in itself, the latter in the Lord.[29]

The heavenly city, for Augustine, is a place of perfection while the earthly is more like the disorderly places we are more familiar with in our urban experience. Nevertheless, these two cities, for Augustine, are intermingled in human history. All human beings are citizens of one or the other, but they are mixed in human history. There are signs of the heavenly city to be found among the earthly, and there are persons who currently

---

[25] Richard Sennett, *Building and Dwelling: Ethics for the City* (New York: Farrar, Straus and Giroux, 2018), 6.
[26] Augustine, *The City of God against the Pagans*, ed. R. W. Dyson (Cambridge: Cambridge University Press, 1998), 448.
[27] Augustine, *The City of God*, 466.
[28] Augustine, *The City of God*, 634.
[29] Augustine, *The City of God*, 630.

appear to be citizens of the earthly city whose final destiny lies with the heavenly. Neither city is fully occupied yet. Human beings in history are pilgrims on their way toward one or the other.[30]

The founder of Augustine's heavenly city might be God, but it is populated by humans and angels. The praise of these inhabitants will constitute the main form of employment in this city. Augustine foresaw this to be the final age of human urban history. Lewis Mumford recognized that it was also the origins of human urban history. In *The City in History*, he writes,

> The city first took form as the home of a god: a place where eternal values were represented and divine possibilities revealed. Though the symbols have changed the realities behind them remain.[31]

Several pages prior to this, Mumford had noted, "The chief function of the city is to convert power into form, energy into culture, dead matter into the living symbols of art, biological reproduction into social creativity."[32] The chief function of the city, in other words, is to transform the material into the spiritual. Mumford concludes:

> The final mission of the city is to further [humanity's] conscious participation in the cosmic and historic process. Through its own complex and enduring structure, the city vastly augments [humanity's] ability to interpret these processes and take an active, formative part in them, so that every phase of the drama it stages shall have, to the highest degree possible, the illumination of consciousness, the stamp of purpose, the color of love. That magnification of all the dimensions of life, through emotional communion, rational communication, technological mastery, and above all, dramatic representation, has been the supreme office of the city in history. And it remains the chief reason for the city's continued existence.[33]

Mumford is not alone in his argument for the origins of cities being found in religion.[34] Eric E. Lampard, a contemporary of Mumford, notes

---

[30] See M. A. Claussen, "'Peregrinatio' and 'Peregrini' in Augustine's 'City of God,'" *Traditio* 46 (1991): 33–75.

[31] Lewis Mumford, *The City in History: Its Origins, Its Transformations, and Its Prospects* (San Diego: Harcourt, 1961), 575.

[32] Mumford, *The City in History*, 571.

[33] Mumford, *The City in History*, 576.

[34] See Paul Wheatley, *The Pivot of the Four Quarters: A Preliminary Enquiry into the Origins and Character of the Ancient Chinese City* (Chicago: Aldine Publishing, 1971) on the ceremonial basis for the first cities of East Asia; and Davíd Carrasco, *City of Sacrifice: The Aztec Empire and the Role of Violence in Civilization* (Boston: Beacon Press, 1999) on the connection between the origin of cities and religion in Meso-America. On the religious origins of cities in Islam, see Nezar AlSayyad, *Cities and Caliphs: On the Genesis of Arab Muslim Urbanism* (New York: Greenwood Press, 1991).

the central role that both temples and priests played in those first cities. Nature and the cosmos were already associated in human consciousness prior to the emergence of cities. The move toward "a more *exclusive* definition of the population and its boundaries and hence toward closure of the system" that cities brought about intensified these connections and extended the range of vision among the human actors, Lampard argues. "At some point, denizens of the temple came to mediate [humanity's] secular relations with the physical and social environment as well as their transcendental involvements in the cosmos."[35] In other words, religion and public policy were synonymous in these first cities. As Mumford puts it, religion took precedence in the emergence of cities as the "general magnification of power" that was part of the initial urban revolution in human experience "transposed into the 'eternal' forms of art."[36] Human beings invented cities not just out of the need or desire for greater protection (military origins), or to build a more complex material economy (commercial origins). They sought to organize and administer material and intellectual resources on a scale that was larger than what any single settlement or village could achieve as a means of recognizing and engaging the forces of nature and the cosmos that they experienced as being greater than what any one tribe or settlement could represent or engage on its own. In Christian terms, one might say that the *imago Dei* found its fuller expression in the *imago urbis*.

Both temple and accompanying ceremonial activities throughout the city are supported by archeological findings from the first cities in Southwest Asia such as Çatal Hüyük, notes Soja. He writes,

> We do not know what guided the overall spatial design of Jericho, what cosmological and religious symbolism was attached to the walled-in urban form, but it is clear that the interior spaces of the shrines and households were elaborately decorated to express and signify a collective belief system, and that the built environment was not simply a random construction. From the very start, then, urban space was designed and produced as a self-conscious expression of local and territorial culture, a materialized "symbolic zone," to use Iain Chamber's term, in which the real and the imagined commingled to comprehend, define, and ceremonialize a much-enlarged scale of social relations and community, the beginnings of *urbanism as a way of life*, to use that famous phrase of the Chicago School of urban studies founded 10,000 years later.[37]

---

[35] Eric E. Lampard, "Historical Aspects of Urbanization," in *The Study of Urbanization*, eds. Philip M. Houser and Leo F. Schnore (New York: John Wiley & Sons, 1965), 535.

[36] Mumford, *The City in History*, 33.

[37] Soja, *Postmetropolis*, 34, emphasis original.

Liliana Gómez and Walter Van Herck in their edited volume, *The Sacred in the City*, make a similar argument for the sacred being diffused throughout the city, not just in the ancient world, but also today. In the introduction to the volume, they highlight their use of the term "sacred" over "religion" precisely to locate it more broadly throughout the city, and not only in specific institutions and structures that are defined as "religious." The sacred, they argue, "as a category is more connected to an embodied attachment to symbols, buildings, monuments, and other cultural manifestations." The sacred is more diffused throughout the city. If religion was public policy, the sacred was and still is more broadly associated with public space and everyday urban life.[38] But, this in turn means that the city shapes the sacred as well. As Gómez and Van Herck note, "The city has a constitutive effect on our relation with the sacred and interacts with the human search for meaning in life and with the sacred in all its many guises."[39] The sacred comes in many guises, they argue. Its diversity is part of the underlying logic of synekism. "It is in the city that different religions and quests for meaning confront one another, ignore one another, communicate with one another, and compete with each other."[40] Today's multifaith urbanism in cities is but the latest chapter to a long urban history.[41]

In her chapter in the book, Gómez argues, "The modern metropolis can be characterized, on the one hand, by the individualization of its subjects, that is, the birth of the so-called modern subject, and on the other, by the emergence of new collective forms and energies." She terms these forms and energies "spirit-force sacred" and the "magical universe."

> The sacred in its manifold modern forms is part of those urban cultures which have been characterized by a performative element, such as celebrations or festivities, or other (para)religious ceremonies and which are relics of the sacred.[42]

---

[38] See Katie Day, "Urban Space and Religion in the United States," *Oxford Research Encyclopedia of Religion,* accessed October 18, 2018, http://religion.oxfordre.com/view/10.1093/acrefore/9780199340378.001.0001/acrefore-9780199340378-e-470; John Chase, Margaret Crawford, and John Kaliski, *Everyday Urbanism.* (New York: Monacal Press, 1999).

[39] Liliana Gómez and Walter Van Herck, eds., "Framing the Sacred in the City: An Introduction," in *The Sacred in the City* (London: Bloomsbury, 2012), 3.

[40] Gómez and Van Herck, "Framing the Sacred in the City," 4.

[41] See Sanjoy Mazumdar and Shampa Mazumdar, "Planning, Design, and Religion: America's Changing Urban Landscape," *Journal of Architectural and Planning Research* 30, no. 3 (2013): 221–43.

[42] Gómez, "The Urbanization of Society: Towards a Cultural Analysis of the Sacred in the Modern Metropolis," in Gómez and Van Herck, *The Sacred in the City* 37.

This immanent presence and pervading force has long been identified in Christian theology with the Holy Spirit, whom the Nicene Creed calls "the Lord, the giver of life."[43] The Spirit has never been entirely confined to ecclesial structures.[44] While it is true that there has long been an effort in certain streams of Christian theology to reduce the Spirit to an ecclesial location, the wider identification of the Spirit working in the world outside the church has never been entirely rejected. As Calvin acknowledges, God "fills, moves, and invigorates all things by the virtue of the Spirit, and that according to the peculiar nature which each class of beings has received by the Law of Creation."[45] Cities are places where this sacred filling, movement, and invigoration are both focused and amplified.[46] They are thus key locations for the transformation that the sacred or the Spirit brings about. As Gómez suggests, "The sacred, indeed, may be a key concept in understanding those modern cultural and social transformations experienced through the city."[47] Rephrasing Cyprian, one is tempted to conclude, *extra urbem nulla salus*.[48]

Gómez and Van Herck open their introduction to *The Sacred in the City* by recounting the design of the new capital of Brazil, Brasilia, from 1957. Lúcio Costa, the architect and urban planner who was mainly responsible for the master plan of Brasilia, laid out the city symbolically on a cross thereby investing this modern metropolis with an ancient sacred symbolism.[49] In his chapter in the same volume, Frank Usarski explores

---

[43] See Jürgen Moltmann, *The Source of Life: The Holy Spirit and the Theology of Life* (Minneapolis, MN: Fortress Press, 1997).

[44] See Stephen B. Bevans, "God inside Out: Toward a Missionary Theology of the Holy Spirit." *International Bulletin of Missionary Research* 22, no. 3 (July 1998): 102–5.

[45] John Calvin, *The Institutes of the Christian Religion*, trans. Henry Beveridge (Edinburgh: Calvin Translation Society, 1846), 237. The passage is from Book II, Chapter 2.16.

[46] See Kathryn Tanner, ed., *Spirit in the Cities: Searching for Soul in the Urban Landscape* (Minneapolis, MN: Fortress Press, 2004).

[47] Gómez, "The Urbanization of Society," 36.

[48] The phrase "extra ecclesiam nulla salus," or "outside the church, no salvation" has long been a staple of Christian theology dating back to Cyprian of Carthage who in his epistle, "Ad Jubajanum de Haereticis Baptizandis," para. 21 wrote: "salus extra ecclesiam non est" or "there is no salvation outside the church." The Latin text can be found online at https://archive.org/details/corpusscriptoru16wiss-goog/page/n8 (accessed March 18, 2019) in a digitalized version of Akademie der Wissenschaften in Wien, ed., *Corpus Scriptorum Ecclesiasticorum Latinorum* (Vienna: Hoelder-Pichler-Tempsky, 1886), 795. For a brief overview of the doctrine, see Gary Macy, "Extra Ecclesiam Nulla Salus," in *An Introductory Dictionary of Theology and Religious Studies*, eds. Orlando O. Espín and James B. Nickoloff (Collegeville: Liturgical Press 2007), 439–440.

[49] Gómez and Van Herck, "Framing the Sacred in the City," 1–2.

the relationship of a particular form of Zen Buddhist walking meditation that is practiced in a number of parks in the city of São Paulo, Brazil to the overall metropolitan context.[50] Filip De Boek's chapter explores the manner in which Pentecostal churches are engaging the dangerous and uncertain world of Kinshasa, capital of the Democratic Republic of Congo. I quote at length from his description.

> Indeed, the Pentecostal narrative has profoundly permeated the public sphere. It has imposed new mental structures onto daily life, but it has also punctuated, marked, shaped, and reconfigured the public urban space in a very physical and material way. There are church buildings emerging on every street corner of Kinshasa, and the sound of prayer accompanies one wherever one goes. It is by no means the exception for bars—these other ultimate urban spaces that are so profoundly linked to the rise of the African city, its popular culture, its notions of leisure, its time (the night), and its politics—to convert into churches, in a movement that infuses the urban public sphere with divine meaning, and visually and auditively stamps the aesthetics and moralities of a new spiritual geography onto its surface. At the same time, this spatial conversion also squarely posits the religious in the urban realm of market, capital, and business. Similarly, the new religious discourse has also engulfed the city's mediascape—it is no coincidence that a majority of the radio and television channels are owned by churches.[51]

De Boek notes that one of the defining features of Kinshasa from its days as a colonial city was the manner in which access to particular areas was denied to particular persons—Africans—by the European colonial rulers. Access to the city continues to be an issue for Kinshasa today. In some places the threat of violence acts as a barrier, while in others the gates around communities of wealth serve such purposes. Such barriers reflect the uneven distributions of power and inequalities of wealth that characterize not just Kinshasa but cities around the world. Such aspects sit in tension with the fact that cities are also places that foster emancipation, or are places where the poor, the disenfranchised, and other persons with less power create a history of their own.[52]

The workings of everyday urban life generate unequal power relations. But, these same creative forces generate resistance against inequalities. This is because the city as a whole is constructed by all who are in it, and not just by those who exercise greater power within it. All urban dwellers carry the urban within them. From within the city itself arises both the

---

[50] Frank Usarski, "*Kinhin* in a Megacity—Implicit Meanings of the 'Walking-in-the-Park' Movement in São Paulo," in Gómez and Van Herck, *The Sacred in the City*, 96–107.

[51] Filip De Boeck, "Kinshasa and its (Un)Certainties: The Polis and the Sacred," in Gómez and Van Herck, *The Sacred in the City* 198.

[52] Sassen, "Who Owns Our Cities".

right and the power to create, not just by some, but by all. Lefebvre calls this "the right to the city."[53] More than an abstract legal right, he considers it "a cry and a demand" for renewed urban life.[54] It arises out of the city itself and is in no small part an expression of its sacredness, or an intensification of its sacred form. Lefebvre writes,

> The right to the city, complemented by the right to difference and the right to information, should modify, concretize, and make more practical the rights of the citizen as an urban dweller (*citadin*) and user of multiple services. It would affirm, on the one hand, the right of users to make known their ideas on the space and time of their activities in the urban area; it would also cover the right to the use of the centre, a privileged place, instead of being dispersed and stuck into ghettos (for workers, immigrants, the "marginal," and even for the "privileged").[55]

For Lefebvre, the right to the city is not something granted by those who occupy positions of privilege and power. It resides in the very fact of our collective and individual humanity. It emerges in the city most clearly because cities are places where this humanity comes into its fullest expression. Cities do not emerge from the thinking of one person. They are instead the result of collective thinking, collective behavior. At the same time, they are unique, as an individual entity. Despite similarities and continuities through time and space that make it meaningful to speak about urban experience generally, no two cities on earth have ever been the same. Lefebvre says that this is because the city as a whole is always an "oeuvre," a work of art, not a product that can be repeated.[56] Cities are collective works of art that ultimately arise not just from their citizens and inhabitants, but from humanity as a whole. The intrinsic right to the city arises from this overall human capacity to build and dwell in them and extends to the right to all to benefit fully from them.

For Soja, the right to the city thus extends beyond its citizens and immediate inhabitants. Soja argues for a more regional spatial understanding of the right to the city that extends to those who live within the suburbs around it that provide its workers and those in the rural areas who provide the foods that sustain it. Given the place that cities have played in creating wealth and in extending the global economy, one can argue that the notion of the right to the city can be extended to all people and even to the overall ecology of our planet. As Soja writes,

---

[53] Henri Lefebvre, *Writings on Cities*, trans. Eleonore Kofman and Elizabeth Lebas (Malden, MA: Blackwell Publishers, 1996), 158, emphasis original.
[54] Lefebvre, *Writings on Cities*, 158.
[55] Lefebvre, *Writings on Cities*, 34.
[56] Lefebvre, *Writings on Cities*, 65–67.

This broadened view of the regional right to the city, as I have been arguing persistently, can be best understood when urbanization and the organized space of the city are seen as generative forces, wellsprings of societal development, technological innovation, cultural creativity, as well as social stratification, hegemonic power, inequality, and injustice. Things do not just happen in cities, they happen to a significant extent because of cities.[57]

In the remaining section of this chapter, I want to argue that the biblical understanding of salvation is fundamentally about the right to the city. One of the reasons for making connections between ancient and modern cities and the urban experiences they foster both at the levels of public policy and everyday urban life is to better facilitate a dialogue between biblical texts and contemporary contexts. The right to the city as figured in the Bible becomes a mandate for the right to the city in contemporary public policy and urban life.

Cities figure prominently in the pages of the Bible from Genesis through Revelation. They dominate the landscape of the Old Testament, even when they are not always explicitly in view.[58] They play an equally important role in the pages of the New Testament, both in the life of Jesus and in the spread of the early Christian movement.[59] In his introduction to *The City in the Hebrew Bible*, James Aitken notes the close connection between cities and the very existence of the Bible itself. He writes,

> An important facet of the city in ancient Israel is scribalism, revealed in the concerns of recent scholarship, even if the city context is not always made explicit. The increase in writing in the eighth century (as evidenced by inscriptions) has been attributed to the need for greater administration within the monarchical system. This would put the cause of writing, and the likely formation of the earliest biblical writings, very much in the city itself. Implicit in the current interest in scribalism is the role of the city as a formative place for schools and the need for a literate bureaucracy. As such our biblical texts come about not only in the city, but thanks to the city.[60]

---

[57] Soja, *Seeking Spatial Justice*, 97.

[58] James K. Aitken and Hilary F. Marlow, eds., *The City in the Hebrew Bible: Critical, Literary and Exegetical Approaches* (London: T&T Clark, 2018); Diana V. Edelman and Ehud Ben Zvi, eds., *Memory and the City in Ancient Israel* (Warsaw, IN: Eisenbrauns, 2014); Volkmar Fritz, *City in Ancient Israel* (Sheffield: Sheffield Academic Press, 1995).

[59] See Edwin M. Yamauchi, *New Testament Cities in Western Asia Minor: Light from Archaeology on Cities of Paul and the Seven Churches of Revelation* (Eugene, OR: Wipf and Stock, 2003); Wayne A. Meeks, *The First Urban Christians: The Social World of the Apostle Paul*, 2nd ed. (New Haven: Yale University, 2003).

[60] James K. Aitken, "Introduction: A City Perspective," in *The City in the Hebrew Bible*, eds. Aitken and Marlow, 5–6.

The Bible opens with the story of creation followed by God planting a garden in which God then placed Adam, the human one (Gen 2:8). Gardens in the ancient world were part of the built environment.[61] Jeremiah 29:5 lists building houses and planting gardens as key tasks for the exiles to perform as they settle in and seek the *shalom* of the new city to which God has sent them. These enclosed urban spaces were for growing vineyards, fruit trees, and other food items, or for holding domesticated livestock such as sheep.[62] Cultivation of food is the announced purpose of the garden God planted for Adam in Genesis 2:15. Gardens were also recreational places where one could go for relaxation. In Genesis 3:8, God was taking a walk in the garden during the time of "the breeze of the day" (*ruach yom*), presumably either in the morning or evening, not the time of day when one is working at cultivating the soil. While recreational gardens could be semi-public spaces (open to members of the aristocracy for the most part), they were most often private property and thus were under the control of their individual owners. As part of the built environment, gardens were located either within the walls of a city or close by enough on the outside of the ways that one could easily get to them to attend them or defend them. The walls around gardens were intended not only to keep unwanted animals out, or if in the case of domesticated livestock to keep the animals in, but also to keep out unwanted intruders who might otherwise steal from them.[63]

In Genesis 4:16, after killing his brother, Cain went out from the presence of God to the land of Nod (or "Wandering" in Hebrew). But then immediately in verse 17, Cain and his unnamed wife had a son whom they named Enoch, and he built a city that he named "Enoch."[64] Always, the city is on the horizon of the rest of the book of Genesis, even when not

---

[61] For an excellent introduction to the history of gardening in the ancient Mediterranean and Persian worlds, and the emerging field of garden archaeology, see Linda Farrar, *Gardens and Gardeners of the Ancient World: History, Myth and Archaeology* (Oxford: Oxbow books, 2016).

[62] Here should be noted the importance of Edward J. Soja's argument that planned cultivation of foods and large-scale domestication of livestock were developed by human beings in the ancient world to meet the need for feeding urban populations. In other words, according to Soja and other urban theorists, the rise of cities and the agricultural revolution happened in tandem, with the former driving the need for the latter. See Soja, *Postmetropolis*, 34–35.

[63] For a social study of contemporary urban gardening in one city in North America and the manner in which enclosure intersects with inclusion and exclusion, see Hilda Kurtz, "Differentiating Multiple Meanings of Garden and Community," *Urban Geography* 22, no.7 (2001): 656–670.

[64] For a fuller discussion of this verse, and the argument that the builder of the city was Cain, see R. P. Gordon, "Contested Eponymy: Cain, Enoch, and the Cities of Genesis 1–11," in *The City in the Hebrew Bible*, eds. Aitken and Marlow, 164–181.

Deus Urbis *and the Right to the City*

explicitly being noted. Israel's formative years as a tribal confederacy in Canaan might not appear to offer much in the way of urban formations, but as Norman Gottwald points out, this entire period is shaped in relation to the surrounding Canaanite cities that at the time were for the most part under Egyptian domination.[65] Eventually, Israel adopted the governing structures of monarchy, which in the ancient world was uniformly an urban formation. One city in particular, that of Jerusalem or Zion, which was the city David chose to make his capital, came to dominate the history, geography, and theology of the Old Testament.[66]

Cities are equally prominent throughout the pages of the New Testament. They figure prominently in the spread of the Christian message in the letters of the New Testament.[67] One encounters in the letters of Paul major urban centers such as Damascus, Antioch, Corinth, and Rome. Extra-biblical sources point to the importance of cities such as Edessa as well in early urban centers in which Christian communities took shape and from which the movement spread further along trade routes. Early Christian community formations were private or voluntary associations of people from various backgrounds who gathered in homes located in urban apartment buildings (the "insula" of the Greco-Roman world).[68]

---

[65] Norman K. Gottwald writes, "In my view it is impossible to understand pastoral nomadism in the ancient Near East, and especially in Canaan, without an appreciation of the political factors at work in its development and experience. At the time of Israel's appearance, centralized government had existed in the ancient Near East for at least two thousand years and probably for a great deal longer. Centralized authority was more or less solidly based in the most prosperous regions of the fertile crescent, operating out of urban centers and extending control into the countryside in the form of taxation in kind and in forced military service and draft labor.... On this way of looking at the political situation in the ancient Near East, the city stands over against the countryside; the centralizing and stratified monarchic and aristocratic classes stand at variance with the peasant and pastoral populations." Norman K. Gottwald, *The Tribes of Yahweh: A Sociology of Religion of Liberated Israel, 1250–1050 B.C.E.* (Maryknoll: Orbis Books, 1979), 449.

[66] See Ben C. Ollenburger, *Zion, the City of the Great King: A Theological Symbol of the Jerusalem Cult* (Sheffield: Sheffield Academic Press, 1987).

[67] See Wayne A. Meeks, *The First Urban Christians: The Social World of the Apostle Paul*, 2nd ed. (New Haven: Yale University Press, 2003); John H. Elliott, *A Home for the Homeless: A Social-Scientific Criticism of 1 Peter, Its Situation and Strategy* (Minneapolis, MN: Augsburg Press, 1997); Rodney Stark, *The Rise of Christianity: How the Obscure, Marginal Jesus Movement Became the Dominant Religious Force in the Western World in a Few Centuries* (San Francisco: HarperSanFrancisco, 1997); and more recently, Steve Walton, Paul Trebilco, and David W. J. Gill, eds., *The Urban World and the First Christians* (Grand Rapids, MI: W.B. Eerdmans Publishing, 2017).

[68] See Bart D. Ehrman, *The New Testament: A Historical Introduction to the Early Christian Writings* (New York: Oxford University Press, 1997), 241–350.

Of the cities mentioned in the New Testament, two dominate: Rome and Jerusalem. By the first century C.E., Rome was more than just a city-state, but had become a full-fledged empire. The city had initially been ruled by a monarch, but for several hundred years had been under a republican form of governance under a senate until Julius Caesar sought to consolidate power under his own rule. After Caesar's assassination, his grand-nephew and adopted son Octavian was granted the title of Augustus by the senate in 31 B.C.E. With Augustus we can date the beginning of Rome as a full-fledged empire, but it was still first of all a city.[69]

Rome might have been a long way from Galilee or Judaea in geographical terms by Jesus's day, but the city was quite present in political and economic terms. Galilee as much as Judaea was engulfed in a wider urban nexus of empire that stretched from Rome to Persia.[70]

The occupation of its armies, or "legions" in regions like the Decapolis might well have been reflected in the name of the demons in Mark 5:9. The image of Caesar on coins used in the region represented well the manner in which rulers were perceived to be immanent in day-to-day material transactions of the realm, reaching into urban marketplaces and even temple courtyards (see Matthew 22:15–22).

By the time of Jesus, Roman citizenship was no longer strictly determined by being a resident of the actual city, but could be extended to those who were residents in other cities throughout the empire.[71] Citizenship in this case was understood to be not so much a function of birth location or even language and culture, but had come to entail a particular urban political experience that brought one into relationship with the emperor who ruled from Rome. The book of Acts (16:37 and 22:25-28) portrays Paul as being a Roman citizen, although his birth home was Tarsus and as far as we know, he never entered the actual city of Rome until toward the end of his life.[72] In his own letters, Paul never referred to himself as a Roman citizen, but he held a clear understanding of the matter when he

---

[69] For a rather engaging account of the history of ancient Rome, see Ferdinand Addis, *The Eternal City: A History of Rome* (New York: Pegasus Books, 2018).

[70] See J. Andrew Overman, "Between Rome and Parthia: Galilee and The Implications of Empire," in *A Wandering Galilean: Essays in Honour of Seán Freyne*, eds. Zuleika Rodgers, Margaret Daly-Denton, and Anne Fitzpatrick-McKinley (Leiden: Brill, 2009), 279–299.

[71] See an excellent brief summary in Steve Walton, "Heavenly Citizenship and Earthly Authorities: Philippians 1:27 and 3:20 in Dialogue with Acts 16: 11–40," in *The Urban World and the First Christians*, eds. Walton, Trebilco, and Gill, 242–243.

[72] See Sean A. Adams, "Paul the Roman Citizen: Roman Citizenship in the Ancient World and Its Importance for Understanding Acts 22:22-29," *Paul: Jew, Greek, and Roman*, ed. Stanley E. Porter (Leiden: Brill, 2009), 309–326.

wrote in Philippians 3:20a, "But our citizenship is in heaven," offering an alternative reading on the same urban theme.

Jerusalem is the other city that has a major presence in the pages of the New Testament.[73] Jerusalem, which David had made his capital, was not just a city, but the location of the temple.[74] For many Jews from across the Persian and Roman empires in the first century, the temple was central to their identity.[75] Even those Jews who were critics of the temple, the ones Josephus called "the Essenes," made its purification a central part of their hope.[76] Jerusalem, both the actual city to which he will turn in the final chapter of his life as well as the ideal city to which all should have access, is a dominant motif in the life and ministry of Jesus of Nazareth, as will be seen below. The right to the city, be it Rome or Jerusalem, is a theme that runs throughout the pages of the New Testament.[77]

The New Testament ends in a city. The *telos* of human history, according to the seer in Revelation 21:22 and again in 22:5, is nothing less than a well-functioning urban reality. The light of divine glory, which will replace the sun and the power grid, is there. Divine life and light will both be immanent in and throughout this alternative "Eternal City." This glory is nothing less than the Spirit of God, which is particularly concerned to shine forth in love. Carrying out their daily urban activities, the inhabitants of this city will participate in the Spirit's work of glorifying God.[78] Furthermore, the glory, with its accompanying love and peace, will be

---

[73] Peter W. L. Walker, *Jesus and the Holy City: New Testament Perspectives on Jerusalem* (Grand Rapids, MI: W.B. Eerdmans Publishing, 1996). For further discussions on the literary and ideological significance of Jerusalem as a city, see Maricel's essay, "Centralization of Religious Power in the City: An Essay Based on 1 Kings 1–11," in this current volume, chapter 3.

[74] James H. Charlesworth, ed., *Jesus and Temple: Textual and Archaeological Explorations* (Minneapolis, MN: Fortress Press, 2014).

[75] Here, I am generally following among others, E. P. Sanders, *Judaism: Practice and Belief, 63 B.C.E.–66 C.E.* (Harrisburg: Trinity International Press, 1994), 59–496.

[76] Sanders, *Judaism: Practice and Belief*, 535–595.

[77] Matthew Sleeman, "Paul, Pentecost, and the Nomosphere: The Final Return to Jerusalem in the Acts of the Apostles," in *The Urban World and the First Christians*, ed. Walton, Trebilco, and Gill, 20–41, draws upon Lefebvre's concept of "the right to the city" to explore how "Paul navigates within Jerusalem" (20) in Acts 21–22. The city of Rome (and the Roman empire it represents) is negatively portrayed as a whoring Babylon, which must be humiliated. As questions of masculinity and femininity clash in and around the city, a feminized Rome is stripped and humiliated, but also morphs into the epicenter of a masculinized Christian empire. See Stephen Moore, *Untold Tales from the Book of Revelation: Sex and Gender, Empire and Ecology* (Atlanta: SBL Press, 2014), 125–154.

[78] Eugene F. Rogers, Jr., *After the Spirit: A Constructive Pneumatology from Resources outside the Modern West* (Grand Rapids, MI: W.B. Eerdmans Publishing, 2005), 176.

unending. According to Revelation 21:25, since the New Jerusalem will be lit by the glory of God, there will be no night and thus the gates will always be open. Gates in cities in the ancient Mediterranean world both along the outer wall and inside the cities themselves that separated districts during times of peace remained open during daylight hours, but were closed and locked at night. Here the gates remain open all day and night, indicating it will truly be a city of peace.

The city will be multicultural in its make-up according to Revelation 7:9. Yet, anxieties about city-zenship abound in the world of Pax Romana. Not all humanity will dwell within the city, but only those whose names are found in the Lamb's book of life. Others who are righteous appear to be free to come and go as they wish, however. Even those who are not citizens of the city will be welcomed to participate in its life and partake of its resources. The divine economy stretches beyond those who are immediately identified as being disciples or believers. They are the primary liturgists of the new Jerusalem, but they do not exhaust its material, social, and cultural life.

In Revelation 11, the seer tells of an angel taking measurements, implying urban planning and code enforcement. Leaders of the nations will bring their taxes to God, indicating an operating economic system for generating material wealth with offices of government administration found in Revelation 21:24. There will be leaves of a tree in the middle of the street for healing (Rev 22:2), suggesting a centralized health care system, while also evoking memory of the tree of life that formed the central part of the first garden (Gen 2:9). The picture is one of a living city that continues to produce and consume. Human beings will be expected to participate in its administration, the most basic form of which will be, as Augustine suggests, liturgy, that is, the ritual work of worship. One foresees a city in which parades and other public ceremonies are central practices, the most common form of daily action, not unlike life in New York City where parades occur almost weekly. The depiction is one of liturgy and ceremonies becoming everyday urbanism. It is significant in this regard that the seer found no temple in the New Jerusalem according to Revelation 21:22, suggesting that the ceremonial activities that had previously been described were taking place in non-temple places, infusing the sacred throughout the entire urban context or process in ways that Gómez and Van Herck suggest.

The text takes care to note that no one who practices abomination or falsehoods will enter the city, implying that such practices will continue outside the city. The general statement in Revelation 22:3 that "Nothing accursed will be found there any more" implies the removal of all anathemas, or the opening of the city to the formerly cursed. This is significant given the place that the Lamb who was slain plays in the New Jerusalem. The implications in the text are of a one formerly accursed, degraded, or humiliated being vindicated and set in a place of high honor. Jesus Christ, who Paul says in Galatians 3:13 was "cursed" is now given a privileged place of honor in the New Jerusalem. Those who were humiliated or cursed for his sake join him. The right to the city becomes extended to those who previously were denied any rights, or who were regarded as being without rights. Christology and ecclesiology both turn toward the wider horizon of the city. Jeremiah's injunction to "seek the *shalom* of the city" (29:7) takes on new urgency as an ecclesiological imperative in light of the right to the city.

The presence of Christ, localized within the city through the figure of the throne, intensifies the manner of sacred immanence in a political direction. This political dimension is what in fact defined the polis in classical Greece. A city in the Greco-Roman world of the New Testament was not just buildings and streets, but a center from which power was exercised over surrounding lands.[79] The New Testament writers drew freely upon their surrounding dominant political experiences to describe the manner in which the risen Christ would exercise power and authority. In the language of the ancient tradition, Jesus would be the monarch, or "king."

A king or queen in the ancient world was an urban figure. A king or queen (and later an emperor) ruled first and foremost over, and from, a particular city, the capital. In a sense, king or queen and state ("kingdom") were mutually constitutive. The glory of a king or queen was the glory of the city-state, and vice versa. The realm over which the authority or power of a king or queen extended was the city and the surrounding regions that person dominated or controlled. It usually included other cities as well as the surrounding countryside whose towns, villages, and trade routes the military forces of the ruling class could secure and from which the rulers extracted tribute or taxes. God, who had long been understood in Israel through the figure of the king, either has or will, according to the book of Revelation hand over the realm of God to Jesus Christ, who up till then sat at the right hand of power. God's glory, in the form or person of the Holy Spirit, extends throughout this urban-centric realm, further diffusing divine presence. The divine realm finds collective urban expression in the Trinitarian figuring of Father, Son, and Spirit. The doctrine of the Trinity is very much an urban construct.

---

[79] See H. Strathmann, "Polis," in *Theological Dictionary of the New Testament*, ed. Gerhard Kittel, trans. Geoffrey W. Bromiley (Grand Rapids, MI: W.B. Eerdmans, 1968), s.v.

Salvation entails a "civitas," a mode of living that takes place in a city or in relation to a city. The right to the city derives not just from the city itself, but from our fundamental humanity of which cities are an expression. As noted above, the right to the city is closely related to the *imago urbis*, which is another name for the *imago Dei*. If this is the case, then we ought to be able to discern the right to the city not just generally in the pages of the Bible, but specifically in the ministry of Jesus Christ who is in the New Testament the privileged figure, the image of God (*eikōn tou theou*, Col 1:15) through whom the salvation of the world is realized. If the *imago Dei* is also *imago urbis*, then we ought to find Jesus asserting the right to the city in fundamental ways.[80]

This turns out to be indeed the case. Emphasizing his identification from birth with those of humble status, Luke nevertheless asserts Jesus's own right to the city in royal terms with the story of Joseph and Mary returning to their native Bethlehem, the city where David, whose identity is closely connected with Jerusalem, was actually born. The right to the city is reasserted again in Luke 2:22–38, in this case in the city of Jerusalem and specifically in the temple that was at the center of the life of the city. For much of first century Judaism, the right to the city was closely tied to the right to the temple, or access to its blessings through rituals of purification. The parents of the child Jesus exercise this right by bringing him to the temple for his blessing. The prophecies spoken over him link his right to the city with the redemption of the city (Luke 2:38).

Soja's regional reading of the right to the city sheds light on the meaning of John the Baptist and his ministry. Matthew 3:5 says that "the people of Jerusalem and all of Judea were going out to him." The message of John the Baptist that the kingdom of heaven has drawn near (Matt 3:2) relocates the right to the city out in the wilderness. A kingdom in the ancient Mediterranean world was an urban construct. When Jesus said the kingdom of God was within, he was in effect talking about that "civitas" or mode of living that characterized life in the divine urban realm. Proclaiming good news to the poor was nothing less than extending to them the right to this city.

The expansion of the right to the city on the part not just of the poor, but of sinners, the ritually impure, and those who generally were relegated to the margins of society or outside the gates was at the heart of Jesus's ministry in Galilee. Galilee was, as noted above, a region that was

---

[80] Sleeman argues that Paul predicates his own right to the city theologically on the basis of the risen Christ's right to the city, Christ now being "Lord of all." Sleeman, "Paul, Pentecost, and the Nomosphere," 36. Sleeman does not explore the manner in which Jesus in the first four books of the New Testament asserts the right to the city, especially of Jerusalem, at the core of his ministry.

embedded in a wider urban construct.[81] The parable of the great banquet in Matthew 22:1–14 and Luke 14:15–23 both cite the failure of those who typically exercised their right to the city to accept the dinner invitation of the king (Matthew) or simply "someone" (Luke, NRSV). Their failure opens the way for those who are from the margins to realize their right to the city, in this instance manifested in the experience of a banquet. In Luke 14:21, the "someone" tells a slave, "Go out immediately into the streets and alleyways of the city (polis) and lead in the poor, the disabled, the halting, and the blind" (translation my own). The slave does so, but there are still seats at the table (v. 22). "Then the master said to the slave, 'Go out onto the highways and along the walls and force them to come in, so that my house may be full'" (v. 23, translation my own). The right to the city, manifested in this instance as an invitation to a great banquet, is extended to those who are found first along both the main streets and back alleys of the city, and then to those who are living outside the city, along the highways or up against the hedges and walls that serve as barriers to keep people out.[82]

According to the first three evangelists, at a particular moment in his public ministry Jesus turned his attention toward Jerusalem in a decisive way. According to John, Jesus's attention was directed toward Jerusalem from almost the beginning of his public ministry. In either case, the turn toward Jerusalem in the first four books of the New Testament was coupled with a profound re-articulation of the notion of the right to the city, in this case, a prophetic right that was closely bound up in the concept of redemption, not just of Israel, but of the world. Jesus's lament over Jerusalem in Matthew 23:37–39 and Luke 13:33–35 expresses a double meaning of the right to the city, that of the prophet who brings a word of judgment against it, as in Isaiah 1, and a word of embrace, especially for those who are most vulnerable within it, which is the other side of the judgment found in Jeremiah in chapters 2 and 22.

Much of what the first four books of the New Testament report Jesus saying in the temple have to do with the right to the temple, which closely

---

[81] See Andrew J. Overman, "Who were the First Urban Christians? Urbanization in Galilee in the First Century," *Society of Biblical Literature: Seminar Papers 27* (Atlanta: SBL Press, 1988), 160–168.

[82] The use of the term *doulos* or "enslaved person" in both Matthew and Luke raises important questions about the manner in which even in the New Testament the notion of the "right to city" was filtered through accepted practices of human enslavement. Enslaved persons in the ancient Greek context exercised to a certain degree a right to the city, but under Roman law they could do so only through the right to the city exercised by their masters, along the same lines as women and children of minority age. See Orlando Paterson, *Slavery and Social Death: A Comparative Study* (Cambridge: Harvard University Press, 1982), 28–33.

parallels for Jesus the right to the city.[83] The incident in the temple reported by all four evangelists where Jesus is supposed to have turned over the tables of moneychangers takes on anti-Jewish implications when read against the long European Christian legacy of anti-Judaism. The story itself is not anti-Jewish, however, but about opening access to the temple to all people. The allusions to Isaiah 56:6–7, which opened the temple to the *nekar*, that is, immigrants or aliens, is itself an expression of the right not just to the temple, but to the city. In John 2:16, Jesus poses the challenge as transforming the house of his Father into a house of commerce (*oikon emperiou*). The marketplace is for Jesus not capable of expressing the fullness of the right to the city, and the right to the temple that is at the heart of the city that he envisions. Mark 11:17 is starker in its contrast between a house of prayer for all nations (*pasom tois ethnesin*) and a den or cave of robbers.

Obery Hendricks argues that Jesus was not expressing anti-Jewish sentiments. Instead, argues Hendricks, he opposed the wealthy temple aristocracy and the hereditary priesthood on the grounds that they closed off access to the temple to the masses, and because they collaborated with the oppressive Roman rulers. Hendricks sees a class divide in terms of wealth between temple aristocracy and the common people who sought access to God through prayer in the temple.[84] The temple priests sought to restrict access to the temple in order to maintain their wealth and religious privilege, and to accommodate their Roman overlords. The revolutionary Jesus challenged them and the temple economy on behalf of the right to the city, and to the salvation that the temple represented. For that he was executed.

Even on the cross Jesus continues, according to accounts in the New Testament, to express the right to the city. He tells one of the rebels along with whom he is being executed, "Truly I tell you, today you will be with me in Paradise" (Luke 23:43, NRSV). Paradise is a resting place within a city. The word made its way into Greek from Persian, where it was the term for a park or garden within a city. In the pages of the New Testament, it became another name for the place where the faithful go after death. In the words of Charles Wesley's hymn, through his resurrection "Christ hath opened paradise," that is, he opened the right to the city.

---

[83] On the manner in which Matthew first asserts the centrality of Jerusalem and the Temple, then moves beyond to it, see Anders Runesson, "City of God or Home of Traitors and Killers: Jerusalem According to Matthew," in *The Urban World and the First Christians*, ed. Walton, Trebilco, and Gill, 219–235.

[84] Obery M. Hendricks, Jr., *The Politics of Jesus: Rediscovering the True Revolutionary Nature of Jesus' Teachings and How They Have Been Corrupted* (New York: Doubleday Books, 2006), 58–60.

The city is more than a sociological form. It is more than a historical development. The city is God's way of divinizing humanity. Another way to say this is that theologically, the city is ultimately the means by which humanity participates in the divine life. According to the biblical witness, the church is not the end of human history. Rather the end is a city in which, according to Hebrews 11:10, God is both the architect (*technitēs*) and builder (*dēmiourgos*). Urbanization and divinization in the end coincide.

This chapter began by noting the manner in which our contemporary world is becoming profoundly urbanized. Urbanization and globalization are indeed, to paraphrase Archbishop William Temple, "the great new facts of our era."[85] Cities are more than incidental conveniences, however. They are means by which human beings amplify their humanity and achieve more in terms of their own human identity. Cities are also places where the sacred becomes amplified, be it through art, culture, religion, or simply everyday human experience. Cities emerged in human history as our ancestors sought to build a better home for their gods. In this sense, religion was the primordial form of public policy. It remains so today, becoming even more evident in our "post-secular" world.[86]

Cities prove to be especially important in the biblical witness and for biblical faith. They shape the biblical imagination in significant ways. Following Lefebvre and Soja, I have argued that the right to the city, to its resources, to the wealth that it produces, and to the benefits that it bestows, extends not just to those who live within specific urban locations, but to all humanity. In a fundamental sense, the Christian doctrine of salvation is also a doctrine of urbanization. Salvation entails a form of urban living, the coming city of God. Salvation is not co-terminal with entering the church. Rather, salvation ultimately means entering into a new city. That experience, combined with the notion of the right to the city being extended especially to the poor, the marginalized, the down-trodden, and the dispossessed, is what constitutes the good news that Jesus was anointed by the Spirit to proclaim in Luke 4:18–19.

---

[85] William Temple referred to the ecumenical movement as "the great world-fellowship," "the great new fact of our era." William Temple, *The Church Looks Forward* (New York: Macmillan, 1944), 2.

[86] See Gregor McLennan, "The Postsecular Turn," *Theory, Culture & Society* 27, no.4 (2010): 3–20; Manav Ratti, *The Postsecular Imagination: Postcolonialism, Religion, and Literature* (New York: Routledge, 2013).

Bibliography

Adams, Sean A. "Paul the Roman Citizen: Roman Citizenship in the Ancient World and Its Importance for Understanding Acts 22:22–29." In *Paul: Jew, Greek, and Roman*, edited by Stanley E. Porter, 309–236. Leiden: Brill, 2009.

Addis, Ferdinand. *The Eternal City: A History of Rome*. New York: Pegasus Books, 2018.

Aitken, James K., and Hilary F. Marlow, eds. *The City in the Hebrew Bible: Critical, Literary and Exegetical Approaches*. London: T&T Clark, 2018.

AlSayyad, Nezar. *Cities and Caliphs: On the Genesis of Arab Muslim Urbanism*. New York: Greenwood Press, 1991.

Augustine. *The City of God against the Pagans*, edited by R. W. Dyson. Cambridge: Cambridge University Press, 1998.

Banfield, Edward D. *Unheavenly City: The Nature and the Future of Our Urban Crisis*. Boston: Little, Brown & Co., 1979.

———. *The Unheavenly City Revisited*. Prospect Heights, IL: Waveland Press, 1990.

Bevans, Stephen B. "God inside Out: Toward a Missionary Theology of the Holy Spirit." *International Bulletin of Missionary Research* 22, no. 3 (July 1998): 102–5.

Calvin, John. *The Institutes of the Christian Religion*, translated by Henry Beveridge. Edinburgh: Calvin Translation Society, 1846.

Carrasco, David. *City of Sacrifice: The Aztec Empire and the Role of Violence in Civilization*. Boston: Beacon Press, 1999.

Charlesworth, James H., ed. *Jesus and Temple: Textual and Archaeological Explorations*. Minneapolis, MN: Fortress Press, 2014.

Chase, John, Margaret Crawford, and John Kaliski. *Everyday Urbanism*. New York: Monacal Press, 1999.

Claussen, M.A. "'Peregrinatio' and 'Peregrini' in Augustine's 'City of God.'" *Traditio* 46 (1991): 33–75.

Davis, Mike. *Planet of Slums*. New York and London: Verso, 2006.

Day, Katie. "Urban Space and Religion in the United States." *Oxford Research Encyclopedia of Religion*, accessed October 18, 2018, http://religion.oxfordre.com/view/10.1093/acrefore/9780199340378.001.0001/acrefore-9780199340378-e-470.

Edelman, Diana V., and Ehud Ben Zvi. *Memory and the City in Ancient Israel*. Warsaw, IN: Eisenbrauns, 2014.

Ehrman, Bart D. *The New Testament: A Historical Introduction to the Early Christian Writings*. New York: Oxford University Press, 1997.

Elliott, John H. *A Home for the Homeless: A Social-Scientific Criticism of 1 Peter, Its Situation and Strategy*. Minneapolis, MN: Augsburg Press, 1997; reprint, Eugene, OR: Wipf and Stock, 2005.

Farrar, Linda. *Gardens and Gardeners of the Ancient World: History, Myth and Archaeology*. Oxford: Oxbow books, 2016.

Fritz, Volkmar. *City in Ancient Israel*. Sheffield: Sheffield Academic Press, 1995.

Gómez, Liliana, and Walter Van Herck. "Framing the Sacred in the City: An Introduction," *The Sacred in the City*. London: Bloomsbury, 2012.

Gottwald, Norman K. *The Tribes of Yahweh: A Sociology of Religion of Liberated Israel, 1250–1050 B.C.E.* Maryknoll: Orbis Books, 1979.

Hendricks, Obery M., Jr. *The Politics of Jesus: Rediscovering the True Revolutionary Nature of Jesus' Teachings and How They Have Been Corrupted*. New York: Doubleday Books, 2006.

International Organization for Migration (IOM). *World Migration Report 2015, Migrants and Cities: New Partnerships to Manage Mobility*. Geneva: IOM, 2015.

Irvin, Dale T. "Migration and Cities: Theological Reflections." In *Contemporary Issues of Migration and Theology*, edited by Elaine Padilla and Peter C. Phan, 73–93. New York: Palgrave MacMillan, 2013.

Kurtz, Hilda. "Differentiating Multiple Meanings of Garden and Community." *Urban Geography* 22, no. 7 (2001): 656–670.

Lampard, Eric E. "Historical Aspects of Urbanization." In *The Study of Urbanization*, edited by Philip M. Houser and Leo F. Schnore. New York: John Wiley & Sons, 1965.

Lefebvre, Henri. *La Révolution Urbaine*. Paris: Gallimard, 1970.

———. *The Urban Revolution*, translated by Robert Bononno. Minneapolis, MN: University of Minnesota Press, 2003.

———. *Writings on Cities*, translated by, Eleonore Kofman and Elizabeth Lebas. Malden, MA: Blackwell Publishers, 1996.

Little, Jo, Linda Peake, and Pat Richardson, eds. *Women in Cities: Gender and the Urban Environment*. London: Macmillan Education, 1988.

Macy, Gary. "Extra Ecclesiam Nulla Salus." In *An Introductory Dictionary of Theology and Religious Studies*, edited by Orlando O. Espín and James B. Nickoloff, 439–440. Collegeville, MN: Liturgical Press, 2007.

Mazumdar, Sanjoy, and Shampa Mazumdar. "Planning, Design, and Religion: America's Changing Urban Landscape." *Journal of Architectural and Planning Research* 30, no. 3 (2013): 221–43.

McLennan, Gregor. "The Postsecular Turn." *Theory, Culture & Society* 27, no. 4 (2010): 3–20.

McNeill, William H. *Plagues and Peoples.* New York: Anchor Books, 1976.

Meeks, Wayne A. *The First Urban Christians: The Social World of the Apostle Paul.* 2nd ed. New Haven: Yale University, 2003.

Moltmann, Jürgen. *The Source of Life: The Holy Spirit and the Theology of Life.* Minneapolis, MN: Fortress Press, 1997.

Mumford, Lewis. *The City in History: Its Origins, Its Transformations, and Its Prospects.* San Diego: Harcourt Inc., 1961.

Myers, Joe. "You Knew China's Cities Were Growing. But the Real Numbers Are Stunning," *World Economic Forum.* Accessed October, 10, 2018. https://www.weforum.org/agenda/2016/06/china-cities-growing-numbers-are-stunning/.

Ollenburger, Ben C. *Zion the City of the Great King: A Theological Symbol of the Jerusalem Cult.* Sheffield: Sheffield Academic Press, 1987.

Overman, J. Andrew. "Between Rome and Parthia: Galilee and The Implications of Empire." In *A Wandering Galilean: Essays in Honour of Seán Freyne,* edited by Zuleika Rodgers, Margaret Daly-Denton and Anne Fitzpatrick-McKinley, 279–299. Leiden: Brill, 2009.

———. "Who were the First Urban Christians? Urbanization in Galilee in the First Century." In *Society of Biblical Literature: Seminar Papers 27* (Atlanta: SBL Press, 1988), 160–168.

Paterson, Orlando. *Slavery and Social Death: A Comparative Study.* Cambridge: Harvard University Press, 1982.

Ratti, Manav. *The Postsecular Imagination: Postcolonialism, Religion, and Literature.* New York: Routledge, 2013.

Rogers, Eugene F., Jr. *After the Spirit: A Constructive Pneumatology from Resources outside the Modern West.* Grand Rapids, MI: W.B. Eerdmans Publishing, 2005.

Sanders, E. P. *Judaism: Practice and Belief, 63 B.C.E.–66 C.E.* Harrisburg: Trinity International Press, 1994.

Sassen, Saskia. "Who Owns Our Cities—and Why This Urban Takeover Should Concern Us All." *The Guardian*, November 24, 2015. Accessed December 21, 2017. https://www.theguardian.com/cities/2015/nov/24/who-owns-our-cities-and-why-this-urban-takeover-should-concern-us-all.

Scott, Allen J., and Michael Storper. "The Nature of Cities: The Scope and Limits of Urban Theory." *International Journal of Urban and Regional Research* 38, no. 4 (2014).

Sennett, Richard. "The Civitas of Seeing." *Places* 5, no. 4 (1989).

Soja, Edward W. *Postmetropolis: Critical Studies of Cities and Regions.* Malden, MA: Wiley-Blackwell, 2000.

———."Writing the City Spatially." *City: Analysis of Urban Trends, Culture, Theory, Policy, Action* 7, no. 3 (2003).

———. "Cities and States in Geohistory." *Theory and Society* 39, no. 3/4 (2010).

Stark, Rodney. *The Rise of Christianity: How the Obscure, Marginal Jesus Movement Became the Dominant Religious Force in the Western World in a Few Centuries.* San Francisco: HarperSanFrancisco, 1997.

Strathmann, H. "Polis." In *Theological Dictionary of the New Testament*, edited by Gerhard Kittel, translated by Geoffrey W. Bromiley. Grand Rapids: Eerdmans, 1968.

Tanner, Kathryn, ed. *Spirit in the Cities: Searching for Soul in the Urban Landscape.* Minneapolis, MN: Fortress Press, 2004.

Temple, William. *The Church Looks Forward.* New York: Macmillan, 1944.

United Nations Human Settlements Programme (UN-Habitat). *World Cities Report 2016, Urbanization and Development: Emerging Futures.* Nairobi: United Nations Human Settlements Programme, 2016.

———. *The State of the World's Cities 2004/2005: Globalization and Urban Culture.* London and Sterling. VA: Earthscan/UN-Habitat, 2004.

Usarski, Frank. "*Kinhin* in a Megacity—Implicit Meanings of the 'Walking-in-the-Park' Movement in São Paulo." In Gomez and Van Herck, *The Sacred in the City*, 96–107.

Walker, Peter W. L. *Jesus and the Holy City: New Testament Perspectives on Jerusalem.* Grand Rapids, MI: W.B. Eerdmans Publishing, 1996.

Walton, Steve, Paul Trebilco, and David W. J. Gill. *The Urban World and the First Christians.* Grand Rapids, MI: W.B. Eerdmans Publishing, 2017.

Wheatley, Paul. *The Pivot of the Four Quarters: A Preliminary Enquiry into the Origins and Character of the Ancient Chinese City.* Chicago: Aldine Publishing, 1971.

Yamauchi, Edwin M. *New Testament Cities in Western Asia Minor: Light from Archaeology on Cities of Paul and the Seven Churches of Revelation.* Eugene, OR: Wipf and Stock, 2003.

2

FAITH, POSTCOLONIALITY, AND SUBJECTIVITY IN EXILE: LATIN AMERICAN INSIGHTS FOR PUBLIC THEOLOGY IN A GLOBALIZED WORLD

Nicolas Panotto

The way in which multicultural relations are understood has considerably mutated throughout history. In recent decades, though, due to the phenomena of globalization and mass migrations, these processes have become even more complex. The notion of globalization encompasses competing positive and negative meanings. On the one hand, it can be understood as a phenomenon that enables the enrichment of processes of mutual knowledge that are formed in connection with exchanges and encounters among a diversity of subjects and cultures. On the other hand, though, it can also be indicative of a scenario of power dynamics where relationships and interconnections among groups and countries have become increasingly asymmetric.

In short, globalization represents a phenomenon that is both inclusive and exclusive. That is, it represents a space where modern power configurations (with its colonial, racial, and subjective matrices) are challenged and transformed. However, far from disappearing, they are concomitantly exacerbated, taking on deeper roots through dynamics and processes of self-reproduction that do not need central powers (in contrast to what dependency theory affirmed decades ago). At the same time, as Byung-Chul Han (2018) indicates, we live in a time of hyperculturality, where the "hyper" (as opposed to the *multi* or *trans*) represents the connection and condensation of complex processes of identity formation and a multiplicity of encounters and dialogues (along with all the political potential they imply).

In the context of such complex relations, one finds numerous "symptoms" that manifest the ambivalent consequences of globalization. For example, the sociopolitical and cultural conflicts that migratory dynamics awaken, like the renewed forms of racism and nationalist sentiments in various national contexts. The Mexico-US border is one of the most known cases in display; one that does not relate only to Mexicans, but also to migrants coming from many Central American countries who experience torturous and many times fatal odysseys to cross the US border in search of a better life.[1] But there are many such cases, in the Americas, which, although not as widely known, evince the complex sociopolitical dynamics in the region. Just to name a few: (1) migration from Andean countries or Paraguay to Argentina and Uruguay; (2) Cuban refugees in the United States; (3) migration of large numbers of Colombians to different countries of the continent, including Canada, caused by a long-lasting civil war and conflicts involving paramilitaries and guerrillas; (4) racial conflicts in Brazil that produce continuous internal movements; (5) migration processes that emerge as a result of conflicts between gangs and drug dealers in places like El Salvador and Honduras; (6) Haitian immigrants arriving in a number of countries of the region (mainly in the Dominican Republic, Panama, and Nicaragua); (7) the growing number of North Africans arriving in the Southern Cone; and (8) the recent displacement of Venezuelan and Nicaraguan groups driven by internal political crises. In addition, one can also mention the constant movements of Latin Americans worldwide—especially their migratory flows in connection with Europe and the United States—as well as circular processes of constant movement between urban centers and rural peripheries, which reflect the clear colonial enclave that still persists in Latin American countries, where the capital cities become places of privilege; the epicenter of political, economic, academic, and social power.

Although these processes are not only urban, they are often connected to movements to and from the main urban centers of Latin America. To understand the complexity of such dynamics, it is necessary to consider that these movements take place within a framework directly related to the colonial enclave in the origins of the main Latin American cities. The most important urban centers in the continent represent three central historical instances: 1) they are the epicenter of the sociocultural and political stratification of each country (and their respective class distinctions

---

[1] For recent insights on the dynamics of Central American migration to Mexico and the US, see the essays by Eduardo Albuquerque, Gioacchino Campese, and Francisco Pelaez-Diaz in *Migration as Public Discourse in World Christianity*, Series: World Christianity and Public Religion, vol. 2, eds. Afe Adogame, Raimundo Barreto, and Wanderley Pereira da Rosa (Minneapolis, MN: Fortress Press, 2019).

commonly identifiable through racialized and territorial demarcations); 2) they are the centers of political power, historically linked to colonial powers; and 3) their economic structures were historically established as provision centers for the colonial market economy.

Therefore, the urban spatiality in which migration processes are inscribed in Latin America today are part of a complex matrix of cultural, social, political, and economic tensions, which must be interpreted from within a historical framework that takes seriously racialized distinctions, also informed by gender and class criteria.

These processes of displacement show that the plurality inherent to Latin America not only represents its cultural wealth, but also the paths where colonial matrices continue to flow, feeding multiple tensions such as those identified through binaries such as center-periphery, city-field, and wealthy-poor, among others. All these tensions contribute to raise the following questions: How should we discern the political dimension of cultural diversity? How can we overcome the contradictions present in the emphases on plurality, which represent both the wealth of the human condition and a signifier that hides historical mechanisms of oppression?

GLOBALIZATION IN POSTCOLONIAL PERSPECTIVE

Two important considerations are crucial for our reflection on globalization. On the one hand, *we talk about globalization vis-à-vis the redefinition of how the construction of individual and social identities is understood.* As Néstor García Canclini has proposed,[2] current Latin American societies are made of *hybrid* communities and subjects. Such hybridity unmasks the fallacy of nationalist, cultural, political, social, and religious essentialisms. Subjects and social groups are built through increasingly diverse and interconnected historical trajectories, intercultural processes involving various geographies, and the conjunction of many existential elements such as specific economic situations, particular places within social hierarchies, and multiple beliefs and ideologies. The plurality that represents a global perspective of social relations is not only a description of the elements that form it, but also a distinct *anthropological worldview* where the diverse, the multiple, and the plural are constitutive fields that converge in all agents.

At least in the context of Latin America, globalization continues to be perceived as being related to colonial and imperial worldviews. In response to that suspicion, postcolonial approaches to globalization entail, before anything else, the recognition of deeply rooted formative elements of constitutive political, social, religious, and economic dynamics in the

---

[2] See Néstor Canclini, *Culturas híbridas* (Buenos Aires: Paidós, 2001).

region. Accordingly, the asymmetry of the globalizing processes is seen as emerging from a long historical heritage, representing deeply rooted power dynamics in our societies. On the other hand, one must pay attention to the fact that these processes cannot be understood unilaterally. They are also generative of power tensions. In other words, they can be seen as processes of asymmetric imposition of power which, while facing resistance, end up turning the diversity of contexts, identities, and relationships into spaces of struggles where tensions between hegemonic inheritances and changes are in friction that produce both continuities and transformations.

Despite the fact that colonialism as such is no longer present in the region, and democracy and the rule of law are often promoted as exemplary policies, Latin Americans continue to attend to post-colonial Western and imperialist dynamics, not only in the actions initiated in countries that are self-proclaimed centers toward "the periphery," but also in the power logics that prevail within various regional contexts. Sociocultural dynamics do not simply represent exogenous processes emanating from "central countries" with the purpose of controlling peripheric subjectivities. They also represent matrices of coexistence, interaction, and subjectivity inscribed in the daily life of all social groups in the region, regardless of their economic condition. Racial stigmas, processes of exclusion, rationalist modes of subjectivation, and traditional parameters of modern and colonial politics continue to be widely implemented.

Reflecting on such a situation, Anibal Quijano[3] speaks of the persistence of three types of colonialities inscribed both in everyday life and in macro-social structures: the *coloniality of being* (through which Western and modern perspectives become fundamental ways for understanding "the human"), the *coloniality of power* (that presents modern social institutions as a monopolistic framework of political exercise), and the coloniality *of knowledge* (that makes Western scientism and academicism the parameters of truth, excluding all other alternative ways of validating reality). In such a context, globalization is also seen as a space of legitimation for these and other forms of power asymmetry.

In contrast with that, Ulrich Beck[4] uses the term *glocal* to point out the interconnection of the local and global, the macro and the micro. According to this understanding of globalization, social communities and human beings transcend any type of national, political, and cultural frontier. Consequently, globalization contributes to make the frontiers that distinguish the cultural from the economic, the private from the public,

---

[3] Anibal Quijano, "Colonialidad del poder y clasificación social," *Journal of World-Systems Research* 2 (2000): 342–386.
[4] Ulrich Beck, *¿Qué es la globalización?* (Buenos Aires: Paidós, 1999).

and the political from the non-political more porous than ever before. Thus, for instance, struggles for economic monopolies can be turned into broader communicational and cultural battles. In the same way, "identity politics" (or the emergence of identitarian non-institutional groups in the public sphere) has a potential to impact economic structures and institutional policies.

As Roland Robertson and Joann Chirico put it,

> There are aspects of the operation of modern—particularly Western—societies which generate a form of transcendence of society at the level of individuals. The combination of alienation from the state and the state's increasing concern—what we call a quasi-religious concern—with "deep" features of life (the definition of life, the organization of death, the "quality of life," aging, the regulation of religion, and so on) increasingly leads to explicitness about the attributes and raison d'etre of human life beyond the particularities of social classification, voluntary religious involvement, even societal membership. The resurgence of "fundamentalistic" promotion of particularistic ideologies and doctrines (local, ethnic, civilizational, and regional) does not by any means constitute counter-evidence. For, [. . .] the recent globe-wide assertion of particularistic ideas is heavily contextualized by the phenomenon of increasing globality.[5]

Two political challenges emerge from such a scenario. First, *the counteracting of decolonization processes of sociocultural practices and worldviews*, which implies the process of unmasking the discourses and actions that legitimize asymmetric power and inequality not only in terms of agonistic "confrontation of forces" ("we" against "them," which would mean the maintenance of colonial political logics), but also in terms of the deconstruction of imaginaries and the rise of new epistemologies based on "otherwise" social, intellectual, relational, cultural, and economic practices that counteract the hegemonic visions.

The second challenge, closely related to the first, is the *necessity to make visible, embrace, and promote plurality, heterogeneity, and diversity as critical approaches to hegemonic powers*. As David Griffin states, a new way of approaching globalization should provide "a base of resistance against homogenization that is now being relentlessly carried out by a globalization captained by corporations."[6] In other words, these processes that involve hybridization, "glocalization," tensions between macro and micro, and exposure of social diversity are both places of visibility of

---

[5] Roland Robertson and Joann Chirico, "Humanity, Globalization, and Worldwide Religious Resurgence: A Theoretical Exploration," *Sociological Analysis* 46 (1985): 233.

[6] David Griffin, "Is a Global Ethic Possible?", in *Global Governance, Global Government: Institutional Visions for an Evolving World System*, ed. Luis Cabrera (Albany: State University of New York Press, 2011), 101–126.

cultural practices and spaces of deconstruction of political hegemonies. In this way, resistance against colonial and global powers occurs through the demonstration of the plurality of ways of living and making the world.

DYNAMIC AND GEOPOLITICAL SENSES IN POSTCOLONIAL PERSPECTIVE

Two emphases summarize the approach advanced in this chapter, namely a particular understanding of the term "postcolonial" and a concern with a dynamic known as "othering." First, we understand the term "postcolonial" as a sociohistorical construct. Postcolonialism argues that despite the processes of national independence in the colonies as well as the various changes in the geopolitical configurations in recent decades, colonial dynamics persist, not only in what relates to the field of the world economy, but also to the sociopolitical (the presence of nation-states), sociocultural (ways of defining citizenship through legal endeavor), and the place of religion in the public sphere, including international affairs. One of the central analytical concepts in this scenario is that of *imperialism*, understood not simply as a mode of centralized power in a specific country or as a bipolar division of the global reality, but also as a set of flows circulating and self-reproducing through transnational social dynamics.

Concurrently, the dynamics called *othering* is understood as the way in which the West constructs its "other"—as Lacanian theory states—through a mirror that legitimizes the closure and suturing of its own (false) homogeneous identity. Edward Said, in his widely known work *Orientalism*, proposes a profound criticism of the European Oriental studies, by the means of an alternative philosophical reading of sociopolitical and literary theory.[7] He shows how Western academia and politics symptomatize the so-called "Orient" based on various stigmas and preconceptions of identity, circumscribing a boundary that imposes alterity. Anibal Quijano, in his turn, has shown that the East-West division brings with it other binomials such as primitive-civilized, magical/mythical-scientific, rational-irrational, and traditional-modern.

In short, postcolonialism evokes an epistemological and methodological framework that aligns with various postmodern and poststructuralist approaches to prioritize analytical categories such as the study of identifying processes, the place of discourse in the construction of sociopolitical practices, and the deconstruction of social imaginary and political visions. These approaches seek to overcome structuralist reductionisms and Manichean approaches that simplify the complex dynamics of world

---

[7] Edward W. Said. *Orientalism*. 25th anniversary edition (New York: Vintage Books, 2003).

power, thus providing a political reading of the place of subjects and the heterogeneity of human groups, which can aid their resistance practices against the borders forced upon them.

Postcolonial theory has many disciplinary derivatives, three of which are important to mention here. First, the *decolonial turn* whose origin is in the Modernity/Colonial Study Group[8] formed by scholars such as Anibal Quijano, Walter Mignolo, Enrique Dussel, Arturo Escobar, and Catherine Walsh. This group began its work with a focus on Latin America, although today it has gradually expanded its reach as a theoretical proposal with a wider impact. The decolonial turn engages social-anthropological analysis vis-à-vis political and economic theories, rather than limiting its analytical partners to literary criticism as other forms of postcolonial studies often emphasize.

Two other important streams in postcolonial studies are worth mentioning. *Border studies* uses postcolonial approaches for the analysis of the sociocultural impact of political boundaries upon identity formation. Border in this sense does not simply represent a geographical demarcation separating nation-states, but also "a sum of social, political, and cultural processes."[9] The second stream, *diasporic studies*, has religious studies, especially in Jewish historiography, as its backdrop. This approach gives more emphasis to literary study and critical hermeneutics in a postmodern perspective. It involves both discourse analysis and sociopolitical criticism, based specifically on the view of diasporic experience as an instance of cultural hybridity.

In short, postcolonial theory offers a complex approach to the dynamics of sociocultural globalization, which surpasses structuralist and economistic readings by including the analysis of heterogeneous and ambivalent processes vis-à-vis cultural, discursive, communicational, and relational processes, among others. Moreover, it evokes a *mimetic* approach to subjects,[10] which sees them not as passive victims of a pervasive system, but as subjects that constantly negotiate and redefine the frames of power from the specificity of their sociocultural location. Finally, it understands cultural dynamics as intercultural encounters, not as a "clash of civilizations."[11]

---

[8] Arturo Escobar, "Mundos y conocimientos de otro modo," *Tabula Rasa* 1 (2003): 51–86.
[9] Marcela Tapia Ladino, "Frontera, movilidad y circulación reciente de peruanos y bolivianos en el norte de Chile," *Estudios atacameños* 50 (2015): 198.
[10] Homi Bahbah, *El Lugar de la Cultura* (Buenos Aires: Manaltial, 1994).
[11] Samuel Huntington, *The Clash of Civilizations and the Remaking of World Order* (London: Simon and Schuster, 1996).

Subjects in Exile: Political Ontology at the Crossroads between Nation-States and Globalization

As stated earlier, globalization poses an ambivalent and paradoxical situation: it purportedly promotes openness and access to what seems to be a borderless world, while, by contrast, facilitating increasingly severe restriction and border control. Perspectives that promote integration as utopian alternatives to address the problem of disintegration—such as those of MERCOSUR, ALCA, and EU—along with political visions that support homogenous notions of cultural dynamics—like the logic of "Patria Grande"—often run the risk of overlooking or even suppressing and excluding diversity. As anthropologist Cardoso de Oliveira points out,[12] these worldviews forget the significance of the constitutive *ethnic friction* in any culture.

The linking of nation-state to identity formation creates its own problems, particularly when one considers the relationship between colonialism and modernity (or sees modernity as inherently connected to colonialism). Here, it is important to remember Hannah Arendt's words,[13] when she stated that ethical judgment against the lack of state does not derive from the lack of civilization. It instead represents a symptom of modernity itself. Such a perspective would help us revisit contemporary analyses of statelessness and stateless persons as symptoms of the modern global condition. As Edward Said states,[14] fear of immigration and refugees does not simply result from pragmatic concerns with containment, but mainly from a perceived threat to the stability of the nation state as a closed identity framework.

In short, the conflicts produced in connection with the presence of refugees, immigrants, and exiles do not come from the structural limitation of a given country and its structure, but emerge as a symptom of double origin: (1) the perception of a threat against the security of belonging that the sense of nationhood offers, and (2) the actions of national states on the geopolitical level, like those connected with the arms industry and its support of regional conflicts (Middle East, Africa, Central America, and Andean countries), and the constant boycott of the economies of smaller nations, which exacerbates poverty and prevents internal development.

All these conflicts can be linked to a colonial matrix that produces ontological constructions of otherness. Coloniality is present within all the social dynamics above, being both legitimized by and productive

---

[12] Roberto Cardoso de Oliveira, "Aculturación y "Fricción" Interétnica," *América Latina* 6 (1963): 33–46.
[13] Hannah Arendt, *La Condición Humana* (Buenos Aires: Paidós, 2013).
[14] Edward Said, *Cultura e Imperialismo* (Sao Paulo: CompanhiaDeBolso, 2011), 495.

of certain ways of understanding and approaching otherness. For this reason, the exercise of deconstructing the senses of identity and cultural belonging that coloniality produces is crucial to address the scenarios presented to us in a variety of "global conflicts," be they primarily socially, politically, or religiously driven.

BORDER SPATIALITY AND SOCIOCULTURAL DISLOCATION

One of the challenges before us is to overcome what is known as *methodological nationalism*,[15] which defines the identity of a group or territory based on the creation of certain patriotic imaginary, corresponding to enrollment in a nation-state.

Border studies have contributed to a critique of this notion through the deconstruction of the meaning of *border*. In accord with this school of thought, border is not merely a line of demarcation between territories, but a social representation that frame spaces of political exchange and cultural mixture. Boundaries have political, strategic, and symbolic significance. Here is the *complexity* of the concept of borders: it represents a condensation of an object and a metaphor. The former refers to physical borders; the latter, to cultural borders.[16] This dyad, therefore, denotes not only existing divisions between two objects/nations/states, but also internal borders of identity frames.

Hence, some prefer to speak rather of *border areas* or *liminal spaces*: places where identities and subjects flow through negotiations, resistances, and reinterpretations of the senses that state cultural delineations. This border dynamics[17] not only refers to the framing of the land, but also to the understanding of identity itself, conceived not as wholly sutured boundaries that circumscribe a homogeneous process of subjectivation, but rather as a set of polyvalent and pluri-valued movements interwoven and in constant interchange. The ambivalences that emerge from such movements project sedimented senses of social, cultural, and political belonging, which are nevertheless constantly joined in a plural and heterogeneous spatiality.

How are "objects" separated by defined and defining boundaries? To what extent are they enclosed? If borders are related to multidirectional flowing and symbolic exchange, how do we identify cultural elements in this encounter? As postcolonial theory suggests, the distinction between

---

[15] Herminio Martins, "Time and Theory in Sociology," in *Approaches to Sociology: An Introduction to Major Trends in British Sociology*, ed. John Rex (London: International Library of Sociology, 1974), 246–294.

[16] Alejandro Grimson, *Fronteras, naciones e identidades: La periferia como centro* (Buenos Aires: La Crujía, 2000).

[17] Walter Mignolo, *Historias locales/diseños globales* (Madrid: Akal, 2013).

"local" and "global" fails to fully represent the complexity of these interactions. Such notions of differentiation still maintain the resolution of homogeneous dynamics (i.e., the global and the local as closed and distinguishable entities). According to this perspective, such a distinction could be used to maintain and legitimize established power relations.

For this reason, it is necessary to speak of a *contingent dialectics* that understands social processes as movements beyond binarisms, represented in a "messy" condensation[18] of multiple—social, cultural, political, ritual, and symbolic—elements that have a fragile historical density within consensual border lines, but whose legitimation is born of the constant tension emanating from the multiplicity of elements that inscribe it. This concept is intended to go beyond understanding of differences as autonomous and isolated circuits, or the understanding of global processes as *ad extra*, as a sort of supra-historical entity that affects sociocultural, personal, and relational dynamics. Rather than talking of "culture" as a seamed entity, we'd rather refer to *the cultural* as a dynamic that goes beyond, responding to formed boundaries (linguistic, historical, territorial, contextual), which in their turn become constantly renegotiated through the encounter with others. As Alejandro Grimson concludes:

> There are not cultures in diaspora, since that would mean saying that there is a culturally homogeneous group that generates enclaves, cloned difference in different areas of the planet (. . .) The diaspora is a cultural transnational configuration space of heterogeneity articulated, where one of the conditions is shared identification.[19]

THE EXCESS OF INTERCULTURAL ENCOUNTERS

Postcolonial theories suggest that cultural differentiation originated in colonial encounters; that is, it emerged in the distinction between nation-states or imperial enterprises and subaltern groups (stateless persons, refugees, immigrants). Such encounters on the border of colonial difference represented not only a dynamic of oppression, but also one of *otherness*, where subaltern identities were not simply subsumed under the hand of the oppressor; they also produced space renegotiation, resistance, and redefinition of boundaries. Here, two things must be noted: (1) borders are not fixed, neither are subjects passive; and (2) any differentiation that emerges, despite the levels of coercion, produces an intercultural dialectical process that facilitates the deconstruction of meaning as resistors and mutual enrichment.

---

[18] John Law, *After Method: Mess in Social Science Research* (Abingdon: Routledge, 2004).

[19] Alejandro Grimson, *Los Límites de la Cultura* (Buenos Aires: Siglo XXI, 2011), 146. Translation by author.

As different de/postcolonial theories and border studies highlight, any intercultural encounter should be evaluated on the basis of its cultural richness and not just as a threat to one's identity. As Walter Mignolo affirms, diasporas create a site of critical enunciation. Similarly, Luis Rivera-Pagan states,

> The displacement of migration creates a new space of liberation from the atavistic constraints and bondages of the native cultural community and open new vistas, perspectives, and horizons.[20]

This perspective is not intended to solve the inherent conflicts present in intercultural encounters or the conditions of oppression that are in play in them. Rather, it aims to evince a process of *mimesis* where the contexts of oppression are re-signified through liminal encounters. Thus, it has the potential to promote and bring other signifiers that are operative in such encounters to the fore, allowing us to deconstruct and challenge the stigma of subjectivities-in-exile. On the other hand, this perspective on flowing cultural identities also presses the (non-existent) homogeneity of national borders, enabling new identitarian imaginative enclaves reflected in new public policies and new practices of citizenship. Decolonial studies refer to this dynamic as *de-linking*, i.e., movements of detachment that emerge within cultural, political, and social borders closed and imposed by the pressure of the subaltern, the others, the internally excluded. As Edward Said once affirmed,

> The great task, then, is to combine the new economic and sociopolitical dislocations and configurations of our time and the amazing reality of human interdependence worldwide.[21]

RETERRITORIALIZATIONS IN THEOLOGICAL TRANSLATIONS IN A COSMOPOLITAN ERA

We can summarize what has been developed so far in three main points. First, the phenomenon of refugees and immigration is a symptom of persistent colonial policies of the West, whose inherent conflicts awake an attitude of occlusion and sociocultural condemnation, exposing the "darker side" of a position presented as neutral or incidental, and avoiding the consequences of their hidden colonialism. Secondly, nationalism and legal definitions of cultural belonging within the nation-state also represent remnants of Western colonial logic, which eclipse various forms of identity formation, inadvertently leading to resistance and rejection, as well as to the recognition of the heterogeneity included in any social and

---

[20] Luis Rivera-Pagán, *Essays from the Diaspora* (México: Publicaciones El Faro, 2002), 5.
[21] Edward Said, *Reflexiones Sobre el Exilio* (Buenos Aires: Debolsillo, 2005), 502.

cultural sedimentation. Finally, a basic principle for building alternative actions of resignification is manifest in the deconstruction of stigmatizing imaginaries based on a notion of identity, which is no longer defined vis-à-vis the nation-state, but through intercultural encounters.

There are some elements on the ethical, sociopolitical, and theological-religious levels of such encounters that allow us to take a further step in approaching them, based on Homi Bhabha's concept of *third space*.[22] This concept originates in Bhabha's experiences with different ways of interpreting meanings and words in the context of translation practices, where gestures, words, and objects question given senses and allow for new ones. It is a dialogical space, an intercultural "fracture" of enunciation, where discourses are relativized through the encounter with others.

The search for this *third space* raises the question about the empowerment of new narratives that originate from dialogue, that is, from a concrete approach to a real and corporal other. The third space represents a locus of listening, which also allows us to speak and re-signify our places. It is a new discursive framework that, as Giles Deleuze indicates, produces the reterritorialization of narratives and imaginaries, creating new loci of meaning, an element that also potentializes new territories of citizenship, based on emerging frontiers of exchange. In the words of Bhabha,

> The lessons of ambivalence are not exhausted in the act of support. The experience of the ambivalent also is a spur to the speech, the need of the word, a way to work as contradictory and no solution, for the purpose of achieving the right to narrate. Even the most extreme forms of cultural ambivalence . . . are moments that coerce the act of supporting up to make claim for the agency of discourse and dialogue.[23]

From the perspective of this approach, exile would not be seen as a fortuitous accident, but instead as a constitutive locus of identity. In the exilic situation, oppression, injustice, and desolation arise. But, the problem does not reside in exile itself, which sometimes is negatively labeled due to a moral judgment based on a sense of threat constructed in connection with the colonial conception of statelessness. The problem addressed here is the rigid concept of identity, which does not take into account the multifaceted constitutive process of subjectivity. This kind of perspective goes against the notion of flowing, walking, and movement, due to the fear of losing security and a false sense of identity homogeneity.

We can identify a third space in the construction of intercultural dialogue, where identity barriers are lifted toward the release of identification processes enriched by the exchange. This third space challenges nationalist

---

[22] Homi Bhabha, *Nuevas Minorías, Nuevos Derechos* (Buenos Aires: Siglo XXI, 2013), 79–87.
[23] Bhabha, *Nuevas Minorías*, 56–57.

and purist visions, which emerge not only from explicit condemnatory speeches, but also from practical, everyday "othering" gestures.

The religious field is one of the most sensitive spaces for encounters and conflicts between different cultures. A close-minded conception in this field often leads to occlusion in the approach to the cultural other, especially when we consider the essentialist views of religion that persist in the West. The rise of social conflicts in recent decades involving the growing Islamic presence in Europe and similar concerns with the revitalization of indigenous and popular religiosity in Latin America are examples of the tensions impacting hegemonic Western cultural and political imaginaries. Likewise, it is worth noting how notions of secularism and laicism have been challenged or stretched in political debates in light of new migratory contexts. An extended discussion of these concepts has been taking place, for instance, in Chile because of the tensions produced in relation to Haitian migrants who are forced to abandon their traditional religious practices when joining shelter and social projects run by evangelical churches.

New theological approaches are needed to promote sociopolitical and cultural sensitivity for religious pluralism. When talking about theology, we do not mean just dogmatic deconstructions, but also new understandings and redefinitions of the divine. As postcolonial studies have shown,[24] Christian missions impregnated with the sense of "manifest destiny" of imperial nations have promoted a colonizing vision of God based on essentialist ontological notions of the divine. Essentialist views of the religious influence the ways images of the divine are constructed (and vice versa!). If culture is a central mediation to define the divine, what does it mean to speak about God from places of liminality, in-between or cultural intersections? Could we imagine a God that is manifested in the fissure where difference is imprinted?

An important step to address this question has to do precisely with *the deconstruction of a central object in the theological task: the image of God*. Christian theology–from its imperial christological images in the fourth century to the business-man Jesus of the prosperity gospel—has fostered hegemonic visions of the divine, which not only have legitimized capitalist economic practices, but also hegemonic projects of domination. They promote the "obvious God," as stated by Hugo Assmann,[25] who presents Godself "in the image and likeness" of subjective interests of people and

---

[24] Marion Grau, *Rethinking Mission in the Postcolony: Salvation, Society and Subvertion* (London: T&T Clark, 2011).

[25] Hugo Assmann, "Por una teología humanamente saludable. Fragmentos de memoria personal," in *El mar se abrió. Treinta años de teología en América Latina*, ed. Luis Susin (Santander: Sal Terrae, 2000), 108–122.

institutions turned into a unique, absolute, and universal representation. A "god" without fissure, just as centralized powers must be: absolute, applicable to all contexts and excluding.

For this reason, *a return to that sense of mystery and alterity about God is urgently necessary*, not as a supra-historical statement, but as images that empower and make visible the possibilities of being, individually and in community, that emanate from a gospel that addresses us in the specific locus where we find ourselves and manifests itself in a pluriform manner. As Catherine Keller concludes, "When the non-human alterity is eclipsed—the non-human that surrounds us and constitutes us in our matter, in our materialization—what kind of humanity is left? One simply reducible to an info-techno-global economy?"[26]

Another important theological step is *the promotion of the Christian community as a locus for building practices of resistance and alternative actions against hegemonic colonial worldviews*. Theologian Juan Luis Segundo, in his book *Masses and Minorities*,[27] states that Christianity is never in favor of the "mass phenomenon," but of the anti-imperial minorities, just as the movement of Jesus was. Likewise, Joerg Rieger affirms, "There is no doubt: the two forms of globalization, one from the top and one from the bottom, do not go together, and it is not an accident that Jesus rejects the devil's offer to rule over 'all the kingdoms of the world and their splendor' (Matt 4:8–10)".[28]

In short, in the face of a globalization that, paradoxically, affirms a sense of diversity, but which in turn is sustained through a set of worldviews and structures that reinforce the homogenization of cultural groups and socioeconomic conditions, we need a theology that flows from the surreptitious narratives and practices produced by excluded/subaltern subjectivities-in-exile. That is, a theology that fosters a vision of a God that stands on the border, turning them into bridges.[29] Such a theology calls for the pluralization of the subjects of faith, which from the location of their specificity and movement create new and different ways of living spirituality, being churches, and sharing their faith as opposed to the rigid discourses of power.

---

[26] Catherine Keller, "Descolonizando la cosmología: Cosmopolitismo en proceso." Conference paper offered at the First Latin American Meeting of Process Philosophy. Xaveriana University of Bogotá, April 2008.

[27] Juan Luis Segundo, *Masas y Minorías* (Buenos Aires: La Aurora, 1973).

[28] Joerg Rieger, *Globalization and Theology* (Nashville, TN: Abingdon Press, 2010), 17.

[29] Devaka Premawardhana uses a similar image in his study of migrant Pentecostals in Northern Zimbabwe. Devaka Premawardhana, *Faith in Flux: Pentecostalism and Mobility in Rural Mozambique* (Philadelphia, PA: University of Pennsylvania Press, 2018).

CONCLUSION

According to Gloria Andalzúa,

> A borderland is a vague and undetermined place created by the emotional residue of an unnatural boundary. It is a constant state of transition. The prohibited and forbidden are its inhabitants. The penetrations live there: the squint-eye, the perverse, the queer, the troublesome, the mongrel, the mulatto, the half-breed, the half dead; in short, those who cross over, pass over, or go through the confines of the standard.[30]

Reinforcing what I have argued throughout this chapter, Andalzúa shows that the processes of conflict over legal and political border delimitation, the role of the nation state, the injustice lived in the complexity of urban centers, and the prejudice against refugees and migrants can be seen as symptoms of broader cultural historical, social, religious, political, and contemporary geopolitical contingencies. Likewise, the dynamics that we experience in Latin America (and other parts of the world) today can be better understood vis-à-vis practices and imaginaries that continue to reflect a colonial imprint that informs the prejudices, stigmas, and preconceptions about "the weird," the different, and the strange, often presented as threats to the perceived cultural suture of our societies.

In light of that, the deconstruction of such meanings and the production of new practices of intercultural relations and translation are crucial for conceiving public and international policies in fresh and more humanized ways. In a world that remains deeply religious, the need for developing a theological vision based on the God-Completely-Other,[31] which inscribes historical and cultural alterity back into public life and moves us to commitment and solidarity toward the excluded, stretching our horizons beyond imposed borders toward new meanings and imaginaries is one of our urgent tasks.

---

[30] Gloria Anzaldúa, *Borderlands/La Frontera: The New Mestiza* (San Francisco: Aunt Like Books, 2007), 25.

[31] Mayra Rivera, *The Touch of Transcendence: A Postcolonial Theology of God* (Louisville: Westminster John Knox Press, 2008).

Bibliography

Adogame A., R.C. Barreto, W. Pereira da Rosa. *Migration and Public Discourse in World Christianity*, World Christianity and Public Religion, vol. 2. Minneapolis, MN: Fortress Press, 2019.

Anzaldúa, Gloria. *Borderlands/La Frontera: The New Mestiza*. San Francisco: Aunt Like Books, 2007.

Arendt, Hannah. *La Condición Humana*. Buenos Aires: Paidós, 2013.

Assmann, Hugo. "Por una teología humanamente saludable. Fragmentos de memoria personal." In *El mar se abrió. Treinta Años de Teología en América Latina*, edited by Luis Susin, 108–122. Santander: Sal Terrae, 2000.

Bhabha, Homi. *El Lugar de la Cultura*. Buenos Aires: Manaltial, 1994.

———. *Nuevas Minorías, Nuevos Derechos*. Buenos Aires: Siglo XXI, 2013.

Beck, Ulrich. *¿Qué es la Globalización?* Buenos Aires: Paidós, 1999.

Canclini, Néstor. *Culturas Híbridas*. Buenos Aires: Paidós, 2001.

Cardoso de Oliveira, Roberto. "Aculturación y "fricción" interétnica." *América Latina* 6 (1963): 33–46.

Deleuze, Giles, and F. Guattari. *Mil Mesetas:capitalismo y esquizofrenia*. Madrid: Pre-Textos, 2015.

Escobar, Arturo. "Mundos y conocimientos de otro modo." *Tabula Rasa* 1 (2003): 51–86.

Grau, Marion. *Rethinking Mission in the Postcolony: Salvation, Society and Subversion*. London: T&T Clark, 2011.

Griffin, David. "Is a Global Ethic Possible?" In *Global Governance, Global Government: Institutional Visions for an Evolving World System*, edited by Luis Cabrera, 101–126. Albany: State University of New York Press, 2011.

Grimson, Alejandro. *Fronteras, naciones e identidades. La periferia como centro*. Buenos Aires: La Crujía, 2000.

———. *Los límites de la cultura*. Buenos Aires: Siglo XXI, 2011.

Han, Byung-Chul. *Hiperculturalidad*. Barcelona: Editorial Herder, 2018.

Huntington, Samuel. *The Clash of Civilizations and the Remaking of World Order*. London: Simon and Schuster, 1996.

Keller, Catherine. "Descolonizando la Cosmología: Cosmopolitismo en Proceso." Conference paper offered at the First Latin American Meeting of Process Philosophy, Xaveriana University of Bogotá, April 2008.

Ladino, Marcela Tapia. "Frontera, movilidad y circulación reciente de Peruanos y Bolivianos en el norte de Chile." *Estudios Atacameños* 50 (2015): 195–213.

Law, John. *After Method: Mess in Social Science Research*. Abingdon: Routledge, 2004.

Martins, Herminio. "Time and Theory in Sociology." In *Approaches to Sociology: An Introduction to Major Trends in British Sociology*, edited by John Rex, 246–294. London: International Library of Sociology, 1974.

Mignolo, Walter. *Historias Locales/Diseños Globales*. Madrid: Akal, 2013.

Premawardhana, Devaka. *Faith in Flux: Pentecostalism and Mobility in Rural Mozambique*. Philadelphia, PA: University of Pennsylvania Press, 2018.

Quijano, Anibal. "Colonialidad del poder y clasificación social." *Journal of World-Systems Research* 2 (2000): 342–386.

Rieger, Joerg. *Globalization and Theology*. Nashville, TN: Abingdon Press, 2010.

Rivera-Pagán, Luis. *Essays from the Diaspora*. México: Publicaciones El Faro, 2002.

Rivera, Mayra. *The Touch of Transcendence: A Postcolonial Theology of God*. Louisville: Westminster John Knox Press, 2008.

Robertson, Roland, and Joann Chirico. "Humanity, Globalization, and Worldwide Religious Resurgence: A Theoretical Exploration." *Sociological Analysis* 46 (1985): 219–242.

Said, Edward W. *Orientalism*. 25th anniversary edition. New York: Vintage Books, 2003.

———. *Reflexiones sobre el exilio*. Buenos Aires: Debolsillo, 2005.

———. *Cultura e imperialismo*. São Paulo: Companhia De Bolso, 2011.

Segundo, Juan Luis. *Masas y minorías*. Buenos Aires: La Aurora, 1973.

3

CENTRALIZATION OF RELIGIOUS POWER IN THE CITY: AN ESSAY BASED ON 1 KINGS 1–11[1]

Maricel Mena-López

INTRODUCTION: FROM POPULAR TO HEGEMONIC RELIGION

The transition from popular religion to hegemonic religion is complex and resists unilinear analyses.[2] When this transition is explored vis-à-vis the epistemological and spatial *loci* of the city, the complexity of its ethical and political ramifications comes to the fore in specific ways. From Cain's constructed human-city to the story of the tower of Babel, anxieties abound about the communities that unfold in and around the city, as well as depictions of the genealogies of city-making, and the limitations of human aspirations about city. What sorts of faith configurations develop in and around the city? How is faith reconfigured in globalizing urban niches? In order to address questions such as these, this chapter focuses on the centralizing model of urbanization manifested in the court of Solomon, the temple, and the city of Jerusalem in 1 Kings 1–11.[3] The temple and the city of Jerusalem represent a cosmopolis where religious diversity converge into a hegemonic and centralizing paradigm. Taking Jerusalem as a trope for this hegemonic model of the city, I will examine the character of a city that still invokes the longing for the *good life* present in peripheral wisdoms. Thus, Jerusalem is examined as a literary

---

[1] This essay was translated from Spanish into English by Stephen DiTrolio.
[2] Mary T. Boatwright, Daniel J. Gargola, and Richard J. A. Talbert (eds.), *Romans: From Village to Empire* (Oxford: Oxford University Press, 2004); Emily Mackil, *Creating a Common Polity: Religion, Economy, and Politics in the Making of the Greek Koinon* (Berkeley: University of California Press, 2013).
[3] Translator's note: All Bible quotations in the English version of this chapter come from the Jerusalem Bible.

and spatial Babel, built in part through extraction of, and alliances with, peripheral resources and beliefs that were simultaneously discredited.[4]

THE ADMINISTRATIVE POLITICAL STRUCTURE OF THE JERUSALEM OF THE TENTH CENTURY: FROM THE HIGH PLACES TO THE CITY

The administrative transition from the peripheral "high places" to the centralized "city" begins to unfold through a dream. God appears to Solomon in a dream at Gibeon (1 Kgs 3:5), then once again upon his completion of the Temple in Jerusalem (1 Kgs 9:2). The narrative of Solomon's dream at Gibeon (1 Kgs 3:4–15) is located strategically between his marriage to the Egyptian princess (1 Kgs 3:1–3), the encounter with the two female prostitutes (1 Kgs 3:16–28), and the description of the administrative (1 Kgs 4), economic (1 Kgs 5), and religious (1 Kgs 6–8) measures that Solomon adopted and implemented. The dream happens after his alliance with Egypt and before the start of his works. Solomon goes to Gibeon and offers there a thousand burnt offerings throughout the night. There, he has the theophany with the angel who, in addition to granting his request of "a discerning and righteous heart," fills him with riches and glories.

Gibeon was known as the city that came under attack from a number of kings, including the king of Jerusalem (Josh 10:5), and also as the place where the "sun and moon stood still" (Josh 10:12), which might be an allusion to the astral character of the local religion. It is from this small Canaanite city that Solomon begins the process of centralization of political, economic, and religious power in the city of Jerusalem and continues the extermination of the Gibeonites initiated by David his father (2 Sam 21:1), but not before showing off his wisdom in the face of a daily problem with two female prostitutes, "*zonoth*," a wisdom based on the power of the sword upon a baby's body, not on argumentative reasoning.

The word *zonah*, whose plural *zonoth* is used to describe the women in this passage, points to a conflict between patriarchal and matrilineal structures. In the meaning it carried prior to the monarchy, *zonah* would be more accurately translated as "autonomous women."[5] As Hannelis Schulte affirms, they were called autonomous women because they did not depend on their father, husband, and much less on a priest, as it was the

---

[4] For an analogous examination of a biblical city and a modern city, see Samuel Tongue, "The Babel Complex: Taking a Turn Around the Tower and the City," in A.K.M. Adam and Samuel Tongue (eds.), *Looking through a Glass Bible: Postdisciplinary Biblical Interpretations from the Glasgow School* (New York: Brill, 2014), 154–173.

[5] Maricel Mena-López, "La herencia de las diosas—Egipto y Sabá en el tiempo de la monarquía Salomónica," *RIBLA–Revista de Interpretación Bíblica Latinoamericana* 54 (2006): 34–47.

case of the sacred prostitutes in the fertility cults.[6] The violent patriarchal scenario is captured and articulated in the narrative's depiction of wisdom founded through the sword—Solomon's capacity to end the autonomous and indigenous life or to subject its existence to the benevolence of his authority. The Jerusalem city-dream both echoes and appropriates the Gibeon dream (I Kgs 9:2), transforming Jerusalem into an imperial site filled with dreams from the "periphery."

Legitimized by a monotheistic theocracy to build the city, Solomon starts his government with an ambitious program of political economy to increase the wealth of his kingdom. Its basic resources were the agricultural surpluses of the peasants, complemented by commercial income through taxes on caravans in transit, and commercial transactions such as the sale of Ethiopian weapons and Egyptian chariots. Lisa Heidorn has shown that Ethiopians settled in the South to train their horses one hundred years after the first domesticated horse appeared in Asia Minor.[7] This suggests that lucrative horse trading was not exclusively from Anatolia, and that Palestinian relations with Egypt and Ethiopia were also based on the horse trade.

To secure his economic empire, Solomon strengthened his military might, and with the wealth derived from tax collection he built his palace and the temple in Jerusalem. He established political and economic structures by dividing the kingdom into twelve administrative districts to ensure the collection of taxes, with each district supervised by a respective minister, in addition to the twelve governors who provided for the house of the king. Furthermore, Solomon extended his borders by subjugating Philistines and Egyptians. This facilitated the centralization of the command structure. With this system, he supplied his palace with food. In addition, to carry out his constructions, he forced his subjects to create forced labor teams. All this was done in the name of God, who, according to the narrative, provided Solomon with extraordinary wisdom and intelligence that surpassed Eastern and Egyptian wisdom. He who owns a numerous harem also composes proverbs and songs (1 Kgs 5: 10–11).

To sustain this increasingly centralized city and its economically privileged social status, Solomon had to resort to agricultural surpluses in order to strengthen trade expansion. For the buildings, Solomon needed wood and metals from abroad, in exchange for which he offered agricultural products, forcing the working class to produce crops for export. Forced labor enraged the people, and prompted Jeroboam to organize

---

[6] Hannelis Schulte, "Beobachtungen zum begriff der zônâ im Alten Testament," in *Zeitschrift für die Alttestamentliche Wissenschaft* (1992), 255–64.

[7] Lisa A. Heidorn, "The Horses of Kush," *Journal of Near Eastern Studies* 56, no. 2 (1997): 105–14.

political and religious resistance. The ideological power of the emerging city was overwhelming, though. Jeroboam was forced to flee to Egypt (1 Kgs 11:26–40). This story reinforces the narrative nexus involving the city and its vibrant/resistant peripheries. Solomon's monopoly on international trade and political power was often compromised and resisted either through political negotiation and or through armed rebellion (cf. Edom and Aram rebelled against Solomon in 1 Kgs 11:14–25; 2 Kgs 8:20).

The construction of Solomon's palace was central to the goals of his administration. The temple was only part of the grounds on which the royal palace was built, much like what also existed in Assyrian palaces.[8] These lucrative endeavors were strengthened after Solomon's dream in the mountains of Gibeon. The path was open to continue replacing the mobile shrines and local religious practices in the mountains (high places) of Israel toward a single mountain, Jerusalem, chosen by his father, David. Political and religious dynasty converged in the making of the city.

Megastructure of the Temple of Israel

The word "temple" in Hebrew, *hêkal*, most likely comes from the Akkadian *ekullu*, or perhaps from the Sumerian *heakal*, which means "great house." The Akkadian term applies more to a royal palace than to a temple. The Temple of Israel was also called "the house," *ha bayith*, or the "House of Yahweh."[9] The idea of the centralization of the Temple came from David, when he established himself in the palace he conquered from the Jebusites in Jerusalem, which became his royal residence (2 Sam 7:1). Nathan's oracle refers to the promise of an eternal Davidic dynasty (2 Sam 7:5–7, 1 Chr 17:3–7), beginning with a call for the Israelite people to abandon the idea that Yahweh lived in tent-like mobile sanctuaries. The oracle also offers a guarantee of authenticity to the Temple, which must be built by David's son. The construction of the Temple lasted seven years (1 Kgs 6:37), but the king's palace, which was a more extensive project, took thirteen years to complete (1 Kgs 7:1). First Kings 6:31–36 speaks of the construction of two doors that opened to a patio, implying that there was a public door to enter the patio of the Temple. This ensured that the faithful would not have to pass through the royal residence. The king had his own entrance to the Temple from his palace.

---

[8] Antonio García Llansó et al., *Historia General del Arte : escrita e ilustrada en vista de los monumentos y de la mejores obras publicadas hasta el día*, Autonomous University of Barcelona (Barcelona, 1886).

[9] Fritz Volkmar, "Temple Architecture: What Can Archaeology Tell Us About Solomon's Temple?," *Biblical Archaeology Review* 13, no. 4 (1987): 38–41, 43–45, 48–49.

From inside the Temple's portico, there were double doors of olive wood that led to the "Holy Place" (1 Kgs 6:33–34). The whole interior was covered in carved cedar with decorative flowers, palms, and cherubim. The room was illumined by windows, which probably had bars. The Holy Place contained furniture for worship: the golden altar for incense, the table for burnt offerings, ten lamps, and other utensils. Two double doors led to the "Holy of Holies" or the most holy place, where the Ark of the Covenant was located. This place was made of cedar overlaid in gold. Two large cherubims of cedar were placed over the Ark, each measuring 4.30 meters high with wings of the same size (1 Kgs 6:26). The courtyard in front of the Temple contained a bronze altar for the burnt sacrifices. Stairs were the only way to reach the top part of the altar. There were also ten bronze mobile shells that held water. These shells were highly adorned and placed on a square support structure.

There seems to be no doubt that the place where Solomon's temple was built was Mount Moriah, known as *Har ah Bayit* in Hebrew and *Haram-al-Sharif* in Arabic.[10] The success of this majestic construction is in part due to the centralization of the power and the justification of a theocracy based on a sole mount (Zion), one city (Jerusalem), one king, one temple, and one God. A sole place to which everyone was to come to worship Yahweh in his house, thus delegitimizing local or mobile sanctuaries. The temple and the city mimic each other as representative sites where the deity is present in special ways.

From the edifice of the Temple, a well-founded theocracy projected itself in such a way that it has lasted for more than two millennia, along with its administrative structures for the collection of taxes. And today, more than ever, it becomes effective given the increase in offers of faith in mega religious structures.[11] In light of this, the question arises about the strategies utilized to captivate the popular masses. The suspicion being that certain elements of the traditions of popular religion were mixed as part of the official religion, as in the case of the common prophecies or divinatory practices in the Bené Hannebî'îm prophetic groups of the Canaanite cults who used music as a means to achieve ecstasy (1 Sam 10:5; cf. 18:10; Exod 15:20; 2 Kgs 3:15), with the spirit resting on the subject until they reached the state of trance (1 Sam 10:10; 19:20–23). These groups lived in community, following the guidance of their teacher, with little resources (2 Kgs 5), or even having difficulty to secure food, as it was

---

[10] Isaac Kalimi, "The Land of Moriah, Mount Moriah, and The Site of Solomon's Temple in Biblical Historiography," *Harvard Theological Review* 83, no. 4 (October 1990): 345–62.

[11] Clifton L. Holland, "Research on the Evangelical Mega-Church Phenomenon in Central America: Facts and Fiction" (PROLADES, 2011).

the case with one of the widows of the disciples of the prophets who had problems with the creditors (cf. 2 Kgs 4:1–7).

However, as Jeremiah 44:15 indicates, women burned incense and made libations to the Queen of Heaven, as did their ancestors in the streets of Jerusalem, feeding on bread and being happy; and nothing happened to them until the arrival of the homogenizing and centralizing Yahweh's prophets. Only then they began to be met with the dagger and the sword.[12] The truth is that Solomon's imperial project failed to remove these cults, assimilated them, and introduced them to the Temple of Jerusalem, under a narrative of unity. Through such narrative, the religious dream at Gibeon was appropriated for the purposes of building the city of Jerusalem.

THE TRANSITION FROM POLYTHEISM TO MONOTHEISM

During the Solomonic period, we find innumerable religious references that allow us to confirm the influence of polytheist religions in the configuration of faith in Israel. One of them was in the structure of the Temple of Yahweh itself, where there were two isolated columns in bronze with decorated capitals (1 Kgs 7:15–22). Although their purpose is unknown, they may be more than just decorations. William Albright suggests that they were luminous pillars with cosmic significance, recalling the smoke column and the fire column from the Exodus.[13] The names *yakin*, "he established," and *booz*, "with strength,"[14] may be the words in their inscriptions, whose meanings remit to astronomical religions such as the Gibeonites and Sabeans,[15] where *yakin* refers to the "sun" and *booz* to "the moon."[16]

The columns of Solomon's temple suggest a hierogamic and sexual relationship, alluding to the moon and the sun as divine partners representing

---

[12] Maricel Mena-López, "Resistencia femenina y religion popular una aproximación a partir de Jr 44,15–19, sentires teológicos en perspectiva liberadora," *Religión Cultura y Sociedad—Universidad Javeriana* 30 (2008): 93–120.

[13] William Foxwell Albright, *Archaeology and the Religion of Israel* (Baltimore: John Hopkins Press, 1949), 148.

[14] Carol L. Meyers, "Jachin and Boaz in Religious and Political Perspective," *The Catholic Biblical Quarterly* 45, no. 2 (1983): 167–78.

[15] In this text, we opt for a focus on Sheba due to the relationship between the Queen of Sheba and Solomon as well as due to the importance of their traditions in the book and the special way it is understood in the Ethiopian Church. Another reason for this decision was that the Canaanite deities have already been the object of much research in the field.

[16] James Bennett Pritchard, ed., *Ancient Near Eastern Texts Relating to the Old Testament* (Princeton, NJ: Princeton University Press, 1954).

the sexed male and female bodies.¹⁷ That is why these columns are linked to another feminine symbolism, the pomegranates. Solomon made these capitals atop the columns: "He also made pomegranates: two rows of them round each filigree, four hundred in all" (1 Kgs 7:17–20). The pomegranates were symbols of the uterus and of the fertility of the seed. This sacred symbolism in architecture was a common practice in Egypt, one of the people that best introduced sacred symbolism in their constructions.¹⁸

Like many contemporary cults, the peoples of southern Arabia worshipped the stars and planets. Therefore, we have no reason to doubt that this pantheon would have been venerated by the sages of the tenth century B.C.E. It is likely that the Queen of Sheba (1 Kgs 10:1–13) may have played the role of "priestess of the faith," "chief astronomer,"¹⁹ or *Mukarrib*, an Arabic title that most likely means "the king-priest," denoting an important role in the cult.²⁰ Presumably, there was also a mythological body and a calendar of religious days and deity festivities as one could see in Mesopotamia and Canaan that had similar religions.

In comparison, southern Arabia revered a large number of deities. Most of them were astral and "acted upon all manifestations of earthly life: light and darkness, heat and cold, drought or rain, prosperity or famine, even influencing human destinies."²¹ Among those divinities, the goddess *Athar* occupies a prominent place. Athar personifies the planet *Venus* for the Greeks and corresponds to the goddesses *Ishtar*, among the Assyrian-Babylonians, and *Isis*, among the Egyptians. We should note that in meridional Arabia, *Athar* was a masculine god, while in the Semitic religions this god was a feminine deity.²²

> Another feminine deity predominant in the Sabean religion was *Astar*, which means "uterus," and corresponds to the Canaanite goddess Ashtoreth. She is the one who has the power to give and to destroy life.

---

17   Antonio Risco, "Las dos columnas del templo de Salomón (Proyecto de Estudio de La Obra de Valle-Inclán)," *Revista Canadiense de Estudios Hispánicos* 10, no. 3 (1986): 433–49.
18   Dieter Arnold, Helen Strudwick, and Nigel Strudwick, *The Encyclopedia of Ancient Egyptian Architecture*, English language ed. (Princeton, NJ: Princeton University Press, 2003); Donald B. Redford, ed., *The Oxford Encyclopedia of Ancient Egypt* (Oxford: Oxford University Press, 2001).
19   Gus W. Van Beek, "The Land of Sheba," in *Solomon & Sheba*, ed. James B. Pritchard (London: Phaidon, 1974), 61–62.
20   Jean-François Breton, *L'Arabie heureuse au temps de la reine de Saba': VIIIe-Ier Siècle Av. J.-C*, La Vie Quotidienne (Paris: Hachette littératures, 1998).
21   M. Gaudefroy-Demombynes, *Mahomet* (Albin Michel, 1957), 35–36.
22   Emiliano Martínez Borobio, "Divinidades de Arameos y Árabes Preislámicos," *Revista Sobre Oriente Próximo y Egipto En La Antigüedad*, no. 2 (1999): 313–18.

Astar was the Queen of Heavens and the mother of all the other deities.[23] She is supposed to have descended from heavens in the form of a ball of fire accompanied by a lioness. She was depicted with horns and a disk in the shape of a sun on her forehead.[24]

The moon was both a masculine and feminine deity. As a masculine sexed deity, it was called *Wadd* amongst miners, *Almaqah* amongst the sages, and *Amm* en Qataban and *Sin* in Hadramaut.[25] This god was portrayed as an old man with a sky-blue beard; his head was covered with a turban and a crown in the shape of the full moon. The function of this divinity was to disperse evil and darkness by inspiring his followers with dreams and prophecies.

On the other hand, the moon as a feminine deity was known as the "Great Goddess" and carried the title of *Shayba*. This moon goddess was represented in three feminine ways: the crescent moon (the young woman), the full moon (the pregnant mother), and the waning moon (the wisdom of the elderly woman). This goddess depicted three stages of a woman's life: youth, maturation, and elderliness. These triple embodied forms (maiden, mother, and old woman) of the female permitted followers to value the feminine body in its various stages. The potentiality of the young woman celebrates the nymph or damsel aspect of the goddess. The mother goddess is presented sometimes giving birth and is seen as a symbol of all the creative and life-generating powers of the universe.[26] The creative power of the goddess was not limited to physical birth; she is also seen as the creator of all the arts and civilizations, including healing, writing, and just laws. The old and wise woman, the one who knows from her own experience what life is, the one whose closeness to death gives her a distance and a unique perspective to address life's problems, is celebrated as the third aspect of the Great Goddess.

The solar god was worshipped in *Sheba (Sabea), Qataban,* and *Hadramaut* as a deity by the name of *Shams,* meaning "sun." Like the Babylonian *Shemesh,* its function was to send powerful rays of benevolence. In the *Kebra Negast,* the sun is a male deity. The Queen of Sheba tells Solomon,

---

[23] The Queen of Heaven appears twice in the Bible in the book of Jeremiah (7:18 and 44:17–24) to refer to the religious practices of popular religion practiced by women, children, and men.

[24] Mena-López, "La herencia de las diosas—Egipto y Sabá en el tiempo de la monarquía salomónica," 46.

[25] Mário Curtis Giordani, *História do mundo Árabe medieval,* 4th ed. (Petrópolis: Vozes, 1992), 27.

[26] James Mellaart, *Earliest Civilization of the Near East* (New York: Thames and Hudson, 1978), 92.

> We worship the sun (…) so that he cooks our food, illuminates our darkness, and takes our fears away; we call him "Our King" and "Our Creator" (…) there are also other practices amongst us (…) where some worship stones, other worship trees, some worship sculpted figures, some images of gold, and also silver ones are worshiped.[27]

The astral religions have remained in Arabia over time. This southern Arabic culture is characterized by its ability to assimilate other divinities. This ability explains the relative ease with which Jewish and Christian beliefs were introduced in the south of the peninsula. This capacity for assimilation is also sustainable due to the fact that Canaanite deities were also worshiped in Yemen. The Canaanite goddess Astarte, as I pointed out, was also part of the Savannah pantheon.

Over long centuries of syncretism, the Deuteronomistic tradition[28] in Israel shows that the "idolatrous cults" in which men participate have "pagan women" as main allies, whether as priestesses, wives, for sacred prostitution, or through polygamy.[29] Women were blamed for seducing men and drawing them away from the worship of Yahweh, and that finds its climax in Solomon, the king of wisdom, who would have taken Israel's prestige to its fullest degree, the one who built a temple that was the pride of his people, restoring an impressive cult with priests, sacrifices, and parties. Solomon who had become the pride of his people by constructing the temple, reestablishing the impressive cultic tradition of priests, sacrifices, and feasts would also be the one who let idolatrous paganism into Israel. Solomon, married to the daughter of the Egyptian Pharaoh and visited and admired by the Queen of Sheba, gradually expanded his harem with "pagan" women who would lead the kingdom into public apostasy. A scandal, a temptation, a sin that mark with fire the history of Israel.

> King Solomon loved many foreign women: not only Pharaoh's daughter but Moabites, Edomites, Sidonians, and Hittites, from those peoples of whom Yahweh had said to the Israelites, "You are not to go among them nor they among you, or they will be sure to sway your hearts to their own gods." But Solomon was deeply attached to them. He had seven hundred wives of royal rank and three hundred concubines. When Solomon grew old his wives swayed his heart to other gods; and his heart was not wholly with Yahweh his God as his father David's had been. Solomon became a follower of Astarte, the goddess of the Sidonians, and of Milcom, the

---

[27] Lorenzo Mazzoni, *Kebra Nagast: La Biblia secreta del rastafari*, Chapter 24 (Málaga: Corona Borealis, 2010).

[28] The books of Kings are part of the so called "Deuteronomist School" whose theology reinforced the worship of one God and one sanctuary by the sole chosen people. Cf. G. von Rad, "Die deuteronomistische Geschichtstheologie in den Königsbüchern en *Deuteronomium-Studien*," FRLAT 40 (1947): 52–64.

[29] Santos Benetti, *Sexualidad y erotismo en la Biblia* (Buenos Aires: San Pablo, 1994).

Ammonite abomination. He did what was displeasing to Yahweh, and was not a wholehearted follower of Yahweh, as his father David had been. Then it was that Solomon built a high place for Chemosh, the abomination of Moab, on the mountain to the east of Jerusalem, and to Milcom, the abomination of the Ammonites. He did the same for all his foreign wives, who offered incense and sacrifice to their gods. (1 Kgs 11:1–8)

This passage reveals three important elements. First, the religious practices of the neighboring peoples were added alongside the worship of Yahweh, the god who would not admit the presence of other gods according to the Deuteronomist tradition; second, these new practices come exactly from conquered peoples and other neighboring peoples, those that the priestly tradition prohibits intermarriages with because it presents a threat to their faith (Ezra 10:1–17); and third, the apostasy is primarily caused by "pagan" women who "seduce" and "tempt" men, perverting them.

For the Deuteronomist redactors, women are responsible for Solomon's decadence. Despite this, they could not erase their memories. These women remain in the narrative, occupied with the transcendental matters such as worship, as they did in their homelands. The foreign women of the court, even during the period of Solomon, achieved a predominant role in the cultural and political life of Israel. One example of this was the case of the queen mother "*gebira*."[30] Even though, the monarchy forced on them stereotyped roles such as docile wives, concubines, or apostates, and they gradually ceased participating in the circulation of power.

It is important to note that in order to justify their relationship to God, the Israelites used myths, symbols, and rituals that explain the origin of life and of the world, birth, marriage, and death, among others, which originated among neighboring peoples, but which were explained in monotheistic perspective. For instance, clay tablets found in 1929 in Ugarit, today Ras Shamra in northern Syria, show myths and legends written in prose that address a wide variety of issues, including legal matters, religious problems, myths, epics, and prayers. These documents dated from between 1,400 B.C.E. and 1,200 B.C.E., and written in Akhadic, Sumerian, Egyptian, and Hittite, they had a strong influence on the religion of Israel as evidenced by the following examples: Exodus 15, which recounts the victorious song of Moses seems to reflect Baal's conflict with the sea; in 1 Kings 17, Baal, known as the god of rain, lightning, and storm, is now unable to produce water, while Yahweh brings "fire of heaven," thus

---

[30] Susan Ackerman, "The Queen Mother and the Cult in Ancient Israel," *Journal of Biblical Literature* 112, no. 3 (1993): 385–401, https://doi.org/10.2307/3267740.

demonstrating his sovereignty over Baal. Numbers 25: 1–9 talks about sexual immorality with Canaanite women in fertility services.[31]

In the Solomonic centralization project, feminine sexuality is stereotyped, removed from its independent domain as sacred, and subjected to the delight of one man, Solomon. One of the institutions that corroborate this is the harem.[32] In the West, the harem has been poorly understood as merely a place of lust where unoccupied women wait for their turn with the king.[33] The confusion seems to stem from the meaning of the Egyptian term *kheneret*, "a closed space,"[34] which scholars translated as "harem" because in those spaces communities of women celebrated rituals in honor of the divinities that protected the harem, such as, Hathor, Isis, or Bastet. The closed nature of the harem, therefore, was linked to its secrecy.

The harem was a well-structured institution that admitted into its walls high ranked functionaries, administrators, artisans, servants, and peasants exploited through taxes on their agricultural products, flocks, and the fruits of fishing, to guarantee the livelihood of this elite. In the harem lived disciple priestesses of the goddess Hathor, patroness of the initiates of the harem[35] who ritually ensured the survival of the soul and the irrigation of earth by celestial powers. In the quality of "wife of God," the royal wife and sovereign over all the priestesses in the kingdom directed this institution in its entirety. She was responsible for all educational programs, appointed teachers, ensured the good economic health of the harem, and the practice of the rhythms.[36] In each harem, an overseer represented the queen as director or delegate, or as an assistant to a director, often as the head of a province, or even as a high priest. The "secondary" queens and wives of the pharaoh had their children raised in the harems, where they received a quality education. The harem as an institution of teaching and instruction was a privileged place for the development of the wisdom of the Egyptians.[37]

---

[31] Gregorio del Olmo Lete, *Mitos y leyendas de Canaan: Según la tradición de Ugarit* (Madrid: Valencia: Institución San Jerónimo, 1981).

[32] Beverly W. Cushman, "The Politics of the Royal Harem and the Case of Bat-Sheba," *Journal for the Study of the Old Testament* 30, no. 3 (March 1, 2006): 327–43, https://doi.org/10.1177/0309089206063438.

[33] Christiane Desroches-Noblecourt, *A mulher no tempo dos faraós* (Campinas: Papirus, 1994).

[34] Christian Jacq, *As Egípcias: Retratos de mulheres do Egito faraônico*, Edição 3 (Rio de Janeiro: Bertrand, 2000).

[35] S. Allam, "Beiträge zum hathorkult, bis zum ende des mittleren reiches," in *Münchner Ägyptologische Studien*, 4 (Berlin: Verlag Bruno Hessling, 1963).

[36] Jacq, *As Egípcias*, 245.

[37] Maricel Mena-López, "Mujeres sabias en 1 Re 3–11," *Concilium* 294 (2002): 27–37.

Solomon offered sacrifice at the high place in Gibeon. But, it is interesting to note that the cult that was initially practiced by all, especially by women, goes through a process of hierarchy. The participation of high priestesses eventually succumbed. The sexual relationship that was necessary for nature to be fertile was now centralized in the figure of the monarch who possesses numerous harems and probably a fairly virile member. The king who in principle maintained a relationship only with the main priestess as a metaphor for sacred marriage with the same divinity, is now the personification of the same monotheistic divinity, thus justifying his polygamy and the submission of women as a divine mandate. The male God of the Israelites is presented as a model that justifies the dominance scheme. As Judith Plaskow clearly points out,

> God as ruler and king of the universe is the pinnacle of a vast hierarchy that extends from God himself ... to men, women, animals, and finally to the earth. As hierarchical ruler, God is a model for the many schemes of dominance that human beings create for themselves. As a holy king, he chooses Israel as his holy people. As holy warrior, he sanctions the destruction of other peoples. As holy legislator, he orders the submission of women in the Jewish community.[38]

The elimination of the goddesses promotes a new relationship of women with Yahweh as their Lord and by imitation with men as their lords. In addition, the idea of sacred marriage undergoes transformation from a hierogamic relationship to a relationship between a patriarchal God and a serving wife.

In the next section, I will further examine this phenomenon by looking at modern megacities and the associated mega spaces of faith. My intention is to create a narrative analogy and parallel between the ancient past and the present forms of city and faith, in order to propose a return to ancestral traditions as an epistemic alternative to dominating power.

On urban religious megastructures: Then and now

Modern city spaces seem to respond to the hegemonic centralizing model of one monarch, one God, one spirit, one nation, and one "I". The edification of the city is a normative political representation, purported to represent the common good in the social, political, economic, and religious order. Yet, in reality, what one sees is the continuous increase of exclusion as part of a global economic model, which denies access to communities on the periphery, paradoxically organized under a normalizing religious model of conduct to which the masses flock. The city today corresponds to a savage neoliberal macro project that emerged from the Washington

---

[38] Judith Plaskow, *Standing Again at Sinai: Judaism from a Feminist Perspective* (New York, NY: HarperCollins, 1997), 132.

Consensus in which a single paradigm of living and thinking prevails. In its highly centralized form, the city projects a model of belonging in which only one paradigm of life and thought governs, compelling submission and re-inscribing a hierarchy.

> It is a phenomenon of exploitation, dispossession, inequality, exclusion, and discrimination whose spatial dimensions are evident. Dual cities of luxury and misery, neighbors separated by fortified walls, thousands of empty rental spaces, and thousands of people homeless without a decent place to live; land without workers, subjugated by agrobusinesses, privatization, and accelerated accumulation and concentration of the wealth produced collectively in the hands of few.[39]

The cities built for the submission of temples-palaces-walls-markets-ramparts are intersected by contrasting urban projects that proclaim urban reform in solidarity to agrarian reform, through alternative practices of production and reproduction of the enjoyment of life. From these scenarios, diverse social groups engage in the dispute for their rights, often negotiated in assemblies and congresses that almost always favor the interests of large capital. These arrangements have implications for the emergence and function of mega churches.

Megachurches gather thousands of followers around the world every day. Their numbers are growing and they increasingly manage huge budgets and financial portfolios. Often led by a charismatic and spiritual leader, a group of associate ministers, leaders for the various programs, and a large number of volunteers, these churches rely on staff and volunteers (in some cases hundreds of them) who offer at least five hours of their time, weekly.[40] As one looks into such structures, questions arise regarding the marketing strategies that have been used to turn these "faith businesses" into one of the most attractive and lucrative businesses in the contemporary world. More importantly for the purposes of this chapter, it is crucial to understand how these mega structures and infrastructures represent part of the character and function of the city. One notices, for instance, how megachurches arrange great technical feats, coordinating musicians and modern sermons in order to attract an expansive audience. They count with gigantic infrastructures and personnel to supply daycare, spaces of relaxation, ample parking, cafes, and other services. These churches hold thousands of people without distinction of class, race, or

---

[39] Maria Lorena Zarate, "El derecho a la ciudad," *Institut de Drets Humans de Catalunya y El Observatori DESC* (2011): 53–70.

[40] Joaquín Maria Algranti, *Política y religión en los márgenes: nuevasformas departicipación social de las mega-iglesias evangélicas en la Argentina*, 1st ed. (Argentina: Ediciones Ciccus, 2010).

culture, all under a hierarchical, authoritarian, dogmatic, and sometimes fanatical discourse.

The mix of power and gender roles in these mega spaces is evident. On the one hand, a majority of the women in these structures tend to hold culturally assigned roles, such as those of service, as manifestation of the distinct sexual division present in patriarchal societies. This patriarchal role of women is maintained and reinforced where they decide to serve God, church, family, and neighbor.[41] These temples become extensions of their private life, where the pastor is the head of the temple, just as at home the man is the head of the household. This idea is reinforced through references to Ephesians 5:23, "as Christ is head of the church and saves the whole body, so is a husband the head of his wife." There is limited female participation in the highest rankings of leadership. In those aspects related to political participation, understood as places of decision-making, the inclusion of women remains marginal, since these spaces are preferably reserved for men and their pastors.

On the other hand, such experience is not universal.[42] Many Pentecostal megachurches offer women a new sense of power and autonomy. In those contexts, women are able to climb to public positions such as preacher, prophet, and leader of women's groups. They attain these positions of leadership through a personal and loving relationship with Jesus.[43] The recognition of women in these roles makes them truly "feel like part" of the community. Sometimes women are able to do things that benefit the church, even while being excluded from participating in the political processes within the church.[44] In Colombia, for example, there are many cases of well-known female evangelical politicians who remain faithful to their religious tradition and continue adopting fundamentalist stances.

I am convinced that women inside these spaces have an important potential and that changes will need to come from within these contexts, that is, from these female leaders. It is necessary to learn our own history, including the processes of adaptation and negation of ancestral traditions that are now part of our own story. One could go as far as to say that the great success of these mega churches resides in their ability to bring together popular practices of women and in turn make them "official" by integrating them into the Christian service. One thinks of the so-called

[41] Zicri Orellana, "Significado de la experiencia religiosa de mujeres pentecostales y su relación con la identidad de género," *Revista Cultura y religion*, no. 3 (2009).
[42] Orellana, "Significado de la experiencia religiosa.
[43] Lindhardt, Poder, "Género y cambio cultural en el pentecostalismo Chileno," *Revista Cultura y Religión*, 3, 2009.
[44] Elizabeth Salazar, "La mujer en el pentecostalismo: entre la ambigüedad y la coherencia," in *Teología, Género y Religión*, eds. D. Agudelo and J. Carrasquilla (Santiago de Cali: Pontificia Universidad Javierana, 2006), 53–82.

"prophecies" that invoke images of divination practices in popular culture; or the cases of "the outpouring of the Holy Spirit" that are comparable to indigenous religious rituals; or African-derived practices of spirit mediation where the ancestors give wisdom from the otherworld or from the terrestrial plane, depending on the circumstance; or the usage and appropriation of modern world dance, which receives a new spiritual value.

Faced with these things, one wonders if it is possible to establish new ecclesial models and new relationships without the need for mediation and that are truly integrative of life in their holistic dimension, that do not exploit the faithful, nor contradict the appearance of inclusivity with exclusivist practices.

> Globalization connects economies and policies into a great knot of macro-capitals whose interests are not in conversation at all with the minimal needs of the masses that inhabit the cities. This is why the result is a hostile environment, a network of services and communications in which one who does not have access to them is out of the game.[45]

This search would be consistent with the notion of an amiable habitat, the category of the "good life" (*sumak kawsay*) from the ancestral wisdom of the Quechua, which the Aymara culture knows as *suma qamaña*.[46] The Guarani *teko pora o teko kavi*, "the good way of being or living," can help us in proposing a city model in which hierarchies are suppressed, because all humans including nature would be in equal conditions, and because we all need everyone else. We can consider these modes of living as being in sync with the time when women participated in leadership in the spaces of Canaan, Sheba, and Egypt; a time when women offered libations to the goddess of the Heavens and of plentiful provision of bread; a time women recounted in Jeremiah 44: "But intend to go on doing all we have vowed to do: offering incense to the Queen of Heaven and pouring libations in her honor, as we used to do, we and our ancestors, our kings and our chief men, in the towns of Judah and the streets of Jerusalem" (v.17). Then, these women assert that "we had food in plenty then, we lived well, we suffered no disasters…" yet because they left their ancestral religion behind, they have "been destitute and have perished either by sword or by famine" (v.18).

The prophetic denunciation on behalf of these women is among many found in the prophetic literature of the Bible. They warn us about the necessity to remember and unmask the patriarchal power that laid the

---

[45] Carmiña Navia, "Ciudades hoy, diálogos con la tradición bíblica," *En Revista Teología y Sociedad*, no. 8 (2010): 17.

[46] This category is part of the ethical principles in the political constitutions of Ecuador and Bolivia. This gives us hope that this is a real life possibility in our urban spaces.

foundations of the "indisputable" monotheism as a system that promotes exclusions and social asymmetries. This reminiscing of better times and of more holistic, harmonious, and distributive models teaches us a different way to live; a new way of better living on this earth and its cities that belong to us all, and not only to a powerful elite. In this way, we want to evoke new forms of socialization in sync with the cosmos, nature, and human beings. These revindications reclaim the cities and the villages, replacing them in joyful harmony, beyond merely extractivist practices destructive to the flora, fauna, and minerals. A return to these "ancient" wisdoms implies rescuing the community and relational dimensions of society and city life. This is a highly political component, for it advances the right to exercise full citizenship, by promoting collective rights, not merely individual ones. This philosophy vindicates the rights of the land, the habitat, ecosystems, cities, and villages. These values reestablish the land as a right and not as a commodity. The search for the "good life" promotes a communitarian rationality—a truly political means that advances our right to exercise citizenship in the city with regard to the collective rather than only to the individual.[47]

Conclusion

The emphasis on possible feminine influences on the religion of Israel is not intended to justify the need for the recognition of women in religion, as the struggle of women is justified in itself. The transition from popular religion to hegemonic religion led to the hierarchization of religion itself and monotheism, while promoting a religious fundamentalism based on the denial of women and their divinities.

The analysis of the megastructure of the Solomonic Temple allows us to understand the success of a Zionist theocracy that centralizes political, economic, and religious power in a city, a hill, a temple, a priest, a king, an elected people, and a retributionist theology under the model of an imperial city.

By recognizing other cultural and religious influences in monarchical Israel, we want to do justice to a human history that is built on the contours of officiality. Thus, in rescuing the symbolism of the goddesses in their political, social, and psychological dimensions, we question the centralization of the spiritual experience in the one, masculine, imperial, and colonialist God. At the same time, we demonstrate the dynamics of exclusion-inclusion, center-periphery at play in the discourse of

---

[47] Maricel Mena-López et al., "Sabiduría ancestral egipcia e israelita: Desafíos éticos para el buen vivir urbano," in *Biblia y Ciudad: Pedagogía Del Buen Vivir En Contextos Urbanos*, ed. Maricel Mena-López, 1st ed. (Madrid: Ediciones USTA, 2017), 89.

political inclusivity and the contradiction of exclusive political and religious practices.

As we concomitantly approached the modern-day mega-religious structures, we identified the similarities of a theocratic model that brings together urban popular masses under a fundamentalist religious discourse that is attractive to the masses for its integration of popular practices. Furthermore, the retributionist theology of prosperity has become a guarantor of the maintenance of worship at the expense of the good of the faithful. Behind this discourse, one finds the desires of wanting to live well, confronted with everything that the capitalist system seems to offer. This essay aims at moving us to think of possibilities beyond those offered by corporate capital. We evoked ideas of the *good life* in a generic manner, as experiences or ways of life that already exist in peripheral communities. One example would be the ways of life advanced by the indigenous communities of the Andes. They seem to point to an alternative model of life in the city, one that accentuates the interconnected relation between humans, the environment, and the divine. In this model of life in the city, "old" and "new" wisdoms are challenged to live together.

Bibliography

Ackerman, Susan. "The Queen Mother and the Cult in Ancient Israel." *Journal of Biblical Literature* 112, no. 3 (1993): 385–401. https://doi.org/10.2307/3267740.

Albright, William Foxwell. *Archaeology and the Religion of Israel*. Baltimore: John Hopkins Press, 1949.

Algranti, Joaquín Maria. *Política y religión en los márgenes: Nuevas formas de participación social de las mega-iglesias evangélicas en la Argentina*. 1st ed. Argentina: Ediciones Ciccus, 2010.

Allam, S. "Beiträge zum Hathorkult, bis zum ende Des Mittleren Reiches." In *Münchner Ägyptologische Studien*. 4. Berlin: Verlag Bruno Hessling, 1963.

Arnold, Dieter, Helen Strudwick, and Nigel Strudwick. *The Encyclopedia of Ancient Egyptian Architecture*. English language ed. Princeton, NJ: Princeton University Press, 2003.

Beltrán Cely, William Mauricio. "La Teoría del mercado en el estudio de la pluralización religiosa." *Revista Colombiana De Sociología* 33 (2010): 41–62.

Benetti, Santos. *Sexualidad y erotismo en la Biblia*. Buenos Aires: San Pablo, 1994.

Breton, Jean-François. *L'Arabie heureuse au temps de la Reine de Saba': VIIIe-Ier Siècle Av. J.-C. La Vie Quotidienne*. Paris: Hachette littératures, 1998.

Cushman, Beverly W. "The Politics of the Royal Harem and the Case of Bat-Sheba." *Journal for the Study of the Old Testament* 30, no. 3 (March, 2006): 327–43. https://doi.org/10.1177/0309089206063438.

Desroches-Noblecourt, Christiane. *A mulher no tempo dos faraós*. Campinas: Papirus, 1994.

García Llansó, Antonio, Lluís Domènech i Montaner, Josep Puig i Cadafalch, Francesc Miquel i Badia, Federico Cajal y Pueyo, Joaquim Fontanals i del Castillo, F. Hottenroth, and Ermenegild Miralles i Anglès. *Historia general del arte: Escrita e ilustrada en vista de los monumentos y de la mejores obras publicadas hasta el día*, 1886.

Gaudefroy-Demombynes, M. *Mahomet*. Albin Michel, 1957.

Giordani, Mário Curtis. *História do mundo Árabe Medieval*. 4th ed. Petrópolis: Vozes, 1992.

Heidorn, Lisa A. "The Horses of Kush." *Journal of Near Eastern Studies* 56, no. 2 (1997): 105–14.

Holland, Clifton L. "Research on the Evangelical Mega-Church Phenomenon in Central America: Facts and Fiction." PROLADES, 2011.

Jacq, Christian. *As Egípcias. Retratos de mulheres do Egito faraônico*. Edição, 3. Rio de Janeiro: Bertrand, 2000.

Kalimi, Isaac. "The Land of Moriah, Mount Moriah, and The Site of Solomon's Temple in Biblical Historiography." *Harvard Theological Review* 83, no. 4 (October 1990): 345–62.

Martínez Borobio, Emiliano. "Divinidades de Arameos y Árabes Preislámicos." *Revista Sobre Oriente Próximo y Egipto En La Antigüedad*, no. 2 (1999): 313–18.

Mazzoni, Lorenzo. *Kebra Nagast: la Biblia secreta del rastafari*. Chapter 24. Málaga: Corona Borealis, 2010.

Mena-López, Maricel. "La herencia de las diosas—Egipto y Sabá en el tiempo de la monarquía Salomónica." *RIBLA—Revista de Interpretación Bíblica Latinoamericana* 54 (2006): 34–47.

———. "Mujeres sabias en 1 Re 3–11." *Concilium* 294 (2002): 27–37.

———. "Resistencia femenina y religion popular una aproximación a partir de Jr 44,15–19, sentires teológicos en perspectiva liberadora." *Religión Cultura y Sociedad—Universidad Javeriana* 30 (2008): 93–120.

Mena-López, Maricel, Jaime Alberto Mancera Casas, Eleazar López Hernández, Hervé Tremblay, Fernando Torres Millán, Mary Betty Rodríguez Moreno, and Alberto Camargo Cortés. "Sabiduría ancestral Egipcia e Israelita: Desafíos éticos para el buen vivir urbano." In *Biblia y Ciudad: Pedagogía Del Buen Vivir En Contextos Urbanos*, edited by Maricel Mena-López, 1st ed. Ediciones USTA, 2017. https://doi.org/10.2307/j.ctvckq9fg.

Meyers, Carol L. "Jachin and Boaz in Religious and Political Perspective." *The Catholic Biblical Quarterly* 45, no. 2 (1983): 167–78.

Navia, Carmiña. "Ciudades hoy, diálogos con la tradición Bíblica." *Colección Revista Teología y Sociedad* no. 8 (2010): 11–30.

Olmo Lete, Gregorio del. *Mitos y leyendas de Canaan: Según la tradición de Ugarit*. Madrid: Institución San Jerónimo, 1981.

Orellana, Zicri. "Significado de la experiencia religiosa de mujeres Pentecostales y su relación con la identidad de género." Tesis de Magíster: Universidad de Chile, 2009.

Plaskow, Judith. *Standing Again at Sinai: Judaism from a Feminist Perspective*. New York: HarperCollins, 1997.

Pritchard, James Bennett, ed. *Ancient Near Eastern Texts Relating to the Old Testament*. Princeton, NJ: Princeton University Press, 1954.

Redford, Donald B., ed. *The Oxford Encyclopedia of Ancient Egypt*. Oxford: Oxford University Press, 2001.

Risco, Antonio. "Las dos columnas del Templo de Salomón (Proyecto de estudio de la obra de Valle-Inclán)." *Revista Canadiense de Estudios Hispánicos* 10, no. 3 (1986): 433–49.

Salazar, Elizabeth. "La Mujer En El Pentecostalismo: Entre La Ambigüedad y La Coherencia." In *Teología, Género y Religión*, edited by D. Agudelo and J. Carrasquilla, 53–82. Santiago de Cali: Pontificia Universidad Javierana, 2006.

Schulte, Hannelis. "Beobachtungen zum begriff Der Zônâ im Alten Testament." In *Zeitschrift Für Die Alttestamentliche Wissenschaft*, edited by Otto Kaiser and Walter de Gruyter, 255–64, 1992.

Van Beek, Gus W. "The Land of Sheba." In *Solomon & Sheba*, edited by James B. Pritchard. London: Phaidon, 1974.

Volkmar, Fritz. "Temple Architecture: What Can Archaeology Tell Us About Solomon's Temple?" *Biblical Archaeology Review* 13, no. 4 (1987): 38–41, 43–45, 48–49.

Weems, Renita J. *Amor maltratado: matrimonio, sexo y violencia en los profetas hebreos*. Bilbao: Desclée De Brouwer, 1997.

Zarate, Maria Lorena. "El derecho a la ciudad." *Institut de Drets Humans de Catalunya y El Observatori DESC* (2011): 53–70.

4

CONFIGURING CHRISTIAN IDENTITIES IN TIMES OF INFORMATION AND COMMUNICATION TECHNOLOGIES

Ernesto Fiocchetto

INTRODUCTION

Information and communication technologies (ICTs) are shaping multiple dimensions of urban life in global societies. This phenomenon, which I refer to as "digitalization of everyday life," also has an impact on religion, including Christianity.[1] Millions of believers perform their Christian faith online on a daily basis, and thus, they configure their Christian identities through processes that are permeated by ICTs. This essay aims to place this trait of Christianity in the broader context of the socioeconomic development of Western societies in order to gain a better understanding of how Christians configure their identities within digitalized societies.

Three questions guide this research. The first one is, what is the context that explains both the digitalization of everyday life and the individuation of beliefs that characterize present Western urban societies? The theoretical framework for this inquiry is drawn mainly from the work of the sociologists of Late Modernity, namely Anthony Giddens, Zygmunt Bauman, and Ulrich Beck, and the different, but complementary perspective of David Harvey. Danièle Heriveu-Léger's notion of religion and individuation is significantly enlightening for my work. Thus, section one

---

[1] This essay focuses in general on Christian believers' identities in Western urban areas. However, I do not mean that the processes that I describe throughout the text are not reproduced in rural areas or in non-Western societies, or that other religious traditions and experiences do not experience them. Although my research does not address these same processes in other geographical and religious contexts, I leave the door open for further research on those relations.

offers answers to this question by showing the entanglement between the advances of capitalism in Late Modernity, the development of religious individuation, and the role of ICTs. Section two introduces the sociological concept of "Augmented Reality," which is crucial to understand new dimensions of the intersection between Christianity and ICT.

The second question I ask in this essay is, how does the context described in the two initial sections influence the ways in which individuals configure their religious identities? Thus, in the third section, following Bauman, I argue that in consumerist societies individuals tend to produce new subjectivities. Digitalized everyday life offers a venue in which individuals configure their identities both as consumers and as products. Fetishized subjectivities, therefore, are turned into performed identities.

Finally, this essay asks how Christians configure their identities within digitalized societies. Based on the growing number of virtual spaces used to perform various kinds of Christian practices online, the fourth and last section of this essay offers an analysis of the intersection between Christianity and ICTs on different levels.

Using virtual-ethnographic research and engaging the theoretical contributions of social scientists from diverse backgrounds, this essay sets out to provide some answers to these questions from a sociological perspective. By examining the causes and consequences of the digitalization of everyday life, we can better understand the resulting new subjectivities and how they contribute to the production of contemporary religious—in the case of this research, Christian—identities.

THE CONTRADICTIONS OF CAPITALISM IN LATE MODERNITY: INDIVIDUATION OF BELIEFS AND THE DIGITALIZATION OF EVERYDAY LIFE

ICTs shape multiple dimensions of urban life in Western societies, including religion and the configuration of Christian identities. Nowadays, we can do countless activities and make innumerable decisions online. For instance, we can invest money, buy and sell, express opinions, sit for exams, stay in touch with relatives and friends who live thousands of miles away, find new and old friends, fall in love, have sex, pray, worship, attend liturgy, and adore Jesus in the Eucharist. Therefore, the analysis of the configuration of contemporary religious identities must be conceived from a perspective that takes ICTs seriously. I argue that in order to understand both the pervasiveness of the ICTs[2] and the process of

---

[2] Marcos De Colsa, "La digitalización de la vida cotidiana: TIC's, consumo y adaptación en el capitalismo," accessed September 14, 2018, https://tinyurl.com/yceke87g . Marcos De Colsa is a Mexican social anthropologist whose work focuses on anthropology applied to business for many years. In 2011, he

individuation[3] that religion has experienced in Western urban areas in the last half-century, it is crucial to examine the socioeconomic dimension of the period known as "Late Modernity."[4]

The digitalization of everyday life and the individuation of beliefs that characterize current Western urban societies can be seen, ultimately, as adaptation mechanisms in response to the contradictions of global capitalism. A classic quote from Anthony Giddens defines capitalism as "a system of commodity production, centered upon the relation between private ownership of capital and propertyless wage labor, this relation forming the main axis of a class system."[5] This system implies its own contradictions. I briefly tackle only two of them in this section because of the importance they have for both adaptation mechanisms.

Global risk society, the rise of individualism, and the individuation of beliefs

Capitalism, as described by Giddens, needs to perpetuate inequality (private owners vs. propertyless wage laborers), which is essential for the existence of the main axis that the British sociologist describes. On the other hand, capitalism—specifically commodity production—depends on the

founded Antropomedia with Axel Mayen and directed the first company of digital Anthropology in Mexico. They considered that their responsibility as social scientists was to re-humanize the internet, since it was a medium that ran the risk of becoming more technological than human. De Colsa is a prolific researcher and has many publications. True to his philosophy, much of his work is only accessible online.

[3] Danièle Hervieu-Léger, "In Search of Certainties: The Paradoxes of Religiosity in Societies of High Modernity," *The Hedgehog Review* 8, no. 1–2 (Spring–Summer 2006): 59–60.

[4] Anthony Giddens, *Modernity and Self-Identity: Self and Society in the Late Modern Age* (CA: Stanford University Press, 1991). Anthony Giddens, Ulrich Beck, and Zygmunt Bauman's approaches to Modernity have dominated sociological theory and imagination from the end of the twentieth century until now. In spite of the nuances that distinguish each of these authors, the three of them agree that the period Giddens calls Late Modernity—a term he prefers in contrast to Postmodernity—does not represent a radical break from Modernity, but instead an adjustment of the Modern project. Furthermore, they assert that one of the main characteristics of Late Modernity—which Ulrich Beck calls "Second Modernity" *Risk Society: Towards a New Modernity* (CA: Sage Publications, 1992), and Zygmunt Bauman "Liquid Modernity" *Liquid Modernity* (Cambridge: Politi Press, 2000)—is that the dynamics of capital is the decisive cause of the main features of globalized societies in the West. In fact, they highlight that all dimensions of Late Modernity, including its urban life, the digitalization of everyday life, religion, and identity formation, are to be understood as shaped by the engine of capitalism.

[5] Anthony Giddens, *The Consequences of Modernity* (CA: Stanford University Press, 1990), 55.

depredation of the resources that are indispensable for its maintenance. In other words, capitalism takes onto itself the signs of its own destruction insofar as it promotes an ideal of equality and development that can never be achieved without challenging its own essence. Thus, the system results in a "global risk society" governed by uncertainty.[6]

According to David Harvey, modernity was constructed under the model of expected stability granted by the ideals of the nation-state and economic development.[7] In contrast, the decades after the 1960s[8] brought a change from stability to permanent mobility, flexibility, and ephemerality. The consequences of this model are that societies turn diffuse—with no boundaries. As a result of such instability and diffusivity, risk and lack of certainties are ubiquitous.[9] Ulrich Beck, indeed, argues that the fellowship of the classes disappears while vulnerability globalizes.[10] The individual is, therefore, the last boundary of responsibility for the sake of one's own and others' survival. "If globalization, detraditionalization, and individualization are analyzed together, it becomes clear that the life of one's own is an experimental life."[11]

Simultaneously, the 1960s saw an urban development of the production of images and signs began to compete with the old modern notion of objects and commodities. These changes in production at the end of the period known as Keynesian-Fordist implied more flexible accumulation of capital.[12] Flexible production requires a system to solve problems

---

[6] Ulrich Beck, "Global Risk Society," in *The Wiley&Blackwell Encyclopedia of Globalization*, ed. George Ritzer (Blackwell Publishing, 2012). doi:10.1002/9780470670590.wbeog242.

[7] He states that "The result is to exacerbate insecurity and instability, as masses of capital and workers shift from one line of production to another, leaving whole sectors devastated, while the perpetual flux in consumer wants, tastes, and needs become a permanent locus of uncertainty and struggle." David Harvey, *The Condition of Postmodernity: An Enquiry into the Origins of Cultural Change* (MA: Blackwell Publishers, 1990), 106.

[8] David Harvey's perspective on this period is different in several aspects from the one of Giddens, Beck, and Bauman. Such differences are beyond the scope of this essay. Many authors have tackled such an issue, for example, see Brian Heaphy, *Late Modernity and Social Change: Reconstructing Social and Personal Life* (NY: Routledge, 2007), 69–92. However, the four authors agree on the thesis, that is essential for this essay, namely, the crucial role that capitalism plays on Western societies in Late Modernity (or Post-Modernity in Harvey's words) and its consequences on the development of the ICTs.

[9] Beck, "Global Risk Society," 2.

[10] Beck, "Global Risk Society," 2.

[11] Ulrich Beck and Elisabeth Beck-Gernsheim, *Individualization: Institutionalized Individualism and Its Social and Political Consequences* (London: Sage Publications, 2002), 26.

[12] De Colsa, "La digitalización de la vida cotidiana," 4.

effectively.[13] Speed and specialization accurately describe this intent to satisfy individual demands. Likewise, societies experienced a change from collective norms and values to a competitive individualism, which ultimately became the central value and necessary condition for this transition.[14] The rise of individualism as a reflection of the fragmentation of the old cultural order has reshaped Western urban societies and how individuals live their faith within them.

In line with the above-mentioned events, French sociologist Danièle Hervieu-Léger claims that we have been also witnessing a process of individuation of beliefs.[15] She observes an increasing loss of control of the established religious institutions, particularly in Western Christianity, over the belief systems and religious practices of individuals; hence, a gap between the official forms of religion and individually accepted religious perceptions and behaviors emerged. Individuals nowadays are increasingly independent from established religious authorities and thus enabled to determine their belief systems autonomously. The broad symbol of the market that has flourished in the West over the last decades is also the fruit of this individuation of beliefs stimulated by the questioning of the absolute regimes of truth that is inherent in the advances of capitalism in Late Modernity.[16] She considers that,

> This putting into perspective of the orthodoxies upheld by institutions is part of a deeper movement in which the governing systems of truth are being displaced. Legitimization of belief is moving from religious authorities, guarantors of the truth of belief, to individuals themselves, who are responsible for the authenticity of their own spiritual approach.[17]

Spatial fixes and the digitalization of everyday life

Capitalism, as described by Giddens, produces overaccumulation when the commodity production registers surpluses of labor and capital side by side with seemingly no way to put them together in new commodity production.[18] Harvey shows how this new contradiction of capitalism leads to crises that, when not solved, result in massive devaluation that can lead to physical destruction and even wars.[19] "But, there are ways to stave off

---

[13] Harvey, *The Condition of Postmodernity*, 170.
[14] De Colsa, "La digitalización de la vida cotidiana," 5.
[15] Danièle Hervieu-Léger, *Religion as a Chain of Memory* (Brunswick, NJ: Rutgers University Press, 2000), 2.
[16] Hervieu-Léger, "In Search of Certainties," 61–63.
[17] Hervieu-Léger, "In Search of Certainties," 60.
[18] David Harvey, "Globalization and the Spatial Fix," *Geographische Revue* 3(2), (2001): 26.
[19] He writes: "Devaluation can sometimes lead to physical destruction (surplus commodities get burned and laborers die of starvation) and even war (the whole

such an outcome. In practice, most crisis phases combine selective devaluations with strategies to alleviate the difficulties. One such strategy is to seek out some 'spatial fix' to the problem."[20] If overaccumulation is chiefly registered as surpluses of commodities, then expansion to new markets of both capital and labor appears the best strategy and, therefore, surpluses of capital and shortages of labor can be "fixed" either by the movement of capital or importation of cheap labor.[21]

Capitalism has, thus, always pushed for faster communication networks that would make distance obsolete as the space between separate spheres of production, distribution, exchange, and consumption was erased.[22] By deploying the term "spatial fix," David Harvey describes capitalism's insatiable drive to resolve its inner contradictions by the means of geographical expansion and geographical restructuring.[23] Harvey's geography of capitalist accumulation shows that,

> (a) capitalism could not survive without being geographically expansionary (and perpetually seeking out "spatial fixes" for its problems), (b) that major innovations in transport and communication technologies were necessary conditions for that expansion to occur (hence the emphasis in capitalism's evolution on technologies that facilitated speed up and the progressive diminution of spatial barriers to movement of commodities, people, information, and ideas over space). [24]

Following the British geographer, I claim that the pervasiveness of ICTs in our society is the best reflection of the capacity of adaptation that is inherent to capitalism. They are open, indeterminate, fluctuant, moving, and constantly transforming entities, which, under the appearance of

sequence of events that occurred in the 1930s and 1940s came close to such a scenario)." Harvey, "Globalization and the Spatial Fix," 26.

[20] Harvey, "Globalization and the Spatial Fix," 26.

[21] He explains: "Surpluses of capital and shortages of labor (or rigidity in labor markets because of political and institutional barriers) can be "fixed" either by the movement of capital to areas of labor surpluses and/or weak labor organization (hence North American capital moving into the maquillas along the Mexican border) or importation of cheap labor (as with guest worker programs in Europe) into centers of capitalist development. Surpluses of wage labor and shortages of capital often generate strong migratory currents (legal and illegal, as with the movement of Mexicans into the USA)." Harvey, "Globalization and the Spatial Fix," 26.

[22] Daniel Greene and Daniel Joseph, "The Digital Spatial Fix," *Triple C* 13, no. 2 (2015): 223.

[23] Harvey, "Globalization and the Spatial Fix," 24.

[24] Harvey, "Globalization and the Spatial Fix," 25–26. He adds a third point: "and (c) its modes of geographical expansion depended crucially upon whether it was the search for markets, fresh labor powers, resources (raw materials), or fresh opportunities to invest in new production facilities that was chiefly at stake." Harvey, "Globalization and the Spatial Fix," 26.

being managed by individuals, are, in fact, reproducing the shape of capitalism.[25] Examples for such digitalization of everyday life are abundant and observable on a daily basis. They go from the increasing capacity and speed of links and communications to the immediacy of the other's presence, which does not require a physical co-presence, through social networks.

Augmented Reality

The advances of capitalism in Late Modernity produce the digitalization of everyday life and reshape religions and religious identities. In the field of Christianity, experiences proliferate, as shown below in the essay. However, the way in which ICTs have affected Western urban societies and their religious communities and individuals does not stop at this point. To gain a better understanding of the relations between ICTs and religion, and more particularly in regard to the configuration of Western Christian religious identities in the context of the digitalization of everyday life, I introduce the term "Augmented Reality."

Although the notion of "Augmented Reality" was born in another field of knowledge,[26] in this essay the term assumes a sociological connotation, referring to the virtual space and time in which we perform actions and dimensions of our being with personal and social real meanings and implications. In the field of religion, the examples of Christian practices in augmented reality abound in our digitalized everyday lives. One can say that live masses, interactive worship, online communities, online churches, eucharistic adorations broadcast via the Internet, guided meditations, and numerous other similar Christian experiences take part in augmented reality. Such virtual religious experiences challenge the widely accepted contraposition between virtual and real.

---

[25] De Colsa, "La digitalización de la vida cotidiana," 3–6.
[26] Although in this essay, I use "Augmented Reality" as a sociological concept, it was born in the field of technology and computer science. However, several authors have applied this concept to other fields, such as, media arts, animation, cinema, architecture, and medicine. See, for example, Abrar Omar Alkhamisi and Muhammad Mostafa Monowar, "Rise of Augmented Reality: Current and Future Application Areas," *International Journal of Internet and Distributed Systems*, 1 (2013): 25–34; Mark Graham, Matthew Zook, and Andrew Boulton, "Augmented Reality in Urban Places: Contested Content and the Duplicity of Code," *Transactions of the Institute of British Geographers* 38, no. 3 (2013): 464–479; John Tinnell, "Computing en plein air: Augmented Reality and Impressionist Aesthetics," *Convergence* 20, no. 1 (2014): 69–84; and Mao-Sheng Lin, Jungle Chi-Hsiang Wu, Hurng-Sheng Wu, and Jack Kai-Che Liu, "Augmented Reality-assisted Single-incision Laparoscopic Adrenalectomy: Comparison with Pure Single Incision Laparoscopic Technique," *Urological Science* 3, (2018): 156–160.

In fact, the taken-for-granted opposition between virtuality and reality needs to be re-thought. It is important that we do not consider digital spaces to be unreal and somehow divorced from the material world. This is the meaning many have in mind when speaking of the "virtual" as a purely representational and platonic plane. In fact, this contrast in the regular use of the term "virtual" might be observed when we look up the antonyms of "virtual" listed in any thesaurus. We find, among others, the following ones: "real," "authentic," and "actual." In contrast, "virtual spaces" are "not spaces of pure representation or imagination, but spaces of Aristotelian potential, spaces to actualize what-might-be."[27] Drastic distinctions between physical and digital are to be challenged since the production and reproduction of many dimensions of individuals' lives are entangled with ICTs, and since these digital technologies produce spatial fixes that embody new forms of affective action.[28]

To put it in simple terms, if we think about our everyday life relationship with ICTs, can we say that virtuality in our lives is not real, authentic, or actual? Can it be denied that the actions and decisions in the virtual spaces affect our everyday lives? Are the relationships that we maintain in social networks not real? In sum, there is a dimension of virtuality that is absolutely real. The real and the virtual are not substitutes that can be understood by mutual negation; rather, they are complements that have maximized our capacity to reshape the boundaries of the world of our everyday life. Thus, there is a process that increases the symbolic value of the intangible and the immaterial.

Such a process is what I call "Augmented Reality." Our online performances are real, even when they are not tangible, material, or physical. Indeed, for this very reason, they are "Augmented Reality," since they have amplified our actual perceptions of the boundaries of reality. Personal and institutional adaptations in religion, therefore, are inevitable consequences of this spatial fix of capitalism. Despite the detailed liturgical rubrics, the preached obligations, the widespread Christian practices that are supposed to be performed inside temples or within the assemblies, every single day, thousands and thousands of Christians perform their religious practices in this online augmented reality.

Cyberspace has become heavily filled with every church imaginable that performs online a wide range of religious initiatives.[29] Indeed, when

---

[27] Greene and Joseph, "The Digital Spatial Fix," 224.
[28] Greene and Joseph, "The Digital Spatial Fix," 225.
[29] A quick search on the web is enough to observe that the number of Christian online experiences has proliferated in the internet. Just a few examples are:
 – Mass-online: https://mass-online.org/
 – The Living Prayer Center: http://prayer-center.upperroom.org/

developing her notion of online religion, Heidi Campbell recognizes that there is an integrating force that bridges and extends online religious spaces and practices with offline religious activity and vice versa. She claims that the term digital religion "describes the technological and cultural space that is evoked when we talk about how online and religious spheres have become blended or integrated."[30] Such is the spatial fix that I call Augmented Reality.

Likewise, Christopher Hellan holds that online religion recognizes a form of participation that

> closely mirrored the ideal interactive environment of the internet itself and allowed for many-to-many communication and interaction. [...] It allowed for greater interaction and collaboration. It also allowed "end users" to contribute, create, and interact with online material in a variety of creative ways. This included online ritual, prayer, worship, and even meditation.[31]

Indeed, he offers a distinction that is illustrative of my perspective. Hellan differentiates "between religion-online and online religion. In the case of religion-online, the internet was utilized to facilitate traditional forms of religious communication to present religion [...] Here, information was presented about religion in a manner that harnessed the internet to communicate in one-to-many fashion. [...] The second classification, online religion, recognized a form of participation."[32] This second notion implies that believers perform their religious actions in augmented reality, that is to say, in real virtual space and time.

"BY YOUR METADATA, THEY WILL KNOW YOU": PERFORMED CHRISTIAN IDENTITIES

The analysis of the wider context of the configuration of Christian identities in Western societies, as portrayed in the previous sections, offers us the foundation for a further step, which sheds light on the second question that this essay addresses: How does the context described in the two previous sections influence the ways in which individuals configure their religious identities?

- St. Clement Eucharistic Shrine: https://www.facebook.com/StClementShrine/
- Marytown Online Adoration Chapel: https://livestream.com/accounts/15529184/events/4408765
- Prayer Chain Online: https://www.prayerchainonline.net/

[30] Heidi Campbell, "Introduction: The Rise of the Study of Digital Religion," in *Digital Religion: Understanding Religious Practice in New Media Worlds*, ed. Heidi Campbell (New York: Routledge, 2013), 3–4.

[31] Christopher Helland, "Digital Religion," in *Handbook of Religion and Society*, ed. David Yamane (Switzerland: Springer, 2016), 178.

[32] Helland, "Digital Religion," 178 (Author's emphasis).

To answer this question, I draw heavily from Zygmunt Bauman's concept of "fetishism of subjectivity." "To put it in a nutshell," the Polish sociologist argues, "'individualization' consists of transforming human 'identity' from a 'given' into a 'task' and charging the actors with the responsibility for performing that task and for the consequences (also the side-effects) of their performance."[33] That task is performed in the context of Western societies, which are governed by consumption. Bauman claims that such a "society of consumers" is characterized by lacking a clear distinction between the consumed object and the entity that consumes it. He calls this characteristic of the society of consumers the "fetishism of subjectivity." In his words,

> "Subjectivity" in the society of consumers, just as "commodity" in the society of producers, is (to use Bruno Latour's felicitous concept) a fait-ishe—a thoroughly human product elevated to the rank of superhuman authority through forgetting or rendering irrelevant its human, all too human origins, together with the string of human actions that led to its appearance and was the sine qua non condition of that appearance... In the case of subjectivity in the society of consumers, it is the turn of the buying and selling of the tokens deployed in the construction of identity—that allegedly public expression of the "self" which is in fact Jean Baudrillard's "simulacrum," substituting "representation" for what it is assumed to represent—to be effaced from the appearance of the final product.[34]

Therefore, in Bauman's "society of consumers," nobody is able to become a subject if one has not previously become a product; that is to say, if one has not previously fetishized one's subjectivity. The essence of the subject in Western societies is to be salable and to be turned into another element within the consumer market. Evidence for this is the increasingly common practice of online dating. Bauman suggests that underpinning the growing tendency toward no physical interaction is the desire to be in control of the interaction. Unlike a seller in a shop who needs to talk, react, and gesticulate (just as a potential partner would do), a screen allows an intended and secure convenience and certainty. The fetishism of subjectivity is, thus, an integral part of the individual that is prompted to switch to internet services as a "safer, more controlled option" that allows them to avoid "the risk and unpredictability of face-to-face encounters."[35] Therefore, the digitalization of everyday life reshapes the configuration of identities. ICTs, rather than resources at hand within digitalized capitalist societies, are a venue in which individuals configure their identities by turning them into a product.

---

[33] Bauman, *Liquid Modernity*, 31.
[34] Zygmunt Bauman, *Consuming Life* (MA: Polity Press, 2007), 14–15.
[35] Bauman, *Consuming Life*, 14–15.

Paradoxically, these fetishized subjectivities, imbued by the fear of insecurity, risk, and unpredictability, in becoming themselves salable products, choose what and how to sell. Therefore, the fetishized subjectivities turn to be mediatized subjectivities and, ultimately, performed identities. "You are your metadata." With this provocative phrase, a group of English researchers of the University College London and the Alan Turing Institute has demonstrated how a set of algorithms is enough to identify one among ten thousand Twitter users with high precision.[36] In this regard, Argentinean anthropologist Paula Sibilia[37] considers that there is a movement in the axis around which we constitute ourselves as subjects. The axis moves from the physical and material to the images and the performance. We start to be recognized and defined by the products of our acts that others can see. The individual faces a new change: from being to acting. In her words, "it is not anymore about being someone or making something, but it is about performing what we are and what we make."[38] In this path from being to acting, the visibility of our person before others turns to be the condition of our existence. Here we see the idea of the character, that is to say of a mediatized subjectivity. We exist insofar as we perform our "being someone" and "making something" in a visible way for others in the media, which find their ground and possibility of existence through ICTs. This is how we configure our identity by fetishizing our subjectivities. In times when identities in general, and religious identities in particular, are fluid, contextualized, and never completely defined, the process of configuration of identities is based on performance in augmented reality.[39] In Western societies, Christians configure performed religious identities in a way that allows us to paraphrase Jesus Christ's words in Matthew 7:16 and state: "by your metadata, they will know you."

---

[36] Beatrice Perez, Mirco Musolesi, and Gianluca Sthinghini, "You Are Your Metadata: Identification and Obfuscation of Social Media Users using Metadata Information," Proceedings of the Twelfth International AAAI Conference on Web and Social Media, 2018, accessed September 14, 2018, https://tinyurl.com/yd372s8u.

[37] Paula Sibilia is an Argentinean anthropologist, teacher, researcher, and essayist. She is based in Rio de Janeiro, Brazil. Her research interests revolve around cultural issues in a genealogic perspective. She focuses on the relations among bodies, subjectivities, technologies, and media and art expressions.

[38] Marta Dillon, "Subjetividad y nuevas tecnologías: Entrevista a Paula Sibilia," Errancia 8 (marzo 2014), accessed September 14, 2018, https://tinyurl.com/yag6rudl.

[39] I have developed this notion in Ernesto Fiocchetto, "Identidades Religiosas: El proceso de configuración de identidades religiosas en el contexto de la individuación de creencias" (Thesis, UNCuyo, Mendoza, 2017).

Configuring Christian Identies in Times of ICTs

After placing the analysis of the relation between the configuration of Christian identities and ICTs in the broader context of the socioeconomic development of Western societies in Late Modernity, and elaborating on the particularities of such a configuration within the context of the digitalization of everyday life, in this final section I present the answers to the third question this essay asks: How do Christians configure their identities in digitalized societies?

The growing number of virtual spaces of many kinds of Christian practices that are performed on augmented reality is unquestionable. I am not referring here to "religion-online," which includes the possibility of acquiring resources for common prayer, Bible study, and reflection (i.e., spiritual writings, religious poems, catechetical material, among the thousands of religious resources that can be obtained online), and facilitating and enlightening face-to-face activities. I am referring instead to "online-Christianity," i.e., virtual spaces of real communal Christian experiences and activities that bring together thousands of believers online daily.[40] Christians gather online to attend liturgies and celebrate their faith together. They extensively use ICTs to pray online and receive preachings and advice from religious leaders of their choice. In augmented reality, many Christians of different denominations perform worship, study the Holy Scripture, participate in Eucharistic adoration, pray the Rosary, meditate, evangelize, perform liturgy, and receive catechesis and spiritual guidance, among other things. Religious leaders take advantage of this phenomenon in thousands of different manners. YouTubers sing and preach, pastors and priests broadcast live celebrations, monasteries teach online-courses and open virtual spaces of prayer, the Pope tweets and is actively present in social media, to mention a few examples.

Considering this growing number of religious experiences of "online-Christianity," it is possible to argue that ICTs are constantly reshaping the processes of configuration of Christian identities. In a panorama in which individuals experiment a loss of external stable points of reference[41] and are the "last boundary of responsibility" for their lives,[42] the process of configuration of identities is transformed from a "given" into a "task."[43] In Late Modernity, individuals do not receive their Christian identity in a closed package. Contrastingly, they find themselves before a constantly renewing horizon, plenty of possibilities in the face of which they have

---

[40] Helland, "Digital Religion," 178.
[41] Hervieu-Léger, "In Search of Certainties," 60.
[42] Beck and Beck-Gernsheim, *Individualization*, 26.
[43] Bauman, *Liquid Modernity*, 31.

to configure "their little personal belief system."[44] This new social context is permeated by ICTs, which add new traits to the individuals' task of reshaping their Christian identities. Such newness does not replace, but coexists with traditional ways of identity configuration. However, due to the pervasiveness of ICTs in the Christian field, they play a crucial role in many aspects of that task.

ICTs are the quintessential example of the movement in the axis around which we constitute our identities in Western societies. The movement from the physical and material to images and performance shapes the religious identity of thousands of Christians who perform their faith online. Within societies that continuously challenge the legitimacy of Christian institutions and question religious authorities, believers overcome the risk, insecurity, and unpredictability that such situation poses by avoiding the materialized boundaries of Christian institutions and configuring their own times and spaces of religious performance through the use of ICTs. Online believers "perform" what they are and what they make in religious augmented reality by fetishizing their subjectivities, thus avoiding being tied by the risks and uncertainties that the physical reality of Christian institutions may produce. Similarly, religious institutions take advantage of this new venue to create an increasing number of religious spaces in augmented reality that sustain and promote these new Christian practices.

In this new religious panorama, ICTs collaborate in the creation of a massive Christian symbolic market within consumers' reach, typical of the flexible production of Late Modernity. By configuring their identities as consumers who are embedded in an immense symbolic market, Christians make use of ICTs to set their "little personal belief system," choosing from the innumerable options that augmented reality offers. The perceived authenticity of Christian augmented reality allows believers to configure their identities through individuation processes of faith marked by the rules of consumption. Thus, while ICTs are useful to believers who individually shape their Christian identities as religious consumers, they also foster a wide religious symbolic market.

One of the consequences of the new dynamics that such huge markets have is that, because they are ruled by the laws of consumption, offerors have lost part of the power to define boundaries within their fields. In other words, the rise of individualism is a reflection of the fragmentation of old cultural orders and, consequently, institutional borders have become increasingly vague. The actuality and certainty offered by augmented reality make it possible for individuated believers to choose beyond the boundaries of the Christian institution or denomination

---

[44] Hervieu-Léger, "In Search of Certainties," 62.

with which they primarily self-identify. Within the broad symbolic field of Christian augmented reality, religious identity configuration is fluid, moving, open, and indeterminate. ICTs deploy new religious experiences for Christians outside institutional and jurisdictional borders, ranging from explicit ecumenical or interfaith practices to unintended eclectic performances. The direct link between Christian identities and Christian institutions is, thus, highly challenged by the pervasiveness of ICTs in Western societies.

Christians who perform their faith in augmented reality do not only easily cross the boundaries of Christian institutions, denominations, and jurisdictions, but also challenge ruling religious mechanisms, particularly in regard to religious authority. When using ICTs to set their individuated system of beliefs, these Christians legitimize their religious identities on their own. They are responsible for the authenticity of their own spiritual approaches. Therefore, religious authorities find themselves in an uncharted situation in which the ruling institutional power that they have is challenged and reshaped. In augmented reality, they experience both the loss of privileges and some benefits of the unique dynamics that online-Christianity implies. On the one hand, in the world produced by ICTs, there are no pulpits to protect the boundaries of authority. Any individual can, for example, contradict and contest the Pope on Twitter or denounce the priest or the pastor without any difficulty or institutional consequence. Any individual can become a religious leader or influencer if they have enough followers on social media. Those who preach, teach, or opine on Twitter have the same power that a regular religious leader has, regardless of their institutional position. On the other hand, religious authorities take advantage of the new dynamics within this religious symbolic market, by weekly or even daily offering online versions of sermons and meditations on the gospel, providing online catechesis, broadcasting liturgies, celebrations, and masses, and promoting online communities for prayer and worship among many other virtual pastoral initiatives. The issue of religious authority, which is constitutive of the configuration of Christian identities, is thus reshaped by the pervasiveness of ICTs in Western societies.

Moreover, individuals' performances and institutional initiatives in augmented reality involve a new perception of space. Places such as temples, churches, and shrines condense a sense of the sacred that is profoundly meaningful for believers. For centuries, those spaces have been exclusively reserved for the performance of holy rituals and communal gatherings. They have visibly embodied the *ekklesia*—the "assembly called out of the world" (cf. 1 Cor 1:2). Thus, for Christian identities, the physical space for meeting with "others who are also called" has been essential. We could never imagine that a factual assembly would not have some kind of material spatial basis. Nevertheless, ICTs have produced new spaces for sacred rituals and communal gatherings, and, therefore, a new dimension of the *ekklesia*. The real virtual spaces in which Christians meet together to pray, worship, and celebrate their faith is somehow a real sacred space that believers experience as actual churches. In this augmented sacred reality, the immediacy of the presence of the others and the Other, which does not require a physical co-presence, expand the pivotal Christian category of *ekklesia*, and consequently, the sacred spaces in which Christians experience the presence of God and the co-presence of their brothers and sisters and configure their identities as part of a church. Via ICTs—through the new augmented reality they produce—Jesus Christ continues to "call individuals out of the world" and to form the *ekklesia*. Via ICTs, Christians are constituting and reshaping the communal experience of the church and configuring their Christian identities in Western societies.

Conclusion

The pervasiveness of ICTs in the individual's everyday life in Western urban societies reshapes how Christians configure their religious identities. The three questions that guided this essay lead us to show aspects of such identity configuration processes. First, I argued that the individuation of beliefs and the pervasiveness of ICTs are only fully understood in the context of the development of capitalism and its contradictions in Late Modernity. Due to the rise of individualism in a global society marked by risk and uncertainty, individuals have become more independent of governing religious systems of truth and, therefore, they individualize their beliefs by producing their "little personal belief system" that they authenticate on their own. The pervasiveness of ICTs is, on the other hand, the best reflex of the capacity of adaptation that is inherent to capitalism. The introduction of the concept of "Augmented Reality" sheds light on the sociological consequences of the spatial fix that implies the digitalization of everyday life. Such concept helps us understand that the real and the virtual are complements that have maximized our capacity to reshape space beyond materiality. In augmented reality, our virtual performances are real, even when they are not tangible.

Second, the identity configuration process implies that fetishized subjectivities, imbued by the fear of insecurity, risk, and unpredictability, move the axis around which they constitute themselves as subjects from the physical and material to the images and the performance. When configuring their identities, the visibility of what they are and make—that is to say, performance rather than being—plays a crucial role. In augmented reality, the process of configuring and reconfiguring Christian identities is based on performance.

Third, given the fact of the plurality of online-Christian experiences, this essay has argued that ICTs continue to reshape the identity configuration of many Christians in their everyday lives. These Christians find themselves before a large religious symbolic market to which they have easy access to configure "their little personal belief systems" beyond the borders of Christian institutions. Thus, ICTs deploy new Christian experiences that challenge the direct link between Christian identities and Christian institutions and reshape the notion of religious authority. Finally, the intersection between ICTs and Christianity also challenges the spatial dimension of the process of identity configuration since the performance of holy rituals and communal gatherings is possible irrespective of the sacred physical spaces.

How do Christians configure their identities within digitalized societies? Christians in urban Western societies increasingly perform their faith in augmented reality. They live out their Christian lives, relate to Christian churches, and perform daily religious acts online. While they renew the manners of living the Christian faith, they configure new Christian identities in real-virtual and virtual-real churches.

Bibliography

Alkhamisi, Abrar Omar, and Muhammad Mostafa Monowar. "Rise of Augmented Reality: Current and Future Application Areas." *International Journal of Internet and Distributed Systems*, 1 (2013).

Bauman, Zygmunt. *Consuming Life*. MA: Polity Press. 2007.

———. *Liquid Modernity*. Cambridge: Politi Press, 2000.

Beck, Ulrich. "Global Risk Society." In *The Wiley&Blackwell Encyclopedia of Globalization*, edited by George Ritzer. Blackwell Publishing Ltd, 2012. doi:10.1002/9780470670590.wbeog242.

———. *Risk Society: Towards a New Modernity*. CA: Sage Publications, 1992.

Beck, Ulrich, and Elisabeth Beck-Gernsheim. *Individualization: Institutionalized Individualism and Its Social and Political Consequences*. London: Sage Publications, 2002.

Campbell, Heidi. "Introduction: The Rise of the Study of Digital Religion," In *Digital Religion: Understanding Religious Practice in New Media Worlds*, edited by Heidi Campbell. New York: Routledge, 2013.

De Colsa, Marcos. "La digitalización de la vida cotidiana: TIC's, consumo y adaptación en el capitalismo," accessed September 14, 2018, https://tinyurl.com/yceke87g.

Dillon, Marta. "Subjetividad y nuevas tecnologías: Entrevista a Paula Sibilia," *Errancia* 8 (marzo 2014), accessed September 14, 2018, https://tinyurl.com/yag6rudl.

Fiocchetto, Ernesto. "Identidades Religiosas: El proceso de configuración de identidades religiosas en el contexto de la individuación de creencias." Thesis, UNCuyo, Mendoza. 2017.

Giddens, Anthony. *Modernity and Self-Identity: Self and Society in the Late Modern Age*. California: Stanford University Press. 1991.

———. *The Consequences of Modernity*. California: Stanford University Press. 1990.

Graham, Mark, Matthew Zook, and Andrew Boulton. "Augmented Reality in Urban Places: Contested Content and the Duplicity of Code." *Transactions of the Institute of British Geographers* 38, no. 3 (2013): 464–79.

Greene, Daniel, and Daniel Joseph. "The Digital Spatial Fix." *TripleC* 13, no. 2 (2015): 223–247.

Harvey, David. "Globalization and the Spatial Fix." *Geographische Revue* 3, no. 2 (2001): 23–30.

———. *The Condition of Postmodernity: An Enquiry into the Origins of Cultural Change*. Massachusetts: Blackwell Publishers. 1990.

Heaphy, Brian. *Late Modernity and Social Change: Reconstructing Social and Personal Life*. New York: Routledge, 2007.

Helland, Christopher. "Digital Religion." In *Handbook of Religion and Society*, edited by David Yamane, 177–196. Switzerland: Springer, 2016.

Hervieu-Legér, Danièle. "In Search of Certainties: The Paradoxes of Religiosity in Societies of High Modernity." *The Hedgehog Review* 8, no. 1–2 (Spring–Summer 2006): 59–68. Academic OneFile.

———. *Religion as a Chain of Memory*. Brunswick, NJ: Rutgers University Press, 2000.

Lin, Mao-Sheng, Jungle Chi-Hsiang Wu, Hurng-Sheng Wu, and Jack Kai-Che Liu. "Augmented Reality-assisted Single-incision Laparoscopic Adrenalectomy: Comparison with Pure incision Laparoscopic Technique." *Urological Science* 3 (2018): 156–160.

Perez, Beatrice, Mirco Musolesi, and Gianluca Sthinghini. "You Are Your Metadata: Identification and Obfuscation of Social Media Users using Metadata Information." Proceedings of the Twelfth International AAAI Conference on Web and Social Media, 2018, accessed September 14, 2018. https://tinyurl.com/yd372s8u.

Tinnell, John. "Computing en plein air: Augmented Reality and Impressionist Aesthetics." *Convergence* 20, no. 1 (2014): 69–84.

PART II

CONTESTED AND NEGOTIATED IDENTITIES

5

CONTESTED SPACES: DIOLA CHRISTIANITY IN RURAL AND URBAN SÉNÉGAL

Aliou Cissé Niang

"Is it still possible to call ourselves Christians without renouncing our deepest African existence at home?"[1]

Introduction

As a Senegalese Diola biblical scholar and follower of Jesus Christ, I have come to appreciate the power of religious innovation. Tracing the movement of Jesus from the first century Palestine to the Graeco-Roman world to the late second century reveals how inculturated the messages of Jesus and the Apostle Paul were.[2] If inculturation is entrenched in the Christian DNA, why did some of the French colonial missionaries of the order of the Holy Ghost Fathers fail to reckon with this incontrovertible reality given the fact that the version of Jesus's message they sought to spread was significantly shaped by their sociocultural optic? Diola Christianity in Senegal, West Africa, is one of the most fascinating examples of the rise and steady growth of a foreign religion in Senegal, especially among Diola people. The seed planted by missionaries, the Holy Ghost Fathers, and the French colonial policies introduced in the Casamance region of Senegal profoundly affected Diola rural life.

Christianity, introduced by Catholic missionaries belonging to the Congregation of the Holy Ghost Father, and colonialism exerted much

---

[1] "Est-il encore possible, chez nous, de se dire chrétiens sans renier son être profond d'Africain?" Nazaire N. Diatta, "Et si Jésus-Christ, Premier-né d'entre les morts, était l'initie?: La personnalité de l'initie joola face au Christ," *Téléma* 57, no. 1 (1989): 50.

[2] Graydon S. Snyder, *The Inculturation of the Message of Jesus on Jewish and Roman Cultures* (Harrisburg, PA: Trinity Press International, 1999), 1–53.

influence on Diola culture. Paulo Palmeri, Constan Vanden Berghen, and Adrien Manga offer unique insights into the life and thought of the Diola of Mof Avvi. The magnitude of their impact was documented by colonial administrators, some missionaries, and ethnographers (foreign and later local).[3] The work of Robert M. Baum offers a good chronological study on the emergence of a Diola Christianity in the Essulalu townships. Gradually, Christianity spread throughout the region being facilitated by subsequent missionary leaders and mostly local converts.[4] Baum's publications provide corrective insights to earlier ethnographic contributions that were conditioned by colonial geopolitical discourse and ideology.[5]

In this essay, I will discuss two main developments in Diola villages: First, Diola encounter with missionaries and the economic policies introduced by French colonial officials that gave rise to increasing seasonal migration from rural to urban contexts such as Ziguinchor and especially Dakar; and second, the gradual contextualization of missionary Christianity with traditional elements of Diola religion that shaped a formidable Diola Christianity. To sustain the weight of my claim, I will offer some thoughts on the sociology of knowledge, Diola Traditional Religion, Diola Christianity, and seasonal migration.

Embodied participation as method

For many years, I tried to understand the constructed image of Africans, not Africa as a continent. I make this distinction based on my research into this troubling matter and my observations on how the continent and its peoples are described by some Western writers and now covered by media outlets. During the transatlantic slave trade, Africa was coveted by

---

[3] Louis-Vincent Thomas, *Les Diola: Essai d'analyse fonctionnelle sur une population de Basse-Casamance* (Tome 1&2; Dakar, SN: Imprimerie Protat FrPres, Mâcon, 1959); Jean Girard, *Genèse du pouvoir charismatique en basse Casamance (Sénégal)* (Dakar, SN: IFAN, 1969); Christian Roche, *Histoire de La Casamance: Conquête et résistance: 1850–1920* (Paris: Éditions Karthala, 1985).

[4] Constan Vanden Berghen et Adrien Manga, *Une introduction a un voyage en Casamance: Enampor, un village de riziculteurs en Casamance, au Sénégal* (Paris: Éditions L'Harmattan, 1999).

[5] Robert M. Baum, "Emergence of Diola Christianity," *Africa* 60, no. 3 (1990): 371–398. See also, Baum, *Shrines of the Slave Trade: Diola Religion and Society in Precolonial Senegambia* (New York: Oxford University Press, 1999), 4, 6, 8, 10, 24, 34, 36–37, 39, 42, 83, 130, 134–5, 143–5, 148, 150, 153 (on Christianity), and 25, 31–32, 146, 154 (peanuts as cash crop).

Europeans for her black people who were objectified as movable property[6] and with the colonial advent, an equally pernicious relationship developed to further wrest the wealth of the continent from her people. Africa is being loved not for her people as human beings, but for the economic resources she offers—precious stones, minerals, oil, animals, timber wood, and the like. Why wasn't she loved for her people, their culture and religious practices? Observations made by Peter Mark provide a chilling answer. He writes,

> English and French attitudes toward Africans in the Senegambia developed and became well-defined during the late sixteenth, seventeenth, and early eighteenth century. These attitudes were influenced by three main factors: European ethno-centrism, the commercial relations which governed European-African intercourse, and the growth of the slave trade. During this period, Europeans expressed increasingly negative characterizations of Africans and their way of life. An ideology of African inferiority served, in part, to validate the Atlantic slave trade. It was easier to justify the enslavement of people who were considered less civilized or even a lower form of humanity. The formation of this ideology was facilitated by ethnocentric perceptions which led to a bias in favor of more Westernized peoples. One important parameter by which Senegambians came to be judged inferior to their European counterparts was in the area of religious beliefs and practices.[7]

African Traditional Religion has been overlooked and sadly misunderstood before and during the colonial period. How Africans practiced their faith traditions was grossly mischaracterized as polytheistic and barbarous superstition. The transfer of culture, Christian beliefs, and practices from civilized Europeans to the uncivilized peoples of the world presupposed that colonists have little, if nothing, to learn from the colonized. Also, methodologically, French and British ethnographers approached Africans, and in particular Senegalese people, differently, especially when exploring the African religious tapestry. Earlier studies inspired by traditional approach tended to trust their direct observation on which they constructed their views of African practices and beliefs. Jan Vansina's

---

[6] Louis Sala-Molins, *Le Code Noir ou le calvaire de Canaan* (Paris: Presses Universitaires de France, 1987), 172 code 44. For a detailed discussion of biblical rationale for slavery and attitudes against people of African descent, see David M. Goldenberg, *The Curse of Ham: Race and Slavery in Early Judaism, Christianity and Islam* (Princeton, NJ: Princeton University Press, 2003) and Winthrop D. Jordan, *White over Black: American Attitudes Toward the Negro, 1550–1812* (Chapel Hill, NC: University of North Carolina Press, 1968).

[7] Peter Mark, "'Marybuckes' and the Christian Norm: European Images of Senegambians and Their Religions, 1550–1760," *African Studies Review* 23, no. 2 (1980): 91.

critique of the shortcomings of the much-hailed Western ethnographic direct field research substantiates my argument with this chilling story.

> The old man stood there in his compound on the top of the hill, silent now, lost in dreams, and gazing over the landscape. He had just retold us how the colonial soldiers came to capture the town and his freedom. He stood there for a long while, recalling perhaps all that happened to him and those he had known since then until this day in the waning years of the era these men had ushered in. If so, his vision of colonial history had certainly very little in common with the standard accounts one finds in textbooks about the period.[8]

What Africans might say about their socioreligious and cultural world is readily suspected as untrustworthy and subjective. Such a distrust has now been challenged by experts such as Vansina and Baum who see some indispensable value in what native people said about their life and thought. Robert M. Baum writes,

> The final source of information from field research grows out of participant observation. By living in a community and joining in religious, work, and social activities, the researcher acquires a wealth of information about the relationships among religious thought, historical consciousness, and daily life. A religion is something that is lived, as well as practiced. . . I had to experience it. . . To understand his shrine, I had to perform its ritual.[9]

Insights from local informants is invaluable as many ethnographers have now come to realize that they have access to the kind of information most local people hold sacred and therefore taboo to be divulged to any foreign experts. My point is, nuanced accounts on Diola identity, socioreligious, cultural, and economic realities inspired by their lived experiences should include informant accounts.[10] It is now commonplace to encounter words such as "concealing"[11] and "secrecy"[12] in recent publications presuming some access to information that can be only be gained from informant participatory agency. Most cultures conceal and hold

---

[8] Jan Vansina, *Being Colonized: The Kuba Experience in Rural Congo, 1880–1960* (Madison, WS: The University of Wisconsin Press, 2010), 3.
[9] Baum, *Shrines*, 17, 21.
[10] Paul Diédhiou, *L'identité Jóola en question (Casamance)* (Paris: Karthala, 2011). See also, Boubacar Barry, *Le sénégambie du XVe au XIXe siècle : Traite négrière, Islam conquête coloniale* (Paris : L'Harmattan, 2017), 384–89.
[11] Robert M. Baum, "Concealing Authority: Diola Priests and Other Leaders in the French Search for a Suitable Chefferie in Colonial Senegal," *Cadernos de Estudos Africanos* 16, no. 17 (2011): 35–51.
[12] Ferdinand de Jong, *Masquerades of Modernity: Power and Secrecy in the Casamance, Senegal* (Bloomington, IN: Indiana University Press, 2007), 3–22, 128–151, 185–94.

secret some features of their cultural memory. Even progressive societies aspiring to much transparency do not share all the elements of their cultural memory—some treasured cultural elements often remain concealed from outsiders and foreigners. What I am saying is this, to access cultural taboos one may have to infiltrate the cultural memory with the help of native informants. It is also true that not all informants would readily divulgate the most sacred beliefs of their societies. To gain insight into the lived experiences of Diola people, one must live and eat with them. Even then, a foreigner will always need the help of informants whose account of local beliefs hinges on their memory of the orally transmitted beliefs. The use of informants or interviews with natives is another form of accessing practical dimensions of "Diola customs"—performed life and thought of Diola people. Though better than just direct observation, a more fully embodied way of accessing Diola customs, Baum understands the Diola expression, "what we do," as meaning the researcher must live with the people and engage in their daily activities; namely, one must "see," "experience," and "perform" Diola rituals.[13] The combination of direct field observations, interviews, and the ritually performed life is what I call *embodied participatory inquiry* that feeds and shapes adequate theory and method.

The need for this method lies in the fact that Diola people, like many sub-Saharan groups of people, are not objects, but humans with pre-colonial robust cultural memory transmitted orally—a process that "seldom included its abstract quantification" since oral traditions were "designed to develop and transmit those aspects of the past which were deemed important, and absolute dating was never, nor could it ever be, one of these."[14] In this *imaginaire*, "*oral traditions are concerned with identifying historical events that are roughly contemporaneous and with establishing sequence of events*"[15] and the purpose has never been based on the exact dating. The importance of relative chronology in this case, "reveals the relative seniority of social groups; legal, social, and economic rights; and ritual precedence that structure contemporary human activity."[16] Although armchair scholarship has its place in academic inquiry, to adequately understand and write about Diola life and thought or other cultural practices, an *embodied participatory inquiry* is indispensable.

---

[13] Baum, *Shrines*, 17.
[14] David Henige, *The Chronology of Oral Tradition: Quest for a Chimera* (Oxford: Clarendon, 1974), 1–2.
[15] Henige, *Chronology*, 1–2.
[16] Steven Feierman, *Shambaa Kingdom* (Madison: University of Wisconsin Press, 1974), 4.

Diola Religion as Lived Experience

Theories about pre-colonial Diola origins and settlement in the Casamance region where they now dwell, in the southwestern region bordering the Atlantic Ocean, is the subject of much debate among Diola ethnographers and anthropologists.[17] Insights from some experts shed much light on how one might make sense of internal movements of African people. Constructions of Diola origins are important, but do not really matter given the diverse unity shared by West Africans of which authors such as Cheikh Anta Diop and Mamadou Fall masterfully speak. The evidence produced thus far shows that Diola people, among other Senegalese groups, emerged from the West African geographical location.[18] In spite of the fact that there was a cohesion between West African groups of people, there were intergroup skirmishes over land as was common to humanity since time immemorial, especially between the Diola and the Baïnunk that lasted for many years.[19]

This essay does not revisit these theories of Diola origins; instead, it addresses Diola religious thought and life, Diola encounter with Christianity during and after the colonial period and how colonization influenced Diola migration. To avoid common mistakes some sociologists and anthropologists made in lumping Diola people into a homogenous group, this essay focuses on the Diola of the southern ridge of the Casamance River, especially the Brin-Séléki and in particular the Enampor and Séléki townships and their Essulalu neighbors.

Dwellers of Enampor and Séléki are monotheists. Their supreme deity is *Émit* (God) or *Ala Émit* (the one who owns the heavens). This is the only deity Diola people revere, but they also believe there are good and malevolent spirits in God's creation. In no way does a Diola of Enampor or Séléki confuse God with these spirits (good or evil) or shrines, visual representations (masks and sculptures), or particular trees as commonly believed. The Diola are faithful to *Ala Émit* and conceive of themselves as a *corporate participatory agent* of the deity as they strive to live

---

[17] Thomas, *Les Diola*; Philippe Méguelle, *Chefferie colonial et Égalitarisme Diola: Les difficultés de la politique indigène de la France en Basse-Casamance (Sénégal), 1828–1923* (Paris: L'Harmattan, 2012); Roche, *Histoire de La Casamance*; Baum, *Shrines of the Slave Trade*.

[18] Cheikh Anta Diop, *The Cultural Unity of Black Africa* (Chicago, IL: Third Word Press, 1959); Anta Diop, *Precolonial Black Africa*, trans. Harold J. Salemson (Chicago, IL: Lawrence Hill Books, 1987); Mamadou Fall, *Les territoires de la Sénégambie entre l'épée et le croissant: $X^{éme}$–$XX^{éme}$ Siècles* (Paris: L'Harmattan, 2016).

[19] Sennen Andriamirado, "La guerre de sept cents ans," *Jeune Afrique* 29, no. 1687 (April/May 1993): 26–30.

symbiotically with the deity's creation—a life meticulously ritualized around rice farming.[20]

As such, Diola life and thought is an expression of African Traditional Religion.[21] The Diola experience the deity as an invisible being who is transcendent as well as immanent—deeply involved in their daily needs, as healer and sustainer of life with abundant rain for rice farming. The rice they farm is a divine gift and thereby sacred. Farming rice, as I noted earlier, has profound religious dimensions not just because of the rituals required, but also the care it demands on the farmers not to abuse the participatory agency of nature (nonhuman creatures). For that reason, many Diola people are reluctant to sell rice for cash.

Diola self-understanding, construction of reality, anthropology-cosmology, and theology cannot be understood without a good grasp of traditional liturgical rituals they practice.[22] In a recent article published in the *Encyclopedia of Christianity in the Global South*, I briefly discussed Diola religion in general and how it is still the lens that most Diola people converted to Islam or Christianity continue to use to observe some aspects of their faith traditions especially when faced with various hardships for which Christianity or Islam has no answer.[23] So, a Muslim or Christian Diola might visit a shrine when faced with natural or human-caused disasters. The supreme deity *Ala Emit*[24] is believed to condescend in order to meet human needs at the shrines where services are officiated by priests on a wide range of needs worshippers might reveal. Diola religion and egalitarian society regulated by their faith traditions would soon be disrupted and nearly abolished by French colonization.

---

[20] Pablo Palmeri, *Living with the Diola of Mof Avvì: The Account of an Anthropological Research in Sénégal* (Padova: Libraria Editrice Univeristà di Padova, 2009).

[21] Laurenti Magesa, *African Religion: The Moral Traditions of Abundant Life* (New York: Orbis Books, 1997).

[22] Nazaire N. Diatta, "Participation du Joola chretien aux rites traditionnels," *Téléma* 46 (avril–juin, 1986): 67–81; Diatta, "Et si Jésus-Christ est, " 49–73; Diatta, "rites funéraires traditionnels et liturgie chrétienne: Lieux du dialogue interreligieux," *Téléma* 67-8 (juillet–décembre, 1991): 61–72.

[23] There are about ten Diola subgroups and their responses to Islam and Christianity is not homogenous. For instance, adherence to Islam is more prevalent among the Diola of the northern ridge of the Casamance River than the southern ridge where Christianity dominates. See Aliou Cissé Niang, "Diola Religion," in the *Encyclopedia of Christianity in the Global South*, vol. 1., ed. Mark A. (Lamport: Rowman and Littlefield, 2018), 221–222; Niang, "Senegal," in the *Encyclopedia of Christianity in the Global South*, vol. 2., ed. Mark A. 710-712.

[24] Since there are many Diola subgroups, one might encounter variable phonetics when it comes to naming the supreme deity. Among the Diola of Mof Avvi, to which I belong, the deity is *Ala Émit*. Others would call the deity *Ata Émit*, *Émitay*, or *Émit*.

Christianity and colonization

Sandwiched between two European powers during the colonial period, the French in Saint Louis and the Portuguese in the south, Senegalese people and their culture were forever changed. The Casamance is the most fertile region of Senegal and as a result became a highly contested space by colonizers not for its people, but its natural resources. The Portuguese who were then based in Cachue controlled the region and founded Ezeguichor as a post to trade slaves, wax, animal skin, and ivory.[25] Portuguese Christian traders were busier enriching themselves than spreading their version of the Christian message. As Lamin Sanneh observed elsewhere, theirs is the kind of Christianity that "marched in step with the profit-seeking machine of Portuguese commerce."[26] The French managed to infiltrate the region from the estuary of the Casamance River and established trading posts on the islands of Diogue and Carabane, transforming the once Portuguese trading post in 1827 and annexed Ziguinchor.[27]

The French gradually infiltrated northern Senegal as the southern ridge of the Casamance River remained undisturbed until the arrival of Émmanuel Bertrand Bocandé who was stationed at Carabane[28]—a strategic island among others (Saint-Louis and Gorée) facilitating French incursion into Diola country. The first missionaries, the Holy Ghost Fathers, to ever set foot in Essulalu townships, as Baum observed, were respectful of some Diola religious practices such as praying for rain, health, and good harvest—an attempt to establish connections later undermined by their zeal to impose Europeanized practices on their catechumen.[29] Over time, the situation changed gradually with the help of the first native Catholic priests who were instrumental in adapting the Christian message to Diola contexts. The so-called Berlin Conference in 1884–85 must have emboldened Europeans and marked their official move to wrestle the continent's goods from her people, as if the transatlantic slave trade had not done enough damage—the French exploitation of Africans started much earlier in 1828. Entry points to Africa have already been decided on (thanks

---

[25] Jacqueline Trincaz, *Colonisations et religions en Afrique noir: L'exemple de Ziguinchor* (Paris: Éditions L'Harmattan, 1981), 2.

[26] Lamin Sanneh, *West African Christianity: The Religious Impact* (New York: Orbis Books, 1983), 23.

[27] Trincaz, *Colonisations et religions*, 2–3.

[28] J. Bertrand-Bocandé, G. Debien, and Y. Saint-Martin, "Notes et Document: Emmanuel Bertrand-Bocandé (1812–1881) un Nantais en Casamance," *Bulletin de L' IFAN* 31, no. 1 (1969): 279–302; Barry, *Le Sénégambie du XVe au XIXe Siècle*, 384–89. Wole Soyinka, *The Burden of Memory, the Muse of Forgiveness* (New York: Oxford University Press, 1999).

[29] Baum, "Emergence of Diola Christianity," 378ff.

to precolonial explorers, traders, and missionary written accounts)[30] that Europeans fought hard to wrest from each other's control as they did in the case of the Island of Gorée.[31]

The Catholic mission led by French priests later established in the Island of Carabane in 1880 had a rough start, but recovered in 1890 and served as the missionary headquarters for most of the townships near the Atlantic Ocean except for the Bandial or Mof Avvi townships.[32] Some French priests from Ziguinchor ministered to the Diola of Mof Avvi in 1926, but ended up leaving due to little success. In the estimation of Berghen and Manga, 85 percent of Mof Avvi dwellers still practiced traditional Diola religion. The number of Christians will gradually increase among the youth not just in Mof Avvi, but also in the surrounding Diola townships. Islam was introduced to Mof Avvi in 1959 by Diola youth seasonal migrants who went to the city to work or to Mandinka Muslim villages to farm peanuts. Christianity will spread to much of the Casamance region from urban to rural spaces—Islands (Saint Louis, Gorée, Diogue, and Carabane).

The doyen on Diola life and thought, Louis-Vincent Thomas, proclaimed the deculturation and acculturation of Diola cultural memory as precipitated by the infiltration of foreign religions and colonization. He opined that,

> Sous des influences diverse: Religions importées (Christianisme, Islam), créations des centres urbains, développement de vie politique, syndicale, affirmation de nouveaux besoins, nécessite de gagner de l'argent pour payer l'impôt, instauration de l'économie de traite, multiples mouvements de population facilites par la réalisation des voies de communication, imprégnation par des idées modern, peut-être aussi un besoin obscure d'autodestruction, la société animiste est en voie de totale dégénérescence. Déjà de nombreuses croyances sont abandonnées ou dénaturées, les chefs coutumiers perdent leur autorité, la mentalité et le comportement

---

[30] Paul Lesourd, *L'Œuvre civilisatrice et scientifiques des missionnaires Catholiques dans les colonies françaises* (Paris: Sous le patronage du commissariat général de l'exposition coloniale internationale de Paris, 1931).

[31] Lucie Gallistel Colvin, *Historical Dictionary of Senegal*, African Historical Dictionary 23 (Metuchen, NJ: The Scarecrow Press, 1981); Jean Delcourt, *Histoire du Sénégal* (Dakar, SN: Éditions Clairafrique, 1976); Pierre Xavier Trincaz, *Colonization and Régionalisme Ziguinchor en Casamance* (Paris: Éditions de L'ORSTOM, 1984); Geneviève Lecuir-Nemo, *Anne-Marie Javouhey: Fondatrice de la congrégation des sœurs de Saint-Joseph de Cluny (1779–1851)* (Paris: Édition Karthala, 2001); Joseph Roger Benoist, *Histoire de l'Église catholique au Sénégal: du milieu du XVe siècle à l'aube du troisième millénaire* (Paris: Édition Karthala, 2008).

[32] Berghen et Manga, *Une introduction a un voyage en Casamance*, 204–5.

évoluent et, plus que jamais, la religion du terroir est soumise à une désagrégation rapide.[33]

[Under various influences: Imported religions (Christianity, Islam), creation of urban centers, development of political life, union, assertion of new needs, and needs to earn money to pay the tax, establishment of the economy of trade, multiple movements of population facilitated by the realization of the ways of communication, impregnation by modern ideas, perhaps also an obscure need of self-destruction, animist society is on the way to total degeneration. Many beliefs are already abandoned or misrepresented, customary leaders are losing their authority, mentality and behavior are changing and, more than ever, the religion of the land is subject to rapid disintegration.]

The changes Thomas enumerates have indeed influenced Diola thought and life since the transatlantic slave trade. It was by no means a surrender to foreign influences. The process was arduous and expanded over centuries into much of the colonial period. Modes of resistance to these changes ranged from refusal to honor contracts they were often forced to sign by colonial authorities, pay taxes,[34] armed conflicts against colonial officials, and resilient attempts to preserve their cultural memory.

The irony is that while village space is contested for what it offers such as rice and other resources coveted by empire, the city was also contested—a space for integrating and participating in the newly introduced economy. Young Diola migrants adjusted to new realities introduced by colonization such as getting the newly introduced mode of exchange—money currency, one of the main tools the empire used to control and exploit the colonized. Western education, styled clothing, and other foreign goods were coveted by many. I will return to this topic later. Similarly, the inculturation of Jesus's message for Diola people was also contested as a handful of Diola people who were converted to missionary Christianity echo much of the scorns and rejections some Holy Ghost Fathers once uttered that reduced Diola faith traditions of animal sacrifice as objectionable. It is not uncommon to hear some Diola, lay and clergy alike, characterize their pre-Christian beliefs as satanic, superstitious, or pagan. French colonial geopolitical discourse managed to reduce Diola people to primitive anarchists—a characterization that did much to color how Diola people are viewed to this day. Civilizing Diola people was an expedient project, especially as French needs for food during World War II increased.

---

[33] Louis-Vincent Thomas, "Les Diola de la Base-Casamance," *Afrique Documents* 51 (Mai 1960): 85–6.
[34] Méguelle, *Chefferie colonial et égalitarisme diola*, 64–116.

Facing French colonization with its inculturated Christianity gave rise to two main developments among Diola villages. The first, Diola encounter with missionaries and the economic policies introduced by French colonial officials gave rise to increasing seasonal migration from rural to urban contexts such as Ziguinchor and especially Dakar. Second, missionary Christianity, especially as introduced by the Holy Ghost Fathers, underwent a gradual contextualization—a process during which key traditional elements of Diola religion reshaped missionary teachings to engender a formidable Diola Christianity.

Diola Christianity

Migration and settlement within the West African context in precolonial times was due to natural (drought and famine) as well as human (intergroup conflicts to control fertile land) phenomena. The religious crisis engendered by imperial missionary Christianity among Diola people underwent a significant novation, right after World War II, as observed by Baum, especially

> with a cadre of Diola Catholic priests and cross-culturally aware missionaries, new possibilities for a new Diola Christianity became possible. Clergy and new laymen alike became aware of the need to root the Christianity of Diola in the concerns and needs of Diola communities. With members of the Diola community in position of authority and with access to the entire Scriptures, this process could begin. The new Christian leaders sought to develop the points of contact between Christianity and Diola traditions and to build their religious edifice on a shared foundation. This implied a reaffirmation of Diola cultural vitality that would distinguish them from other Christians and an involvement of Christian beliefs and practices in the daily lives of Diola Christians.[35]

Conceivably, the novation Baum is referring to is not limited to Essulalu Diola Christianity, but most of Diola country. To say these changes are comprehensive would be overdrawn. Some Diola did in fact abandon traditional values and it would be naïve to generalize the resulting novation. Inculturated Christianity is what Father Nazaire N. Diatta, one among many Senegalese-born priests reading the Bible with some of his Diola faith traditions, passionately called for. Unfortunately, much of his language echoes a Western theological worldview. For instance, in pinpointing how the process of inculturation of the church in Diola culture might look, Diatta opines that it is the church's role to "elevate and heal

---

[35] Baum, "Emergence of Diola Christianity," 394–5.

peoples' cultures."³⁶ The verb "élever" which Diatta uses transitively could mean to "raise" or "increase" the standing of a person or a thing from inferiority to a superior stature and status. I am surprised about Diatta's use of this word since it recalls much of the colonial missionary objectifications and denigration of African Traditional Religion—a practice legitimating assimilation policy and French missionary Christianization from the colonial towns (Saint Louis, Gorée, Dakar, and Rufisque) to Diola county.

In spite of my reservation about some of Father Diatta's terminologies, he offers some key insights on how a Diola might inculturate the biblical message. At stake is how might a Diola Christian participate in traditional Diola rituals and still be Christian. As is clear, this question of participation in traditional rituals was raised about a century earlier, as Baum documented, when the Holy Ghost Fathers attempted to convert Diola people. Diola responses to the gospel preached by these earliest missionaries were mixed. Christianity was either embraced by a handful of Diola people (especially youth seeking education), inculturated by others, and rejected by most elders. Diola initiation rituals are not just festive occasions for conspicuous consumption. They include an interwoven tapestry of practices that proclaim life from birth, initiation rites, marriage, work, death, and salvation. In the reflections Diatta made, one cannot understand the Diola without a good grasp of Diola initiation rituals. I concur.

This conclusion resulted from his attempt to address a question that puzzled many Diola Christians since, I would argue, the beginning of Christianity in Diola country: "Is it still possible, at home, to call ourselves Christians without renouncing one's deepest African being?"³⁷ A related question he also discussed is, should Diola Christians participate in the traditional rites?³⁸ The efforts of Diatta to inculturate the gospel should be admired, but Diatta does not go far enough. The Diola male rite of passage known as *buhut* has a profound religious dimension, which Diatta knows is a ritual process through which they symbiotically assimilate with nature/cosmos. Diola religion is not Satanism, idolatry, or superstition antagonistic to the ministry of Jesus, but proclaims human and nature relations, wellbeing, and communalism under the aegis of *Ala Emit*.

The Negritude movement might be credited with paving the way for such a momentous change, as Baum observes.³⁹ Ironically, some elements

---

36 Diatta, "Participation du Diola Chrétien," 72; Moustapha Tamba, *Histoire et sociologie des religions au Sénégal* (Paris: L'Harmattan, 2016); Théodore Ndok Ndiaye, *Quel Sénégal pour demain?: Une vision chrétienne et citoyenne* (Paris: L'Harmattan, 2012).
37 Diatta, "Et si Jésus-Christ," 50, "Est-il encore possible, chez nous, de se dire chrétiens sans renier son être profond d'Africain?"
38 Diatta, "Participation du Diola chretien," 67–81.
39 Baum, "Emergence of a Diola Christianity."

of the Holy Ghost Fathers' Europeanized Christianity still flare up to this day as I noted earlier. Europeanized marriages, associations of expressions of African Traditional Religion with Satan, evil, paganism, and backwardness can be heard from many Sunday sermons and Bible studies to this day. In spite of these setbacks, the resolute task of making a home for Jesus's message among Diola people is alive and well. Father Diatta's work sheds much light on how a Diola who is not *dépaysé* "rootless" might engage the Bible contextually. Insights on how a Diola Christian and Diola traditionalist might participate in each other's rituals has been a key concern of his as well as a handful of Catholic priests currently serving in the Casamance.[40] In Diatta's estimation, Diola beliefs and initiation rituals would help them understand the function and significance of Jesus in their lives.[41] His observation on what I might term the cultural construction of reality is clearly stated in the following words:

> Si la culture définie la personne, alors la participation aux grands rites liturgiques est une est volonté de se reprendre dans sa culture même, une volonté de se situer, de se découvrir comme être relationnel en participation. Si l'être Joola se définir comme maillon d'une structure sociale, économique, religieuse, alors quand les jeunes repartent aux initiations--lieu d'expression de la culture où ils découvrent qui ils sont structurellement--ils se découvrent des existants.[42]

> [If the culture defines the person, then the participation in the great liturgical rites is a will to take again in its very culture, a will to be located, to discover itself as to be relational in participation. If the Diola is defined as a link of a social, economic, religious structure, then when the young people return to the initiation—place of expression of the culture where they discover who they are structurally—they discover themselves as human beings.]

A recovery of some demonized Diola beliefs and practices, in Father Diatta's estimation, is an indispensable rehabilitation optic through which a culture lives on and innovates. Diola traditional rituals are foundational to how Diola people understand themselves, the world, and the deity they worship. Repositioning themselves into the matrix on their traditional liturgical rituals neither questions, nullifies, nor contradicts their faith in Jesus Christ. Father Diatta adds,

---

[40] See Tamba, *Histoire et sociologie des religions au Sénégal*, and Ndiaye, *Quel Sénégal pour demain*.

[41] Diatta, "Participation du Joola chretien," 67–81; Diatta, "Et si Jésus-Christ est," 49–73; Diatta, "rites funéraires traditionnels et liturgie chrétienne," 61–72; Diatta, "Nécessité d'une formation adéquate des pasteurs: Quelle formation pour les gens de pastoral en Afrique?" *Téléma* 61(Janvier–mars, 1990): 39–51.

[42] Diatta, "rites funéraires traditionnels et liturgie chrétienne," 77.

> Mais c'est justement en étant présent que le Joola chretien, parce que chrétien, va sentir la réorientation effective à donner à impulser, à la coutume et dans le fond et dans la forme, pour arriver à décentrer le Joola de lui-même et le recentrer sur Dieu; pour passer donc de l'anthropocentrisme de la religion traditionnelle au théocentrisme chrétien. Voilà le devoir du chretien et ce qui justifie sa participation aux rites funéraires, aux initiations . . . Voilà à quoi, on doit, en tout cas le former aujourd'hui.[43]

> [But it is precisely by being present that the Christian Joola, because Christian, will feel the actual reorientation to give impulse, custom, and in the background and in the form, to arrive to decenter the Joola of itself and refocus on God; to go from the anthropocentrism of traditional religion to Christian theocentrism. This is the duty of the Christian and what justifies his participation in funeral rites, initiations . . . That is in what we should, at least, train him today.]

Instead of Christianity reorienting Diola Christians, as Father Diatta contends, I would say Diola Christians were contextualizing the Christian message, as the catechism taught by some of the first Catholic missionaries was increasingly being Europeanized. This phenomenon was not unique to Diola people. Most of sub-Saharan Christianity was and is still affected by a Western-shaped Christianity to this day.

I was struck by an essay I read on interreligious dialogue that echoes the damages caused by missionary discourse against African Traditional Religion.[44] The experience of SimonMary Asese Aihiokhai illustrates my point clearly. He recounts what I believe recalls the Petrine conversion recorded in the Acts of the Apostles (Acts 10–11) while serving as a Catholic missionary in Nigeria. The biblical text I am referring to has Peter saying to Cornelius: "I truly understand that God shows no partiality, but in every nation anyone who fears him and does what is right is acceptable to him" (Acts 10:34–35 NRS). Aihiokhai learned how Indigenous Religion and its priestess were objectified by Christians as "devil worship"; he visited, against the advice of his guide, and befriended a "devil worshipper."[45] As it turns out, like the supreme deity she worships, the priestess was "just, honest, kind, loving, hospitable, and respectable of everyone."[46]

---

[43] Diatta, "rites funéraires traditionnels et liturgie chrétienne," 79.

[44] SimonMary Asese Aihiokhai, "Interreligious Friendship: A Path to Conversion for a Catholic Theologian," in *Interreligious Friendship After Nostra Aetate*, Interreligious Studies in Theory and Practice, ed James L. Fredericks and Tracy Sayuki Tiemeier (New York: Palgrave MacMillan, 2015), 187–200.

[45] Aihiokhai, "Interreligious Friendship," 188.

[46] Aihiokhai, "Interreligious Friendship," 189. See also, Marinus Chijioke Iwuchukwu, "Interreligious Friendship: Symbiosis of Human Relationship vis-à-vis Religious Differences—A Christian Encounter with Two African Traditional Religionists," in *Interreligious Friendship After Nostra Aetate*, Interreligious Studies in

In spite of being pushed into liminal space by the very Christians who were supposed to have received the priestess with love and compassion, her temperament, which many Christians would identify with Christian virtues, is exemplary for followers of Jesus.

Village and city as contested spaces

Two phenomena explain Diola youth seasonal migrations to cities. First, Diola youths migrate for economic reasons. Peanut farming did affect much of Diola life and thought, especially among converts to Islam of the northern ridge of the Casamance River, as noted by many ethnographers. Many Diola of the southern ridge, especially of Mof Avvi still prioritize rice farming to this day, but there were increasing pressures to join peanut farming due to the lucrative economic gains it promises—monetary currency and participation in the world market. It also introduced an unusual competition for monetary control that threatened Diola egalitarian society. Single and married men began to clear the forest to make room for larger peanut farms to increase capital. Since then, many turned away from their rice fields to farm peanuts that engendered two problems: a move that led to the impoverishment of the land. But, a complex set of factors contributed to the increasing flow of Diola youth migrants to cities from the time before colonization to this day. The introduction of peanuts as the main cash crop, foreign religions (Christianity and Islam), cultural encounters, and frequent droughts have been cited by ethnographers as key reasons for migration. In spite of the many changes Diola people faced, many still consider work, especially rice farming as sacred, and courage, honesty, and mutuality are valued virtues.[47]

Second, impoverished land, cleared forests, and increasingly rare rain forced many Diola people to leave their villages to cities during the dry season. Immigration and migration are perennial dynamic human phenomena. Natural and human caused disasters are the main drivers in either case. This is true especially in the case of realities that are unfolding before us today with global immigration crises. Economic needs and conflicts (such as war) are responsible for human movement. Reasons often cited by many immigrants include the desire to improve life conditions—economics or safety (especially in war-torn countries) as being the reasons for leaving their villages, cities, or countries. In this essay, I focus on seasonal migrations from village to city, from city to village, and from village to another village of many Diola youth and adults from Enampor

---

Theory and Practice, eds. James L. Fredericks and Tracy Sayuki Tiemeier (New York: Palgrave MacMillan, 2015), 201–214.

[47] Berghen et Manga, *Une introduction*, 277–8. See also Baum, *West Africa's Women of God*, 112–13.

and Séléki. Senegalese people call these movements *nawetaan*—a Wolof meaning "working away from home during the rainy season."[48] The reverse meaning applies to young and adult seasonal Diola migrants who would return home to farm rice only during the rainy season (see map).

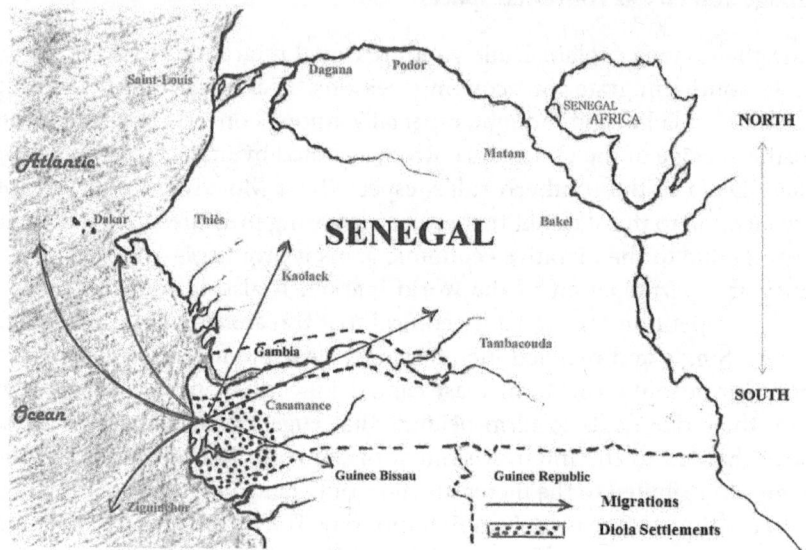

Diola migration destinations within Senegal, to other African countries, Europe, and the Americas some of which are permanent, but most remain seasonal.

The phenomenon occurs during a specific period of each year. Rice farming begins in the earliest rainfall (mid to late May) and ends with harvest (mid to late November). From December to early May, many young people migrate to cities where they often work as maids, watchmen, masons, and the like. As soon as the first rain began to fall, many young Diola who migrated to the cities would stop their city jobs to return to their villages to farm their rice fields.[49] In the village, all activities carried out in the dry season would be halted and everyone refocuses on a single

---

[48] Jean-Léopold Diouf, *Dictionnaires Wolof-Français et Français-Wolof* (Paris: Éditions Karthala, 2003), 238. Wolof is the only national language widely spoken besides French. The transitive verb *nawet*, "to spend the rainy season," is not to be confused with its noun form which simply means "rainy season." Also, the antonym of *nawetaan* (*naweta:n*) has come to mean "sport games held during the rainy season," especially soccer. My translation of the French text.

[49] Louis-Vincent Thomas, "Esquisse sur les mouvements de populations et les contacts Socio-culturels en pays Diola (Basse-Casamance)," *Bulletin de L' institut Français d'Afrique noire"* (1960): 486–507.

task, rice farming—preparing rice nurseries, and fields for planting the paddies. Aline Sitoé Diatta worked in Dakar as a maid and it was there that she received her prophetic call.[50]

Diola youths and adults negotiated the natural seasonal conditions and new realities imposed on them by the French empire. Many youths were attracted to the new possibilities and hope for a better life, away from their arduous rice farming world, urban life promises, and migrate seasonally to cities for economic reasons taking on jobs that range from higher education to army, police, nursing, hotel attendants, gatekeeping, etc. Girls worked as maids. Most adults tend to remain, but some do migrate to other villages bordering the Casamance River or Lagoons in search for better fisheries or forests with dense palm tree tap wine to improve their economic livelihood. Marie-Christine Cormier sees in these seasonal movements a gradual move from seasonal migration to a full-blown rural exodus toward cities. Fortunately, government organizations and church charities are gradually slowing down the flow of seasonal migrations with the creation of rural job opportunities.[51] Christian charities, social organizations, and associations team up to contribute to the needs of villagers in the areas of fishing, gardening, digging fresh water wells, donating wheelbarrows, means of transportation, construction of anti-salt dams, hotels, and tourist camps. Measures discouraging seasonal or permanent migrations range from baiting youths with incentives and imposing fees on those who tended to abandon rural life.

Most traditionalist Diola of the southern ridge of the Casamance River are known for their strong attachment to their ancestral traditional beliefs that they often practice in urban rather than rural settings. Those who resettle in cities such as Ziguinchor, Kaolack, Dakar Saint Louis, or overseas do return for about a month or two vacation or to observe traditional women and men rituals. Low paying job rates are mitigated with the creation of migrant associations corporate accounts designed to meet financial needs such as living expenses, funerals, and burial expenses (in cases where the dead are transported and buried back in their native village), marriage and other festive expenses, and remittance. To date, Diola country is heavily Christianized with more Catholics, lay and clergy, than any other Christian group of the Protestant denominations in Senegal.[52] This Senegalese Christianity is lived with an African traditional garb as debates as to whether it should reflect African religious rituals

---

[50] Girard, *Genèse du pouvoir charismatique*, 226.
[51] Marie-Christine Cormier, "Les jeunes Diola face à l'exode rural," *Cahier ORSTOM. Séries Sciences Humaines* xxi/2–3 (1985): 267–73.
[52] Ndiaye, *Quel Sénégal pour demain?*, 130–135; Tamba, *Histoire et sociologie des religions au Sénégal*, 296–298.

continue.⁵³ Today, many jobs are held by Diola people in both administrative and private sectors. Whether Protestant or Catholic, many Diola who embrace Christianity are in many cases *rehabilitated Diola Christians* who learn to be proud again of their identity and most of their traditional practices. It is often noted that another factor cited that encouraged Diola Christian migration to cities was their new status due to literacy imparted by missionaries. A combination of the two phenomena forced some Diola youths to migrate to Europe and America.

Conclusion

I hope I have clearly presented how colonization and Europeanized Christianity influenced Diola culture and religion and how both phenomena engendered cultural, religious, identity, and economic crises and continue to be the strong spurs for not just seasonal, but also permanent migrations to this day.⁵⁴ The roots of these crises reach back to the onset of European and African encounters, namely the transatlantic slave trade, colonization, and *global user-satellization*.⁵⁵ From the conversation I had with some hotel staff while I was in Dakar in May 2018, I learned that most of them were Diola Christians. They talked about the preparations they were making to return to their respective villages by the first rainfall to farm their sacred crop—rice. Similarly, Diola Muslims look forward to their seasonal homecoming for the same reason—helping their family members farm either rice or peanut field. Almost all would return to their respective villages to observe traditional rituals their forefathers and foremothers practiced since time immemorial. They were seasonal migrants. To date, Diola country is one of the most Christianized of the Senegalese regions. These Diola Christians have neither forgotten nor abandoned their most cherished religious traditions—a reality shared by many Senegalese—both Muslims and Christians. As for the future of Diola Christianity, it depends on how much Senegalese people of faith negotiate a way out of and yet, in a balanced conversation with Western influence.

---

[53] Tamba, *Histoire et sociologie des religions au Sénégal*, 297–298.
[54] Thomas, "Les Diola de la Base-Casamance," 85; Baum, *West Africa's Women of God*, 110–12.
[55] Ndiaye, *Quel Sénégal pour demain?*, 132–133.

Bibliography

Aihiokhai, SimonMary Asese. "Interreligious Friendship: A Path to Conversion for a Catholic Theologian." In *Interreligious Friendship After Nostra Aetate*. Interreligious Studies in Theory and Practice, edited by James L. Fredericks and Tracy Sayuki Tiemeier, 187–220. New York: Palgrave MacMillan, 2015.

Andriamirado, Sennen. "La guerre de sept cents ans." *Jeune Afrique* 29, no. 1687 (April/May1993): 26–30.

Barry, Boubacar. *Le Sénégambie du XVe au XIXe Siècle: Traite négrière, Islam conquête coloniale*. Paris: L'Harmattan, 2017.

Baum, Robert M. "Concealing Authority: Diola Priests and Other Leaders in the French Search for a Suitable chefferie in Colonial Senegal." *Cadernos de Estudos Africanos* 16, no. 17 (2011): 35–51.

———. *Shrines of the Slave Trade: Diola Religion and Society in Precolonial Senegambia*. New York: Oxford University Press, 1999.

———. "Emergence of Diola Christianity." *Africa* 60, no. 3 (1990): 371–398.

———. *West Africa's Women of God. Alinesitoué and the Diola Prophetic Tradition*. Bloomington, IN: University of Indiana Press, 2016.

Benoist, Joseph Roger. *Histoire de l'Église catholique au Sénégal: du milieu du XVe siècle à l'aube du troisième millénaire*. Paris: Édition Karthala, 2008.

Berghen, Constan Vanden et Adrien Manga. *Une introduction a un voyage en Casamance: Enampor, un village de riziculteurs en Casamance, au Sénégal*. Paris: Éditions L'Harmattan, 1999.

Bertrand-Bocandé, J., G. Debien, and Y. Saint-Martin. "Notes et Document: Emmanuel Bertrand-Bocandé (1812–1881) un Nantais en Casamance." *Bulletin de L' IFAN* 31, no. 1(1969): 279–302.

Colvin, Lucie Gallistel. *Historical Dictionary of Senegal*. African Historical Dictionary no. 23. Metuchen, NJ: The Scarecrow Press, 1981.

Cormier, Marie-Christine. "Les jeunes Diola face à l'exode rural." *Cahier ORSTOM. Séries Sciences Humaines* 21, no. 2-3 (1985): 267–273.

De Jong, Ferdinand. *Masquerades of Modernity: Power and Secrecy in the Casamance, Senegal*. Bloomington, IN: Indiana University Press, 2007.

Delcourt, Jean. *Histoire du Sénégal*. Dakar, SN: Éditions Clairafrique, 1976.

Diatta, Nazaire. "Participation du Joola chretien aux rites traditionnels." *Téléma* 46 (avril–juin, 1986): 67–81.

———. "Et si Jésus-Christ est, le premier ne d'entre les morts, était l'initie?: La personnalité de l'initie Joola face au Christ." *Téléma* 57 (janvier–mars, 1989): 49–73.

———. "Rites funéraires traditionnels et liturgie chrétienne: Lieux du dialogue interreligieux." *Téléma* 67–8 (juillet–décembre, 1991): 61–72.

———. "Nécessité d'une formation adéquate des pasteurs: Quelle formation pour les gens de pastoral en Afrique?" *Téléma* 61(Janvier–mars, 1990): 39–51.

Diédhiou, Paul. *L'identité Jóola en question* (Casamance). Paris: Karthala, 2011.

Diop, Cheikh Anta. *The Cultural Unity of Black Africa*. Chicago, IL: Third Word Press, 1959.

———. *Precolonial Black Africa*. Translated by Harold J. Salemson. Chicago, IL: Lawrence Hill Books, 1987.

Diouf, Jean-Léopold. *Dictionnaires Wolof-Français et Français-Wolof*. Paris : Éditions Karthala, 2003.

Fall, Mamadou. *Les territoires de la Sénégambie entre l'épée et le croissant: Xème -XXème Siècles*. Paris: L'Harmattan, 2016.

Feierman, Steven. *Shambaa Kingdom*. Madison: University of Wisconsin Press, 1974.

———. *Peasant Intellectuals: Anthropology and History in Tanzania*. Madison: University of Wisconsin Press, 1990.

Girard, Jean. *Genèse du pouvoir charismatique en basse Casamance (Sénégal)*. Dakar SN: IFAN, 1969.

Goldenberg, David M. *The Curse of Ham: Race and Slavery in Early Judaism, Christianity and Islam*. Princeton, NJ: Princeton University Press, 2003.

Henige, David. *The Chronology of Oral Tradition: Quest for a Chimera*. Oxford: Clarendon, 1974.

Iwuchukwu, Marinus Chijioke. "Interreligious Friendship: Symbiosis of Human Relationship vis à vis Religious Differences—A Christian Encounter with Two African Traditional Religionists." In *Interreligious Friendship After Nostra Aetate*: Interreligious Studies in Theory and Practice, edited by James L. Fredericks and Tracy *Sayuki Tiemeier*. New York: Palgrave MacMillan, 2015.

Jordan, Winthrop D. *White over Black: American Attitudes Toward the Negro 1550–1812*. Chapel Hill, NC: University of North Carolina Press, 1968.

Lecuir-Nemo, Geneviève. *Anne-Marie Javouhey : Fondatrice de la congrégation des sœurs de Saint-Joseph de Cluny (1779–1851)*. Paris: Édition Karthala, 2001.

Lesourd, Paul. *L'Œuvre civilisatrice et scientifiques des missionnaires Catholiques dans les colonies Françaises*. Paris: Sous le patronage du commissariat général de l'exposition coloniale internationale de Paris, 1931.

Magesa, Laurenti. *African Religion: The Moral Traditions of Abundant Life*. New York, Orbis Books, 1997.

Mark, Peter. "'Marybuckes' and the Christian Norm: European Images of Senegambians and Their Religions, 1550–1760." *African Studies Review* 23, no. 2 (1980): 91–99.

Méguelle, Philippe. *Chefferie colonial et Égalitarisme Diola: Les difficultés de la politique indigène de la France en Basse-Casamance (Sénégal), 1828–1923*. Paris: L'Harmattan, 2012.

Ndiaye, Théodore Ndok. *Quel Sénégal pour demain ?: Une vision chrétienne et citoyenne*. Paris: L'Harmattan, 2012.

Niang, Aliou Cissé. "Diola Religion." In *The Encyclopedia of Christianity in the Global South* volume 1, edited by Mark A. Lamport, 221–222. New York: Rowman and Littlefield, 2018.

———. "Senegal." In *The Encyclopedia of Christianity in the Global South* volume 2, edited by Mark A. Lamport, 710–712. New York: Rowman and Littlefield, 2018.

Palmeri, Pablo. *Living with the Diola of Mof Avvi: The Account of an Anthropological Research in Sénégal*. Padova: Libraria Editrice Univerістà di Padova, 2009.

Roche, Christian. *Histoire de La Casamance: Conquête et résistance: 1850–1920*. Paris: Éditions Karthala, 1985.

Sala-Molins, Louis. *Le Code Noir ou le calvaire de Canaan*. Paris: Presses Universitaires de France, 1987.

Sanneh, Lamin. *West African Christianity: The Religious Impact*. New York: Orbis Books, 1983.

Snyder, Graydon S. *The Inculturation of the Message of Jesus on Jewish and Roman Cultures*. Harrisburg, PA: Trinity Press International, 1999.

Soyinka, Wole. *The Burden of Memory, the Muse of Forgiveness*. New York: Oxford University Press, 1999.

Tamba, Moustapha. *Histoire et sociologie des religions au Sénégal*. Paris: L'Harmattan, 2016.

Thomas, Louis-Vincent. "Les Diola de Basse-Casamance." *Afrique Documents* 51 (Mai 1960): 73–90.

———. "Esquisse sur les mouvements de populations et les contacts Socio-culturels en pays Diola (Basse-Casamance)." *Bulletin l'institut Français d'Afrique noire* 22, no. 3–4 (1960): 486–508.

———. *Les Diola: Essai d'analyse fonctionnelle sur une population de Basse-Casamance*. Tome 1&2; Dakar, SN: Imprimerie Protat FrPres, Mâcon, 1959.

Trincaz, Jacqueline. *Colonisations et religions en Afrique noir: L'exemple de Ziguinchor*. Paris: Éditions L'Harmattan, 1981.

Trincaz, Pierre Xavier. *Colonization and Régionalisme Ziguinchor en Casamance*. Paris: Éditions de L'ORSTOM, 1984.

Vansina, Jan. *Being Colonized: The Kuba Experience in Rural Congo, 1880–1960*. Madison, WS: The University of Wisconsin Press, 2010.

6

DANGERS AND POSSIBILITIES OF THE CITY: SEXUAL MIGRATION, SEXUAL AND GENDER DIVERSITY, AND THE PARABLE OF THE PRODIGAL SON[1]

André S. Musskopf

BIBLE, GENDER, AND SEXUALITY

The present reflection on the parable of the prodigal son follows two basic principles: (1) the methodology known as Popular Reading of the Bible, and its search for the relationship between life (experience) and the biblical text in the context of a hermeneutical perspective that is not primarily concerned with the "final truth" of the text in itself, but which asks for its truth in relation to the one or the ones who interpret it; and (2) the perspective of gender and sexual diversity that specifies this experience, searching not only for the ways in which sexual and gender relations and identities are presented in the text, but also asks in what ways they relate to that which is understood as liberating sexual and gender relations in the context of sexual migration. This way, the text is not an end in itself, but a dialogical-relational element in the process of becoming aware of and transforming reality.[2]

---

[1] A previous version of this article was published in Portuguese and Spanish in RIBLA, vol. 56, 2007, 141–157.

[2] These statements presented here, in an extremely simplified manner, have been developed in Latin America over the last decades, and are quite evident for any reader familiarized with Liberation Theology, Popular Reading of the Bible, Popular Education, and Latin American Feminist and Queer Theologies. I put them here at the outset as theoretical references, so as to inform the approach to the specific issues discussed in this essay.

To accomplish this exercise, it is important not to lose sight of what many feminist and queer biblical scholars have already pointed to: the biblical texts have been conceived, selected, canonized, and interpreted in patriarchal contexts and from a patriarchal ideological point of view.³ Besides, this context can also be defined as heteronormative, notwithstanding the difficulty and anachronism of applying contemporary concepts to the biblical world.⁴ In any case, the sexism and misogyny characteristic of patriarchalism are intimately related to heterosexism and different forms of LGBTIQ phobia,⁵ with important consequences for the reading and interpretation of biblical texts using categories of gender and sexuality.⁶

More specifically, the re-reading of the biblical text of Luke 15:11–32 is done from the experience of gay men, in this case through the story of Henrique.⁷ This way, it doesn't look for validation for "homosexuality"⁸ through the various hermeneutical strategies adopted even by many gay theologians. Instead, as Robert Goss states, "it is the horizon or social location from which I enter into the text, queer it, and bring it into my own

---

3   See for example, the work of Elisabeth Schüssler Fiorenza, *In Memory of Her: A Feminist Theological Reconstruction of Christian Origins* (New York: Crossroad, 1983); Elisabeth Schüssler Fiorenza, *Sharing Her Word: Feminist Biblical Hermeneutics in Context* (Boston: Beacon Press, 1998); and Ken Stone, *Practicing Safer Texts: Food, Sex, and Bible in Queer Perspective* (New York: T&T Clark, 2005).

4   On the use of concepts such as homosexual/heterosexual and other related terms in the interpretation of biblical texts from a gay/queer perspective, see André S. Musskopf, *Talar Rosa* (São Leopoldo: Oikos, 2005), 128; André S. Musskopf, "Bíblia, Cura e Homossexualidade," *RIBLA*. 49 (2004); and also Robert Goss, *Queering Christ* (Cleveland: Pilgrim, 2002), 204–220.

5   LGBTIQ+ is here used as a designation for gender and sexual diversity as expressed through the experience of Lesbian, Gay, Bisexual, Transgender, Transsexual, Intersex, Queer and other non-heteronormative and non-conforming sex, gender, and sexual identities and expressions; when followed by "phobia," it indicates all forms of prejudice, discrimination, and violence toward those persons because of their sex, gender, and sexual identities and expressions.

6   See Beverely Harrison, "Misogyny and Homophobia," in Carol S. Robb, ed., *Making the Connections* (Boston: Beacon Press, 1985), 3–73.

7   Henrique's story does not depict the experience of a particular person. In many ways, it condenses the experiences of many people I have met or stories I have heard, including my own.

8   I am aware of the problems of using categories such as "gay men" and "homosexuality" in the context of queer studies and movements. Even so, I use those categories in this text to refer to very specific contexts and realities that are many times labeled this way, nonetheless questioning the idea of a unified and stable meaning and pointing to the possibility of applying them to a range of experiences in the context of gender and sexual diversity.

queer world of meaning and empowered Christian practice."⁹ Also, it sets the experience of gay men in the context of sexual migration, understood broadly as the reality of people who move from one place to another as a consequence of their sexual orientation and/or gender identity. Although there are usually many intersecting issues in the decision of people to migrate (and many times it is less a decision than a survival strategy or even a forced and violent situation), gender and sexuality often are not considered as part of or as a central cause in this process.

History of interpretation

Luke 15:11–32 is surely one of the most well-known texts in the Bible. Its use in indoctrination and in sermons makes its plot known and its symbolism effective. Apparently, there are no great doubts about the message transmitted by this parable: It is the story of a father and his two sons; the younger, seen as a rebel, naively asks for his part in the inheritance, leaves the father's house, and discovers that life outside it is cruel; he behaves irresponsibly, reaching disaster, and goes through humiliating situations that make him decide to return to his father's house; the father, instead of imposing his authority and power, receives the son with open arms, without resentment, and throws a party to celebrate; the older son, knowing what has happened, revolts against the father's mercifulness, since he feels treated in an unfair way.¹⁰

In fact, the message seems very clear: the younger son goes through a process of learning that will lead him to conversion, making him return to his father's house; the older son also needs to go through a process of conversion, although this one will have to liberate himself from the rigidity of the system he serves. The sons, each one in his own way, represent attitudes that need to be corrected, one for despising the father's house and abandoning it, and the other one for his lack of compassion and flexibility. The father is the great hero of the plot. He is the model of the one who gives freedom for his sons to act in their own way and welcomes them and forgives them when things go wrong. His attitude is associated with the image of a compassionate God.¹¹

---

[9] Robert E. Goss, *Queering Christ*, 215. On the several gay/queer biblical hermeneutical strategies, see Andre S, Musskopf. "Queer: Teoria, Hermenêutica e Corporeidade," in *Teologia e Sexualidade*, ed. Jose Transferetti (São Paulo: Átomo, 2004), 179–212.

[10] Most commentaries about the text agree with the general ideas of this interpretation, although they usually highlight specific aspects of the parable. Barbara J. Essex presents a brief overview of those interpretations. *Bad Boys of the New Testament* (Cleveland: Pilgrim 2005), 25.

[11] All the commentaries mentioned in the bibliographical references at the end of this essay support this interpretation.

Many scholars have highlighted the newness that the text suggests: In the context of a patriarchal structure, where the father holds the power over everything and everybody, this father breaks away from those patriarchal ties and, in compassion, receives back the son who denied him. But, is there really a subversion of the patriarchal and heteronormative family model in this text? And, who is the one who breaks away from this structure? The goal of this essay is to look at the text from the perspective of the gender and sexual relations that take place in it and point to the possibilities of resistance to the patriarchal/hetero-centric system, particularly in the context of sexual migration in relation to gender and sexual diversity.

Some (exegetical) introductions to the text

As stated above, there is significant—though not absolute—consensus over the meaning of this text in its ancient context.[12] Scholars and interpreters agree that the central theme is the need for repentance and conversion to the exercise of discipleship and the experience of the abundance of God's merciful and gracious love.[13] In general, the text is put in the wider context of Luke 9:51–19:28, affirming that this part of the book deals with the implications of following Jesus, spoken on the way to Jerusalem.[14] Specifically in chapter 15, in the form of a "parabolic triptych," Jesus is presented as speaking to the "large crowds [that] were traveling with [him],"[15] (14:25) to the "tax collectors and sinners [who] were all gathering around to hear [him]," and (15:1) to "the Pharisees and the teachers of the law," (15:2) preaching about the role of each of those groups in their relation to God. The focus lies in that which has been "lost," and the importance they have before God.

The two previous narratives (parables) prepare the ground for the parable of the lost son. The first one (v. 3–7) presents an example from the world of the peasant pastor of sheep and the second one (v. 8–10) from

---

[12] David A. Holgate, *Prodigality, Liberality and Meanness in the Parable of the Prodigal: A Greco-Roman Perspective on Luke 15:11–32* (Sheffield, England: Sheffield Academic Press, 1999).

[13] Joel Huffstetler, *Boundless Love: The Parable of the Prodigal Son and Reconciliation* (Lanham: University Press of America, 2008).

[14] See João Inácio Wenzel, *O caminho do seguimento no Evangelho de Lucas* (São Leopoldo: CEBI, 1998), 44; Carlos Mesters and Mercedes Lopes, *O Avesso é o Lado Certo* (São Leopoldo/São Paulo: CEBI/Paulinas, 1998), 76ff; Alois Stöger, *O Evangelho Segundo Lucas* (Petrópolis: Vozes, 1985), 13; and Josep Rius-Camps, *O Evangelho de Lucas* (São Paulo: Paulus1991), 181.

[15] All Bible quotes are taken from the New International Version.

the domestic world of women.¹⁶ Their function is to show to the scribes and Pharisees the importance of the "lost ones" to the kingdom of God, contradicting the accusation they make to Jesus: that he eats with sinners and tax collectors. (v. 15:2b) According to scholars, those two previous parables, dealing with "lost objects," are taken to their culmination in the parable of the prodigal son, due to its human character and the contrasting of the experiences of the two sons with the mercy of the father, here identified as God, and the joy in face of repentance and return.¹⁷

The central theme of chapter 15, thus, is the repentance and conversion of those who have been "lost." This is even more evident at the end of the two previous narratives: "I tell you that in the same way there will be more rejoicing in heaven over one sinner who repents than over ninety-nine righteous persons who do not need to repent;" (15:7) and "In the same way, I tell you, there is rejoicing in the presence of the angels of God over one sinner who repents" (15:10). But, the parable of the prodigal son broadens this need of repentance to include those who feel righteous and observant of the law, presenting the older son's intransigence and moralism as an example of the attitude of the scribes and Pharisees. Both need to repent and convert, change their ways.

In the face of all this, what is the innovation in analyzing this theme from the perspective of gender and sexuality and sexual migration as suggested above? Traditional readings of the text of Luke 15:11–32 depict the son who leaves his father's house through negative lenses, many times inferring information that is not presented in the text. Also, those readings tend to associate his "lostness" with some kind of sexual practices considered not appropriate, even if any reference to sexuality (spending his money with prostitutes) is only made by his older brother, also depicted as somebody who needs to change his ways. The father, on the other hand, is presented as an understanding and forgiving person (usually identified as a merciful God), never being questioned about his virtual silence in the face of his son's departure and return, or in relation to what this return represents for the future of the relationships in the context of this family. The reading of this biblical narrative through the lenses of the history of Henrique and the reality of sexual migration provides new insights both to the reading of the text itself and to current theological reflections on migration.

---

16   This parable has been used by feminist scholars to talk about the possibility of thinking about God from the perspective of women's experience. Here, God is a woman who lost a coin, cleaned the house, found the coin, and called her friends to celebrate.

17   See Essex, *Bad Boys*, 28; Stöger, *O Evangelho*, 59; and David L. Tiede, *Luke* (Minneapolis, MN: Augsburg Fortress, 1998), 273.

Reading from Experience: Intercontextual Analyses

Leaving

> Henrique grew up with the feeling that there was something wrong with him. Jokes at school, and complaints from his father who wanted him to take interest in what he considered more masculine activities were some of the things that annoyed him. During adolescence the situation only got worse. He didn't take interest in many things that his friends used to do and felt pressured to take part in them in order not to be excluded from the group and ridiculed. He studied a lot, dreamt of growing up and earning the affection and respect of people, becoming someone successful. In the small town in which he lived, this meant having a good job, getting married, and having children. Since he liked to study, he thought that for this to happen he would have to go to college and prepare himself well. At the age of 18, he had a good job with chances of professional growth, but decided to leave everything behind and move to the capital to study. He didn't have major conflicts with his family and had the respect of the community. Many people thought he should have continued at his job since there were possibilities of ascending. But, leaving the familiar and known environment opened a new world of possibilities for him.

The parable of the prodigal son starts without many explanations. The younger son asks for his part in the inheritance and leaves to a "distant land." We don't know anything about the family relationships and only later the text will talk about the father's compassion, the jealousy of the older son, and the latter's readiness to follow the family structure as he understands it. The older son worked as the father's servant, taking care of what, for the most part, would be his at the death of his father according to birthright.

The text is not interested in offering information about the relationships in this family. Thus, it leaves the possibility to imagine them open, an exercise so dear to feminist and gay/queer theologians.[18] Actually, the gaps in the text about several aspects of the family relationships are always filled by exercises of imagination, even when interpreters don't make it explicit or acknowledge it. João Inácio Wenzel, for example, states that "the happiness that [the younger son] experienced at the father's house is nothing that can be compared with the emptiness left by the experience of being a foreigner."[19] Barbara Essex states that "this boy has been gone all this time (we don't know how long) and doing only God knows what (but we have our suspicions)."[20] David Tiede states that "the *youngest* son is

---

[18] Goss, *Queering Christ*, 212. The author refers to the use of the categories of "phantasie" (Dorothee Soelle) and "hermeneutics of creative actualization" (E.S. Fiorenza) by the gay theologian Robert Williams in *Just as I am*.
[19] Wenzel, *O Caminho*, 61.
[20] Essex, *Bad Boys*, 30.

headed for trouble, and everyone knows it."²¹ Alois Stöger states that "life at the father's house, with his orders and instructions, became hard on the son who seeks autonomy and who desires to live at his free will."²² All those suspicions and suppositions are a result of the imagination of the interpreters, since that information is not explicitly given by the text. The critical point here is the starting point for interpretation, and the ideological and contextual assumptions made in analyzing the characters in the story.

We do not know the reasons that led the younger son to ask for his part of the inheritance and leave for a distant land. The history of interpretation leads us to question his character, since the end of the text presents him as someone irresponsible and reckless. We only know that the family structure he is part of follows traditional patriarchal patterns. Being the younger son, his part in the inheritance is smaller than his older brother's and his father makes it available, despite having no obligation to do it. When he receives his part, according to the social custom at the time, it is as if the father had died, so that when his son returns he says: "This brother of yours was dead and is alive again" (Luke 15:32).²³

Based on this information, we can establish some of the aspects of the family structure. In the Greco-Roman world, the *oikos* is the family structure where the *pater familias* has authority and power over all the other members of the family. It is a hierarchical structure that does not imply dialogue, but obedience to the different levels of the family structure.²⁴ As much as we can point to the benevolence and openness of the father who divides his possessions and makes them available to his son, in the first place it is the son who breaks away from the family by asking for his part. He decided to make his own journey, far away from the vigilance and power of the father, the *pater familias*. Maybe he was irresponsible, or wanted to have another experience, felt anxious, bound to the family context. The truth is that the parable does not present any resistance by

---

[21] Tiede, *Luke*, 278.
[22] Stöger, *O Evangelho*, 66.
[23] For the proceedings on the division of inheritance according to Jewish laws, see Marcos A. Armange, "A experiência do perdão," Unpublished Monograph (São Leopoldo: IEPG, 2005), 6; Stöger, *O Evangelho*, 66; Essex, *Bad Boys*, 31; and Michael D. Goulder, *Luke* (Sheffield, Sheffield Academic Press, 1994), 613.
[24] For studies about the Greco-Roman family structure, see: Marga J. Ströher "A Igreja na Casa Dela," in *Série Ensaios e Monografias*, no. 12 (São Leopoldo: IEPG, 1996), 18–19; Marga J. Ströher, *Caminhos de resistência nas fronteiras do poder normativo*. Tese de Doutorado (São Leopoldo: IEPG, 2002), 151–156; L. William Countryman, *Dirt, Greed & Sex* (Philadelphia: Fortress, 1988), 147–167; Elisabeth S. Fiorenza, *As origens Cristãs a partir da hulher* (São Paulo: Paulinas 1992), 322–359.

the father, no attempt to dissuade the younger son, and no dialogue about the apparently unexpected request.[25]

Henrique does not live in a Greco-Roman family structure, although his family is not exempt from prejudices and a hierarchical division of power. But, he feels cloistered in his family and in his community. He wants to go to distant lands searching for something he doesn't quite know yet. He wants to know the possibilities, he wants to discover himself, have the freedom of getting to know himself, and grow as a person. And so, it happens,

> Henrique managed to get a job at the capital and soon made friends at college. He started to go out and get to know life in a big city. He ended up getting close to Antônio and they became good friends. In one of those conversations about college and life in the city, Antônio told Henrique he is gay. Henrique was surprised, since he didn't know much what that meant, but he liked Antônio a lot and little by little understood that that was just part of who Antônio was. More than that, he started to go out with Antônio to gay sites, coming out himself. The feeling that he was different, that he didn't fit, so strong during childhood and adolescence, started to make sense. He was also gay and his being away from his family, lost in the anonymity of a big city, allowed Henrique to come out as a gay man, although not without conflict.

In her book *A Mobilidade da Senzala Feminina* [The Mobility of the Feminine *Senzala*], Ivone Gebara presents and analyzes the issue of poor women from the Brazilian Northeast region and their vocation to be on the move. She describes the patriarchal and oppressive context in which those women live and run from by migrating to other places. With all the specific aspects that this mobility presupposes, Gebara helps us to think beyond the purely economic reasons that make those women move from one place to another in search of "a better life." She speaks of the gendered and sexual character of this migration of women who want to break away, consciously or unconsciously, from the oppressive patriarchal system.[26]

When analyzing the gay community in Brazil, Richard Parker puts its developments in the wider context of economic, political, and cultural changes that took place in Brazil during the nineteenth and twentieth centuries. The fast population growth at the end of the nineteenth century and the accelerated urbanization and industrialization during the twentieth century transformed the structures of Brazilian society. So, "during the most part of the last fifty years (…) the main source for the provision

---

[25] Tiede, *Luke*, 277. The author speaks of the lack of sensibility on the part of the father who does not dialogue with the son who wants to leave, nor listens to him when he comes back.

[26] Ivone Gebara, *A Mobilidade da Senzala Feminina* (São Paulo: Paulinas, 2000).

of the industrial labor force was internal migration."[27] But, in the same way as Gebara, Parker's interest is to add an element that goes by unnoted in the researches about migration in Brazil: its sexual component. As Parker puts it so well, the motivations for those migrations are not singular, but complex. Thus, it is important not to lose sight of the sexual issue in the decision of people to move from one place to another. According to him, "for many gay or bisexual men, issues connected to sexuality are part of the decisions to move and of the experiences they live after moving."[28]

In the context of those motivations, a factor that appears very often, as in Henrique's story, is the feeling of inadequacy, the difficulty of the family in dealing with differences in their patriarchal and heteronormative structure, including sometimes experiences of discrimination and violence, and the search for a better life. As Parker puts it,

> since urban life is constructed in the social imaginary as a place of relative freedom and opportunity, as an alternative to the oppressive characteristic of life in the country or small towns, maybe one should expect those images to be translated into sexual freedom.[29]

Life away from home

> Henrique got to know all about the gay life at the capital. He went out almost every night and came back early in the morning. He went to saunas, bars, and discos. He got to know many people and had many sexual encounters. Some with men he never saw again, others became short relationships. He was robbed many times walking in the dark streets in the middle of the night and even by a man he met at a disco and took to his apartment. One night, he was stopped by the police and insulted because of the suspicion that he was gay. He spent all his money on fashion clothes, drinking, and eventually used recreational drugs with his partners. He missed work a few times and when he wasn't late, he barely managed to accomplish his tasks, which resulted in his discharge. His academic life went bad, and in some courses, he failed in consequence of too many absences. The new world full of seductions that Henrique was getting to know, and his lack of experience and naïveté, pushed him to dangerous and sometimes dehumanizing situations. The money his father used to send barely paid college and rent.

Luke 15 once again does not reveal explicitly what happened to the younger son after he left his father's house. It only states that he "squandered his wealth in wild living" (v. 13b). His circumstances were aggravated by the country's economic situation that was experiencing "a severe

---

[27] Richard Parker, *Abaixo do Equador* (Rio de Janeiro: Record, 2002), 178. For the wider context, see pages 145–174.
[28] Parker, *Abaixo do Equador*, 260.
[29] Parker, *Abaixo do Equador*, 247.

famine" (v. 14), which led him to a situation of need. Forced to look after pigs, his situation became so deplorable that "he longed to fill his stomach with the pods that the pigs were eating, but no one gave him anything" (v. 16). According to David Tiede,

> Exactly how he squandered the money is not clear, even if the elder brother accuses him of whoring (v. 30). When the RSV says in loose living, it is translating a rather vague term which says "living in an unsalutary way" (Gk: asotos). Certainly, that is not good, and he did blow the inheritance. But, it is not so lurid as the elder brother and many interpreters imagine.[30]

There is an attempt, in the text itself, and more so in the history of interpretation, to blame the younger son for his tragedy. The older brother himself uses the supposed way the other brother lived his sexuality to ground his indignation and establish guilt. His is the only accusation raised in the text, stating that his younger brother squandered the money with prostitutes. At any place in the text, the question for the reasons that made the son leave his father's house and that led him to get involved in situations that caused him harm, resulting in the fact that he lived an "un-salutary life," is raised.

Gay men, such as Henrique, know just too well those accusations. In the booklet *Igreja e Homossexualismo* [*Church and Homosexualism*], Arzemiro Hoffmann presents "some cases of people [pastors] who were accused (or caught in the act) of homosexual proceedings." These are the cases he cites:

> **Case I.** The pastor was caught in the act of attempting to seduce minors (pedophilia). (…)
>
> **Case II.** The pastor was caught in the [homosexual] act with a partner in his own apartment on the occasion when his wife was traveling. (…)
>
> **Case III.** The pastor was never caught in the act or in any relationship, although his attitudes caused an environment of suspicion in the congregation. Because of his complicated, despotic, star personality, he never stayed for a longer period at the same parish.

---

[30] Tiede, *Luke*, 278 (RSV=Revised Standard Version). According to the author, referring to the use of "Parable of the Prodigal Son" as a title for this text, "Since the word 'prodigal' refers primarily to the son's extravagant wasting of his inheritance, that traditional title draws attention to the son's immorality, perhaps even stressing a moralistic interpretation. But then, the elder brother's understanding may have the last word. He had the moral of the story well in hand" (276). According to Essex, the word *asotos* "occurs only three other times in the New Testament and its meaning refers to indulging in vices and a lack of moral discipline (Eph 5:18; Titus 1:6; and 1 Pet 4:3). The text does not spell out the young man's activities in detail, but he may have indulged in drunkenness, licentiousness, carousing, and total rebelliousness." Essex, *Bad Boys*, 27.

Case IV. The pastor with highly suspicious attitudes managed to relate only to the boys in the youth group, exposing the girls to ridicule. He used his ministry status to open accounts and did not honor the payments.[31]

Supported by his interpretations of specific Bible texts, the analysis of those cases led the author to conclude that "it is evident that the Church should disrecommend the ordination of practicing homosexuals to the ecclesiastical ministry."[32] This kind of moralist understanding and reductionism of gay men's experiences and of those of other gender and sexually diverse persons would be intriguing, if it wasn't so common and popularized.

Those who have minimum knowledge and interest in understanding the processes of coming out and constructing identities outside of heteronormative patterns need to inquire about the reasons that lead people to act in such a way. This is not the place to explain this process, since there is a wide range of publications about it.[33] For the purpose of this essay, it is enough to state that the vulnerabilities to which many LGBTIQ+ persons (including gay men) are exposed, are intrinsically connected to the heteronormative system that structures societies. The fear of prejudice, discrimination, and violence, the lack of positive models, and the invisibilization of the LGBTIQ+ community circumscribed to ghettos and marginal places are some of the factors that generate those vulnerabilities.[34]

Hasty and prejudiced judgments about the experience of non-heterosexual and gender non-conforming people, such as Henrique and the pastors described by Hoffmann, relating all the unfortunate situations in which they end up involved as a logical consequence of the way they express their gender identity or live their sexuality, may well be identified with the blaming of the younger son in Luke's text. A reading done from the perspective of gender and sexual diversity wants to know the reasons why he decided to leave his house and how he ended up involved in an "un-salutary" way of living.

---

[31] Arzemiro Hoffman, "Como lidar com a homossexualidade na comunidade?," in *Igreja e homossexualismo*, ed. Martin Weingartner. *Série A Caminho do Reino* (Curitiba: Encontro, 2000), 56–57.

[32] Hoffmann, "Como lidar," 57.

[33] See, for example, Larry K. Graham, *Discovering Images of God* (Louisville: Westminster John Knox Press, 1997); Robert Goss, *Jesus Acted Up* (New York: HarperCollins, 1994); Richard Cleaver, *Know My Name* (Louisville: Westminster John Knox Press, 1995); Chris Glaser, *Coming Out as Sacrament* (Louisville: Westminster John Knox Press, 1998).

[34] See, for example, Larry K. Graham, *Discovering Images of God* (Louisville: Westminster John Knox Press, 1997) for a non-moralist study of the gay experience.

Returning

> Henrique's life became truly hell. Everything he had imagined to accomplish going to the capital had gone. He was unemployed, his studies went bad, and he felt that the fact that he was gay was connected to his tragedy. He prayed to God asking to "free him from this condition" so that he would be able to reconstruct his life, get married, have children, get a nice job, be respected, as he had always imagined. The more he tried to "run away from his homosexuality," the more he felt his sexual attraction to men was part of himself. He dated girls and felt like a trifler, misleading them in order to run away from himself. His financial condition got worse and worse. He didn't manage to get a job and even had no money to buy food. He had left his town a long time ago and had never gone back. The new life in the capital seemed incompatible with the life he had at his father's house and his home town. He wondered about going back to his father's house, where he wouldn't be in need, but he didn't know how his father would deal with his homosexuality. Maybe the only way out was to go back and hide it from his family, but that would mean renouncing his sexuality or living a double life, full of lies.

The difficulties faced by the younger son in Luke 15 may be viewed as a function of the larger social structures that ultimately prevent him from flourishing away from the father's house, resulting in him regretting his initiative and denying himself. He feels lost, frustrated, and sees no other plausible possibility besides returning. He imagines that at his return, the father will react according to the patriarchal order. That's why his strategy is to play according to the system, and before being denied by his father he denies himself as a son: "Father, I have sinned against heaven and against you; I am no longer worthy to be called your son; make me like one of your hired servants" (v. 18b–19).

The option to return to the father's house is unthinkable for many LGBTIQ+ persons in Brazil and in similar contexts. In the face of the fear of rejection and the relative freedom and tranquility they experience away from their family, this return becomes impracticable. In Henrique's experience, and in the experience of other LGBTIQ+ persons, however, this may seem the only way out. In the face of public and cultural rejection (the prodigal son is associated with pigs), the most viable option seems to be "to go back into the closet" and hinder the confrontation with the family and possible expulsion. For many, it is difficult to imagine an openness on the side of the family, especially from the father, the one who usually expresses the model of normativity they betrayed by "coming out."

The younger son of Luke 15, when leaving the father's house in search of his identity, ended up denying and losing that which grounded his identity up to then. He lost his status of son, he became a foreigner and, at last, the job of looking after pigs denied also the rules of his religion.³⁵ For Marcos Armange, the idea of "getting real" represents the son's self-forgiveness. It is necessary to forgive oneself in order to be able to receive the father's forgiveness. According to him, "the young man notices his mistake of abandoning the family and all the abundance that was offered there."³⁶ Forgiveness, repentance, and conversion walk hand in hand. In the experience of LGBTIQ+ persons and in the discourse of most churches, this means denying their gender and sexual identities and expressions.

There isn't anything in the text that leads to the conclusion that the younger son wishes to go back home for any other reason than the desire to fulfill basic needs. The young man reflects: "How many of my father's hired servants have food to spare, and here I am starving to death!" (v. 17) The relationships and the family structure are not, at any moment, qualified in an affirmative way nor as oppressive. For gay men and other gender and sexually diverse people, the option between a marginal life and the possible/probable need to adjust to a patriarchal and heteronormative model puts them at a crossroad.

> Henrique, at last, decided to go back to his father's house. To his surprise, his father received him with open arms. He didn't ask any kind of question. He was immensely happy with his son's return, after such a long time, and invited all the neighbors for a welcome party. His brother, Cláudio, when told about it, didn't like the idea. He had always thought Henrique was irresponsible and did not approve the idea of his brother studying in the capital, leaving him alone helping his parents. Besides, the money his father sent every month to pay for Henrique's college and rent had made the family budget short, so that Cláudio had to postpone his dream of buying a motorcycle. He confronted his father and didn't even show up at the party.

Not only the younger son was surprised with the attitude of the father. The older brother even confronted his father and accused him of being unfair. This is also not the experience of most LGBTIQ+ persons who reveal their gender and sexual identity to family members. Ostracism, denial, silence, and even violence are very common. Breaking away from the heteronormative system involves a reconstruction of the family and community structure that seems to be beyond the possibility of most families.

Truly, the father's attitude receiving his son back in his house has a subversive potential to challenge the patriarchal and heteronormative family structure. He lets his son free to experience the world—although he seems to choose silence when he could have given recommendations

---

35 Stöger, *O Evangelho*, 67.
36 Armange, "A experiência do perdão," 8.

and helped his son to live this experience positively. He also receives him back without restrictions when he faces his frustrated attempt to make his own life away from home.[37] He seems to question, or at least render flexible, the patriarchal family structure in the face of the older son's attitude, whose revolt is justified by his desire to keep and strengthen that structure. According to Barbara Essex, "the elder brother in this parable represents all of us who feel displaced by God's embrace of those whom we reject."[38] From the point of view of the relationships, this means to question the patriarchal and heteronormative patterns based on God's welcoming.

The text ends without solving the issue. We don't know what the older son did after confronting his father and not taking part in the party, how the relationship between the younger son and his father and with his other brother developed, or in which ways the relationships went on being constructed and reconstructed. It is this openness of the text to the answers and experiences of the ones who read it that allows imagining and constructing new relations in our lives.

THE POSSIBILITY OF NEW RELATIONS

The goal of this essay is to accomplish a re-reading of Luke 15:11–32 from the standpoint of the relations that take place in it in terms of gender and sexuality, and to reflect on the issue of sexual migration in relation to gender and sexual diversity. In this sense, its first statement, based on the information that the text itself presents, is that the family structure presented in it is essentially patriarchal. All the characters are male, and the plot evolves around the issue of the rights (inheritance) those men have in that structure. In the patriarchal world of hegemonic masculinities, men own the power and they are the ones that actually matter.[39]

---

[37] This interpretation seems to be a consensus, even by gay theologians who mention the text. See, for example, Robert Goss, *Jesus Acted Up*, 73; Countryman, *Dirt, Greed & Sex*, 183.

[38] Essex, *Bad Boys*, 36. In her analysis of the text, she emphasizes exactly the role of the older brother, referring to the "eternal rivalry between brothers" so common in biblical narratives (24, 31–32).

[39] Feminist scholars have pointed to the absence of the mother in the text. It might be that the father was a widower or just that any female character is not relevant for the writers' intent, strengthening the argument of a patriarchal perspective assumed and naturalized. In an imaginative exercise, one could also ask what the mother would have done in relation to the son's leaving and to the other son's complaint when he comes back. However, in the process of deconstructing patriarchalism, the fact that the father does not behave in the way it was expected of him in the patriarchal family system might also be an important clue to question traditional and hegemonic models of masculinity.

In this essentially patriarchal/masculine context, we are faced with the decision when one of them breaks away. This breaking away is not treated with much relevance by the other men, but it is the central motor of the whole plot. It is his return, and the way he is received by his father, that troubles the patriarchal structure and causes the revolt of the older son. The way his life was outside home/family is presented, but mostly interpreted, by scholars as a logical consequence of the betrayal to this system. His mistaken choices generate disastrous consequences, and his only way out is returning to the "safety" of the family structure.

Many interpreters suggest that the way this strayed son is received by his father presupposes, or invites reflection on, a change in the way this structure is understood. Breaking away from such hierarchy, the father accepts and welcomes the son in love. This is no doubt a valid and important interpretation, and also seems to be in agreement with Luke's attitude regarding family structures (see Luke 8:19–21).

LGBTIQ+ persons in general, and gay men in particular, are usually seen as betrayers of heteronormativity. Because of the way they construct their identity, and the potential creation of new relations that this construction engenders, they are excluded from the heteronormative universe and punished severely because of it.[40] The adversities faced outside this system are blamed on them, imputing them guilt for their subversive "option." A re-reading of Luke 15:11–32 from the experience of gender and sexual diversity implies asking other questions of the text.

Barbara Essex, using Freudian and Jungian psychological interpretations, affirms that the premise of this parable is the search for reconciliation and integrality of the family. According to this analysis, the younger son as well as the older one are alienated from the family that can be reconstructed through the unmeasured love of the father.[41] Josep Rius-Caps also speaks of "a new affection relationship" in relation to the way the father receives the younger son.[42] But, the questions gay men and other gender and sexually diverse people might ask to the text are: what kind of new relationship is established between those men? What kind of concessions will the one who leaves have to make in order to be reintegrated to the family? In what way will this family unit be reconstructed? The answers to those questions are not given by the text. They need to be constructed by the community of readers.

---

[40] As for the relationship between masculine homosexuality and models of masculinity, see André S. Musskopf, *Uma Brecha no Armário*, 2nd ed. (São Leopoldo: CEBI, 2005), 77–119.

[41] Essex, *Bad Boys*, 34–36. She bases her argument on the works by Mary A. Tolbert and Dan O. Via.

[42] Rius-Camps, *O Evangelho*, 254.

In the context of the relations between those three men, this means thinking about what kind of conversion is necessary. It is not the simple conversion of the younger son who, repenting from his liberating initiative, returns to the ties and chains of a closed family system, but the conversion of the family system that needs, in fact, to be a safe place, with not just material abundance, but affection to the point of welcoming new identity constructions.

In terms of sexual migration, it is necessary to understand that the process of leaving is not simply a betrayal of the family, but, many times, a necessary part of the process of constructing one's identity. Based on the text and on the experience of many LGBTIQ+ people, the "distant land" or the big cities and urban centers might present many dangers and drive them to "un-salutary" experiences. Nonetheless, it might also be a context that presents possibilities in terms of exploring and constructing alternative identities, especially in the context of LGBTIQ+ subcultures and communities. As Richard Parker states about the gay communities in Brazil:

> As they become more constant, the gay subcultures and communities create for many men the possibility to imagine a new and different life, and clearly stimulate some men to move. The structures that support those communities at their turn strengthen the men who move—offering them access to networks of friends, employment possibilities, residence opportunities, and things like that.[43]

But, it is also important not to lose sight of the risks and dangers that this leaving and those "distant lands" can represent to those who leave, and especially for those who leave without knowing exactly what they are searching for.[44] The act of leaving and the life in the city is full of possibilities, but also full of risks. And the text perhaps hints at the dangers of assuming a welcoming space in the "distant land" of self-definition and identity; it certainly draws attention to the need for structural systems that allow for and support non-heterosexual identities as coexistent with heterosexual structures.

The intention here is not to create a dichotomy between the "city" and the "small town," or the urban and the rural, and characterize them as more or less welcoming to gender and sexual diversity. This would be misrepresenting the diverse and plural realities of those contexts and how life is experienced in them. Sexual migration and gender and sexual diversity can be and are experienced in those contexts in different ways; or it might

---

[43] Parker, *Abaixo do Equador*, 260.
[44] For an analysis of the limitations of the gay ghettos from a theological perspective, see J. Michael Clark, *Beyond Our Ghettos* (Cleveland: Pilgrim, 1993).

not be an issue at all. The proposed reading is just one possibility of opening up this text to discuss issues that are relevant to many people like Henrique.

That is to say, an intertextual and intercontextual reading allows Luke's text to be in intimate conversations with experiences such as Henrique's and many other gay men and/or other nongender conforming people. Such analyses of gender and sexually diverse practices allow for the visualization of the construction of non-heteronormative identities in the context of sexual migration,[45] when the process of constructing one's identity also means "to be on the move" geographically. It points to the dangers and possibilities of being in a different place, be it cities and urban centers. It also points to the challenges of "going back" when that becomes less of a desire and more of a need, a compulsion from the reality of an unwelcoming world.

The fact that the plot is left open at the end of the narrative calls the reader to imagine new possibilities of relations among the characters and between them and God. If the father represents God in the symbolic imaginary that this text evokes, the direct consequence is the possibility of an image of God outside the heteronormative pattern. Not just a heterosexual-male-father-God that kindly welcomes "despite of" their experiences, but a God that takes part in those relationships, is mixed in them, leaving open the possibility of multiple identifications and constructions. The journey of the younger son links the traditional space with the non-traditional space; it connects the rural and the urban in intimate ways around the issues of sexuality and identity.

---

[45] In this essay, we are not dealing with or reflecting on issues of human and sexual trafficking, forced displacement, or other related issues. Those are also situations that might be triggered and discussed in the context of re-reading the text. However, in this reflection we are considering that the initiative to go to another place is taken by the subject that moves (not necessarily in the perspective of a completely free and autonomous choice, as this migration might still be understood as "forced").

Bibliography

Armange, Marcos A. *A Experiência do Perdão.* Unpublished Monograph. São Leopoldo: IEPG, 2005.

Comstock, Gary D. *Gay Theology without Apology.* Cleveland: Pilgrim, 1993.

Countryman, L. William. *Dirt, Greed & Sex.* Philadelphia: Fortress, 1988.

Clark, J. Michael. *Beyond our Ghettos—Gay Theology in Ecological Perspective.* Cleveland: Pilgrim, 1993.

Cleaver, Richard. *Know My name—A Gay Liberation Theology.* Louisville: Westminster John Knox Press, 1995.

Essex, Barbara J. *Bad Boys of the New Testament.* Cleveland: Pilgrim 2005.

Fiorenza, Elisabeth S. *As origens cristãs a partir da mulher.* São Paulo: Paulinas 1992.

Gebara, Ivone. *A mobilidade da senzala feminina.* São Paulo: Paulinas, 2000.

Glaser, Chris. *Coming Out as Sacrament.* Louisville: Westminster John Knox Press, 1998.

Goss, Robert E. *Queering Christ.* Cleveland: Pilgrim, 2002.

———. *Jesus Acted Up.* New York: HarperCollins, 1993.

Goulder, Michael D. *Luke—A New Paradigm.* Sheffield: Sheffield Academic Press, 1994.

Graham, Larry K. *Discovering Images of God—Narratives of Care Among Lesbians and Gays.* Louisville: Westminster John Knox Press, 1997.

Harrison, Beverly. "Misogyny and Homophobia." In *Making the Connections—Essays in Feminist Social Ethics*, edited by Carol S. Robb, 3–73. Boston: Beacon Press, 1985.

Hoffmann, Arzemiro. "Como lidar com a homossexualidade na comunidade?" In *Igreja e Homossexualismo*, edited by Martin Weingartner. Série A Caminho do Reino. Curitiba: Encontro, 2000.

Holgate, David A. *Prodigality, Liberality and Meanness in the Parable of the Prodigal: A Greco-Roman Perspective on Luke 15:11–32.* Sheffield: Sheffield Academic Press, 1999.

Huffstetler, Joel. *Boundless Love: The Parable of the Prodigal Son and Reconciliation.* Lanham: University Press of America, 2008.

Mesters, Carlos, and Mercedes Lopes. *O avesso é o lado certo—Círculos Bíblicos sobre o Evangelho de Lucas.* São Leopoldo/São Paulo: CEBI/Paulinas, 1998.

Musskopf, André S. "Bíblia, cura e homossexualidade—'Homens sejam submissos ao seu próprio marido. Da mesma forma, mulheres sejam submissas ás suas esposas,'" *RIBLA.* 49 (2004): 93–107.

———. "Queer: Teoria, hermenêutica e corporeidade." In *Teologia e sexualidade–um ensaio contra a exclusão moral*, edited by José Transferetti, 179–212. São Paulo: Átomo, 2004.

———. *Talar Rosa—Homossexuais e o ministério na igreja*. São Leopoldo: Oikos, 2005.

———. *Uma brecha no armário—Propostas para uma teologia gay*. 2nd ed. São Leopoldo: CEBI, 2005.

Parker, Richard. *Abaixo do Equador*. Rio de Janeiro: Record, 2002.

Rius-Camps, Josep. *O Evangelho de Lucas—O Êxodo do homem livre*. São Paulo: Paulus, 1991.

Schüssler Fiorenza, Elisabeth. *In Memory of Her: A Feminist Theological Reconstruction of Christian Origins*. New York: Crossroad, 1983.

———. *Sharing Her Word: Feminist Biblical Hermeneutics in Context*. Boston: Beacon Press, 1998.

Stöger, Alois. *O Evangelho Segundo Lucas*. Petrópolis: Vozes, 1985.

Ströher, Marga J. *"A Igreja na casa dela."* Série Ensaios e Monografias, no 12. São Leopoldo: IEPG, 1996.

———. *Caminhos de resistência nas fronteiras do poder normativo*. Tese de Doutorado. São Leopoldo: IEPG, 2002.

Stone, Kenneth. *Practicing Safer Texts: Food, Sex, and Bible in Queer Perspective*. New York: T&T Clark, 2005.

Tiede, David L. *Luke—Augsburg Commentary on the New Testament*. Minneapolis, MN: Augsburg Fortress, 1998.

Wenzel, João Inácio. *O caminho do seguimento no Evangelho de Lucas*. São Leopoldo: CEBI, 1998.

7

HETEROGENEITY'S MIDWIFERY ROLE IN IDENTITY TRANSFORMATION

Sunder John Boopalan

Introduction

Optimism for a better world often enlivens the human spirit. The Enlightenment was one such period, filled with optimism and purpose. Many at the time thought that industry, information, travel, connection, and the inherent human power to reason would make humans overcome narrow worldviews and identity affiliations. They opined that religion would give way to secularism and identity-based politics would give way to rational approaches that thought of the collective human good, not just of "one's own."

However, contrary to the Enlightenment optimism that particular human identities would give way to rational approaches in democratic practice, what we find today is that identities—religious, racial/ethnic, and a number of others—are increasingly becoming rigid and antagonistic, setting communities over against one another, rather than in relation to one another. Thinking about identity in the context of urbanization and migration, therefore, is a worthwhile task.

When new waves of migrants locate themselves in urban contexts in the US, they add a layer of heterogeneity to already-existing racial/ethnic identity formations. Partly due to being conditioned by negative stereotypes in circulation in their "home" countries and partly because of the fundamentally racialized landscape of the US, the consequent complex heterogeneity—filled with affect—that migrants find themselves in is one in which social arrangements are reassessed. This essay is in part devoted to highlighting unhelpful and regressive reifications and reenactments of problematic identities in the context of urbanization in the United States.

Having established such unhelpful and regressive identity formations, the second part of the essay describes how heterogeneity might play a midwifery role in positive transformation of self and world.

Migrants do participate in unhelpful reifications of problematic identities. This is the focus of the first part of this essay. However, one cannot stress enough that the situation is severely complicated by the ubiquitous presence of America's original sin, racism. Paula Ioanide's insightful commentary on racism serves, therefore, as a helpful starting point for framing this conundrum. Ioanide, now a professor and commentator on race and ethnicity, reflects on her Romanian immigrant experience as she enters the US along with her family at the age of ten. The racial undertones she notices—almost as if having stumbled upon some long-kept skeleton in the closet—soon emerge, upon closer observation and analysis, as having sinews and flesh. Ioanide writes,

> I felt that Americans around me (who were predominantly white middle- and working-class suburbanites) spoke to each other in superficial and contrived tones. At first, I thought this tonal difference had to do with my limited knowledge of the English language. Even after I became fluent, however, the tonal quality continued to bother me, and I kept waiting for the moment when they would stop pretending. I had the constant suspicion that people were hiding something and were talking in exaggerated, strained inflections in order to cover up some secret. I felt as if I were in a game where everything white Americans said had a secondary, coded meaning that I could not grasp.[1]

Ioanide continues,

> I sensed notes of hollowness in their overly jovial, high-pitched tones. They would exchange pleasantries and profess love and fellowship. But, their words seemed to be very abstract, divorced from actual realities, and deeply concerned with appearances. I was disoriented by the churchgoers' pre-occupation with the aesthetics of looking like a loving church because I could not understand what motivated this preoccupation. Even as a teenager, the social interactions felt fake to me, and therefore spiritually inauthentic, but I could not locate what prompted this feeling.[2]

In the first quote, Ioanide describes the racial climate that she encountered when entering the US. Ioanide's experience can, however, be seen as representative of what a great number of migrants themselves suspect, observe, and feel around them. In and through these encounters, migrants undertake a reassessment of identities—both others' and their own. What are the consequences of such a reassessment? While there are persons and communities that embrace positive consequences of such reassessment,

---

[1] Paula Ioanide, "The Alchemy of Race and Affect," *Kalfou* 1, no. 1 (2014): 152.
[2] Ioanide, "Alchemy," 153.

this essay, as already indicated, focuses on unhelpful reifications of identities experienced during such reassessments. The second quote more directly describes her experience in the encounter of religious communities, offering itself as a framework to help discern what is inauthentic and then consider what may be authentic. The two parts of this essay are framed around these quotes.

ANTI-BLACKNESS: REGRESSIVE REIFICATIONS OF IDENTITY IN THE PROCESS OF URBANIZATION

Whiteness[3] hides the everyday realities of racism in no less part because of the incentives gained from investments in its power. The practice of whiteness, as the first block quote describes it, thus entails speaking and acting in ways that circumvent brutalities of oppression. In the end, because of such hiding and circumventing, superficiality is one of its key characteristics. This superficiality, precisely because of its subconscious logic to cloak the malevolence of racism, causes a dissonance in both its practitioners and also in migrants who enter this dissonance.

Because of my South Asian social location, let me start with an Indian American example of the unhelpful reifications of problematic identities when migrants enter this dissonance. Prema Kurien, author of *Ethnic Church Meets Mega Church*, observes a trend in large American evangelical churches to move toward an embrace of diversity.[4] Kurien's ethnographic work on Indian American Christians in the Mar Thoma Church—also called Syrian or St. Thomas Christians—shows that these immigrant Christians, especially their younger, perceive such a trend as inclusive.

The Syrian Christians of India continue to operate for the most part as an endogamous community that has historically established itself as a dominant caste group in India. From a sociological point of view, they are thus a narrowly caste-based ethnic church. In an effort, perhaps, to steer away from this homogeneity, the younger among them perceive the white

---

[3] Whiteness includes "both a mechanism that protects the organizing logics of race" and "a category of identification (i.e., white people, or whites)." Racism in relation to whiteness is thus a "result of deeply embedded constructs that create oppressive social conditions that work to favor whiteness." See Samuel Jaye Tanner, *Whiteness, Pedagogy, and Youth in America: Critical Whiteness Studies in the Classroom*, Routledge Research in Educational Equality and Diversity (New York: Routledge, 2018), 18; Margaret Pfeil's observation that it "functions systematically, invisibly, and without name, while at the same time conferring power" is also a good definition, cited in Katie Walker Grimes, *Christ Divided: Antiblackness as Corporate Vice* (Minneapolis, MN: Fortress Press, 2017).

[4] Prema A. Kurien, *Ethnic Church Meets Megachurch: Indian American Christianity in Motion* (New York: New York University Press, 2017), 6.

American evangelical trend to embrace diversity as something that offers a way out of their exclusivity, allowing for them to have a seat at a more diverse table.

While the intention to shed exclusivity in favor of inclusivity might be good for a migrant community that finds itself in urban America, the logics of such a move, when critically viewed, reveals investments in whiteness. First of all, it makes one ask if the trend toward multiculturalism on the part of the aforementioned evangelical churches is reflective of the best of Christian tradition, or if it is merely a desire to make cosmetic changes to look a certain way, as Ioanide's commentary observes. Second, if these Mar Thoma Christians sought to escape exclusivity and embrace inclusivity, they could have easily found the sought diversity in an inclusive Indian American church elsewhere. In other words, because Indian Americans come from different ethnic and linguistic communities, an Indian American church that represented this diversity could have been an equally viable option. When this option is not pursued, the gravitation toward predominantly white churches, despite the perceived inclusivity therein, makes the move suspect.

This is where migrants run into the danger of reifying problematic identities. One could ask if the move away from the multiethnic Indian congregation option is a way to avoid mingling with those whose identities may not be equal in the social hierarchy that these dominant Indian Christians are used to inhabiting. While Kurien's commentary, staying faithful to ethnographic data, does not directly touch on this point, it does note other identity-based entanglements that highlight problematic reifications of identity. For instance, Kurien points out, "In the informal discussions that I was privy to during the course of my fieldwork, the marriage of their children to African Americans was always discussed as the worst-case scenario a family could ever face. Like other Indian immigrants, Mar Thomites have a lot of negative stereotypes about black Americans and their culture."[5] Mar Thomites' anti-blackness is particularly complicated by their dominant caste identity that is often tied to colorism in India. Anti-blackness, nevertheless, does cut across ethnic lines and is rampant among Indians.

Consider the following example. Upon seeing a group of African Americans walking toward us on a busy downtown street sidewalk in the US, an Indian friend of mine turned his body toward me and moved close to my ears to ask, "Are they Americans?" As I came to terms with what I just heard and gathered myself for a response, he moved his body away from the center of the sidewalk where we were and located himself to one side of the path. While the question shocked me, his bodily

---

[5] Kurien, *Ethnic Church*, 120.

movement away from the line of oncoming black bodies was embarrassing. Nevertheless, he persisted. In the midst of this shocking and embarrassing bodily reaction to heterogeneity in urban America, I managed to respond at some point, saying, "Yes, they are Americans; there are black people in America."

The behavior of my Indian friend pursuing graduate study in the US is indicative of how persons from other countries bring with them racialized frameworks of what the US represents. As Wendy Roth and Nadia Kim rightly argue, the heterogeneity that immigration brings about also reshapes racial dynamics.[6] As they note, "the racial attitudes [immigrants] hold toward other groups, and vice versa, shape racial dynamics, tensions, and interactions in neighborhoods, local politics, schools, shops, and workplaces."[7] This merits elaboration.

A quick anecdote comes to mind. I know of an instance in which the extended family of an Indian immigrant man prayed that he might be "delivered" from the hands of a woman he fell in love with. The woman happened to be African American. When this anecdote is seen through the lenses of the above commentary, it raises the question of whether problematic reifications of identity among immigrants in the process of urbanization are better understood in the context of anti-blackness. Following Katie Walker Grimes'[8] recent analysis of such phenomena, this particular lens does help to uncover—to recall Paula Ioanide's language—some secrets.

Notwithstanding my critique of Indian Americans in relation to whiteness, other migrant communities seem to face similar problems.

Take, for instance, a sample of Arabic speaking Protestant churches. While the data is limited in its scope and sample, it does allow for some informed commentary on identity formations of migrants in urban settings in the US. Based on her research on Arabic speaking churches in the New Jersey area, Deanna Ferree Womack notes how some youth, dissatisfied with their conventional church structure in the US, state their preference for an "American pastor." When clarification is sought, these youth are clear in stating that they "do not [merely] want an Arab American pastor with perfect English," but rather prefer "an American pastor."[9] Without a doubt, Arab Americans, irrespective of religion, con-

---

[6] Wendy D. Roth and Nadia Y. Kim, "Relocating Prejudice: A Transnational Approach to Understanding Immigrants' Racial Attitudes," *International Migration Review* 47, no. 2 (2013): 330.

[7] Roth and Kim, "Relocating Prejudice," 331.

[8] See Grimes, *Christ Divided*.

[9] Deanna Ferree Womack, "Transnational Christianity and Converging Identities: Arabic Protestant Churches in New Jersey," in *Religion, Migration and Identity:*

tinue to face discrimination, especially after September 11.[10] Perhaps due to this and other accentuating factors, there is a desire to be part of a dominant cultural group in the US. Also, as Womack importantly notes, not all Arab Protestant immigrants seek to move closer to mainstream American churches.[11] Nevertheless, the gravitation toward whiteness is real and when the phrase "an American pastor" is used, the implicit racialized connotation is often "white."

If we shift attention to other immigrant communities, other racial entanglements are unraveled. Take, for example, Dominican and Korean immigrants. Roth and Kim's research focuses on these groups because Latinx and Asian-origin groups make up some of the largest incoming immigrants to the US. They are aware of the fundamental differences between these groups. Koreans, for example, come from a generally homogeneous context while Dominicans come from a setting in which intermixing of various racial and ethnic groups have "produced a continuum of appearances and racial terminology."[12]

Despite these fundamental differences, there are similarities in the formation of their racial attitudes. As Roth and Kim rightly argue, "both South Korea and the Dominican Republic have undergone racial formation processes, stemming from histories of imperialism and colonialism, that place darker individuals at the bottom of racial hierarchies."[13] Because of such historical processes of socialization, including current portrayals in mass media,[14] anti-black stereotypes and attitudes are formed even before migrants enter the United States.[15]

Based on historical data, Elizabeth Hordge-Freeman, in an article titled "What's Love Got to Do With It?," notes that in colloquial use, "Brazilians may use over 100 different terms when asked to describe themselves by

---

    Methodological and Theological Explorations, ed. Martha Frederiks and Dorottya Nagy (Leiden: Brill, 2016), 263.

[10] For a good collection of essays, see Amaney A. Jamal and Nadine Christine Naber, eds., *Race and Arab Americans before and after 9/11: From Invisible Citizens to Visible Subjects* (Syracuse: Syracuse University Press, 2008). For a more recent monograph, see Saher Selod, *Forever Suspect: Racialized Surveillance of Muslim Americans in the War on Terror* (New Brunswick, NJ: Rutgers University Press, 2018).

[11] Womack, "Transnational Christianity," 265.

[12] Roth and Kim, "Relocating Prejudice," 333.

[13] Roth and Kim, "Relocating Prejudice," 347.

[14] For a good overview of anti-blackness in mass media, see Alice Mikal Craven, *Visible and Invisible Whiteness: American White Supremacy through the Cinematic Lens* (Cham: Palgrave Macmillan, 2018).

[15] Roth and Kim, "Relocating Prejudice," 359.

phenotype."[16] The logic inherent in this wide repertoire of words is based on anti-black perceptions of bodily features. Interestingly, her commentary focuses on these dynamics within familial relationships and thus the title of the essay. As Hordge-Freeman notes, the role of affection and the entailing emotional investment in these processes of "racial socialization" cannot be ignored and reveal "the centrality of the body."[17] In close familial circles, much before a child is even born, the child's skin color and appearance are discussed openly.[18] To make this commentary even more accessible, she offers a case study.

Damiana is a pregnant mother in her 20s with "caramel brown skin and naturally straight black hair" and identifies as a black woman. Her husband is dark skinned. Damiana has dreams about the possible phenotype and outward appearance of her unborn child. She sometimes dreams of her child as white and at other times sees her as a brown child.[19] What Damiana has to say in response to her dreams is this: "I hope she gets her nose and straight hair from me. That's why I sit here all day and watch 'gente bonita' [pretty people] on television. If an ugly person walks by, I try not to even look in their direction."[20]

While these details may seem striking to some readers, the logic in all of these above-mentioned communities is similar in its anti-blackness. Anti-blackness is a global disease and migrant communities bring racialized baggage with them as they enter the US. While taking stock of this problem is a project in itself, the particular aspect that this essay is interested in is how the frameworks and affective dispositions migrants bring with them react to "maneuvers of whiteness."[21]

This section has clued us in on some problematic reactions to heterogeneity among migrants in the process of migration when seen through the lens of anti-blackness.[22] If regressive reifications of identity are better understood through the lens of anti-blackness, then understanding the constricting conditions that disable heterogeneity's liberatory promise is vital.

---

[16] Elizabeth Hordge-Freeman, "What's Love Got to Do with It?: Racial Features, Stigma and Socialization in Afro-Brazilian Families," *Ethnic and Racial Studies* 36, no. 10 (2013): 1510.

[17] Hordge-Freeman, "What's Love," 1509.

[18] Hordge-Freeman, "What's Love," 1511.

[19] Hordge-Freeman, "What's Love," 1512.

[20] Hordge-Freeman, "What's Love," 1512.

[21] I borrow this phrase from Moore and Bell's essay. Wendy Moore and Joyce Bell, "Maneuvers of Whiteness: 'Diversity' as a Mechanism of Retrenchment in the Affirmative Action Discourse," *Critical Sociology* 37, no. 5 (2011): 597–613.

[22] For a good discussion on related matters, see Grimes's chapter, "Nonwhiteness Will Not Save Us: The Persistence of Antiblackness in the 'Brown' Twenty-First Century, " in Grimes, *Christ Divided*, 147–76.

WHITENESS: THE CONDITION THAT CONSTRICTS HETEROGENEITY'S LIBERATORY PROMISE

This essay, in the end, is interested in heterogeneity's liberatory promise. Some ground clearing, nevertheless, is necessary before we can do that.

Urbanization has brought together a group of very different people that makes it seem as if the resultant multiculturalism is inclusive. Racial reifications, nevertheless, will continue to hold power unless and until the spell of white innocence is broken. For communities of color, breaking such a spell includes deconstructing the notion of diversity and multiculturalism that does not ask questions about history, power, and inequalities.[23]

The spell of whiteness—as Ioanide's earlier commentary describes—involves hiding and masking. This superficiality is further buttressed by a chosen ignorance and a presumed innocence that knows what not to know. "Knowing what not to know"[24] is internal to the mechanism of whiteness. An important element in this chosen ignorance is the lack of reference to the country's racial wound that is often bandaged, but never healed.

As Eduardo Bonilla-Silva notes in his book, *Racism Without Racists*, today "the white commonsense view on racial matters is that racists are few and far between, that discrimination has all but disappeared since the 1960s, and that most whites are color blind."[25] This is part of what Ioanide calls "knowing what not to know." Whiteness' mechanism would rather have people believe that whiteness as a racist culture of dominance does not exist.

The brutality of racism in the US has been well documented.[26] As important as it is to come to terms with the unhealed racial wound of the US, "it is not enough to declare that race matters or that racism endures."[27] "The more demanding challenge, as Lawrence Bobo rightly argues, is to

---

[23] Moore and Bell, "Maneuvers of Whiteness," 600.
[24] Michael Taussig, cited in Ioanide, "Alchemy, " 154.
[25] Eduardo Bonilla-Silva, *Racism without Racists: Color-Blind Racism and the Persistence of Racial Inequality in America*, 4th ed. (Lanham: Rowman & Littlefield, 2013), 25.
[26] In addition to Bonilla-Silva's work, see also Joe R. Feagin, *The White Racial Frame: Centuries of Racial Framing and Counter-Framing*, 2nd ed. (New York: Routledge, 2013); Leslie Picca and Joe Feagin, *Two-Faced Racism: Whites in the Backstage and Frontstage* (New York: Routledge, 2007).
[27] Lawrence Bobo, cited in Tyrone A. Forman, "Color-Blind Racism and Racial Indifference: The Role of Racial Apathy in Facilitating Enduring Inequalities," in *The Changing Terrain of Race and Ethnicity*, eds. Maria Krysan and Amanda Lewis (New York: Russell Sage Foundation, 2004), 58.

account for how and why such a social construction comes to be reconstituted, refreshed, and enacted anew in very different times and places."[28] Tyrone Forman's commentary on this insight is helpful: "Clearly," Forman avers, "our efforts to eradicate racial and ethnic inequality will not be successful until we better understand the precise mechanisms reproducing it."[29]

One common mechanism of whiteness is to pit various migrant communities against one another.[30] When a man from Haiti is told by his African black friends that he would do well to retain his Haitian accent because that distinguishes him—for the better, from their perspective—from African Americans, the subtleties of racism in the US begin to reveal themselves.[31]

Responsible work by people of color can advance only when "the enduring reality of ethno-racial prejudices, asymmetries, and ideologies of power" are acknowledged[32] in historic context. Given that color-blindness—and, by extension, blindness to the continuing effect of oppressive historical particularities—is a central theme in the post-civil rights era in the highest courts of the US,[33] this becomes all the more important. If immigrants are to be responsible citizens and faithful Christians, intentional efforts are to be made to identify sources and sites of suffering and oppression so that one does not become complicit in "knowing what not to know."

What Ki Joo (KC) Choi notes about the effect of whiteness on Asian Americans is a good reminder for other immigrant groups as well. "To be disciplined into a kind of quiet submission to the prevailing ideals and norms of race and personhood"—by putting us in our place over against other groups—"preempts our capacity to determine our own agency and what it means to be full participants in American society."[34]

Choi goes on to make another astute observation about the effect of succumbing to such sort of disciplining by whiteness. He argues

---

[28] Lawrence Bobo, cited in Forman, "Color-Blind Racism," 58.
[29] Forman, "Color-Blind Racism," 58.
[30] Susan Abraham, "Asian/Asian North American Feminist Theology and the Secular Academy," *Journal of Feminist Studies in Religion* 31, no. 1 (2015): 124. Abraham's commentary is specifically on the maneuver of colonialism, but the logic is similar.
[31] This example comes from first-person testimony.
[32] Ki Joo (KC) Choi, "Racial Identity and Solidarity," in *Asian American Christian Ethics: Voices, Methods, Issues*, ed. Grace Kao and Ilsup Ahn (Waco: Baylor University Press, 2015), 131.
[33] Moore and Bell, "Maneuvers of Whiteness," 601.
[34] Ki Joo (KC) Choi, "Asian American Christian Ethics: The State of the Discipline," *Journal of the Society of Christian Ethics* 38, no. 3 (2019): 37.

rightly that "rendering Asian Americans [and by extension other immigrant groups as well] as model minorities [in one way or another] (or, more specifically, as 'almost white') also functions to discipline African Americans and Hispanics by manipulating their perceptions of Asian Americans [and others] as 'other,'—as socially different from them."[35]

If whiteness pits different minoritized groups against each other to perpetuate dominance, this mechanism needs to be seen for what it is. It is important to remember that this pitting of various communities against each other is done by dangling the "American Dream" carrot in front of immigrant communities. Reaching for this carrot means centering one's identity as close as possible to whiteness.

Indian Americans, for example, historically argued that they were white because they had "Aryan" origins. To make a long story short, Indian Americans were considered white for three full decades in the twentieth century. Over time, with gains made through civil rights struggles of African-Americans and others that suffered brutal oppression in the US, dominant caste Indian Americans sought to be included under the category "Asians" in order to reap the benefits of affirmative action.[36]

Immigrant communities need to work with each other not merely to get a piece of the metaphorical carrot, but in order to forge authentic solidarities that make them full and responsible participants in American society. Such authentic solidarities are forged when immigrant communities bypass the condition—namely the veneer of innocence of whiteness and the corresponding sinister mechanics of its operation—that constricts heterogeneity's liberatory promise.

Heterogeneity's midwifery role

Let us briefly return to the second block quote from Paula Ioanide cited in the Introduction. The quote's direct reference to religious communities allows this section to name what's inauthentic, thereby making space for us to outline a possible midwifery role for heterogeneity.

Ioanide finds the "overly jovial" tones, "pleasantries," profession of love, and the deep concern with appearances disorienting and names these interactions as "spiritually inauthentic." Importantly, such inauthenticity in whiteness, according to Ioanide, masks the realities of racism. In thus masking the realities of racism, differences are flattened, inequalities

---

[35] Choi, "Asian American," 37.
[36] Sunder John Boopalan, *Memory, Grief, and Agency: A Political Theological Account of Wrongs and Rites*, New Approaches to Religion and Power (New York: Palgrave Macmillan, 2017), 64, 190–91; Also see Kamala Visweswaran, "Diaspora by Design: Flexible Citizenship and South Asians in U.S. Racial Formations," *Diaspora: A Journal of Transnational Studies* 6, no. 1 (1997): 5–29.

are misrepresented, and, finally, "secrets" are maintained. In the end, this "unwittingly produce[s] spiritual emptiness, since a society that denies the unjust outcomes of its past and present actions cannot stand on ethical grounds."[37]

To positively restate the problem of spiritual emptiness hinted at by Ioanide above, differences encountered through heterogeneity are opportunities to eschew inauthenticity and embrace an authentic spirituality. As urbanization continuously adds to the heterogeneity of the US landscape, encounters of various sorts of differences are opportunities to decode public secrets. These opportunities are what this essay terms as midwifery roles.

When encounters mask and sentimentalize otherwise oppressive racialized realities, they become complicit in maintaining society's "secrets." An authentic spirituality overcomes this. Part of this authentic spirituality includes overcoming notions of "world" that are abstract and devoid of particular references to societal realities.[38] Referring to this concern and following Johannes Baptist Metz, Henry Kuo makes an astute observation. As followers of Jesus, "by bearing the dangerous memory of Jesus Christ's suffering, murder, and resurrection, the church provides Christians with resources to maintain society's dangerous memories and to ensure that past sins do not become future sins."[39] Bearing the memories of the particularities of social sin, therefore, is central to the identity of Christians. In other words, as bearers of the dangerous memory of Jesus, Christians need to constantly remind themselves that we are in the business of paying attention to suffering and oppression.

Ioanide's commentary on similar matters is instructive. Referring back to the conversations she had with her own immigrant family about the racialized nature of US history—past and present—Ioanide observes that many of her family members lift up "innocence" as a response to racism.[40] Perhaps, readers are able to relate to the oft-heard retort, "Well, I was not here when that happened," which captures the desire for such innocence. When Christian migrants from various social locations across the globe enter the racialized landscape of the US, this move to a false innocence is to be avoided at all costs. This is important not only for overcoming the pernicious gravitational pull of whiteness, but also to be faithful to the

---

[37] Ioanide, "Alchemy," 161.
[38] Henry Kuo, "The Dangerous Memory of the Crucified People: The Church as Critical, Liminal Space" (unpublished paper), presented at the 9th Ecclesiological Investigations Network International Conference, entitled "Vatican II: Remembering the Future" on May 22, 2015, at Georgetown University. Thanks are due to Kuo for sharing this essay with me.
[39] Henry Kuo, "Dangerous Memory."
[40] Ioanide, "Alchemy," 157.

memory of Jesus that poses dangers for any system—in this case, whiteness—that maintains secrets about itself.

Ioanide also notes another significant obstacle inherent in an inauthentic spiritual disposition. The above mentioned "innocence" is often coupled with a claim about human wretchedness in particular. As the author rightly observes, "one of the most powerful arguments the 'innocents' make is that humans are generally wretched, and the four-hundred-year history of white supremacy in the United States is merely another example of that."[41] The implied meanings and implications in such a resort to "innocence" and "wretchedness" are many. Such a resort, for instance, could avoid naming and redressing wrongs while simultaneously employing, as Kuo notes, "the virtue of mercy and grace as a cover."[42] I have addressed similar concerns elsewhere.[43]

As I bring this essay to an end, what I would like to focus on are the challenges of the label "people of color" as we seek to unlock heterogeneity's liberatory promise. Mari Matsuda reminds us that, historically, heterogeneous people did come together, discovering their particularities, uncovering secrets of racism, and finding ways to work together in order to raise the collective good.[44] Recovering this dangerous memory is perhaps essential even as one problematizes the term "people of color" today.

The term "people of color," nevertheless could fall into the danger of collapsing power differences and flattening particularities by subsuming several immigrant groups under its label. Given the Christian commitment to uncover secrets through dangerous memories, describing the limitations of the term is internal to embracing an authentic spirituality.

When immigrants enter the US, they encounter other immigrants. The particularities in such encounters are extraordinary. These various groups simultaneously collide with the mechanics of whiteness. On the one hand, it is understandable, therefore, how the term "people of color" can be helpful to come together to resist racism. On the other hand, however, this desire may unwittingly undo the necessity of encountering each other in and through our differences, learning particular histories, and critically analyzing chosen and unchosen power imbalances that whiteness confers differently on different migrant groups.

---

[41] Ioanide, "Alchemy," 157.
[42] Henry Kuo, "Dangerous Memory."
[43] See Boopalan, *Memory, Grief, and Agency*, 7–16; see also Sunder John Boopalan, "Doing Constructive Theology with B. R. Ambedkar: Where Theology and Ethics Kiss," *Bangalore Theological Forum* 48, no. 2 (2016): 58–69.
[44] See Mari J. Matsuda, "We Will Not Be Used: Are Asian Americans the Racial Bourgeoisie?," in *Where Is Your Body?: And Other Essays on Race, Gender, and the Law* (Boston: Beacon Press, 1997), 149–60.

Heterogeneity's midwifery role lies in enabling such encounters, learning, and analysis. Each time migrants encounter each other, it is an opportunity to uncover secrets of complicated histories of oppression. Therefore, encountering one another in our particularities is essential.

As an Indian from South Asia, for instance, I need to come to terms with the privilege I enjoy vis-à-vis other immigrant groups. In addition, such coming to terms also involves assessing my standing in relation to other ethnic groups from within the subcontinent. This both-and posture is essential. Such coming to terms cannot be a solipsistic endeavor. It is simultaneously public in nature. Herein lies heterogeneity's promise as midwife in birthing a fresh reality where identities are employed in the service of full and authentic participation.

When heterogeneity is embraced as an opportunity for reassessment of self and collective identities, it fosters the uncovering of the mechanics of oppression. It is in this way that "past sins do not become future sins." Immigrants would do well, then, to encounter one another not merely as "people of color," but rather in the fullness of their ethnic and racial particularities.

To spark thinking on heterogeneity's midwifery role in identity transformation, a set of questions may be posed. How might we tell and re-tell our stories of identity and discover ourselves anew? Could we start by paying attention to bodies? In gatherings of various kinds, whose bodies do we see? Who are present? Who are absent? Does everyone look, dress, or sound the same? Who has authority? Who does not? Whose bodies and voices form the center and whose are marginal? If Christian communities and churches are to serve as receptacles for engendering a new reality by embracing heterogeneity's promise, what conditions are to be present? What are the means by which dangerous memories are catalyzed? How may such dangerous memories uncover society's secrets?

Bibliography

Abraham, Susan. "Asian/Asian North American Feminist Theology and the Secular Academy." *Journal of Feminist Studies in Religion* 31, no. 1 (2015): 121–126.

Boopalan, Sunder John. *Memory, Grief, and Agency: A Political Theological Account of Wrongs and Rites*, New Approaches to Religion and Power. New York: Palgrave Macmillan, 2017.

———. "Doing Constructive Theology with B. R. Ambedkar: Where Theology and Ethics Kiss." *Bangalore Theological Forum* 48, no. 2 (2016): 58–69.

Choi, Ki Joo (KC). "Racial Identity and Solidarity." In *Asian American Christian Ethics: Voices, Methods, Issues*, edited by Grace Kao and Ilsup Ahn. Waco: Baylor University Press, 2015.

———. "Asian American Christian Ethics: The State of the Discipline." *Journal of the Society of Christian Ethics* 38, no. 3 (2019): 33–44.

Craven, Alice Mikal. *Visible and Invisible Whiteness: American White Supremacy through the Cinematic Lens*. Cham: Palgrave Macmillan, 2018.

Feagin, Joe R. *The White Racial Frame: Centuries of Racial Framing and Counter-Framing*. 2nd ed. New York: Routledge, 2013.

Forman, Tyrone A. "Color-Blind Racism and Racial Indifference: The Role of Racial Apathy in Facilitating Enduring Inequalities." In *The Changing Terrain of Race and Ethnicity Maria and Amanda Lewis*, edited by Maria Krysan and Amanda Lewis. New York: Russell Sage Foundation, 2004.

Grimes, Katie Walker. *Christ Divided: Antiblackness as Corporate Vice*. Minneapolis, MN: Fortress Press, 2017.

Hordge-Freeman, Elizabeth. "What's Love Got to Do with It?: Racial Features, Stigma and Socialization in Afro-Brazilian Families." *Journal of Ethnic and Racial Studies* 36, no. 10 (2013):1507–1523.

Ioanide, Paula. "The Alchemy of Race and Affect." *Kalfou* 1, no. 1 (2014).

Jamal, Amaney A., and Nadine Christine Naber, eds. *Race and Arab Americans before and after 9/11: From Invisible Citizens to Visible Subjects*. Syracuse: Syracuse University Press, 2008.

Kurien, Prema A. *Ethnic Church Meets Megachurch: Indian American Christianity in Motion*. New York: New York University Press, 2017.

Matsuda, Mari J. "We Will Not Be Used: Are Asian Americans the Racial Bourgeoisie?" In *Where Is Your Body?: And Other Essays on Race, Gender, and the Law*, 149–60. Boston: Beacon Press, 1997.

Moore, Wendy, and Joyce Bell, "Maneuvers of Whiteness: 'Diversity' as a Mechanism of Retrenchment in the Affirmative Action Discourse." *Critical Sociology* 37, no. 5 (2011): 597–613.

Picca, Leslie, and Joe Feagin. *Two-Faced Racism: Whites in the Backstage and Frontstage*. New York: Routledge, 2007.

Roth, Wendy D., and Nadia Y. Kim. "Relocating Prejudice: A Transnational Approach to Understanding Immigrants' Racial Attitudes." *International Migration Review* 47, no. 2 (2013): 330–373.

Selod, Saher. *Forever Suspect: Racialized Surveillance of Muslim Americans in the War on Terror*. New Brunswick, NJ: Rutgers University Press, 2018.

Tanner, Samuel Jaye. *Whiteness, Pedagogy, and Youth in America: Critical Whiteness Studies in the Classroom* Routledge Research in Educational Equality and Diversity. New York: Routledge, 2018.

Visweswaran, Kamala. "Diaspora by Design: Flexible Citizenship and South Asians in U.S. Racial Formations." *Diaspora: A Journal of Transnational Studies* 6, no. 1 (1997): 5–29.

Womack, Deanna Ferree. "Transnational Christianity and Converging Identities: Arabic Protestant Churches in New Jersey." In *Religion, Migration and Identity: Methodological and Theological Explorations*, edited by Martha Frederiks and Dorottya Nagy, 112–131. Leiden: Brill, 2016.

PART III

CONFLUENCES: MIGRATION, URBANIZATION, AND INTERCULTURALITY

8

POLYCENTRIC WORLD CHRISTIANITY COMES TO WINNIPEG, MANITOBA: THE RESPONSES OF EURO-CANADIAN CONGREGATIONS

Peter Bush

Pastors and Leaders Prayer is a monthly gathering of 150 pastors, youth pastors, directors of parachurch organizations, and other church leaders in Winnipeg, Manitoba, Canada. The draw of the group is the encouragement, prayer, and networking it offers to those who attend. Those gathered include Filipinos, Koreans, Africans, South Asians, Arabs, Metis, and Euro-Canadians for Winnipeg is a multiethnic city. This month, those speaking to the gathering include a Nigerian church planter, a Mennonite who grew up in Belize, a first-generation immigrant from the British Isles, and a Euro-Canadian who is a long-time Winnipegger. The music sung was firmly rooted in a North American worship style, showing little influence from the variety of cultures present in the room. The prayers in small group were entirely in English, although speakers of many other languages were present in the room.

Growing attention is paid by the scholarly community to the various expressions of World Christianity being brought by migrant groups arriving in North America and Western Europe. Jehu J. Hanciles's significant work provides a lens through which to explore the connections between migration and the spread of Majority World Christianity.[1] Mark Gornik's description of African Independent churches and other African churches in New York not only provides a case study, but also gives people outside New York ways of framing what is taking place in their own community.[2]

---

[1] Jehu J. Hanciles, *Beyond Christendom: Globalization, African Migration, and the Transformation of the West* (Maryknoll, NY: Orbis Books, 2008).

[2] Mark R. Gornik, *Word Made Global: Stories of African Christianity in New York City* (Grand Rapids, MI: W.B. Eerdmans Publishing, 2011).

The essays published in *Church in an Age of Global Migration* push the story beyond African migration to North America to highlight the worldwide nature of migration and its impact on the church and other religious institutions.[3] These studies and others like them have allowed Afe Adogame and James Spickard to discern seven patterns among the case studies and academic descriptions of the migration of world Christian communities to new contexts.[4] The seven patterns are: Ellis island, religious bi-localism, religious cacophony, reverse mission or missionary rebound, South-South religious trade, transnational organization theory, and deterritorialized religious identity.[5]

The Ellis Island model, named for the island in New York City harbor through which millions of new arrivals to the United States passed, describes an assumption that immigrants will leave behind patterns of life from the Old Country, including religious practices, to become American. This was previously the dominant way of understanding immigration.[6] Gleaning their research on "a very complex transnational religious scene," Adogame and Spickard identify six additional patterns.

Religious bi-localism occurs when immigrants bring religious practices from their home country and maintain those practices in the host country through the establishment of institutions and social structures. The migrants, while living in the host community, maintain a vibrant connection with the home country and its practices and religious developments.[7] Transnational religious communities living out this bi-localism seek partners in the host country with whom to engage. As will be discussed, that engagement can take a variety of forms. A second form of religious bi-localism, religious cacophony, identifies bi-local religious groups that have not engaged with the host society or partnered with the religious groups with an established presence in the host community; instead these bi-local groups have become additional religious presences in the crowded buffet of religious offerings already present in many multi-ethnic nations.[8] The lack of partnership with religious groups established in the host community may be the result of not finding a welcoming partner as much as a desire from the bi-local religious community wishing to hold the host culture at arm's length.

---

[3] Susanna Snyder, Joshua Ralston, and Agnes M. Brazal, eds., *Church in an Age of Global Migration: A Moving Body* (London: Palgrave Macmillan, 2016).

[4] Afe Adogame and James V. Spickard, eds., *Religion Crossing Boundaries: Transnational Religious and Social Dynamics in Africa and the New African Diaspora* (Boston: Brill, 2010), 7–20.

[5] Spickard, *Religion*, 11.

[6] Spickard, *Religion*, 9–10.

[7] Spickard, *Religion*, 11–12.

[8] Spickard, *Religion*, 13.

The next three approaches are clustered together for they "break the stereotype that places the North Atlantic at the center of the religious universe," each illustrating "a kind of religious action that may include the West, but which does not privilege it."[9] Reverse missions, or missionary rebound, describe the phenomenon where parts of the world that once received missionaries are now sending missionaries to the regions from which the first missionaries came.[10] For example, having adopted the missionaries' message, Asian and African Christians have migrated to North America and Europe taking the gospel with them. Some reverse missionaries migrate with the understanding they are missionaries; others arrive in what they perceived to be a Christian country and discover it is not and begin the work of evangelization. South-South religious trade occurs when a religious community in the Global South sends missionaries to another country or region in Global South.[11] Finally, some religious organizations that cross-national boundaries find themselves shaped by their transnational nature.

The diverse ethnic and national voices bring unexpected agenda items to the conversation, such as economic inequality and power imbalances. In addressing these challenges, the transnational religious organization as a whole is changed.[12] Finally, transnational imagined community allows deterritorialized migrants from a number of regions to find connection in an imagined community. Some migrants' experience of moving frequently from place to place for work or to be free from danger leaves them without a place of stability and belonging, a place to call "home." Joining with others, of diverse ethnic and cultural backgrounds, who share the same unsettled life, they create home in an imagined community. A diaspora community, sharing dislocation as a common element turns to corporate religious practice to find a place of belonging. Living in hope, the community gathers to worship and to encourage one another in a space of belonging and safety, reminding each other that a better world awaits.

The research on "a very complex transnational religious scene" has generally focused on the newly arrived expressions of World Christianity. The response of the recipient culture, and more specifically the Christian churches in the recipient culture, has not been brought to the fore. This essay interrogates how older, established congregations in the Euro-Canadian receiving culture respond to the arrival of a variety of expressions of World Christianity in their community. These established congregations, in addition to having been worshipping communities for

---

[9] Spickard, *Religion*, 13.
[10] Spickard, *Religion*, 13–14.
[11] Spickard, *Religion*, 15.
[12] Spickard, *Religion*, 15, 16.

often many years, frequently have buildings, links in the community, and physical and spiritual presence in their neighborhoods. The discussion will use the list from Adogame and Spickard to give theoretical context for the approaches that will be highlighted. Given the complex nature of the transnational religious scene, there will not always be a one-to-one correlation, at times an overlapping of approaches will be observed.

To make the exploration manageable, the question is being asked of primarily Protestant and Pentecostal Euro-Canadian congregations in Winnipeg, Manitoba. The choice of Winnipeg is the result of two factors: First, it is where I live, making it easier to do the research. Second, Winnipeg is a culturally diverse city. The cultural diversity produces a variety of intercultural connections that provide a rich collection of cross-cultural contexts to analyze in seeking to find patterns and common approaches in those connections between established congregations in the receiving culture and the newer arrived world Christian communities. Generally, Pentecostal and Protestant congregations have an administrative autonomy that provides opportunity to compare and contrast different congregations within the same theological family.

Situating Winnipeg

Winnipeg, Manitoba, is a city of 705,244 (2016) in the east-west center of Canada. Once called "the Chicago of the North," it is 500 miles away from the next community of equal or greater size. The first people at the forks of the Red and Assiniboine Rivers, which is the heart of the city, were the indigenous people of the Plains. The Oodena, a sacred site at the meeting of the two rivers, is a reminder of the spiritual life in this place before the arrival of the fur traders and the settlers. Eighty-four thousand Winnipeggers, 12 percent of the population, self-identify as indigenous people, just over half of whom are Metis, having both indigenous and settler ancestors.[13] Throughout the discussion, indigenous will be used referring to the first people of Canada, sometimes called aboriginal people or native people.

During the years of settlement (1870–1914), Winnipeg was the gateway to Canada's West. As successive waves of migrants passed through the city, some stayed, establishing roots, and contributing to the complex mix of cultures present in the city. Annually, Winnipeg hosts Folklarama, a two-week celebration of the cultural diversity of the city, with over twenty-five cultures celebrated. The migrant communities have established places of worship and so churches, mosques, synagogues, temples, and other sacred meeting places are part of the city's landscape.

[13] "Census Profile, 2016 Census, Winnipeg, City [Census subdivision], Manitoba," accessed September 2, 2018, https://tinyurl.com/y6q7dcmq.

The first Christian witnesses were French Roman Catholics, followed by English Anglicans, and then Scottish Presbyterians. None of that makes Winnipeg unique. Following the 1896 election of the Liberals under Prime Minister Wilfrid Laurier, Clifford Sifton as Minister of the Interior, opened Canada's doors to mass immigration. German speakers, Mennonites and Lutherans and Baptists, established their presence on the church scene of Winnipeg. Lutherans remain a strong presence in the city. Forty congregations in the city identify themselves as Mennonite. Opening the doors to mass immigration also meant the arrival of significant numbers of Ukrainian Orthodox in Winnipeg and on the Canadian prairies. Here was the beginning of a polycentric Christianity. Ukrainian Orthodox priests were slow in following the migrants and there was competition within the existing Winnipeg church community in doing ministry with people coming from the Ukraine. The Roman Catholics claimed the Ukrainians as theirs, but did little to adapt to the linguistic or liturgical preferences of Ukrainian Orthodox parishioners, which alienated many who were skeptical of Roman Catholic motives. The Methodists welcomed any Ukrainian who attended their churches, but did little to adapt to their linguistic and liturgical practices. The Presbyterian Church in Canada created a separate hybrid denomination, the Independent Greek Church, within the Presbyterian denomination that blended Presbyterian and Orthodox liturgies and theology. The Independent Greek Church, so named because of its liturgical practices rooted in John of Chrysostom, had a catechism that, while affirming a thoroughly Protestant understanding of justification, named seven sacraments while holding up communion and baptism as the most important. This experiment collapsed in the early 1910s as the Presbyterian Church became an increasingly centralized modern denomination. The distinctive church domes of Ukrainian Orthodox architecture bear witness to the ongoing presence of Ukrainian Christianity in Winnipeg.[14]

During the two world wars and through the 1950s, immigration to Winnipeg came largely from Europe, with new arrivals fitting into the existing denominational networks. For example, many Dutch immigrants who came following the Second World War became Presbyterian, while others established Reformed Church congregations. During the 1960s, a new story began to be written as immigrants from non-European countries became a growing presence in Winnipeg. The 2016 Census reported 25 percent of Winnipeggers had been born outside of Canada or the United States.

---

[14] Peter Bush, *Western Challenge: The Presbyterian Church in Canada's Mission on the Prairies and North, 1885–1925* (Winnipeg, MB: J. Gordon Shillingford Publishing, 2000), 141–150.

The largest group of more recent immigrants in Winnipeg is Filipino. In 1959, four Filipino nurses arrived in Winnipeg. The flow of immigration from the Philippines that remained slow through much of the 1960s had grown by 2005 to become an annual influx of 4,000 and 5,000 Filipino immigrants. By 2016, 73,000 Winnipeggers (10 percent) identified ethnically as Filipino. Africans are migrating to Winnipeg in significant numbers; over 7,000 between 2011 and 2016. The same census reveals that 16,000 Winnipeggers were born in Africa, primarily from Nigeria and Rwanda/Burundi/Congo, with a significant Egyptian presence. Since 2016, Syrians, Somalis, and Sudanese have been among the new arrivals to Winnipeg. The Filipinos and the African community are having a visible impact on the church in Winnipeg. The Filipinos are filling the pews of the Catholic churches in the city and leading to the opening of new Protestant churches, Egyptians have made Saint Mark Coptic Orthodox Church one of the largest congregations in the city, and sub-Saharan Africans are opening new congregations, sometimes independently and sometimes in partnership with established congregations.[15]

Fifteen percent of Winnipeggers (100,000) are immigrants to Canada, having arrived between 2001 and 2016, with half (50,000) of them arriving in the last five years. Some further census data will provide a fuller picture of the multiethnic face of Winnipeg. South-Asian is the way 37,500 people in Winnipeg identify their ethnic background, half of whom claim Punjabi as their mother tongue. China (including Hong Kong) is the birthplace for 9,000 Winnipeggers; with almost 15,000 Winnipeggers having either Mandarin or Cantonese as their mother tongue. The self-identifying Arab population is 4,500.[16]

The new arrivals are coming to a city full of churches. Thus, congregations have responded to the new arrivals in a variety of ways. Five patterns of response are outlined and placed in conversation with the seven approaches noted by Adogame and Spickard. No claim is being made for the six patterns being definitive; hopefully, the categories will stimulate a conversation about how congregations in host cultures welcome new arrivals from polycentric Christianity. These patterns arise from observation and reflection on what is taking place in Winnipeg, a community in which I have lived for twelve years. The observations arose through participant observation, conversation with church leaders (both lay people and ordained) in both the newly arrived communities and the existing communities, and my functioning for three years as crosscultural liaison for the Presbyterian Presbytery of Winnipeg.

---

[15] "Census Profile, 2016, Winnipeg," accessed September 2, 2018.
[16] "Census Profile, 2016, Winnipeg," accessed September 2, 2018.

Denying or ignoring polycentric Christian communities

For some Christians living in Winnipeg, the idea that there are Christians in the Middle East or China, as examples, is unimaginable. Shocked looks appear on the faces of some regular church attenders when they are told that there are Arabs living in Winnipeg who are Christians. Many churchgoers are committed to the narrative that says North America and Europe are Christian and Arabs coming to Canada are homogeneously Muslim. Many Euro-Canadian Christians in Winnipeg are unaware of the size and dynamism of World Christianity. As a result, they brush aside, as aberrations from the norm, any signs of World Christianity in their own congregations let alone recognize the presence of World Christian communities in their neighborhoods. The myth that Western Christianity is majority Christianity is fed by the media's frequent portrayal of Christianity as a Western religion. When Christians from the majority world receive media attention, the stories frequently highlight the ways in which the World Christian community being described is different than Western Christianity, leaving the impression that the World Christian community is somehow syncretistic and not "really" Christian. Such a viewpoint links with Adogame and Spickard's comments about the three approaches that "break the stereotype that places the North Atlantic at the center of the religious universe."

Central to denying or ignoring the presence of World Christian communities from the majority world is the contention that the World Christian communities are not "our kind of Christian." One of the largest Christian congregations in Winnipeg is Saint Mark Coptic Orthodox Church. Yet, only in the last five to seven years have Euro-Canadian Protestant church leaders in Winnipeg generally become aware of their presence. This awareness has not been because of a growing appreciation for the presence of Saint Mark in Winnipeg, but because the persecution of Coptic Christians in Egypt has led to an awareness of Coptic Christians present in Winnipeg. Almost no Protestant church leaders have sought to build bridges to this large Christian presence in Winnipeg.

Even more unacknowledged is the presence of African Initiated Churches in the city. The Deeper Life Bible Church, part of Pastor W.F. Kumuyi's Deeper Life Ministry that originated in Nigeria, purchased a closed Presbyterian church building in May 2013 to be the home for their Winnipeg ministry. The members of the selling congregation, when asked at a presbytery meeting about the congregation purchasing the building, could describe almost nothing about Deeper Life Ministry. They spoke in such a way that hearers were left wondering if the members of Deeper Life were Christians. Despite having a building and a campus ministry at the

University of Manitoba in Winnipeg, Deeper Life remains unknown to most Euro-Canadian Christians largely because the church is linked to an African denomination and not a Euro-Canadian one.[17]

Glory and Peace International, an independent congregation led by a clergy couple from Nigeria, is known for its building on Main St., but few of Winnipeg's Euro-Canadian Christians know about its back story or its ministry in the north end of the city. Apostle Mike Efezino, the leader of Glory and Peace, nurtured a connection with Elijah Harper, a significant indigenous political figure, an outspoken Christian who served in both the Manitoba Legislature and the Canadian House of Commons. When Harper died in May 2013, much to the surprise of many, Efezino led the funeral service.[18] This connection between a Nigerian Christian leader and an indigenous Canadian Christian politician happened completely outside the awareness of the dominant Euro-Canadian church, a variation on the "South-South religious trade" from Adogame and Spickard's list.

Euro-Canadian Protestants in Winnipeg who are convinced that Christianity is a Western religion are frequently ignorant of the polycentric forms of Christianity present in the city.

Assimilating persons from world Christian communities into existing Euro-Canadian expressions of church

For many years, church leaders in North America have declared the large-scale immigration from other parts of the world to be God's action bringing the mission field to the very doors of the North American church.[19] North American Protestants were encouraged to reach out to their neighbors who were coming from Africa and Asia, the Middle East, and Latin America; an approach based on the assumption that these new arrivals were not Christian and were in need of conversion. Confusion arises when Euro-Canadian Christians in bearing witness to their neighbors about their faith in Christ discover that their neighbors are Christians, but with a denominational affiliation they have never heard of before. Being welcoming, the Euro-Canadians invite the new arrivals to their congregation, providing rides, introducing them to people at the church, all the time anticipating the day the stranger will be like everyone else.

---

[17] Regarding "Deeper Life Bible Church," accessed September 24, 2018, www.dclm-ca.org/locations/manitoba/. Information about the sale of the property from author's notes, Minutes, Presbytery of Winnipeg, The Presbyterian Church in Canada, May 16, 2013.

[18] "Harper's Body to Lie in State Today," *Winnipeg Free Press*, May 19, 2013, 3.

[19] See for example, Terry Muck, *Alien Gods on American Turf* (Wheaton, IL: Victor Books, 1990).

This approach is a variation on the Ellis Island assimilationist model identified by Adogame and Spickard that is present in wider culture and seeks to assist new arrivals in acclimatizing to the dominant culture. A congregational lay leader expressed the view succinctly when she said of a Congolese in the congregation, "I thought that when his English improved, he would be just like us."[20] These congregations and individuals while being genuinely welcoming provide limited space for expressions of Christian practice that are markedly different than the ones present in the dominant Euro-Canadian Christian culture. A Congolese pastor who broke into song in the middle of his sermon was chastised by elders in the congregation.[21] A Korean pastor who sought to introduce the practice of early morning prayer to the Euro-Canadian congregation he served, was accused of creating divisions in the church between those who were more spiritual and those who were less spiritual.[22] These Euro-Canadian congregations celebrate the multicultural cuisine on offer at the congregational potluck, but offer little space for expressions of polycentric Christianity in worship or preaching.

This lack of space for alternative expressions of Christianity leaves the new arrivals with three choices: 1) leave to find a worshipping community where there is room for their Christian practices, 2) assimilate into the congregation, becoming part of the dominant church culture, or 3) remain on the edge of the congregation's life always feeling like an outsider. Examples of congregations offering welcome to new arrivals willing to "be like us" abound in Winnipeg. Appeals to anecdotal evidence are notoriously inaccurate for producing anything approaching statistical certainty. However, in most gatherings of pastors of Euro-Canadian Protestant or Pentecostal congregations, half of those present will have stories of non-Euro-Canadian church attenders some of whom stayed briefly and moved on, and others who stayed putting down roots in the congregation. Often, individuals in the visible minority groups have assimilated into the congregation, at times even becoming leaders. A Trinidadian joined a Euro-Canadian congregation, and over time was elected an elder of the congregation, serving as the congregation's representative in the higher levels of the denomination. When asked how others in the congregation saw him, the Trinidadian replied, "I am Caucasian, they think I am from Canada."[23] The assimilation is so complete that the individual's minority status is unrecognized by the dominant culture of the church. "They are like us," is the way the Euro-Canadians in the congregation describe them.

[20] Gretta Redahl, interview by author, June 20, 2015.
[21] Gretta Redahl, interview by author, June 20, 2015.
[22] Sean Kim, interview by author, April 15, 2014.
[23] Sam Raman-Nair, interview by author, May 17, 2012.

Creating space for groups from world Christian communities within a Euro-Canadian culture congregation

Some Euro-Canadian congregations, recognizing the presence of World Christianity in Winnipeg, give space to those various expressions by creating opportunities for those groups to have worshipping communities within the larger congregation. In particular, larger and multi-site Euro-Canadian congregations have the resources and flexible structures to do this. The World Christian worshipping communities are not independent of the host congregation.

Calvary Temple, a large downtown Pentecostal Assemblies of Canada congregation, has sought to develop this approach. The church's location places it in the midst of a large community of newly arrived French-speaking Africans. Calvary Temple employs Pastor James Okot, a French-speaking Congolese, to lead a congregation of predominantly Africans who meet Sunday afternoons for worship. Two English language services take place in the morning. Okot has ongoing connections with Christian communities in Congo and has led preaching missions back to Congo. Under the umbrella of the English-speaking Euro-Canadian congregation, the French-speaking African congregation has space to express its worship style and approach. The congregational structures are clear; Calvary Temple is a Euro-Canadian congregation with an ethnic ministry.[24]

Riverwood Church in Winnipeg is a multi-site congregation with seven worship gatherings, one is described as "African Worship Community" that is led by two immigrants from Africa, Pastor Joseph Bagaza and Pastor Richard Mufaridji. Riverwood is an independent Pentecostal congregation. These two had their pastoral gifts recognized after their arrival in Canada and took some theological training in Canada, however, they wanted to be ordained by a leader from Congo so that their receiving a blessing from their homeland would be evident to all. This is a form of bi-localism—fully aware of the Canadian context, but also wanting the blessing from the church in Africa.[25]

Both Calvary Temple and Riverwood Church are creating contexts where the first generation of immigrants can find a place where they are comfortable to worship within the aegis of a Euro-Canadian congregation. The decision-making power of these ethnically-distinct worship communities is limited, and both Calvary Temple and Riverwood offer youth programming where young people from all backgrounds are in one

---

[24] "Our Team, Calvary Temple," accessed September 2, 2018, www.ctwinnipeg.com/who-we-are.

[25] Pastor Joseph Bagaza and Pastor Richard Mufaridji, interview by author, August 22, 2018.

context. As Hanciles notes, the future of such ethnically-distinct worshipping communities depends on the decisions made by the second and third generations, "a great deal will depend on how much the second and third generations follow in the footsteps of the first."[26] The approach Calvary Temple and Riverwood have taken is to create temporary spaces for expressions of World Christianity within the larger entity as way stations for the first-generation of arrivals. In relationship to Adogame and Spickard's list, the approach taken mitigates against World Christian communities becoming simply part of the "religious cacophony," for they have a place in the life of an established congregation, yet they face the very real possibility of assimilation as pointed to by the Ellis Island approach.

Nurturing the development of polycentric expressions of the church as self-determining congregations

As a range of expressions of World Christianity have arrived in Winnipeg, some Euro-Canadian church leaders have actively supported the development of congregations that worship in languages other than English and French, led by pastors from various parts of the world. This support has led to the establishment of what are sometimes referred to as "ethnic" congregations. This approach is deeper than the landlord-tenant relationship that a number of Euro-Canadian congregations have with the ethnic congregations that meet in their buildings. Sometimes, as in the case of Whyte Ridge Baptist Church and Winnipeg Somang Presbyterian Church (a Korean-speaking congregation), a landlord-tenant relationship may evolve into something more significant. These two congregations have moved from being landlord (the Baptists) and tenant (the Presbyterians) to being partners on mission trips to South America and working together to offer conversational English classes. As Whyte Ridge Church builds a new building, the blueprints have always included an office for the pastor of Somang Church, for as the Baptist pastor said, "They are coming with us to the new building."[27]

Presbyterian, United, and Mennonite denominational judicatories have encouraged and financially supported the development of non-Euro-Canadian congregations in the city, giving these new congregations full status within the denomination.[28] The Presbytery of Winnipeg of the Presbyterian Church in Canada, aware of Arabic-speaking Presbyterians

---

[26] Jehu J. Hanciles, "Migration and Mission: Some Implications for the Twenty-first Century Church," *International Bulletin of Missionary Research* 27, no. 4 (October, 2003): 146–153.

[27] Pastor Terry Janke, interview with the author, March 20, 2016.

[28] For further discussion of how various denominations have done this in Canada, see Paul Bramadat and David Seljak, eds., *Christianity and Ethnicity in Canada* (Toronto: University of Toronto Press, 2008).

in Winnipeg, arranged for a pastor from Jordan to come to lead a newly formed congregation. Euro-Canadian congregations within the presbytery provided some funding and used their connections to help this congregation come into being. The resulting congregation, Lighthouse Evangelical Arabic Church, is taking its place at the table as a full status congregation. It therefore plays a role in defining the policy and direction of the denomination and thereby impacts Euro-Canadian Presbyterian congregations through its presence in the decision-making processes of the church. Two examples of the impact of Lighthouse Church is the discussion started by the congregation's name: First, evangelical has quite different meanings in the Middle East and in mainline Protestant circles in North America. Second, conversations about Syrian refugees take on new meaning when those refugees are found in one of the congregations of presbytery.

Some of the communities of faith arriving in Canada from other parts of the world have links to denominational missions that had their genesis in North America or were staffed by missionaries from North America. When immigrants who have Presbyterian roots, for example, arrive in Canada and approach a congregation for services in Korean, as an example, the default position is to help them form a worshipping community that will evolve into a Korean speaking congregation. Often, these newly arrived immigrants have in their midst persons who are willing and able to lead the newly formed congregations, using the language and cultural practices of the church in the homeland. While Euro-Canadian church leaders offer worship, meeting and office space free of charge or at a reduced cost, arrange for the direct provision of financial grants, and assist the independent congregations in dealing with government and, at times, church bureaucracies, the newly formed congregations remain independent entities. These self-propagating, self-governing, and frequently self-supporting congregations have autonomy. This autonomy is important as these congregations seek to maintain their distinct expression of World Christianity.

In relation to the approaches that form the background of our discussion, this approach connects with bi-localism as these World Christian congregations stand in two contexts simultaneously. Further, it also bears the marks of reverse mission as those impacted by missions to their home countries now come bringing their faith to the countries who sent missionaries in the first place. As members of denominations with international scope or transnational relationships move to Winnipeg, they do so as part of transnational organizations.

Assisting immigrant congregational leaders from polycentric Christianity understand the Canadian context

The old narrative declared the mission field had come to North America.[29] The new reality is North America is the mission field and polycentric Christianity is coming to share the good news of the gospel with North Americans. A significant number of the newly arrived Christian communities in Winnipeg, especially those with African roots or Korean roots, have a desire to proclaim the gospel in the new land they call "home." Shalom Christian Outreach, started in 2011 as a congregation for refugees from the Rwandan genocide, within three years of starting had stopped using any African language because as Pastor Mutabazi Shadrack said, "We want to tell Canadian culture the good news and that means we need to use English."[30]

A Baptist pastor in Winnipeg, the Rev. Joe Welty, who served for five years in a research capacity in a megachurch, recognized some church leaders from Africa were making significant missteps in relating to the patterns and cultural norms of Canada as they sought to proclaim the gospel.[31] For example, the use of inclusive language for people, and the role of women in general. Welty connected with Carey Hall (the Baptist theological college in Vancouver) and arranged for the Carey Institute to be established in Winnipeg. The program teaches intensive courses using congregational pastors from Winnipeg as faculty. Courses include Canadian History, Canadian Church History, Systematic Theology, Biblical Exegesis, and Pastoral Counseling. All these courses are taught highlighting the Canadian context. The program does not seek to turn students into Canadian pastors, rather the goal is to help participants understand their new context so they can more effectively do crosscultural ministry.

I have taught in the program, and found myself challenged by the students to deepen my awareness of how my theological understanding is limited by my context. In conversation about Canada's failure to live up to treaties signed with the First Nations in Canada, I was forced to confront the fact that Canada's reneging on the treaties was a violation of the biblical injunction to keep one's oath even to one's hurt (Ps 15:4). Further, the evangelistic zeal of the pastors forced me to re-examine my commitment to answering the call to go and tell. This training provides a context in which Euro-Canadian teachers open themselves and Canadian culture to critique offered by pastors from World Christianity.

---

[29] See Muck, *Alien Gods*, 4–11.
[30] Pastor Mutabazi Shadrack, interview by the author, January 15, 2015.
[31] Pastor Joe Welty, interview by the author, November, 12, 2014.

A number of Korean clergies have demonstrated a desire to reach out to the indigenous peoples of Winnipeg and beyond. This provides an interesting reversal in roles. The Euro-Canadian church with its dismal track record of failure regarding engagement with indigenous peoples is being shown new ways of living out mission by the Korean church. The Rev. Saehoon Lee takes a group from Winnipeg Somang Church to a community two hours outside of Winnipeg to provide a meal, offer hairdressing, and make connection with aboriginal people.[32] The Rev. Jeanie Lee does a similar thing, leading her ethnically mixed congregation to provide monthly services and a meal at the Birdtail Reserve.[33] These examples of service and long-standing commitment challenge Euro-Canadian congregations, many of whom have little connection with indigenous people, to engage with aboriginal communities.

The reverse mission vision of many within the World Christian community is evident in the students in the Carey Institute and in the outreach of the Korean Christian community. The Carey Institute and such training programs, have the goal of allowing new arrivals to Winnipeg to do more than just add to the religious cacophony.

Creating an intercultural congregation

Creating an intercultural congregation is an exercise in calling participants to an imagined community; to a de-territorialized religious identity.

The Church of the Rock in Winnipeg describes itself as "a charismatic, interdenominational, evangelical church of people from a huge variety of backgrounds."[34] Hung from the rafters of the sanctuary are the flags of more than 150 countries, a statement that Christians of every country in the world are welcome to attend this imagined community that is beyond national lines. However, the congregation's worship style is contemporary Euro-Canadian showing little impact from the polycentric Christianity present in the congregation each Sunday. The leadership at the front each Sunday is Euro-Canadian, even as the congregational leadership seeks to promote itself as being beyond national lines.

City Church, the creation of Grant Memorial Baptist Church, also seeks to be an intercultural church, "a place of equality for the nations to meet and passionately worship Jesus Christ."[35] Leaders at Grant Memorial realized two things. First, a large number of new arrivals to Winnipeg were Christians, and second, these new arrivals could not be easily assimilated into the existing life of Grant Memorial Church, a middle-class

---

[32] Rev. Saehoon Lee, interview by the author, September 15, 2018.
[33] Correspondence with the Rev. Jeanie Lee, March 10, 2019.
[34] "Church of the Rock," accessed September 2, 2018, www.churchoftherock.ca/.
[35] "City Church, Winnipeg," accessed June 18, 2019, http://citychurchwinnipeg.ca/.

Euro-Canadian congregation. Therefore, Grant Memorial provided the funds for a new congregation to be formed that, from its inception, would be multiethnic. As City Church passes its tenth anniversary, it is now a selfsupporting congregation, steering its own course.[36]

City Church says of itself: "We like to describe ourselves as an intentionally international and intercultural church. We believe that a church must be more than multicultural in its ministry; it must be intercultural. To only be multicultural is to exist in groups near each other, but to be intercultural is to develop friendships between cultures and to see this diversity naturally reflected in ministry, worship, and leadership."[37] English is the language of worship at the 10:30 a.m. service on Sundays; however, some songs are sung in the original language they were written in with an English translation displayed on a screen. Simultaneous translation is offered in a variety of languages. Prayers are invited to be made in the mother tongue of the prayer. Additional fellowship gatherings occur on Sunday afternoons in Swahili, Karen, Chin, and Eritrean. The leadership at City Church is very aware that many who attend share a common experience of suffering. This common experience grounds "the unity in the ethnically diverse church, whose members have suffered so much," an imagined, a de-territorialized religious community.[38]

Conclusion

The monthly gathering of pastors and church leaders for conversation and prayer is a context where Euro-Canadian and non-Western expressions of Christianity meet. Yet, the circle of those present has yet to move beyond the Protestant and Pentecostal. Further, the leadership of the gathering remains firmly in the hands of Euro-Canadian pastors. Five of the six approaches described are present among those who gather each month. (The presence of World Christian communities in Winnipeg is hard to deny when representatives are beside you in song and prayer.) No claim is being made that these six categories are somehow definitive. Rather, they describe the range of approaches Euro-Canadian Protestant and Pentecostal churches have used to respond to the arrival of polycentric, World Christianity in Winnipeg. The degree of openness that Winnipeg's existing churches show to Christians coming from other parts of the world will remain an important question moving forward. If most Euro-Canadian congregations continue to deny or ignore the presence of

---

[36] Rev. Joe Welty, interview by the author, November 12, 2014.
[37] "About Us, City Church," accessed September 25, 2018, http://www.citychurch winnipeg.ca/about-us/.
[38] "About Us, City Church," accessed September 25, 2018, http://www.citychurch winnipeg.ca/about-us/.

polycentric, World Christian communities in the city there will be little opportunity for Western expressions of Christianity to be enlivened by engagement with non-Western expressions of Christianity. At the same time, the non-Western expressions of Christianity will not be able to benefit from the encouragement and nurturing that leaders from existing expressions of Christianity might be able to offer. The continuing disconnection would leave the emergence of intercultural congregations where people of every tongue and ethnicity join together for worship and prayer a distant hope.

Bibliography

Adogame, Afe, and James V. Spickard, eds. *Religion Crossing Boundaries: Transnational Religious and Social Dynamics in Africa and the New African Diaspora*. Boston: Brill, 2010.

Bramadat, Paul, and David Seljak, eds. *Christianity and Ethnicity in Canada*. Toronto: University of Toronto Press, 2008.

Bush, Peter. *Western Challenge: The Presbyterian Church in Canada's Mission on the Prairies and North, 1885–1925*. Winnipeg, MB: J. Gordon Shillingford Publishing, 2000.

Gornik, Mark R. *Word Made Global: Stories of African Christianity in New York City*. Grand Rapids, MI: W.B. Eerdmans Publishing, 2011.

Hanciles, Jehu J. *Beyond Christendom: Globalization, African Migration, and the Transformation of the West*. Maryknoll, NY: Orbis Books, 2008.

———. "Migration and Mission: Some Implications for the Twenty-first Century Church." *International Bulletin of Missionary Research* 27, no. 4 (October 2003): 146–153.

Muck, Terry. *Alien Gods on American Turf*. Wheaton, IL: Victor Books, 1990.

Snyder, Susanna, Joshua Ralston, and Agnes M. Brazal, eds. *Church in an Age of Global Migration: A Moving Body*. London: Palgrave Macmillan, 2016.

9

DEMANDS OF URBANISATION AND RURAL MIGRATION IN INDIA: A CALL FOR MULTICULTURAL LEADERSHIP[1]

Atola Longkumer

INTRODUCTION

Cities are centers of economic growth, activity, and innovation. They are hubs of education, the arts, and the sciences. Cities are also the forward edge of emergent matters facing our world in the environment and changing climate, culture, housing, and health. And some of the most immense challenges of urban life are faced by the over one billion people who live in favelas, townships, and shantytowns of Africa, Asia, and Latin America. Others live in refugee camps that have become cities.... Because cities are central to our world, we must also see their vital potential for addressing the future.

Mark R. Gornik and Maria Liu Wong[2]

The authors of the book *Stay in the City*, Mark R. Gornik and Maria Liu Wong, articulate succinctly the inevitable centrality of urban spaces in the modern world and the multiple intersections they provide to flourishing communities across the globe. Given that cities are places where people from diverse cultures come together, being also crucial centres of economic and political power, they challenge individuals and communities

---

[1] An earlier essay on leadership in the context of theological education was published in *Transformative Leadership and Theology of Life: Festschrift for Dietrich Werner*, eds. Uta Andree, Atola Longkumer, and Po Ho Huang (Oxford: Regnum Books International, 2016).

[2] Mark R. Gornik and Maria Liu Wong, *Stay in the City: How Christian Faith is Flourishing in an Urban World* (Grand Rapids, MI: W.B. Eerdmans Publishing, 2017), 11.

to practise tolerance and fairness. In other words, urbanisation to some extent provides opportunities to live the ethos of inclusive hospitality. Cities are not, however, places of blissful harmony. In fact, cities can be places of contest and conflict between different constituents. Furthermore, as much as they are centres of power, cities are also places of brokenness, instability, and vulnerability. Therefore, urbanisation also demands critical assessment and calls for a deeper understanding of the factors that generate rapid urban growth.

Cities are the epitome of urbanisation. Therefore, as one considers the gathering of Christians from different sociocultural landscapes, ecclesiastical traditions, political locations, and economic positions, cities present a dynamic context for conversation on World Christianity. The witness and lived expression of the *evangelium* is made possible in a space with significant possibilities for the pursuit of the good life, which must be fundamentally inclusive and marked by compassion. On the other hand, the possibilities of urbanisation can also be perilous, in that the reproduction of structures of inequalities and exploitation remains a threat, especially if practices of conventional discrimination—for instance, caste practice and gender inequalities—remain unchecked.

Discussing the complexities and ambivalence of cities, Dale T. Irvin highlights the crucial possibilities they create. As he surmises,

> Cities have always been places of differentiation, places where strangers became neighbors, and neighbors became strangers. One form of differentiation that they fostered and intensified was what we call "class." The extremes of rich and poor were—and are—in fact a function of the city.[3]

The intensity of this differentiation is most observable in the growing disparities between the uber-wealthy and the homeless as evident in some of the global cities of the world such as San Francisco, London, Mumbai, and New York etc.

Apart from class, cities are also places that attract immigrants from rural areas as well as professionals and traders from other urban places.[4] Global cities, in particular, are heterogeneous spaces comprised by a cacophony of cultures, classes, ethnicity, and aesthetics as represented by the multicultural convergences that is urban in essence. They are major

---

[3] Dale T. Irvin, "The Church, the Urban, and the Global: Mission in an Age of Global Cities," *International Bulletin of Missionary Research* 33, no.4 (October 2009): 177.

[4] As Irvin points out, "The merchants from afar contributed much to making the urban a multicultural reality. The modern industrial city accelerated the processes of cultural differentiation by attracting immigrants from distances far away, not only to come and trade, but also to come and work." Irvin, "The Church, the Urban", 178.

sites of economic globalisation. In "global cities," productions are spread beyond an immediate locale, just as consumption is sourced from almost every corner of the globe.[5] Due to the vibrant economic activities in these urban centres, people from all kinds of background are drawn to them for purposes of production and survival.

The rise of metropoles across different regions of the world, their global links, and other phenomena crucial for the reality known as Late Modernity, such as the phenomenon of mass migration, have drastically transformed human societies. The movement of people from village/rural locations to economic and political centres of powers in search of higher education and more opportunities for production and consumption has been central to such changes. Furthermore, due to their size and concentration of power and opportunities, cities have become not only the destination of migrant populations, but also important "passageways."[6]

While there have been movements of people across cultural borders in different periods in history, migration in modern times is unique in its scale and extensive reach to almost every region of the world. People from different regions, nation-states, religiocultural traditions, and diverse socioeconomic locations comprise the movement of people from their domicile to another region or country for a variety of purposes, not least for security and economic reasons. Migration occasions encounters and interactions with different cultures more intensely.[7]

It is also worth noting that the phenomenon of migration is often not discussed as an issue central to the Global North, with political undertones and not without racist connotations. Nevertheless, migration is a global phenomenon that is evident across different nation-states. The contemporary mass movements of people cannot be limited only to migration from the Global South to the Global North; there are massive movements of population also between Global South countries and within nation-states as well. India, for instance, is a nation that produces millions of migrants both outbound and inbound, from within the country as well

---

[5] For a critical discussion on the impacts of globalisation on the need of "spatial" and "territorial" ascendency, see Saskia Sassen, "The Global Cities: Introducing a Concept," *Brown Journal of World Affairs* XI, no. 2 (Winter/Spring, 2005): 1–18.

[6] A phenomenon that, as Dale Irvin shows, was also true to ancient metropoles. Irvin, "The Church, the Urban," 178.

[7] For an excellent theological analysis of the phenomenon of migration, wherein the magnitude and the experience of migrants make it imperative to make migration as a locus of theology, see Gemma Cruz, *An Intercultural Theology of Migration: Pilgrims in the Wilderness* (Leiden: Brill, 2010); Daniel G. Groody and Gioacchino Campese, eds., *Promised Land, Perilous Journey: Theological Perspective on Migration* (Notre Dame, IN: University of Notre Dame Press, 2008).

as from the neighbouring nations such as Nepal, Bangladesh, Sri Lanka, and Myanmar.

The contemporary reality of migration has turned urban centres and their inherent levels of differentiations and plurality into important loci for the study of Christianity, particularly as one takes into consideration their intrinsic demand for the engagement and embracing of diversity through a praxis which is inclusive and just. Moreover, one should not forget that the accelerated process of urbanisation, its links to globalisation, and the advent of global cities took shape in the same era when Christianity has seen a seismic development, observable in its drastic demographic changes in recent decades.[8] Consequently, the reality of urbanisation has significant implications for the conditions, expressions, and challenges of a dynamic World Christianity. As Irvin notes, when "city and world are converging formations," there are enormous implications for mission and ministry."[9] Likewise, because of their complexity and diversity, "Cities can be places where signs and countersigns alike of the coming reign of God" can be found.[10]

Anchored on the urban reality of India, this essay will focus on a particular aspect of World Christianity which needs our attention in these times of mass migration and rapid urbanisation: intercultural leadership. As noted earlier, migration brings people from diverse backgrounds to centres of power and possibilities. Migration both creates and feeds urbanisation. Urbanisation, on the other hand, generates conditions for migration. Therefore, urbanisation and migration are intertwined and need to be explored as a pair.

The convergence of people from diverse backgrounds in urban centres is a central mark of contemporary migration across various geographical regions. Generally, migration flows from rural agriculture-based economies to urbanised, industrialised, and highly technologised metropolitan

---

[8] The mission historian Andrew F. Walls was one of the earliest scholars to make this observation, and was followed by other detailed books and statistics. See Andrew F. Walls, *The Missionary Movement in Christian History: Studies in the Transmission of Faith* (Maryknoll, NY: Orbis Books, 1996); Philip Jenkins, *The Next Christendom: The Coming of Global Christianity* (Oxford: Oxford University Press, 2011); Todd M. Johnson and Kenneth R. Ross, eds., *Atlas of Global Christianity* (Edinburgh: Edinburgh University, 2009); for more recent data and analyses, see https://www.gordonconwell.edu/ockenga/research/Quick-Facts-about-Global-Christianity.cfm. It is important to note that numerical realities might not correlate to the power and influence Western nations and Christianity continue to hold sway on global affairs as well as global Christianity, and the social realities of the Global South nations might differ between contexts, particularly, from social and inclusive justice index perspectives.

[9] Irvin, "The Church, the Urban," 177.

[10] Irvin, "The Church, the Urban," 177.

centres, where myriads of cultures converge. Such a convergence does not necessarily diminish existing cultural identities and lived expressions among the migrant groups. The struggle to sustain cultural, religious, and linguistic traditions in urbanised centres is particularly visible in the lives of migrant churches in many urban areas, including major cities in India such as Bangalore, Delhi, and Chennai.[11] As sites of multiethnic friction and intense intercultural relations, these churches necessitate a leadership that can understand the complexity of such locations and properly address the challenges that arise in those contexts.

Considering the Indian context, this essay will discuss the role and nature of Christian leadership that is tuned to the challenges and opportunities of multicultural convergences. The intersection of multiple cultures, plurality of religions, and myriad layers of social class calls for community leaders who are interculturally equipped to advocate for the most vulnerable and for an inclusive way of life.

A discussion of migration that highlights the terrains and conditions of urbanisation forms the backdrop of the essay. The quest for a leadership that is thoroughly intercultural follows the initial section. I conclude with a non-exhaustive list of defining leadership skills that can contribute to mutual coexistence among different identity groups.

WORLD CHRISTIANITY

The study of World Christianity has emerged concomitantly with the demographic shift of Christianity to the Global South. The fact that Christianity has become a world religion,[12] embraced and practised in a variety of ways in almost all the regions and cultures of the world, has augmented the necessity of understanding the phenomenon of Christianity in multiple global locations. By most statistical surveys, Christians in the Global South have outnumbered those in the Global North (Europe and North America) for the first time in more than a thousand years. The exponential growth of Christianity in the Global South as its sway declined in the Global North has been described, analysed, and interpreted in various studies underlining its multiple implications for the expressions, experiences, contours, and features of Christianity in the coming decades.[13]

[11] Bengt G. Karlsson and Dolly Kikon, "Wayfinding: Indigenous Migrants in the Service Sector of Metropolitan India," *Journal of South Asian Studies* 40, no. 3 (2017): 447–462.

[12] Sebastian Kim and Kirsteen Kim, eds., *Christianity as a World Religion* (London: Continuum Books, 2008); See also, Dana L. Robert, *Christian Mission: How Christianity Became a World Religion* (Chichester, UK: Wiley-Blackwell, 2009).

[13] Lamin Sanneh, *Whose Religion Is Christianity? The Gospel beyond the West* (Grand Rapids, MI: W.B. Eerdmans Publishing, 2003); Jehu J. Hanciles, *Beyond Christendom: Globalization, African Migration and the Transformation of*

But, what is World Christianity? One of the earliest attempts to provide a frame for World Christianity came from Dale Irvin, who defined World Christianity as,

> An emerging field that investigates and seeks to understand Christian communities, faith, and practice as they are found on six continents, expressed in diverse ecclesial traditions, and informed by the multitude of historical and cultural experiences in a world that for good and ill is rapidly globalizing. It is concerned with both the diversity of local or indigenous expressions of Christian life and faith throughout the world, and the variety of ways these interact with one another critically and constructively across time and space. It is particularly concerned with under-represented and marginalized communities of faith, resulting in a greater degree of attention being paid to Asian, African, and Latin American experiences; the experiences of marginalized communities within the North Atlantic world; and the experiences of women throughout the world.[14]

World Christianity thus defined has a primary orientation to the understanding of Christianity in cultures which encountered Christian mission and went through multifaceted processes of conversion.[15] A common presumption which accompanied the narrative of conversion for a long time was the reductionist notion that the embracing of Christianity in those contexts created *in toto* a replica of the mission church, without traces of the converts' agency either in the conversion process per se or in the expression of the newly adopted religion, i.e., Christianity. Numerous studies have adequately illustrated that this presumption flies in the face of the evident diversity of expressions of Christianity among the converts which demonstrate the active participation of converts in

---

the West (Maryknoll, NY: Orbis Books, 2008); Afe Adogame, *The African Christian Diaspora: New Currents and Emerging Trends in World Christianity* (London: Bloomsbury, 2013); Jonathan Y. Tan and Anh Q., trans. and eds., *World Christianity: Perspectives and Insights, Essays in Honor of Peter C. Phan* (Maryknoll, NY: Orbis Books, 2016).

[14] Dale T. Irvin, "World Christianity: An Introduction," *The Journal of World Christianity* 1, no.1, 2008, 1–26.

[15] While Christianity consolidated as a powerful movement entangled with political influence by its earliest centuries, and found itself expanding globally by the sixteenth century, notably with the intrepid Jesuits armed with fundamental cultural curiosity, Christianity became a world religion espoused by more cultures, ethnic groups, and languages during the Great Century of Christianity, to use a term coined by Kenneth Scott Latourette. The role of the modern nation of America was no less significant, as many studies have demonstrated. For a recent study, see David A. Hollinger, *Protestants Abroad: How Missionaries Tried to Change the World but Changed America* (Princeton, NJ: Princeton University Press, 2017), 3.

making Christianity their own.[16] World Christianity therefore provides the platform to investigate the nuances, intricacies, and complexities of Christianity in cultures which were introduced to the faith in different historical periods by diverse Christianising movements.

Irvin's definition delineated the salient features of World Christianity, which include the recognition of "indigenous expressions of Christian life and faith" and experiences of the "under-represented" and "experiences of women."[17] World Christianity shifts the lens from an Eurocentric understanding of Christianity, mostly patriarchal and entrenched with a social hierarchy which privileged existing powers, to the borders, being more attentive to the nuances one can find in Christian inception and development in a variety of contexts.

The critical need to lend meaning to the diversities inherent in World Christianity is further explored in the recent book *World Christianity: A Historical and Theological Introduction*, by the mission historian from Northeast India, Lalsangkima Pachuau, who teaches at the Asbury Theological Seminary. According to him, "World Christianity expresses the worldwide character of Christianity as it came to be owned at heart by people of diverse cultures and societies from every region and every continent, and portrayed in the multiplicity of church traditions, cultural expressions of faith-practices, and doctrinal voices. This worldwide, diverse, and multifaceted character of Christianity as a (single) religion is what we have come to call World Christianity."[18]

Despite its connection with globalising and imperialist civilisations, Christianity in its essence is compatible with diverse cultures. Pachuau continues to remark, "An important mark of World Christianity is the multiplicity of the religion's self-expressions in different contexts, traditions, and practices. Christianity's essential nature is to be able to incarnate itself in any context to transform such contexts for the knowledge and likeness of God in Christ."[19] World Christianity, therefore, differentiates itself from Western Christianity by its recognition and retrieving of indigenous expressions, symbols, languages, and practices. The necessity for World Christianity is twofold, as Pachuau underlines: the failure to

---

[16] The work of anthropologists Jean and John Comaroff among the Tsawana of South Africa fundamentally shifted the lens, shedding light on the active involvement of the natives in the process of both conversion and modernisation. See Jean Comaroff and John Comaroff, *Of Revelation and Revolution: Christianity, Colonialism, and Consciousness*, vol. 1 (Chicago, IL: The University of Chicago Press, 1991).

[17] Irvin, "World Christianity."

[18] Lalsangkima Pachuau, *World Christianity: A Historical and Theological Introduction* (Nashville, TN: Abingdon Press, 2018), 3.

[19] Pachuau, *World Christianity*, 3.

recognise indigenous expressions as meaningful, and the imposition of the older Western form of the religion on others as if it represented a universal form.[20]

World Christianity, thus, is comprehensive in its scope. It envisages correcting the wrongs of exclusion of local expressions and dominance of a Euro-centric Christianity. The fact that the diversity of local expressions of Christianity is reckoned with and that women's experience of and within Christianity is considered makes the study of World Christianity promising. Thus, the rise of World Christianity as a way of studying Christianity, which is more inclusive and accommodative of the diversity of human knowledge, experience, and meaning. From this perspective, World Christianity has become a fulcrum to explore the phenomenon of urbanisation wherein intersections of multiple socioeconomic and religiocultural traditions take place.

Raimundo Barreto Jr., in introducing the volume *World Christianity as a Public Religion*, brings a critical point to the category of World Christianity. He cautions against the threat of "idealized notions of World Christianity."[21] It is important therefore to underline that a discourse on World Christianity should not be just a triumphant count of population which makes up the category of World Christianity and a token nod to the so-called indigenous expressions of Christianity in the erstwhile under-represented and excluded communities.[22] Recognising the shift in Christianity and diversities of local expressions of Christianity as World Christianity entails a significant change in the study of Christianity, which is not only limited to expressions conditioned by local cultural symbols, but also include critical re-evaluation of historiography and theological articulations.

The phenomenon of World Christianity also parallels the process of urbanisation, given the projections of sizeable populations inhabiting urban centres in the third millennium. As noted earlier, urbanisation is characterised by diversity and multicultural convergences, and World Christianity incorporates the local expressions and articulations conditioned by different contexts. Pairing World Christianity and urbanisation is crucial to the project of being attentive to the underrepresented and the local nuances of Christian communities. The following section will briefly

---

[20] Pachuau, *World Christianity*, 3.
[21] Raimundo C. Barreto Jr., "Introduction," in *World Christianity as Public Religion*, eds. Raimundo Barreto, Ronaldo Cavalcante, and Wanderley P. da Rosa (Minneapolis, MN: Fortress Press, 2017), 7.
[22] For instance, although Todd M. Johnson and Kenneth R. Ross's edited book *Atlas of Global Christianity* is an excellent resource, it does not throw light on social realities such as women's participation and the persistence of male-centric Christianity.

discuss the relationship between urbanisation and World Christianity, with particular attention to migration as illustrated by the case of India.

Urbanisation and World Christianity

Where World Christianity attends to local variants and hierarchies, urbanisation brings multiple locals to converge together in the making and sustenance of urban spaces. Migration is one of the major phenomena intertwined with the era of urbanisation in human history. The annals of history and archaeological discoveries provide evidence of movement of people, settling in new places, and setting up new infrastructures and social networks from immemorial times.[23] While migration is not a phenomenon exclusive to the late modern era, in the present age it is unique in its comprehensive reach of human communities forced to migrate and the tremendous multicultural encounters it engenders. The unequal economic realities exacerbated by environmental vagaries which are largely a by-product of anthropocene activities is a major cause of contemporary global migration.[24]

From the perspective of globalisation and its needs for modernised infrastructure, migration is linked to urbanisation as an inevitable socioeconomic condition of globalisation. The need of labour in the urban space on one hand, and, on the other hand, the transformation of rural space by the development of urban centres for the machine of globalisation produce the intrinsic relationship between migration of labour and the unstructured growth of urban centres. Furthermore, the dilemma of navigating the tension between ultra-technologised urban centres and the neglected rural areas remains a challenge.

India, the most populous country in the world, with a diversity of cultures and languages, is home to many ancient world religions and numerous textual and oral based spiritualities.[25] India presents a kaleidoscopic canvas of cultures, economic positions, social realities, and millions of

---

[23] Stephen Castles, Hein de Haas, and Mark J. Miller, *The Age of Migration: International Population Movements in the Modern World*, 5th ed. (New York: Palgrave Macmillan, 2014); Immanuel Ness, ed., *The Encyclopedia of Global Human Migration* (Oxford: Wiley-Blackwell, 2013).

[24] For the statistics of migration from different countries and regions of the world, including data for women migration, see "International Migration 2017," accessed on October 29, 2018, http://www.un.org/en/development/desa/population/migration/publications/wallchart/docs/MigrationWallChart2017.pdf.

[25] For a helpful source on the encounters and intersections of many religions in the region, see Peter Frankopan, *The Silk Roads: A New History of the World* (New York: Vintage Books, 2015); For a perspective of Christianity in the region, see Peter Phan ed., *Christianities in Asia* (Oxford: Wiley-Blackwell, 2011).

younger people seeking quality employment and better lives than their parents' generation.[26]

The case of India illustrates vividly the intrinsic relationship between urbanisation and migration. Since India joined the liberal economy in the last decade of the twentieth century, it has launched itself wholeheartedly towards urbanisation, notwithstanding the impact on the environment and the displacement of rural population. As India quickly urbanises, the demand for workers in every sector of the society is growing, which in turn brings people from different sociocultural locales of the country to the urban centres to feed and sustain the process of urbanisation. The movement of workers make the metropolitan cities the heart of the country.

Furthermore, India is a nation with multilayered social and economic realities which produce both an outflow of migrants crossing international borders and an inflow of migrants from within the nation as well as from neighbouring regions.[27] For labour as well as educational purposes, India is a destination of migrants from the neighbouring developing nations, and further afield such as from African countries and the Gulf region. The cities in India, therefore, have become urban spaces wherein multiple identities converge and intersect.

From the perspective of the macro history of modern India, urban centres, migration, and multicultural encounters are not a new phenomenon. Religious pilgrims, traders, and sages have traversed the borders of the region for centuries.[28] Western imperialism and the modern missionary movement, however, were major forces of urbanisation, in that the transfer of Western values, commerce, and the creation of mission centres contributed to the rise of modern urban spaces which became new terrains of multicultural encounters. For instance, an urban space in southern India is directly related to Christian mission. Anandpur in Karnataka

---

[26] India has a sizeable younger generation, with aspirations to participate in the growing economy of the country and the global trends. The challenges and the potentials of the young population is developed in a new book. See Snigdha Poonam, *Dreamers: How Young Indians are Changing the World* (Cambridge: Harvard University Press, 2018).

[27] For migration in the region of South Asia, the International Labour Organisation provides a detailed index, see https://www.ilo.org/wcmsp5/groups/public/---asia/---ro-bangkok/---sro-new_delhi/documents/publication/wcms_645314.pdf. See also, Philip Connon, "India is a Top Source and Destination for World's Migration," accessed July 10, 2019, https://www.pewresearch.org/fact-tank/2017/03/03/india-is-a-top-source-and-destination-for-worlds-migrants/.

[28] For instance, Al-Biruni (973–1048), Faxian (337–422), and Xuanzang (600–664) are some important personalities known for their travels, seeking religious cultures and teachings in the region.

is a town connected to the famous Brahmin convert Anandarao Kuandiya, who converted to Christianity through the work of Basel Missionaries in the nineteenth century. After his conversion, Anandarao took the name of his mentor Hermann Moegling, and came to be known as Hermann Anandarao Kaundiya. Anandarao was trained in Basel and ordained in 1851. Mrinalini Sebastian sheds light on Anandarao's work among the most marginalised, writing about the new settlement for Christian converts, mostly among Dalit communities, as "The new settlement of the converted Christians in Anandapur, a place named after Anandarao Kaundiya because this parcel of land was bought with his money."[29] Initially a new settlement for new converts, mostly from the most marginalised community, Anandapur became an urban space for commerce and industry.

Given its diversity of cultures and religions, in essence, urbanisation in India calls for a code of "plurality and creativity" to aid peaceful and dignified mutual existence. Considering all intersections of diversities in such a context, the Christian faith will only be fully meaningful if in its expression as a world religion, it incorporates the local and universal commitment to the flourishing of "every tongue, tribe, and nation."

As was discussed earlier, urbanisation brings peoples and cultures from different contexts to converge. Therefore, the challenge of urbanisation for the church as an instrument of God's mission for the peaceful flourishing of the whole of creation requires a World Christianity with interculturally equipped leaders; i.e., a World Christianity committed to the nurturing of leaders with intercultural leadership skills, beyond a particular language or denomination.

World Christianity, urbanisation, and intercultural leadership

The fast-paced urbanisation of the late modern era has been paradoxical. With the undeniable comforts and conveniences brought about by material and technological progress, and the more regular interaction among a plurality of cultures, urbanisation also ushered in dreadful isolation,

---

[29] For more details, see Mrinalini Sebastian, "Localised Cosmopolitanism and Globalised Faith: Echoes of 'Native' Voices in Eighteenth and Nineteenth Century Missionary Documents," in Judith Becker, ed., *European Missions in Contact Zones: Transformation through Interaction* (Gottingen: Vandenhoeck and Ruprecht, 2015), 47–64; see also Albrecht Frenz, *Freiheit hat Gesicht: Anandapur, eine begegnung zwischen Kodagu und Baden-Wurttemberg* (Stuttgart: Staatsanzeigler fur Baden-Wurttemberg, 2003); Mrinalini Sebastian, "The Scholar-Missionaries of the Basel Mission in Southwest India: Language, Identity and Knowledge in Flux," in Heather J. Sharkey, ed., *Cultural Conversions: Unexpected Consequences of Christian Missionary Encounters in the Middle East, Africa and South Asia* (Syracuse, NY: Syracuse University Press, 2013), 176–202.

debilitating hostility, and an assertion of dominance that created conditions of vulnerability for many. In contexts like India, with its quintessential heterogeneity and "eclectic plurality"[30] as described by Wendy Doniger, urbanisation gathers the diversities into more intense interactions. In contrast to the isolation of parochial locations, the urban spaces become cosmopolitan sites of convergence. However, urbanised centres also concentrate many paradoxes, as poverty, injustice, and homophobia amass, residing together with unprecedented social interaction and collaborations. Christianity, by contrast, articulates God's love for humanity expressed in the life and work of Jesus. To articulate a persuasive message of God's intent of goodness for all, Christian churches in urbanised centres are required to be a crucial source for nurturing interculturally equipped leaders.[31] If World Christianity's marked feature is attentiveness to the neglected and the marginalised in both the historiography and theological articulations, it must contribute to enable and engender leaders who can faithfully traverse the terrain of urban spaces with all its heterogeneity. Urbanised contexts, with their constant frictions and negotiations of identities, thirst for community leaders who are tuned to multicultural ethos. Such leadership is essential for the church's missional commitment to the flourishing of all creation.[32]

Leadership is a crucial component of faith communities such as those which comprise World Christianity located in different local contexts such as the Indian urban centres. The character of its leadership often reflects the condition of the community within pluralistic urban societies. In urban spaces, leadership and its charisma are essential as a fulcrum for the communities to articulate a code of mutuality. The nature and quality of leadership is, therefore, foundational for the flourishing of communities in urban terrains wherein multiple cultures intersect.

In its basic sense, what I call intercultural leadership is one which is formed by individuals organic to particular communities who bridge among different communities and individuals, channeling values that are inclusive, just, and accountable to all. Intercultural leadership in the context of World Christianity is Christ-centred, characterised by compassion to the vulnerable, inclusive of the marginalised, embracing of the excluded, and promoter of radical friendship with the other. This Christ-centred

---

[30] Wendy Doniger, *The Hindus: An Alternative History* (Delhi: Viking Penguin, 2009), 44.
[31] Douglas Hall, "Theological Education in the Urban Context," in Eldin Villafañe, *Seek the Peace of the City: Reflections on Urban Ministry* (Grand Rapids, MI: W.B. Eerdmans Publishing, 1995), 97–102.
[32] Jooseop Keum, *Together Towards Life: Mission and Evangelism in Changing Landscapes* (Geneva: WCC Publications, 2013), 15.

intercultural leadership overcomes the boundaries and borders urbanisation produces through fencing off the different other.

Intercultural leadership is best expressed in contexts of human relationships brought together in urban spaces marked by respect and inclusion of the "other," be that alterity categorised on the basis of gender, class, caste, race, clan, or any other sort of sociocultural difference. Intercultural leadership practises compassion and empathy through an attitude of humility towards the members of the community and the larger world.

The challenges and opportunities of urbanisation call for leadership equipped in intercultural ways of living. I propose four characteristics such leadership needs to develop in the context of World Christianity.

Intercultural leadership must be prophetic

The intensity of urbanisation calls for leadership that promotes a way of life which embraces multifaceted and even at times contesting views of life. As urban spaces are a terrain wherein diversities interact, often with dominant assertion prone to exploitation of the weakest, an intercultural leader is often called to be prophetic. If prophets are individuals who see existing reality through a justice-oriented lens and announce an "alternative reality," intercultural leadership helps mediate this alternative reality in urbanised contexts. Where there are precarious conditions of competition and potential conflicts, a leadership tuned to intercultural ethos is needed. To be an interculturally-equipped leader is to be prophetic; that is, be able to see beyond the immediate context and to guide the community towards being just and accountable to all. A word of caution on the usage of the term prophetic, though, comes from J. Andrew Kirk, since "prophetic" is usually associated with denunciation.[33] Kirk cautions against the risk of becoming a self-righteous prophet who announces judgements against transgressors.[34] While it is critically important to note such a risk, the role of a prophet is fundamental to Christian communities.[35] Located in the variegated urban centres, risking being overwhelmed by compelling forces of power, prophets emerge particularly in contexts where power is being misused, wherein rulers and leaders of nations have exploited and victimised the people. Prophets declare God's purposes for all to flourish, hence the prophetic message encompasses every aspect of community life: religious life, economic practices, moral convictions,

---

[33] J. Andrew Kirk, *Mission under Scrutiny: Confronting Contemporary Challenges* (Minneapolis, MN: Fortress Press, 2006), 157.
[34] Kirk, *Mission under Scrutiny*, 157.
[35] Abraham J. Heschel, *The Prophets* (New York: Harper Collins, 1969), 5; Walter Brueggemann, *The Prophetic Imagination* (Minneapolis, MN: Fortress Press, 2001).

and political policies.³⁶ Finally, the prophetic message also includes the condemnation of the unjust actions, the warning of the consequences of one's actions, and the promise of new beginnings.³⁷ In the same way the prophets of the Judeo-Christian tradition were called in a sociopolitical context of oppressive regime, misuse of power, and economic exploitation, Christian communities living in contemporary urbanised contexts marked by intense competition and conflicts also need leaders to be prophetic, denouncing destructive forces and announcing God's reign.

There is an ethical element in announcing God's purpose to the community. The individuals entrusted to leadership position must make a conscientious effort to take actions and make decisions that are inclusive of all, inspired by the vision of an alternative reality wherein all members are supported to flourish. An intercultural leadership that is prophetic engenders a community of justice and compassion. In the context of urbanisation, such leadership points to an alternative reality wherein values of the gospel and God's reign are presented as counter-reality to the distortion and destruction of creation by exploitative and selfish attitudes. Intercultural leaders are invariably located within structures pervaded by and bequeathed with certain power. A prophetic leadership exemplifies the just stewardship which grounds power in accountability to and transparent governance of the community.

Intercultural leadership is interreligious

One of the implications for mission and ministry in urbanised contexts, as Irvin rightly points out, is the "level(s) of growing engagement with other religions" characteristic of global cities.³⁸ Indeed, one of the most defining landscapes of contemporary urbanisation is the convergence of different religions and their practices in urban settings. Urbanisation presents the challenge of religions in both their best and worst interpretations and praxes. At different historical periods and diverse contexts, there have been ample examples of both the vices and virtues of religions lived out in human encounters. As urban spaces create more interactions between different religions, the role of community leaders to be aware and skilled towards constructive encounters and exchanges among different religious traditions is immensely vital.³⁹ Eboo Patel and Cassie Meyer underline the primary mark of interfaith leadership as possessing "knowledge and skills necessary to navigate religious diversity toward a positive end in various

---

[36] Kirk, *Mission under Scrutiny*, 158.
[37] Kirk, *Mission under Scrutiny*, 158–160.
[38] Irvin, "The Church, the Urban," 180.
[39] Michael Barnes, S.J., *Interreligious Learning: Dialogue, Spirituality and the Christian Imagination* (Cambridge: Cambridge University Press, 2011), 202.

applied settings."[40] Leaders embedded in particular religious communities simultaneously learn about other religions and apply that knowledge in forging relationship with other religious communities.[41] Furthermore, intercultural leaders share the knowledge of other religions with their communities, assisting the community in turn to navigate and organise in pluralistic urban settings.

Global religious organisations have noted the potential of this reality. In 2011, the World Council of Churches, the Pontifical Council for Interreligious Dialogue, and the World Evangelical Alliance prepared and produced a document to encourage and provide guidance for Christian witness. Titled "Christian Witness in a Multi-Religious World: Recommendations for Conduct," the document succinctly summed up the primary foundation for faithful witness as followers of Christ, in the following paragraph:

> Jesus Christ is the supreme witness (cf. John 18:37). Christian witness is always a sharing in his witness, which takes the form of proclamation of the kingdom, service to neighbour, and the total gift of self even if that act of giving leads to the cross. Just as the Father sent the Son in the power of the Holy Spirit, so believers are sent in mission to witness in word and action to the love of the triune God.[42]

Because God in his all-encompassing generosity revealed his love for all in Jesus Christ, those who profess this truth are called to relate with neighbours of other religions with compassion and freedom. Based on a principled theological foundation, the document provides a list of recommendations for implementations on the ground level.

[Along with study of the document, churches are encouraged to]
1. Build relationships of respect and trust with people of all religions, in particular at institutional levels between churches and other religious communities, engaging in ongoing interreligious dialogue as part of their Christian commitment. In certain contexts, where years of tension and conflict have created deep suspicions and breaches of trust between and among communities, interreligious dialogue can

---

[40] Eboo Patel and Cassie Meyer, "Teaching Interfaith Leadership," in *Teaching Interreligious Encounters*, eds. Marc A. Pugliese and Alex Y. Hwang (Oxford: Oxford University Press: 2017), accessed July 10, 2019, https://www.oxfordscholarship.com.

[41] For a discussion on the role of religious leaders in organising towards a common cause, see Luke Bretherton, *Resurrecting Democracy: Faith Citizenship, and the Politics of a Common Life* (Cambridge: Cambridge University Press, 2014), 21–56.

[42] "Christian Witness in a Multi-Religious World," *World Council of Churches*, accessed January 14, 2019, https://tinyurl.com/y3wnue37.

provide new opportunities for resolving conflicts, restoring justice, healing of memories, reconciliation, and peace-building.

2. Encourage Christians to strengthen their own religious identity and faith while deepening their knowledge and understanding of different religions, and to do so also taking into account the perspectives of the adherents of those religions. Christians should avoid misrepresenting the beliefs and practices of people of different religions.

3. Cooperate with other religious communities engaging in interreligious advocacy towards justice and the common good and, wherever possible, standing together in solidarity with people who are in situations of conflict.

4. Call on their governments to ensure that freedom of religion is properly and comprehensively respected, recognising that in many countries religious institutions and persons are inhibited from exercising their mission.

5. Pray for their neighbours and their well-being, recognising that prayer is integral to who we are and what we do, as well as to Christ's mission.[43]

Christianity has a complicated history of encounters with other religions,[44] and in the context of urbanisation and convergence of diverse religions in condensed terrains, community leaders must be intercultural in their commitment to practise hospitality and openness in heterogeneous urban spaces. The role of ecclesiastical leaders as intercultural leaders is crucial to bridge the gap between local Christians and people of other faiths towards cooperation and mutual recognition and respect.

Intercultural leadership is gender sensitive

The process of urbanisation, its demands on labours, and the opportunities it creates have consequences across the web of human relationships. While urbanisation brings adherents of different religions to live and work together sharing spaces and seasons, it also brings changes to established norms and social roles. Situations of exploitation and discrimination inherent to certain contexts can sometimes go unchallenged. Caught in the complexities of urbanisation, in the intensity of living in global cities, gender hierarchies often continue entrapping Christian communities. Uncritical urbanisation reproduce structures of inequalities and normative discriminations, particularly from a gender perspective. The demands

---

[43] "Christian Witness in a Multi-Religious World," *World Council of Churches*.

[44] Among the many excellent sources on the topic, Timothy Yates' book offers a judicious reading and analysis of Christian mission's engagement with other religions. Timothy Yates, *Christian Mission in the Twentieth Century* (Cambridge: Cambridge University Press, 1994).

and opportunities of urbanisation impact every individual. Analysts of migration and labour have noted the growing feminisation of migration across the globe.[45] The feminisation of migration means that there are more women workers leaving their homes and moving to work in urban spaces. A lesser attended issue is that of those individuals who are marginalised because of their sexuality, including transgender persons who might seek safe spaces in urban settings. These realities of gender translocations and experiences in urban spaces challenge the communities of faith to make deliberate efforts to embrace and include every member of the community.[46]

A leadership sensitive to feminist visions is marked by an attitude of praxis-oriented collaboration and flexibility in the face of struggles with differences.[47] As shown earlier, World Christianity in its essence attends to the perspectives of excluded and suppressed voices. Thus, an intercultural leadership formed in such a context must enable a vision of inclusion of every individual in the community, prioritising neglected and suppressed voices, including the leadership of women.[48] Intercultural leadership must also lead the community in living out the ethos of compassion, embracing especially those members who are often isolated or alienated because of their sexual identity. As urbanisation and its demands breaks conventional gender roles and relationships, churches existing in urbanised settings need an intercultural leadership that is sensitive to the challenges presented by those changing realities.

Intercultural leadership is missional

The mission document adopted by the World Council of Churches in 2012, titled "Together Towards Life," succinctly articulates the mission

---

[45] Sourced from data generated by the World Bank, the following blog provides regional and country-wise statistics of female migrants. See Eliana Rubiano-Matulevich and Kathleen Beegle, *Women and Migration: Exploring the Data*, accessed July 11, 2019, https://blogs.worldbank.org/opendata/women-and-migration-exploring-data.

[46] Nicola Piper, *Gender and Migration* (Geneva: Global Commission on International Migration, 2005).

[47] Lynn N. Rhodes, "Leadership from a Feminist Perspective," *Word and World* XIII, no. 1 (1993): 13–18.

[48] In a previous volume of this series, the matter of gender sensitivity was discussed in the contexts of Germany and Brazil, shedding light on the complexities of women participation and leadership in the church and in theological education. See Uta Andree, "Church and Gender in Germany," in *World Christianity as Public Religion*, ed. Raimundo Barreto, Ronaldo Cavalcante, and Wanderley P. da Rosa. (Minneapolis, MN: Fortress Press, 2017), 121–130; and Claudete Beise Ulrich, "Women and Academic Theological Education," in Barreto, Cavalcante, and da Rosa, *World Christianity*, 133–152.

of the church as reconciliation and restoration of humanity. It states, "mission begins in the heart of the Triune God and the love which binds together the Holy Trinity overflows to all humanity and creation. The missionary God who sent the Son to the world calls all God's people (John 20:21), and empowers them to be a community of hope. The church is commissioned to celebrate life, and to resist and transform all life-destroying forces, in the power of the Holy Spirit...."[49] The fundamental basis of World Christianity is the gathering of people sharing a common faith in the Triune God, revealed in the life and work of Jesus Christ. As a community that bears witness to the good news of all creation flourishing, World Christianity cannot be anything but missional. The proclamation of the good news and the demand of putting the message into lived actions of compassion and solidarity are midwifed by intercultural leaders.

Urbanisation calls for the church to discern its mission in the reality of complex encounters and interactions often marked by contest and conflict. Leaders, who are transformed and inspired by the good news in Christ are called to bear witness to the goodness of God across the diverse realities and urban spaces.

Conclusion

As a defining mark of the anthropocene age, urbanisation is an inevitable process in contemporary societies, which brings with it both good and ill. The convergence of diversities and the intersections of multiple identities in the urban spaces bring to the fore the potential of World Christianity to participate in the making of a more just world where inclusion, embrace, and hospitality towards the other are the marked features of its pronouncements. World Christianity and its commitment to attend to the underrepresented and the ignored are challenged by the realities of urbanisation. Attention and inclusion begin by being available and present. As Gornik and Liu Wong exhort, "the vocation of urban Christians begins with presence. It is a calling to be present with and open to God in the local context, attending to what is in front of us with all of our senses."[50]

The interstices between urbanisation and World Christianity are bridged by intercultural leaders who are organic to the communities and assist the negotiations between existing and converging diversities towards a society marked by solidarity and presence for one another. The capacity of being present as the beginning of Christian witness is highlighted by Robert Lupton. Writing in the context of reviving urban ministry in the late twentieth century aftermath of suburbia, Lupton states, "almost all [urban ministries] grow out of contact with poor and disenfranchised

---

[49] Keum, *Together Towards Life*, 4.
[50] Gornik and Wong, *Stay in the City*, 6.

people. They are often multiethnic or multiracial. They are reinstituting early church practices of sharing food, home, and material possessions with those in need. And there is a rediscovery of the importance of spiritual gifts which are distributed to all believers and give special significance to even the least in the body."[51] Being present and sharing urban spaces require the crossing of boundaries and borders. The fundamental message of Christianity is God's presence in the whole world, and urbanisation, with its complexities and challenges, calls exactly for God's presence, a hope that is fulfilled in the promise of God's presence in the human Christ.[52]

---

[51] Robert Lupton, *Theirs is the Kingdom: Celebrating the Gospel in Urban America* (San Francisco, CA: HarperCollins Publishers, 1989), 120.

[52] Karl Rahner, one of the wise theologians during the turmoil of the twentieth century, has aptly articulated this as he stated, Christianity "calls for a wholehearted and straightforward profession of hope, amidst all the mysterious twists and turns of our life, and assures us that in this mystery lies what we call God, eternal life, ultimate value, and the salvation of our being." Quoted in Michael Barnes, *Interreligious Learning: Dialogue, Spirituality and the Christian Imagination* (Cambridge: Cambridge University Press, 2012), 6.

Bibliography

Adogame, Afe. *The African Christian Diaspora: New Currents and Emerging Trends in World Christianity*. London: Bloomsbury, 2013.

Barnes, Michael. *Interreligious Learning: Dialogue, Spirituality and the Christian Imagination*. Cambridge: Cambridge University Press, 2012.

Barreto, Raimundo, Ronaldo Cavalcante, and Wanderley P. da Rosa, eds. *World Christianity as Public Religion*. Minneapolis, MN: Fortress Press, 2017.

Bretherton, Luke. *Resurrecting Democracy: Faith Citizenship, and the Politics of a Common Life*. Cambridge: Cambridge University Press, 2014.

Brueggemann, Walter. *The Prophetic Imagination*. Minneapolis, MN: Fortress Press, 2001.

Castles, Stephen, Hein de Haas and Mark J. Miller, *The Age of Migration: International Population Movements in the Modern World*. 5th ed. New York: Palgrave Macmillan, 2014.

Comaroff, Jean, and John Comaroff. *Of Revelation and Revolution: Christianity, Colonialism, and Consciousness*. Vol. 1. Chicago, IL: The University of Chicago Press, 1991.

Cruz, Gemma. *An Intercultural Theology of Migration: Pilgrims in the Wilderness*. Leiden: Brill, 2010.

Doniger, Wendy. *The Hindus: An Alternative History*. Delhi: Viking Penguin, 2009.

Frankopan, Peter. *The Silk Roads: A New History of the World*. New York: Vintage Books, 2015.

Frenz, Albrecht. *Freiheit hat Gesicht: Anandapur, eine begegnung zwischen Kodagu und Baden-Wurttemberg*. Stuttgart: Staatsanzeigler fur Baden-Wurttemberg, 2003.

Gornik, Mark R., and Maria Liu Wong. *Stay in the City: How Christian Faith is Flourishing in an Urban World*. Grand Rapids, MI: W.B. Eerdmans Publishing, 2017.

Groody, Daniel G., and Gioacchino Campese, eds. *Promised Land, Perilous Journey: Theological Perspective on Migration*. Notre Dame, IN: University of Notre Dame Press, 2008.

Hall, Douglas. "Theological Education in the Urban Context." In Eldin Villafañe, *Seek the Peace of the City: Reflections on Urban Ministry*, 97–102. Grand Rapids, MI: W.B. Eerdmans Publishing, 1995.

Hanciles, Jehu J. *Beyond Christendom: Globalization, African Migration and the Transformation of the West*. Maryknoll, NY: Orbis Books, 2008.

Heschel, Abraham J. *The Prophets*. New York: Harper Collins, 1969.

Hollinger, David A. *Protestants Abroad: How Missionaries Tried to Change the World but Changed America*. Princeton, NJ: Princeton University Press, 2017.

Irvin, Dale T. "The Church, the Urban, and the Global: Mission in an Age of Global Cities." *International Bulletin of Missionary Research* 33, no. 4 (October 2009): 177–182.

———. "World Christianity: An Introduction." *The Journal of World Christianity*, vol. 1, no.1 (2008): 1–26.

Jenkins, Philip. *The Next Christendom: The Coming of Global Christianity*. Oxford: Oxford University Press, 2011.

Johnson, Todd M., and Kenneth R. Ross, eds. *Atlas of Global Christianity*. Edinburgh: Edinburgh University, 2009.

Karlsson, Bengt G., and Dolly Kikon. "Wayfinding: Indigenous Migrants in the Service Sector of Metropolitan India." *Journal of South Asian Studies* 40, no. 3 (2017): 447–462.

Keum, Jooseup. *Together Towards Life: Mission and Evangelism in Changing Landscapes*. Geneva: WCC Publications, 2013.

Kim, Sebastian, and Kirsteen Kim, eds. *Christianity as a World Religion*. London: Continuum Books, 2008.

Kirk, J. Andrew. *Mission under Scrutiny: Confronting Contemporary Challenges*. Minneapolis, MN: Fortress Press, 2006.

Lupton, Robert. *Theirs is the Kingdom: Celebrating the Gospel in Urban America*. San Francisco, CA: HarperCollins Publishers, 1989.

Ness, Immanuel, ed. *The Encyclopedia of Global Human Migration*. Oxford: Wiley-Blackwell, 2013.

Pachuau, Lalsangkima. *World Christianity: A Historical and Theological Introduction*. Nashville, TN: Abingdon Press, 2018.

Patel, Eboo, and Cassie Meyer. "Teaching Interfaith Leadership." In *Teaching Interreligious Encounters*, edited by Marc A. Pugliese and Alex Y. Hwang. Oxford: Oxford University Press, 2017.

Phan, Peter, ed. *Christianities in Asia*. Oxford: Wiley-Blackwell, 2011.

Piper, Nicola. *Gender and Migration*. Geneva: Global Commission on International Migration, 2005.

Poonam, Snigdha. *Dreamers: How Young Indians are Changing the World*. Cambridge: Harvard University Press, 2018.

Robert, Dana L. *Christian Mission: How Christianity Became a World Religion*. Chichester, UK: Wiley-Blackwell, 2009.

Rhodes, Lynn N. "Leadership from a Feminist Perspective." *Word and World* XIII, no. 1 (1993): 13–18.

Sanneh, Lamin. *Whose Religion Is Christianity? The Gospel beyond the West.* Grand Rapids, MI: W.B. Eerdmans Publishing, 2003.

Sassen, Saskia. "The Global Cities: Introducing a Concept." *Brown Journal of World Affairs* XI, no. 2 (Winter/Spring, 2005): 1–18.

Sebastian, Mrinalini. "Localised Cosmopolitanism and Globalised Faith: Echoes of 'Native' Voices in Eighteenth and Nineteenth Century Missionary Documents." In *European Missions in Contact Zones: Transformation through Interaction*, edited by Judith Becker. Gottingen: Vandenhoeck and Ruprecht, 2015.

———. "The Scholar-Missionaries of the Basel Mission in Southwest India: Language, Identity and Knowledge in Flux." In *Cultural Conversions: Unexpected Consequences of Christian Missionary Encounters in the Middle East, Africa and South Asia*, edited by Heather J. Sharkey, 176–202. Syracuse, NY: Syracuse University Press, 2013.

Tan, Jonathan Y., and Anh Q. Tran, eds. *World Christianity: Perspectives and Insights, Essays in Honor of Peter C. Phan.* Maryknoll, NY: Orbis Books, 2016.

Walls, Andrew F. *The Missionary Movement in Christian History: Studies in the Transmission of Faith.* Maryknoll, NY: Orbis Books, 1996.

Yates, Timothy. *Christian Mission in the Twentieth Century.* Cambridge: Cambridge University Press, 1994.

10

"ETHIOPIANISM IS MOST RAMPANT IN CITIES"—AFRICAN CHRISTIANITY BETWEEN MIGRATION AND URBAN SETTLEMENT: SOUTH AFRICA AROUND 1900

Ciprian Burlacioiu

INTRODUCTION

South Africa saw in the last decades of the nineteenth century the formation of new urban centers. Different from the older ones, these new cities were neither harbor towns, nor centers of political colonial, or white Boer power, but they were—as Kimberley and Johannesburg—industrial areas. These cities were, consequently, not primarily the habitat of the colonial elite and the bourgeoisie. These were places where the labor force of migrant workers was extracted and managed in the best way possible. Except for the colonial situation, they were very similar to the late eighteenth and nineteenth century industrial cities in Europe. Under these conditions, a colonial, non-European working class—composed to a large extent of a circular migratory labor force—came into being.

In the following pages, I will focus on the conditions of these African migrant workers basically in the city of Johannesburg and try to understand how the general frame—marked by industrialization and migration—influenced the emergence of a missionary independent African Christianity at the end of the nineteenth century and during the first decades of the twentieth century. Far from intending to set with this case in point a typical pattern of understanding (South) African Christianity, I consider the dynamic of native Christianity in such urban areas as exemplary for the evolution of Christian religion in different areas in Africa and in the Global South during this period.

For the scope of this essay, I choose to rely largely on the Rand Daily Mail[1] (RDM) as my primary source. For sure, a comprehensive picture of the topic must use primary sources of different types. Nevertheless, relying—as an exercise—largely only on a newspaper, has the advantage of introducing researcher and reader—more than other sources—to the daily debates of the society. Small reports and comments or letters to the editor provide an intimate picture of the gossips and rumors circulating among the public, which—sometimes even more than official information and formal decisions—contributed to the formation of public opinion. As a matter of fact, journal materials show how fluid and disputed public opinion regarding these churches was and how fluid their real situation was.

Since the issue of religion in the South African context (as elsewhere in Africa) draws for this epoch, to a large extent, basically from missionary and white churches primary sources, and—where available—on testimonies of independent churches as well, the recourse to a secular newspaper as a main source of information for the religious field is diversifying the spectrum of historical information. As a newspaper of colonial society, the RDM aired debates and opinions of different actors of this milieu and could be regarded as a representative sample of white public opinion in Transvaal. As such, this newspaper had no special interest in religious issues. However, precisely for this reason its materials are mirroring the average interest of public opinion on this issue.

THE EMERGENCE OF INDUSTRIAL, URBAN AREAS

After the discovery of the most significant reef deposit of gold on the Rand[2] in 1886, a gold rush was set in motion. In the first ten years, the alluvial surface exploitation opened a field for thousands of small diggers, employing small capital and rudimental equipment. In 1896, the area becoming Johannesburg gathered already 100,000 residents and one year later, the Kruger government reluctantly granted the growing settlement municipal status. The depression occurring in these years due to the end of mass alluvial exploitation brought a crucial change to the structure of the Rand gold industry (the geological structure of the reef forced a deep level mining and, as an additional difficulty, the known chemical process by the extraction of gold from ore was becoming less efficient). Due to the exploding production costs, a large number of undercapitalized diggers

---

[1] Rand Daily Mail (RDM) was a secular journal that began publication in 1902 in Johannesburg. During the first decades of the twentieth century, the RDM was one of the major newspapers in the Rand, touching on all important local, transregional, and international issues.

[2] For this part, I rely on the classic work of Charles Van Onselen, *Studies in the Social and Economic History of the Witwatersrand 1886-1914*, vol. 2 (London: Longman, 1982).

went bankrupt and sold their premises, making way for a small number of stock mining companies, some of them having the experience of diamond mining in Kimberley. Consequently, the mining industry settled on this base caused an industrial revolution on a large scale, creating in the Rand and beyond its urban settlements a new economic environment of a modern industrial type. The large digger camp, which was Johannesburg's form in its first decade, transformed itself due to the demands of the mining industry into a rapidly growing mining town, having by 1914 over a quarter of a million residents. At the same time, other different economic branches—such as coal mining, transportation, construction, and agriculture—also rapidly developed at an industrial level, changing the traditional farming and pastoral profile of the region.

Beyond the necessary financial capital, another element was crucial to a positive industrial development: a permanent flow of cheap labor force, which was mainly provided by unskilled natives. Its importance is revealed by the effort on the part of economic and political actors to provide it. R.F. Fricker, the chairman of the Simmer and Jack Gold Mine Co., at the annual general meeting of 1902, stated: "These mines have been brought to their present state of efficiency by cheap labor, and can only retain that efficiency so long as cheap labor is assured to them. ... If we find that we cannot supply ourselves from the African Continent [with cheap labor], we cannot afford to hinder the development of the country or stifle its industries..."[3] Such statements were repeatedly made during this period: "the scarcity of native labor has retarded the development of business"[4]; "It is recognized that the agricultural and industrial development of South Africa is retarded by lack of sufficient labor, and that the importation of labor is thereby necessary."[5] As a matter of fact, the demand for unskilled workers was calculated in 1905 as being 782,000. Estimations about the male native workers available in all South African British territories came to only 474,000.[6] However, the real number of the employed natives might have been at that time something around 100,000.

Labor Migration

Recruiting labor force in the desired number was always a complex and at times even a difficult task. Prior to the South African War (1899–1902), the flux of native unskilled workers proved to be—for different reasons—quite reliable. In September 1899, just before the beginning of the hostilities, some 100,000 native workers were employed in the Rand mines.

---

[3] RDM, 30.09.1902, 3.
[4] RDM, 01.10.1902, 3.
[5] RDM, 09.02.1905, 8.
[6] RDM, 09.02.1905, 8.

The war brought the mining industry to a quasi-standstill in Transvaal, with many mines practically closing their activities, which forced almost all native migrant workers to return to their homes. But, some of them subsequently found employment as auxiliary forces during the war. After the slow restart of the mining operations in 1901, by September of the following year only 42,000 native workers were back at work.[7]

To fill that gap, a comprehensive network of recruiting agents was mobilized. The most important player was doubtless the Witwatersrand Native Labour Association (WNLA), the labor organization operating in the name of the Chamber of Mines with the support of the South African government. Already in 1902, only one year after starting its operations, the activity of the WNLA was described in the following way:

> Their agents are everywhere, like Oom Paul's [Paul Kruger, the president of the Transvaal republic] secret service men in the ante-war days. The southern half of Africa is being scraped with a fine comb to discover "boys." From Quillimane north to the borders of German territory and inland right to the shores of Lake Nyasa the recruiting officer goes with his native "runners" and inspans that muscular savage for service on the Rand. A quite recent report from Mombassa states that a considerable number have been enrolled and will be sent round by sea to Lourenco Marques. Permission is also being sought to recruit in the Congo Free State, Rhodesia, among the Zanzibaris, and some day we may hear of the "fuzzies" enlisting at Berber and Khartoum as drill-bays. Meanwhile the East Coast tribesmen in Gazaland are finding the largest contingents.[8]

As a matter of fact, the WNLA operated effectively for most of the twentieth century almost in the entire southern half of the African continent. Its network included local collecting stations with food supply, train, and later bus, and even airplane transportation. Its importance both for South Africa and for the countries where it operated brought WNLA to the position of making contracts with many governments in Africa. The lucrative field of labor recruitment was, however, disputed by many other agents.

Even if labor migration was known long before 1900 among Africans, their reasons for engaging it changed with time. Before 1900, this phenomenon was largely deliberate, wage labor being seen as a means to get cash, to buy guns, and to enjoy the products of civilization. Sometimes, for young males, this was the way to avoid the control of elders. Thus, this experience became a rite of passage to adulthood. After 1900, due to the changing political and social situation, the wage labor increasingly became quasi-compulsory due to the taxes imposed upon natives or

---

[7] This figure is provided by the RDM, 30.09.1902, 3.
[8] RDM, 30.09.1902, 15.

because of large land expropriation and loss of cattle. Even in this situation, the willingness of natives to engage in wage labor was low. Solutions for the insufficient labor supply were to be found. *From Cape to Cairo*, an influential book written by E.S. Grogan,[9] was quoted in regard to the necessity of even introducing forced labor as a last resort: "Wither we give up the country commercially or we must make them work. ... Compulsory labour in some form is the corollary of our occupation of the country, and the sooner we grasp this essential fact the better chance there will be that South Africa will settle down contented in the shadow of the flag."[10]

From the beginning of shortage of the local cheap labor force—or of laborers from nearby regions such as from Portuguese East Africa—migration from afar was considered as a possible solution. Besides African labor, some regions in Asia—in particular India and China—were also considered for the import of workers. In 1902, shortages in labor supply for the coal mining and the railway led to the initial introduction of some 700 Indians in the coal industry in Natal.[11] In the subsequent years, tens of thousands of Indian coolies, and some 50,000 Chinese indentured labors, followed. At the same time, on the political and social arena, hot debates like this one in the Cape Parliament were taking place:

> Mr Forst, Secretary for Agriculture, admitted that there were very strong prejudices against the importation of Asiatic labour, but he favoured the importation of Italian peasants, for which purpose a sum of £10,000 would be placed on the supplementary estimates. He assured the House that the Government would do everything in its power to meet the demand for labour. Mr. Oats said they must swallow their prejudice. The development of the country was now being hampered through the want of labour. It would be simply foolishness to bow to the existing prejudice against Asiatic labour.[12]

Such debates took place not only in the Cape Province. At the first session of the Second Legislative Council in Rhodesia, the following opinion was aired: "On the Immigration Amendment Ordinance, Mr. Frames spoke strongly in regard to the failure of the Government to provide restrictions to prevent the country being flooded by Chinese, Indian, and other undesirable immigrants. The Attorney-General replied that the danger was not great, and not so threatening as in the Transvaal and O.R.C."[13]

---

[9] E.S. Grogan, *From Cape to Cairo: The First Traverse of Africa from South to North* (London: Hurst and Blackett, 1902).
[10] RDM, 29.09.1902, page unreadable.
[11] RDM, 01.10.1902, 3.
[12] RDM, 17.10.1902, 6.
[13] RDM, 10.11.1902, 5.

As a matter of fact, these and other statements testify to the contemporary ambivalent perspective on migration: on the one hand, necessary for the industrial development of the country; but at the same time, in some cases, undesirable, depending on the origin of migrant workers. British or Australian immigrants, or even other white groups such as Italians or East Europeans were welcomed and their settlement was encouraged by different means such as financial support for the initial settlement and land donations; "Asiatics" were, however, generally undesirable. The employment of migrant Africans was encouraged as well, under the condition that whites and blacks were not "mingling" and the social control of the white leading class was not threatened. For this reason, both temporary accommodation and long-term settlement of native migrant workers in urban industrial areas were closely observed and controlled.

Residence in Urban Areas

In 1948, the Fagan Commission, inquiring into the issue of racial segregation in South Africa, made the following statement:

> In our urban areas, there are not only native migrant labourers, but there is also a settled, permanent, native population. These are simply facts which we have to face as such. The old cry "Send them back!"—still so often raised when there is trouble with natives—therefore no longer offers a solution. A policy based on the proposition that the natives in the towns are all temporary migrants, or can be kept in the stage of temporary migrants ... would be a false policy, if for no other reason than because the proposition itself has in the course of the time proved to be false."[14]

The dynamic described here already began shortly after 1900. Upon this time, constant change of the legal status of native residents in urban areas occurred. Mostly, debates concerning "natives in town" are witnessed related to the three large urban and industrial areas: Johannesburg, Cape Town, and Durban. All these debates and, sometimes, subsequent new municipal regulations had to deal with the bias of being extremely dependent (both in the public and private sector) on a reliable native labor force and the desire of avoiding any social mingling between the two "races"—in the language of the period. For the largest part of the white society, "the great object was to prevent the natives mixing up with the white people."[15]

"Segregation" proved to be the desired goal even for white Christian charitable and missionary organizations. In September 1915, a joint deputation of several Christian and secular bodies was received by the Johannesburg Town Council, asking for legislation allowing natives to

---

[14] RDM, 30.03.1948, 6.
[15] RDM, 07.01.1916, 6.

buy properties in so-called native locations as a means to improve their housing conditions. Their argument proved to be quite interesting: "The fulfilment of this scheme was most strongly desired by the native population. They did not want to live among the whites; they wished to live apart and asked to be provided with such reasonable facilities as would enable them to do so. ... Both whites and natives were agreed that it was advisable that they should live apart."[16] Further on, in the opinion of the deputation, establishing such a location would be as well the premise for dealing with the insanity and criminality in the city.

On the eve of the Native Urban Area Act from 1923, the following state of affairs was reported:

> Since 1905 the town native population has increased enormously, and, on the Witwatersrand and elsewhere, the housing problem has become exceedingly acute. [...] We are so accustomed to think of natives as living in kraals or compounds that we forget that in 1911 there were 508,142 [natives] resident in urban areas—forming 34.4 per cent of their total population. There were 31 towns with a native population of over 2,000."[17]

Generally speaking, there were different forms of residence and legal conditions for natives in towns. A large number of native workers were provided accommodation by big companies or the municipality in so-called compounds. These consisted generally of barracks of different standards and capacity, housing hundreds and, frequently, thousands of native workers. Barracks were divided in large rooms for dozens of people, where sleeping places were provided along the walls in the form of niches on several levels. Since the work was organized in shifts, a "bed" was shared sometimes by two or more persons. A fireplace was arranged in the middle of the room both for heating or cooking necessities, and sanitary facilities were shared.

In some compounds, the companies allocated to small groups a few square meters plot and provided them with a minimum of building material for erecting a "hut" in a more traditional way. Largely, the working population consisted of single males, but for "married" workers some companies provided a special compound area, where families could erect their own hut. The main feature of the compound life was the lack of privacy and a life in permanent company of fellow workers with a rhythmicity given by working shifts and "leisure time" interrupted only on Sunday, when the majority of workers chose to rest. The existence of cash and the lack of alternative for other activities led, very often, to consumption of alcohol and other vices.

---

[16] RDM, 22.09.1915, 1.
[17] RDM, 15.02.1922, 6.

Small businesses, shopkeepers, and private persons chose to provide accommodation on their property to their native employees, or rent for them such a space in the town. This was called residence on "business premises" and was organized by the white employer. This form of residence was convenient for the employer, since labor was accommodated in the proximity of the working place, this being an economic advantage. In the eyes of the white population, police, and municipal administration, the vicinity between whites and natives was regarded as a serious threat due to an alleged criminal behavior of natives and the improper sanitation conditions. This form of residence reduced the control over natives significantly. It was estimated that on such business premises, a larger number of natives was gravitating due to the fact that the legal residents were accommodating occasionally or semi-permanent over the night, a number of friends or relatives without the permission of their employer. Generally, the urban premises accommodated legally a large number of natives. In 1912, this form of native residence was described as such:

> Nearly ten thousand such permits have been issued and in every warehouse, foundry, or factory within the centre of Johannesburg there is to be found today a native compound. The condition of affairs has been condemned by the police authorities, and the Municipal Council has been blamed ... for the difficulty which the police has in controlling natives in Johannesburg, for the reason that the Council has not provided suitable places for the residence of natives within the municipal area.[18]

After discussing this situation for years, by 1904 the Johannesburg municipally introduced a by-law for "regulating the number of natives allowed to reside on business premises to five."[19] In the same year, in the opinion of the Public Health Committee, "no large body of natives should be allowed to live within the close neighborhood of the town."[20] Such measures had not the desired effect and the "problem" only deepened. New regulations tried to put pressure equally on natives and white owners or employers. In 1913, a new by-law was approved:

> Any person who without permission in writing from the Council establishes or maintains any compound or other place for the housing of natives or coloured persons, not being domestic or household servants, shall be guilty of a breach of these bye-laws, and shall be liable to a penalty of not exceeding £20, and to a further penalty not exceeding £2 for every day during which such offence shall continue, providing that nothing in this bye-law shall be held to refer to the housing upon the property of any mining company of natives of coloured persons employed in the mining industry. It is further notified that all previous permission

---

[18] RDM, 14.05.1912, 5.
[19] RDM, 30.01.1904, 4.
[20] RDM, 21.07.1904, 9.

granted to storekeepers and others for the housing of natives in their employ upon their premises are hereby cancelled, and fresh applications should be submitted wherever necessary by the persons concerned to the Chief Sanitary Inspector.

A figure from 1915 gives a sense about the dimension of the problem: "There were 7,500 natives about the town. There were 5,300 living on premises occupied by employers; 641 on premises hired by employers; and 1,500 on premises hired by natives themselves. The Municipality's difficulty was that it had no power at present to compel the two former classes to go into locations."[21]

Next to compounds and business premises, a third form of residence in urban areas was given in the already mentioned "native locations." Compared with the business premises, such locations were regarded by authorities as the better solution. Natives were supposed to reside in distinct, segregated areas. The control of such locations on the part of authorities was considered as better, and mingling between natives and whites was avoided. In such locations, natives were supposed to rent or even buy a plot, where they could erect small houses with a provisory or permanent character. The municipality was responsible for setting a proper sanitation and transportation system. The hardest difficulty proved to be the search for a suitable area. Even if plans for developing one or multiple such locations were discussed already in the early 1900s, nothing could be done for years. The reason was the strong opposition of white population against such areas—or even only access roads—in their vicinity.

> It cannot be forgotten that these open locations in close proximity to large white populations are very difficult to police and control. They are the haunts of loafers and criminals, both white and black, who are a source of great trouble to the police authorities. [...] In regard to locations, Johannesburg cannot be compared to a small town with large vacant areas surrounding it. Johannesburg up to a radius of five miles from the Post Office is almost completely occupied by white persons, and wherever an open location may be situated in Johannesburg it will be in close contact with white persons who, as well as the natives, will have practically free access to the location. [...] The white people in this district [Brixton] put forward very strong objections to the proposed location, but through the Ratepayers' Association they indicated they would agree to the location on certain conditions, some of which, however, such as that no persons will be allowed to trade within the location.[22]

A letter to the editor aired a similar opinion and a later article on this issue stated the mood of the white population.

---

[21] RDM, 16.06.1915, 8.
[22] RDM, 14.05.1912, 5.

> Have those who have suggested this site taken the slightest trouble to consider what such a site would mean to the town and especially to the white people living all round it? ...would mean that drunkenness would be rampant, the morals of the natives would drop to zero, the black peril cry of the past would sink into insignificance compared to what would happen, and should unfortunately some disease break out amongst them, the results would be most appalling.[23]
>
> On the other hand, whenever it has been mooted that the Council should establish a location in any quarter, the white inhabitants in the particular area or on the routes which might be used by the natives going between town and the proposed location have been up in arms against the proposal.[24]

When Southwood and the New Highlands were proposed by the municipal committee of such locations, opposition was raised and the committee was accused for selecting Southwood "because the people there were poor and Dutch. ... [W]hy they should have the north and south taking the scum of other parts?"[25]

A last form of—uncontrolled—residence in urban areas were private, unofficial "compounds" or slums, organized on the property of (mostly) white owners. These were interested in extracting as much money as possible from their property by renting rooms to anybody able to pay—sometimes even an inflated—price. Over such backyards, where the owner himself imposed no other control except the collection of his rent, any kind of regulation was difficult. This situation was favored due to an alleged incapacity of laws: "the native in the town having lived so long in absolute freedom, without any proper supervision, either in private compounds or in slum areas."[26] The Germiston Town Council, dealing with the problem, stated: "people actually let rooms to natives, and frequently harboured the criminal and undesirable class."[27]

In conclusion, any kind of racial interaction, except those caused by services brought by natives as wage laborers, was to be avoided. Even establishing segregated native locations in the proximity of the town proved difficult, and authorities and white population favored an even more restrictive system: "This committee is strongly of [the] opinion that the housing of natives in barracks under proper supervision is a much preferable method to the establishment of open locations."[28] Even

---

[23] RDM, 10.06.1912, 8.
[24] RDM, 27.06.1916, 5.
[25] RDM, 04.07.1916, 8.
[26] RDM, 14.05.1912, 5.
[27] RDM, 07.01.1916, 6.
[28] RDM, 14.05.1912, 5.

if this remained generally only a crude "vision," such an aim influenced considerably the real conditions of the natives in urban areas. At the same time, the daily lives of many poor whites in cities proved to be similar to that of the natives, but comparably better from the legal point of view.

CHRISTIANITY AND NATIVES IN URBAN CONTEXT

Ignoring the developments of this period, the Christian mission toward the natives focused further on the countryside. Rural mission stations remained for a long time the favored environment of Western missions. However, emerging industrial urban areas along the Rand attracted a huge number of natives. Shortly before 1900, as many as one hundred thousand people were already working there. The situation is described by a contemporary in the following way: "More than one hundred thousand of the young manhood of all the tribes of South Africa gathered in groups of (from) three to five thousand, and all accessible to the Gospel."[29] About 1895, acting as an attorney in the nearby Pretoria, Albert Weir Baker, the author of the following lines, became interested in mission.

> I began to be interested in the compounds on the Rand and sent Mr. Shemeld over to enquire what, if any, evangelistic work was being done in the compounds. He reported that, apart from fortnightly open-air meetings being held by a Miss Usher and a few friends in the Wolhuter and Meyer and Charlton compounds, he could hear of none. The various churches seemed satisfied with having provided places of worship in the town, to which their members and adherents could come on Sundays.[30]

Consequently, Baker renounced his legal career and became involved in mission work for the next forty plus years. Focusing initially on natives in the compounds, Baker made an application at the City and Suburban Company and got approved "a site adjoining the compound for a church, and another not far distant for a cottage for myself and family."[31] Shortly, a hall was erected "at the compound" and the activity of the interdenominational South African Compounds Mission started in 1896. This seems to be one of the earliest missionary involvements in the Rand industrial areas on the side of a white controlled body.

The slow beginning of missionary work among natives on the Rand is confirmed by information in the RDM regarding the activities of churches in the region. The "Church Notes" periodically counted all the places where churches were holding Sunday services. Those notes included

---

[29] A.W. Baker, *Grace Triumphant: The Life Story of a Carpenter, Lawyer and Missionary in South Africa from 1856 to 1939* (London: Pickering and Inglis, 1939), 102.
[30] Baker, *Grace Triumphant*, 101.
[31] Baker, *Grace Triumphant*, 102.

information regarding activities in mines or among the natives, along with report about their beginnings. In May 1903, a short note mentioned: "The Wesleyan Church has secured as evangelists Mr. Barrett, who before the war was stationed in Johannesburg in charge of the Salvation Army. Mr. Barrett is engaged in working among the miners along the reef, and has started a series of entertainment(s) at Cleveland, which promise to be very successful."[32] Regarding another church body, the note stated: "The Rev. W. Rubusana [native African], from East London, has been for the past month organizing the native church on the Reef, in connection with the Congregational Union. He has been met with much success in his work."[33]

On top of these few references to work among natives, some weeks earlier, the same journal had mentioned the inception of a Baptist mission. "[The] Baptist Union Church of South Africa will commence work at Germiston tomorrow. Services will be held in the Magistrate's Court… I also feel sure that there are many Baptists in and about Germiston, both from the Homeland and the Colonies, and it is to be hoped that they will rally round and support Mr. Heard."[34] In the subsequent years too, there were some other testimonies in similar tones. Based on the context of the last quotation, it is clear that the activities described here concern white miners and their families. Only indirectly and slowly, white governed societies engaged in native work in the area.

Summing up the missionary activities in the newly established Johannesburg around 1900, the following conclusion can be drawn: Due to the reluctance of missionaries to engage in urban areas and because of the fast-growing number of African migrant workers in a short period of time, these urban, industrial areas became, in a certain way, the new missionary frontier. In the absence of consistent missionary activities (sometimes hindered by compound managers or mining companies) and, to a certain extent, as a reaction to the missionary paternalism, the native migrant population came over time to create Christian alternatives to the missionary Christianity.[35]

---

[32] RDM, 30.05.1903, 5.
[33] RDM, 30.05.1903, 5.
[34] RDM, 02.05.1903, 5.
[35] Cf. T. Maloka, "The Struggle for Sunday: All-male Christianity in the Gold Mine Compounds," in *Christianity in South Africa: A Political, Social, and Cultural History*, ed. Richard Elphick and T.R.H. Davenport (Cape Town: David Philip Publishers (Pty), 1997), 242–252; The information given here for the period around 1900 is very general and, regarding missionary early engagement, it represents a projection of later times. Only the non-denominational South African Compounds Mission of A.W. Baker could be regarded for this period as a serious attempt of white mission among compound workers.

In the jargon of the time, these alternatives became known as the "Ethiopian Movement."[36] Shortly after 1900, the South African public was filled with information, rumors, and debates about it. Among the white public, the feelings were overwhelmingly negative. Regarding the dynamic of Ethiopianism in urban areas, opinion was expressed in the RDM that "Ethiopianism is most rampant in cities."[37] The reason for this opinion was the fact that "semi-educated" natives—responsible for the spread of Ethiopianism—were generally attracted to urban areas. Nevertheless, still more important than that was the enormous number of natives living in the urban context and the new challenges related to this situation. As far as known, it was here where a specific form of non-missionary, ethnic-overarching African Christianity emerged as a mass phenomenon.[38] A large number of African migrant workers learnt to vindicate their marginal status—not least—by creating such religious bodies, representing their desires and needs. This was not simply an intellectual exercise, but a concrete means to cope with the daily ordeal. African workers were eager to overcome their status as uneducated, exploited, still "half pagans," "poor sinners"—as they were treated by both employers and missionaries. Missionary independent churches gave them the feeling of spiritual empowerment and vindication they were looking for.

As a prime example, the influential "Ethiopian Church" of Mangena Maake Mokone came into existence in 1892 in Pretoria, close to the Rand urban region. Mokone was himself a migrant (even if not an industrial worker) and worked among fellow migrant workers. This church was not the first missionary independent one, but became known as the cradle of Ethiopianism in South Africa, being successful basically for two reasons: First, the amalgamation with the African Methodist Episcopal Church in

---

[36] Cf. Hennie Pretorius and Lizo Jafta, "'A Branch Springs Out': African Initiated Churches," in *Christianity in South Africa*, Elphick and Davenport, 211–226; J.T. Campbell, *Songs of Zion. The African Methodist Episcopal Church in the United States and South Africa* (New York: Oxford University Press, 1998).

[37] RDM, 06.07.1904, 6; The context of this statement is the following one: "But possibly the real and most effective remedy is a thorough overhauling of the system of the native education which exists in South Africa to-day. The lines along which the Lovedale College and most of the schools in the native territories are worked are worse than useless [,] they are dangerous. Every year hundreds of natives are turned out of these places, cursed with the rudiments of an education which suffices only to make them despise manual labour as degrading. Crammed as they are with a knowledge which fades like a breath on a looking-glass, they drift to towns and cities in search of employment, sloughing their primitive virtues and absorbing most white vices. ... And so *Ethiopianism is most rampant in cities*, where this type of native concentrates, and the native territories are almost bare of the precious American breed."

[38] Cf. Pretorius and Jafta, "'A Branch Springs Out,'" 213.

the US dramatically increased its prestige among Africans; second, and of equal importance, the Ethiopian church developed in the urban context as an African-universal, non-tribal church, repealing widespread ethnic parochialism. In other words, one of the fundamental conditions for the emergence of a successful non-missionary African Christianity resulted from the broad African migration into the new industrial urban areas. The timing and the topographical coincidence of these two developments—namely the rise of the non-missionary African Christianity simultaneously with the expansion of the Rand urban areas—are not accidental.

A list compiled in 1924 at the office of Director of Native Labour in Johannesburg, containing sixty-five names of independent churches, is the evidence of the growing number of such churches in the next decades.[39] In 1940, a similar list with some 800 church names testifies the same for the entire union.[40] From the simple names of these churches, as they were listed in 1924, we learn that a number of them represent communities of migrant workers: African Gaza Church, African United Gaza Church, East African Gaza Church, Gaza First Found Church, Gazaland Zimbabwe Ethiopian Church, Central African Church, Rhodesian Seventh Church Mission, and African Pentecostal Mission (of the Province of Moçambique). To these can be added other known church names such as Egreja Luzo Episcopal (known as Episcopal Egreja Luzo-Africana as well), the Gaza Mission Church or the National Ethiopian Church of Moçambique, proving that the said list was incomplete.

The Director of Native Labour in Johannesburg compiled in 1916 with the assistance of local inspectors a list with all the places in the Transvaal mines, where European-controlled or missionary independent churches were active. According to it, the different Gaza-churches were present at least in nineteen locations.[41] In comparison, the Church of the Province (the Anglican Church) was represented in forty-six locations and the Dutch Reformed Church only in thirteen places. Regarding the way the church life was organized under the compound conditions, we learn that missionary independent churches are holding their services "in rooms in compound," having "native local preacher[s]." On behalf of one church was mentioned: "There is a self-appointed conductor of services who works and lives on the mine."[42] This model should be regarded as the usual way of existence in compounds.

---

[39] National Archives and Records Service of South Africa (Pretoria Repository), GNLB 205, Native Separatist Churches.
[40] Cf. Bengt G.M. Sundkler, *Bantu Prophets in South Africa* (London: Oxford University Press, 1961) 354–356.
[41] GNLB 216, Native Churches and Missions—General, June 1916.
[42] GNLB 216, Native Churches and Missions—General, June 1916.

The leader of Episcopal Egreja Luzo-Africana, Mott Munene Scobele, made in 1929 the following statement for the Native Affairs Department: "We have regular Evangelists [in] nearly every Compound in the Gold minings where our workers have also established our work [...]. [O]ur work was established already in Transvaal by those [of] our members who are working in the mines both Gold and Coal [in Natal]. ... Our people in Transvaal, along the Rand and Collieries [in Natal] are crying for their ordained ministers."[43] The General Superintendent of the African Pentecostal Mission (of the Province of Moçambique) affirmed in 1922 that "the majority of the natives in connection with this religious movement are now found here as mine employees."[44]

Conclusion

Ethiopianism has been regarded by scholars largely as a reaction to the complex of missionary paternalism and political colonialism. It has been seen as an African version of Christianity, as a reaction to the frequent bankruptcy of the moral economy of mission churches, and as a response to European nationalism. Furthermore, Ethiopianism was regarded both in its religious and political dimension in connection with the experience of forced-migration and diaspora of African slaves, free black people, and colonial subjects looking for emancipation on different shores of the Atlantic.

Regarding South Africa, the golden age of Ethiopianism can be seen as the period between the 1890s and 1920. Yet, attempts of religious emancipation are to be found even before 1890. This is the case of a small group of Africans leaving the Paris Mission in Basutoland in 1872, of another one in Natal two years later, of the Nehemiah Tile Tembu "national" church in the Cape Colony since 1883, and of a number of African converts departing in 1890 from the German Lutheran mission in northern Transvaal. However, these "remained tied to particular ethnic groups and hence were not the seeds of a national movement."[45] For South Africa, the cause of Ethiopianism was seen in a set of reasons ranging from racial segregation and lack of perspective for able African churchmen as leaders in mission-controlled churches to secular elements as the decline of opportunities for natives in agriculture, manufacturing, and business due to restrictive laws of white governments. While it is true that such reasons represent, in the long term, the soil for the rise of such a religious and secular protest movement as Ethiopianism, this does not explain why the boom of Ethiopianism took place in the 1890s. The reasons lay not

---

[43] GNLB 384.
[44] GNLB 205, African Pentecostal Mission, 9.11.1922.
[45] Pretorius and Jafta, "A Branch Springs Out," 213.

in dramatic changing conditions on the side of politics and missionary Christianity during this decade, since the erosion of status in church and society for Africans is a process advancing differently in the four colonies and republics before 1910, and accelerating with the foundation of the Union. The answers to the question, why to this time and to this place (Transvaal, and more specifically the Rand region), are obvious: due to growing labor migration and emerging urban settlements in the course of the development of mining industry in the region.

Even if this aspect has been largely overlooked in the discussion about Ethiopianism, this should be recognized if we agree on the role of African migrants as missionaries with O. Kalu: "South Africa was like a nodal point from which many migrant laborers, as black missionaries, fanned into the contiguous countries."[46] The urban environment, as described previously, offered the condition for the emergence and propagation of missionary independent Christianity: Ethiopianism as a mass movement with local weight and transregional missionary outreach is only the result of exchange and transformation of religious ideas, ideals, and claims in the expanding urban context. It was only with the boom of the Rand as an industrial zone, with the rapid expansion of urban settlements as a melting pot and communication hub due to the mass migration of cheap African labor force that Ethiopianism got a platform of interaction between actors coming from different regions and departing as multiplicators and "missionaries" to different corners of the continent as far as Kenya and Uganda. In the absence of this explanation, statements such as that "[b]y 1893 Ethiopianism was outgrowing its earlier ethnic particularism and was developing a pan-African vision"[47] remain without clarification. The first important group to engage on this path was the Ethiopian Church of M.M. Mokone founded in 1892, in Pretoria, in the proximity of the industrial and urban centers on the Rand. A real boost of the Mokone's church was the affiliation with the African Methodist Episcopal Church in the US, a fact that flamed up imaginations and hopes of a large number of Africans.

In the religious economy of South Africa, this process had tremendous consequences: religious emancipation went together with religious diversification. Even if for a period of time African churches replicated the confessional spectrum of missionary Christianity, mainly by holding principles, doctrines, and rituals of their archetypes and as such remaining at their core Presbyterian, Methodist, Lutheran, Baptist, Reformed,

---

[46] Ogbu U. Kalu, "Ethipianism in African Christianity," in *African Christianity: An African Story* edited by Ogbu U. Kalu (Pretoria: Department of Church History, University of Pretoria, 2005), 258-277 (276).

[47] Pretorius and Jafta, "'A Branch Springs Out,'" 214.

etc., after a while, these churches began to experience the shaping of their "confessional" profile. Identities were shaped over a process of selection and combination of religious ideas in such a way that missionary independent churches produced new Christian profiles compared with the Western confessional catalogue. This new Christianity emerged from responding to the needs of marginalized and oppressed African Christians. The fact that such ideas did not remain confined to urban settings, having spread rapidly in rural contexts, demonstrates the range of the triggered religious innovation. During this process, no stone of the traditional Western Christian edifice—in Bible study, teaching, piety, rite, church order, ministry etc.—remained unturned. In South Africa, this second "African Reformation,"[48] as it was called, very similar to the first one in the sixteenth century, emerged as an urban phenomenon. But, different from the first one with academic and religious elites at its core, this one erupted among migrant workers.

From all different consequences of Ethiopianism in South Africa, one should be still mentioned here briefly. In an analysis of the dynamic of Islam in South Africa, Robert C.H. Shell[49] recounts some fears of Christian missionaries around 1900. One of the voices quoted was Thomas F. Lightfoot, Anglican missionary in charge of the "Mission to Moselems," who testified in 1900 to a wide-spread contemporary opinion: "*Slam's kerk is die zwart man's kerk*"[50] (the Islamic church is the black man's church). Shell mentions in the same context the 1915 estimation of Gustav Bernhard Gerdener, a Stellenbosch missionary: "thousands of Moslems in the Rand [goldmine] compounds are enthusiastic propagators of their religion" and "many of the raw natives return to their homes strongly under the influence of Islam."[51] Even if such reports might have included some exaggeration, as Shell and his source is further suggesting, the presence of Muslim migrant workers on the Rand is well known. In his analysis of the spread of Islam in the Cape Colony before 1820, Shell stressed the fact that the overwhelming majority of the non-European population in the urban centers of this region was Muslim. This included Asians (such as Malaya or Indians) and Africans. According to Shell, only the substantial European migration to this region during the following decades and the end of slavery in the 1830s changed the largely Muslim

---

[48] Allan Anderson, *African Reformation: African Initiated Christianity in the 20th Century* (Trenton: African World Press, 2001).
[49] R.C.H. Shell, "Between Christ and Mohammed: Conversion, Slavery, and Gender in the Urban Western Cape," in *Christianity in South Africa*, Elphick and Davenport, 268–277.
[50] Shell, "Between Christ and Mohammed," 276.
[51] Shell, "Between Christ and Mohammed," 276.

profile of the Cape-born urban population of the early nineteenth century into a Christian one.

Considering the mentioned testimonies about the Muslim presence on the Rand around 1900 and extrapolating from the base of Shell's analysis for the earlier time, it could be possible that the competition between Christianity and Islam in the emerging urban regions on the Rand would have been a close one, if we consider the initial incapacity of mission churches to cope with the massive and rapid growth of population in this region. In the absence of Ethiopianism as the authentic expression of an African Christianity, Islam could have been regarded as an African religion and possibly adopted by a large number of natives. This could have been favored by the fact that Islam represented to natives a religious alternative to Christian colonial society. In conclusion, Ethiopianism—emanating from urban centers—made a major contribution to the spread of Christianity on the southern part of the continent. In South Africa, Islam remained until today a sizable reality mainly on coastal regions like Cape Town and Durban.

Bibliography

Anderson, Allan H. *African Reformation: African Initiated Christianity in the 20th Century*. Trenton, NJ: Africa World Press, 2001.

Baker, A.W. *Grace Triumphant: The Life Story of a Carpenter, Lawyer and Missionary in South Africa from 1856 to 1939*. London: Pickering and Inglis, 1939.

Campbell, James T. *Songs of Zion: The African Methodist Episcopal Church in the United States and South Africa*. Chapel Hill: Univ. of North Carolina Press, 1998.

Grogan, Ewart Scott. *From the Cape to Cairo; the First Traverse of Africa from South to North*. London: Hurst and Blackett, 1902.

Kalu, Ogbu U. "Ethipianism in African Christianity." In *African Christianity: An African Story*, edited by Ogbu U. Kalu (Pretoria: Department of Church History, University of Pretoria, 2005), 258-277 (276).

Maloka, T. "The Struggle for Sunday: All-Male Christianity in the Gold Mine Compounds." In *Christianity in South Africa: A Political, Social, and Cultural History*, edited by Richard Elphick and T.R.H. Davenport, 242–52. Perspectives on Southern Africa 55. Berkeley, CA: University of California Press, 1997.

Shell, R.C.H. "Between Christ and Mohammed: Conversion, Slavery, and Gender in the Urban Western Cape." In *Christianity in South Africa: A Political, Social, and Cultural History*, edited by Richard Elphick and T.R.H. Davenport, 268–77. Perspectives on Southern Africa 55. Berkeley, CA: University of California Press, 1997.

Sundkler, Bengt. *Bantu Prophets in South Africa*. London: Oxford University Press, 1961.

Van Onselen, Charles. *Studies in the Social and Economic History of the Witwatersrand, 1886-1914, vol. 1: New Babylon*. Studies in the Social and Economic History of the Witwatersrand, 1886-1914. London: Longman, 1982.

———. *Studies in the Social and Economic History of the Witwatersrand, 1886-1914, vol. 2: New Nineveh*. Studies in the Social and Economic History of the Witwatersrand, 1886-1914. London: Longman, 1982.

Primary Sources

GNLB. Government Native Labour Bureau (1904–1950). National Archives and Records Service of South Africa, Pretoria.

RDM. "Rand Daily Mail." *Rand Daily Mail*. n.d. https://www.readex.com/content/rand-daily-mail-1902-1985.

PART IV

CREATIVE TRANSFORMATIONS: AGENCY, CITIZENSHIP, AND PUBLIC RELIGION

11

CHRISTIANITY AND URBANISM: THE ECUMENICAL TRAINING AND ADVISORY CENTER (CECA) AND THE FORMATION OF THE POPULAR LEGAL AGENTS[1]

Claudete Beise Ulrich
Nivia Ivette Núñez de la Paz

Established in 1973, during a time when Brazil was ruled by an authoritarian military dictatorship, the Centro Ecumênico de Evangelização, Capacitação e Assessoria (CECA)[2] aimed at contributing to the process and possibility of re-democratization in light of the Christian faith. Based in São Leopoldo, this ecumenical organization initially developed two programs that intersected with each other: (a) Solidarity and Citizenship; and, (b) Faith and Citizenship. Nowadays, under a new name, Centro Ecumênico de Capacitação e Assessoria,[3] CECA's programs function around three emphases: ecumenism, gender, and human rights. The center's key objective continues to be the development of an understanding and practice of citizenship that is guided by a faith that summons and articulates itself through a sense of ecumenicity and interreligious engagement. This essay reflects on CECA's action in the formation of civically active women through the program called Popular Legal Agents (PLPs),[4]

[1] This essay was translated from Portuguese into English by Caio César da Silva Barreto. Throughout this essay, the expression "Popular Legal Agents" is used to translate the Portuguese Promotoras Legais Populares (PLPs).
[2] Ecumenical Center for Evangelization, Training and Counseling.
[3] Ecumenical Training and Advisory Center. For more information, see: https://cecadh.wordpress.com/.
[4] Editors' note: PLPs is the acronym for the plural Promotoras Legais Populares. The Portuguese word "promotora" is feminine. The gender-neutral nature of the word "agents," which we are using as the English translation of "promotora," must not hide the gender-specificity of this program. This program equips

seeking to demonstrate how the formation of these female Popular Legal Agents is articulated within the broader framework of the People's Access to Justice Projects.[5] By focusing on CECA's actions through this particular lens, this essay addresses the question of how this ecumenical organization has been instrumental in confronting and overcoming violence against women through actions grounded on a public theology that points to new forms of ecumenical urban Christianity.

Violence against women

The first important fact to highlight when we talk about violence against women is that this word/concept/reality always denotes "a plural"; there is no violence in the singular. When it happens, we always witness a set of actions, a process (circular or spiral, depending on the authors working on the theme),[6] but always a complex process in which, in practice, different types of violence (physical, psychological, patrimonial, moral, symbolic,[7] religious[8]) are intertwined. The number of cases of violence against women worldwide is alarming,[9] despite the many actions that have been implemented to combat this kind of violence in the past decades. Since what is at stake and in danger is life, *the life of women*, one must not

---

and empowers grassroots women to offer legal counsel and education in impoverished communities, taking into account, especially, the legal system's bias against women. According to *THEMIS—Gênero, Justiça e Direitos Humanos*, an NGO created in 1993 by a group of feminist lawyers and social scientists "to address discrimination against women in the justice system—The Popular Legal Agents (PLPs) are community leaders trained in basic notions of law, women's rights, and the organization of the state and the judiciary, among other pertinent themes, depending on the context of the neighborhood or region in which they are inserted." Their work bridges between the state and their communities, contributing to expand the protection of their neighbors' rights as well as improve their access to public services. See "Promotoras Legais Populares," *THEMIS— Gênero, Justiça e Direitos Humanos*, accessed June 10, 2019, http://themis.org.br/fazemos/promotoras-legais-populares/.

[5] Projetos de Acesso Popular à Justiça.
[6] Nivia Ivette Núñez de la Paz, ed., *Da Violência de Gênero para Relações Humanizadas* (São Leopoldo: CEBI, 2010).
[7] Pierre Bourdieu, *A Dominação Masculina*, trans. Maria Helena Kühner. 3rd ed. (Rio de Janeiro: Bertrand, 2003).
[8] Abdruschin Schaeffer Rocha and Claudete Beise Ulrich, "A dessacralização da violência contra as mulheres a partir dos conceitos de desejo mimético e bode expiatório em René Girard—desafios para a educação teológica latino-americana." *Reflexus—Revista Semestral de Teologia e Ciências das Religiões*, ano XII, no. 19 (2018): 15–38, accessed November 20, 2018, http://revista.faculdadeunida.com.br/index.php/reflexus/article/view/718.
[9] Key facts can be found at World Health Organization, "Violence against Women," https://www.who.int/news-room/fact-sheets/detail/violence-against-women.

downplay the importance fighting all sorts of violence against women and much less give up on confronting it. Ivone Gebara wonders,

> What do we women have that attracts so much violence"? [. . .] I am convinced that there is not a single cause to explain and understand something about the aggression that we humans do to each other and particularly the violence done to women. There are multiple causes that are intertwined, complex situations in which the given reasons do not [fully] explain all what happens.[10]

In the case of the Latin American churches, and, more specifically, in the Brazilian case (the context in which the authors of this chapter live and work), there are multiple and diverse examples of initiatives to cope with and respond to this sort of violence. Some of these initiatives include preparing guidebooks to work with the communities, opening and maintaining shelter homes or temporary houses for women facing imminent risk of life, and offering lessons and workshops. However, given their hierarchical structures and their participation in a cultural and patriarchal system that fosters and perpetuates this type of behavior, Brazilian churches, despite showing some degree of commitment to such initiatives, have never made the theme of violence against women a priority for their practice of the gospel. Moreover, some denominations do not address this problem at all, while others do not take relevant actions in response to it.

By contrast, social movements and ecumenical and interreligious organizations, which include many women and men who are part of different Christian denominations, having a more horizontal structure (formed by networks), have generated more decisive forms of confronting this problem. Because they are not tied to a dogmatic view of the world and do not need to respond to pyramidal institutional structures, social movements such as the movement for the decriminalization and legalization of abortion[11] tend to be more incisive and consistent in their work to stop violence against women. Also, social movements are usually more affirmed and supported by ecumenical organizations than by the churches that form those organizations. The struggle to end violence against women needs to consider the different contexts in which such violence happens as well as the particularities of each context. Even if it is important to think about global actions (since, as the World Health Organization and many other advocacy groups have shown, this is indeed

---

[10] Ivone Gebara. "Quando as mulheres atraem violência," In Ivone Gebara, *Teologia Urbana: ensaios sobre ética, gênero, meio ambiente e a condição humana* (São Paulo: Fonte, 2014), 163–167.

[11] For a discussion of abortion in the Brazilian context, see Alcilene Cavalcante and Dulce Xavier, eds., *Em defesa da vida*: aborto e direitos humanos (São Paulo: Católicas pelo Direito de Decidir, 2006).

a global problem), both macro and micro actions need to be considered (a denomination in a particular country, a specific municipality or neighborhood, etc.), taking into account that what may work in a given context or place will not necessarily work in others. With regard to global actions, which are crucial, one must be aware that this is a problem/situation that touches all people, bringing the lives of more than half the planet's population to the center of public policy concerns, since these lives (women's lives) have been constantly threatened by a system that has normalized and perpetuated a particular and cruel kind of oppression both in the past and in the present. This system considers natural that a large part of humanity sees themselves as history's protagonists (men), while the other half (women) are seen as objects, or as inferior and incapable, thinking of them, therefore, as beings subject to subalternization and domination.

We are aware that this is not an easy topic to discuss, neither in terms of identifying its roots nor in terms of setting up actions to address and confront its reality. Due to centuries of habituation, it is difficult to help others understand—to show that what happens is not a natural behavior, but rather the result of rules established by male, androcentric, and patriarchal societies, and by kyriarchal institutions that offer all kinds of privileges to a certain group of people over others. An example of such privileges in our churches is the discussion of female ordination, which is a recent practice in most countries, still prohibited in many places and contexts, such as the case of the Anglican province of the Southern Cone of America (now the Anglican Church of South America). Even when we think about mainstream Protestant churches like the IEAB[12] and the IECLB[13] in Brazil, it was only in the year 2018 that a female reverend was made bishop for the first time (Marinez Rosa dos Santos Bassotto), and only then a female pastor was elected president (Silvia Beatrice Genz), even after decades since these churches started ordaining women. Can we truly view this as a "natural" process? Can we truly view it "as God's will" and consider it a surprise that these two churches had their "first time" choosing women to this level of leadership so recently, in the same year? The feminist suspicion leads us to other questions, readings, and findings. If we affirm this fact as natural, as God's will, as a surprising fact, we would be ignoring how the patriarchal system interferes in our lives, and how power relations cross across our bodies and the spaces we inhabit.

In 2016, Brazil's National Council of Christian Churches—CONIC,[14] held an ecumenical meeting of women with the theme "Women: Rights

---

[12] Igreja Episcopal Anglicana do Brasil.
[13] Igreja Evangélica de Confissão Luterana no Brasil.
[14] CONIC—Conselho de Igrejas Cristãs do Brasil.

and Justice."[15] This event, the first of its kind at the national level, revisited the history of women in the Latin American ecumenical movement, asking the women participants in that meeting about our place as women in the "history line," i.e., when and where we appeared, when and where we were silenced, erased; and which spaces are still being denied to us. At the time we were discussing these matters, President Dilma Vana Rousseff, the first woman ever to be elected president of Brazil, was undergoing an impeachment process. In our discussions, we understood that the "impeachment" perpetrated against her was a sexist and misogynistic coup. Thus, fueled by a sense of prophetic indignation and denunciation, we decided to include that general perception in the meeting's final document. We were surprised to hear, however, that the leadership of a certain church represented in the event, which in the previous day had delivered a beautiful speech on gender as the denomination's guiding principle, was opposed to the use of the word coup, requesting it to be removed from the document while threatening not to sign it. Unfortunately, cases like this remind us of the fragility of actions against power structures that dictate rules and establish the limits of the denunciation of oppression.

Although the number of actions confronting oppression against women has increased in the past years, they are not sufficient if we consider the absurdly large number of cases of violence against women in Latin America and the world.[16] If on the one hand, we have become more aware of the importance of being able to name, understand, recognize, and denounce such violence, on the other hand, the elevated number of cases of violence and violent deaths of women (femicide) alerts us to the insufficiency of our actions to confront it. Hence, it is crucial that this matter does not become a subject of the past, nor a thematic of secondary concern. It has to be seen for what it is, i.e., a daily life-threatening situation that affects women all around the world, literally every minute. It is noteworthy that the recognition of women as human beings and citizens is not a gift; such a recognition results from the continuous struggle of women. It is in this spirit of the continuous struggle for the recognition of the full humanity and citizenship of women that we present the work of CECA.

---

[15] São Paulo, November 17–20, 2016.
[16] Brazil alone reported 65,000 cases of violence against women in 2017. See IPEA, "Atlas da Violência: Brasil registra mais de 65 mil homicídios em 2017," accessed January 30, 2020, http://www.ipea.gov.br/portal/index.php?option=com_content&view=article&id=34786&Itemid=8.

Ecumenical Training and Advisory Center, CECA

The Ecumenical Training and Advisory Center, CECA[17] is a civil society organization (CSO)[18] formed in 1973, during a time of authoritarian military rule in Brazil. CECA was originally constituted as a training center for pastoral agents created to support and encourage popular movements, especially the Base Ecclesial Communities (CEBs), in the state of Rio Grande do Sul. Its mission had two pillars: evangelization and catechesis. These pillars should go hand in hand. The theoretical matrix informing the center's programs was Paulo Freire's methodology of popular education and liberation theology. The courses offered by CECA trained many community organizers to oppose the dictatorship, forming spaces of resistance and social transformation.

After the years of military rule, CECA gradually became a reference for churches and organized social movements involved in the rebuilding of a democratic society. CECA described itself as an ecumenical organization focused on training and advising the grassroots with the aim of strengthening democracy. CECA's mission was to contribute to social transformation and to the development of a democratic, just, and participatory society. Its work was based on the formation and articulation of a critical consciousness in the face of multiple forms of inequality and oppression in order to achieve the "utopia of oikomene." Through its training and advising services, CECA impacted social and popular movements, ministries, church groups, ecclesial and community leaders, and public agencies.

In the years after 2000, in order to respond to the complexity of new challenges, many civil society organizations had to reinvent themselves, revising their theoretical and methodological paradigms of social intervention. CECA underwent such a process, developing and implementing new praxis models, with a focus on three lines of action: ecumenism, gender concerns, and human rights. The word "evangelization" was sacked from its social and legal name in 2010 in order to facilitate access to government funds, since that word was no longer welcomed in the secular milieu. Furthermore, the poor, the central axis of liberation theology, had new and multiple faces. Because of that, Latin American liberation theology itself was turned into a plural theology, a theology representative of the diversity of bodies emerging from multiple individualities. However,

---

[17] For more on CECA and its history, see José Carlos Stoffel, *Centro ecumênico de evangelização, capacitação e assessoria. Ecumenismo de justiça: reflexão e prática* (São Leopoldo: CECA, Oikos 2006).

[18] For an understanding of CSOs, see United Nations Development Program (UNDP), *A Guide to Civil Society Organizations Working on Democratic Governance* (Oslo: UNDP Oslo Governance Centre, 2005).

another theology was also emerging and began to guide the daily life of CECA, i.e., public theology, specifically the brand of this theological stream that aims to promote citizenship. This citizenship-oriented public theology does not use theological discourse so overtly as it addresses a broader interreligious and/or secular context, offering guidance, and contributing to an understanding of abundant life for all people. It was at this stage of revising its mission that CECA decided to turn its focus to the formation of Popular Legal Agents (PLPs), giving birth to a new phase of its history, which intertwines Christianity, urbanism, citizenship, and human dignity to cement life—in particular the life of women.

Popular Legal Agents—PLPs

In 1998, CECA offered its first Popular Legal Agents Training Course, thus giving birth to the PLPs. This program was named under the broader rubric "People's Access to Justice," because it was born as one initiative among other similar programs that already existed in other parts of Brazil in organizations such as the Women's Union of São Paulo (SP) and Themis (PoA). In the case of CECA, the PLPs trained women for leadership in the Vale dos Sinos region, providing them with the necessary empowerment to qualify and validate the work they carry out. The objectives of this program are the following: (1) to train women for actions to prevent violence and defend human rights in favor of marginalized sectors of the population, especially women and girls; (2) to empower women so they may succeed in their own life projects; and (3) to qualify their interventions in the discussion and implementation of public policies related to gender. The Popular Legal Agents Training Course is a space for building citizenship and autonomy in the struggle for women's human rights, being a legitimate space for women's social organization and freedom.

PLPs are women who combat violence against women through listening, orientation, follow-up, and referrals. They act directly in neighborhoods and communities where violence against women occurs on a daily basis, many times in subtle ways. At the same time, they also participate in existing councils, forums, and Redes de Atendimento e Enfrentamento (Care and Coping Networks) in the municipalities where they live and work.[19]

After the first twenty years of implementation of this program and eleven Popular Legal Agents Training Courses that qualified more than 270 women, we noticed the consolidation of leadership roles, with women

---

[19] For more on these networks formed accross the nation, see Secretaria Nacional de Enfrentamento à Violência contra as Mulheres, *Rede de Enfrentamento à Violência contra as Mulheres* (Brasília: Secretaria de Políticas para as Mulheres—Presidência da República, 2011).

who graduated from the program taking greater responsibility. Over the years, Popular Legal Agents have participated in the coordination of the Women's Forum, the Health Forum, the Black Movement, and the Municipal Council for Women's Rights, among other important networks for coordinated action in Vale dos Sinos. These women have become community leaders, educators, and coordinators in social projects, being also active participants in the Municipal Secretaries of Women in the region, in church ministries, and in neighborhood associations.

The broader umbrella under which the PLPs are placed, the People's Access to Justice Projects, are organized in multiple stages, which start with a Training Course comprised of one hundred hours of classes (eighty-four hours of which take place in a classroom under a more theoretical format while sixteen hours are devoted to visits to public offices). A typical Training Course is organized in the following manner:

1. It begins with a four-hour introductory session titled "Presentation of the Ecumenical Training and Advisory Center—CECA." This is the time when participants are introduced to the People's Access to Justice Project more broadly.

2. A second four-hour session follows with a focus on the PLPs program, under the rubric "Popular Legal Agents—Function and Action."

3. The two four-hour introductory sessions are followed by daily eight-hour sessions on diverse topics of significance for the work of the PLPs. On the second day, that eight-hour session covers the following topics: civil, political, and social human rights, international law, and women's rights (in the morning). In the afternoon, they are introduced to notions of law, justice, and legislation; the organization of the judiciary power; fundamental rights—the public prosecutor's office and collective demands.

4. On the following day, another eight-hour session covers the topics of feminism, gender, race, and ethnicity, patriarchy, and power relations (morning); and violence (concept/types/spiral-cycle), in the afternoon.

5. The eight-hour pattern is repeated on the fourth day, with the morning being devoted to the study of the National Pact for Combating Violence against Women, and the afternoon to discuss the Maria da Penha Law[20] (humanized care).

---

[20] This is the popular name of the law, 11.340/2006, a law passed in connection with a brutal case of domestic violence against Maria da Penha Maia Fernandes, in 2002, with the goal of creating mechanisms to combat and reduce domestic violence in Brazil. For more on this law, see Wânia Pasinato, "The Maria da Penha Law: 10 Years On," *SUR International Journal on Human Rights* 13, no. 24 (2016): 155–163.

6. The fifth day has only a half-day lesson, complemented with an afternoon visit to the Municipal Women's Secretariat and Coordination.
7. The sixth day of training goes back to the eight-hour pattern, with the morning session focusing on conflict mediation/resolution and the afternoon on sexual and reproductive rights—concept, family planning, STD/HIV prevention, rape/sexual abuse/harassment, and abortion.
8. On the seventh day, the morning session discusses women's rights in family relations, marital relationships, stable union, and civil union for same sex couples. The afternoon is devoted to the themes of dissolution of marital relations/separation/divorce, sons/daughters, and alimony/ custody/regulations of visits.
9. The eighth day includes a four-hour lesson and a visit to the Referral Center.
10. The ninth day involves morning lessons on police stations, law offices, and sheltering services, while the Child and Adolescent Statute (ECA) is studied in the afternoon.
11. The tenth day offers a four-hour lesson and a visit to the police station.
12. That pattern is repeated on the following day, which includes a visit to the Child Protection Council.
13. The morning session on the twelfth day focuses on drugs (prevention/care network), while the afternoon session discusses the topics of masculinities/homosexuality, and discrimination.
14. The eighth-hour session on the penultimate day of the training course focuses on churches, religions, and interreligious dialogue.
15. On the last day, participants have a full eight-hour session on restorative justice.

The second stage of the program happens through monthly meetings, in which participants discuss key concepts or themes on topics such as feminism, citizenship, human rights, and democracy in connection with the day-to-day realities in which they meet those concepts both at the local and the national levels. At this stage, PLPs share some reports (on their community actions, or their contributions in the different civil or political groups or movements they participate in or represent). These reports and testimonials aim to foment dialogue and the search for joint solutions for the problems mentioned at the meetings. These reports also help shape and effect the articulation of networks of community care and resistance to gender-based violence.

The third stage of the program is the Follow-up Course, which aims to deepen previously acquired knowledge. These courses are implemented every two years, as follow-ups for the initial training courses. Their duration is of approximately twenty hours. The Follow-up Course is the training space that brings together the newly formed PLPs and the older practitioners, i.e., those PLPs that have already been active. In those courses, themes proposed by the PLPs themselves are discussed. This stage of the program constitutes an opportunity for reencounter, recycling, and joint planning of the group's journey after the training sessions.

After that stage, PLPs are sent out to advice/work on other CECA projects such as the *Youth Working against Gender-based Violence Project*, the *Not So Sweet Home Project*, and the *Awareness-raising Project*.

Youth Working against Gender-based Violence is a project that is implemented primarily in state and municipal schools in Rio Grande do Sul, being carried out also in private schools, although less often. High school students (fourteen to eighteen years old) are the ones mainly reached by this project. Utilizing a methodology based on the popular education movement,[21] the groups sit in a circle where participants are encouraged to interact on the basis of the reality they experience both at school and at home. Dance, poetry, singing, and drama are used as pedagogical dynamics to propose new relations and new behaviors emphasizing respect for diversity and the construction of humanized relationships.

Not so Sweet Home is a project that was born out of a partnership with another entity, the Lutheran Foundation of Diaconia—FLAD,[22] created by the council of the Igreja Evangélica de Confissão Luterana no Brasil (IECLB) in 2000. CECA and PLPs have been working on this project since its inception, in 2006, during the World Council of Churches Assembly gathered in the city of Porto Alegre. The project consists of assembling a house with four spaces: a living room, a kitchen, a double bedroom, and a children's room, using the placement of objects of daily use in those spaces to encourage dialogue and reflection through written sentences on the side of each object, all revolving around the issue of domestic violence. For example, a knife in the kitchen is commonly associated with cutting food. Yet, for participants coming from a home where relationships are marked by violence, it may also be associated with a weapon

---

[21] Popular education is a pedagogy developed in the 1960s by the Catholic left, including its best-known articulator, Paulo Freire. It has become a pillar for numerous popular movements in Brazil and in other parts of the world since the 1970s. See, for instance, Scott Mainwaring, "The Catholic Church, Popular Education, and Political Change in Brazil," *Journal of Interamerican Studies and World Affairs* 26, no. 1 (1984): 97–124.

[22] Fundação Luterana de Diaconia.

that threatens or kills. The Bible on the bedroom nightstand, a book that can be associated with love and peace, and which many families have in their homes, can also be turned into an object that enables and perpetuates psychological violence—that produces, reproduces, and many times sacralizes symbolic violence. *Not so Sweet Home* is an interactive house, open to the public for visitation, where formation happens in a different, lively way. Trained PLPs are often on duty in the house in pairs or trios. In this kind of activity, PLPs develop skills such as listening, counseling, training, accompaniment, and referral (when necessary) to other services offered in the care network.

The *Awareness-Raising Project* reached 1,120 people in different districts of the city of São Leopoldo in 2010. The purpose of this project was to raise awareness and prevent violence against women. It was developed by the Municipal Department of Public Policies for Women, implemented by CECA, and financed by the federal government through the Secretariat for Women's Public Policies. The project contemplated actions to prevent violence, giving publicity to the Maria da Penha Law and to other services available through the municipal care network. PLPs were placed in charge of the project's execution, serving as advisors in the districts where it was implemented. Such experience sedimented their role as community leaders. The workshops gathered families, using the same methodology of popular education mentioned above: a circle for sharing and dialogue based on personal and communitarian daily experiences. Life stories were told and analyzed through a dynamic of knowledge exchange in the midst of laughs, tears, smells, gestures, and silences. Together, they conceived possible "family and community movements" that could generate real change, transform that violent reality, and build different, humanized relations. Didactic booklets[23] were elaborated specifically for the implementation of this project, which still exists and has experienced new developments in different neighborhoods and institutions in the region.

PLPs and the delicate moment that Brazil is experiencing

What does "People's Access to Justice" mean? Which are the guidelines that mark and define the execution of this program? What has unfolded from it? To answer these questions, we will offer a brief historical survey of what this formation has meant for the empowerment and action of women, through the prism of what has transpired in the last three years in Brazil (2016–2019).

---

[23] Graciela Patrícia Cornaglia, ed., *Prevenção à Violência contra as Mulheres*: Caderno I (São Leopoldo: CEBI, 2010); Graciela Patrícia Cornaglia and Karine Santos, eds., *Pacto nacional pelo enfrentamento à violência contra as mulheres*. Caderno II (São Leopoldo: CEBI, 2010).

In the training evaluations, PLPs have highlighted what they have gained from the program. An analysis of those evaluations leads to the following conclusion:

a) On the personal level, the program provides a space for active speaking; fosters the empowerment of women (as they find themselves as subjects of a right that is reflected in the demands for autonomy and freedom); and promotes the recognition of the need to confront and/or leave situations of violence that immobilize them, so they can be true subjects of their own history;

b) On the collective level, the PLPs' formation program is recognized as a legitimate space for the social organization of women in the struggle for freedom and justice, having the purpose of equipping women to become advocates for women's rights and consolidating new leadership roles, as those women take on broader commitments and greater responsibilities in their communities. As mentioned earlier, Popular Legal Agents have been involved in the coordination of the Women's Forum, the Health Forum, the Black Movement, and the Municipal Council of Women's Rights, among other civil society forums and movements. They have become educators and coordinators of social projects, and taken on leadership roles in the Municipal Women's Secretariat, in church ministries, and in neighborhood associations.

As we previously discussed, Brazilian democracy was impacted by a tragic coup in 2016. A president elected by more than 54 million votes (the first woman to have ever been elected president in the country) was removed from office through an abusive use of impeachment proceedings.[24] The vice president, a white male politician who participated in the collusion to bring President Dilma Rousseff down, quickly started the implementation of a full-fledged neoliberal program of government, radically different from the platform that elected his predecessor in 2014.

---

[24] Editors' note: A 103-page report of a fact-finding delegation of the Latin American Studies Association (LASA), composed by scholars of different political and ideological orientations, came to the following conclusion about the legitimacy of Rousseff's impeachment: "While technical rule-following was a concern at certain key junctures, even supporters of the outcome would have difficulty today defending its substantive basis in the terms that were formally adduced." See Chalhoub, Sidney, et al., "Report of the Lasa Fact-Finding Delegation on the Impeachment of the Brazilian President Dilma Rousseff," accessed by the editors on October 30, 2019, https://lasa.international.pitt.edu/members/reports/BrazilDelegationReport-2017.pdf.

Much needs to be said about this recent history.[25] But in this essay, we limit ourselves to assess the misogynistic and chauvinistic aspects of the coup. There are many points of entry for that discussion. We could, for instance, highlight the sexist approaches used in respect to the candidate Dilma Rousseff (months before her election) by her political adversaries; or we could refer to the very composition of the cabinet formed by the vice president who succeeded her, which put only men in charge of the executive ministries (right after Dilma Rousseff had made history by placing eleven women as her top cabinet advisors, something unprecedented in Brazil).

However, to keep with the focus of this essay, among the many aspects of how the 2016 coup on Brazilian democracy negatively impacted women, we have chosen to highlight the dismantling of public policies that advanced women's rights,[26] since the swift take-down of those policies has been pivotal to the recent rise in the numbers of cases of violence against women in Brazil, including grotesque cases of femicide.[27] This dismantling of public policies put in place to protect and advance women's rights directly impacts the articulation and execution of the activities in the networks formed by civil society organizations to combat violence and support women at the municipal, state, and federal levels. At the same time, it reinforces the importance of having an organized civil society and the difference it makes to have well-equipped women fighting for their rights.

In addition to creating women's secretariats at the municipal, state, and federal levels, in the 14 years when the federal government was led by the Workers' Party (PT), the Brazilian congress passed the Law 11.340/2006, known as the Maria da Penha Law, for the specification of domestic violence against women as a particular type of crime subject to punishment, and the Law 13.104/2015, known as the Law of Femicide, which qualifies a murder as heinous when it is practiced against a woman due to the

---

[25] For instance, see Nivia Ivette Núñez de la Paz and Romi Márcia Bencke, eds., *Presidenta Dilma: Em Sororidade Mulheres Resgatam a História*. (São Leopoldo: Karywa, 2017); For an assessment in English, of the role evangelicals played in the impeachment process, see Claudio Carvalhaes and Raimundo Barreto, "A Coalition to Impeach: How Evangelicals Helped Oust Brazil's President," *The Christian Century* 33, no. 23 (November, 2016), accessed January 30, 2020, http://christiancentury.org/article/2016-10/coalition-impeach.

[26] For more information on the implementation of public policies to protect women's rights, see CFEMEA. *Guia dos direitos da Mulher* (Brasília: CFEMEA, 1994).

[27] "Brazil, Organizations on Alert after Rise in Number of Women Killed," *Agencia Brasil*, accessed January 30, 2020, http://agenciabrasil.ebc.com.br/en/direitos-humanos/noticia/2019-02/brazil-organizations-alert-after-rise-number-women-killed.

simple fact that she is a woman.[28] In order to strengthen the implementation of these laws and the work of the secretariats, a National Pact for Combating Violence against Women was signed. The Pact represented the signed commitment on the part of the federal, state, and municipal authorities to develop joint actions for the implementation of the National Policy to Combat Violence against Women. The Pact had four emphases: (1) consolidating the National Policy to Combat Violence against Women and the implementation of the Maria da Penha Law; (2) combating sexual exploitation and women trafficking; (3) promoting women's human rights in prison; and (4) promoting reproductive rights and confronting the feminization of HIV/AIDS and other STDs. On top of that, the Workers' Party-led federal administration created the Casas da Mulher Brasileira (the Brazilian Woman Houses), one in each of the twenty-seven states, in a coordinated effort to provide a network to protect women in situation of risk.

Of all these public policies implemented before 2016, only the two laws mentioned above still remain in place at the time of this writing,[29] and they are constantly under the threat of being reversed. Secretariats in the federal government have been disbanded and others at the state level have merged into broader ministerial portfolios such as the Human Rights Secretariat. The National Pact for Combating Violence against Women no longer exists. No new Brazilian Woman House has been established since 2016, and only five of the existing ones are still functioning across the entire country. These five houses are currently operating in very precarious conditions, since they no longer have the support they used to get from the women care networks. The dial-up number 180 still exists, but no further referrals are offered when women denounce violence against them. The dismantling of such networks has left women significantly more vulnerable to violence. Recent data have shown that Brazil records a case of assault on women every four minutes.[30]

Due to the formation and power of the women's movement in civil society, the Women's Forum, the Municipal Council for Women's Rights, the Popular Legal Agents, and other initiatives mentioned in this essay, the municipality of São Leopoldo in the state of Rio Grande do Sul has

---

[28] See *Lei Maria da Penha e feminicídio. Comissão de cidadania e direitos humanos* (Assembleia Legislativa RS, 2017).

[29] Nivia Ivette Núñez de la Paz, "Sólo la Ley no Basta! Ley María da Penha: análisis de su aplicación en el contexto brasilero," in *Desigualdade de gênero e as trajetórias Latino-Americanas: reconhecimento, dignidade e esperança*, ed. Amanda Motta Castro and Kathlen Luana de Oliveira (São Leopoldo: EST, 2014).

[30] Marina G. Cubas et al., "Brasil registra 1 caso de agressão a mulher a cada 4 minutos, mostra levantamento," *Folha de S. Paulo*, accessed January 30, 2020, https://tinyurl.com/y3hguuar.

guaranteed the survival of policies protective of women's rights (at the municipal level) in the midst of the neoliberal drilling we are currently immersed in. In other words, São Leopoldo has a Municipal Department of Policies for Women and a Women's Referral Center (Centro Jacobina)[31] that offer psychological, social, and legal assistance to women who suffer violence. The dismantling of these networks at the federal level inevitably influences all the prevention and care services offered at the municipal level. But, the existence of a strong organization of empowered women in particular contexts shows that such dismantling can be resisted, and is meeting resistance in municipalities such as São Leopoldo.

The training of women as PLPs has empowered them to not stay silent, but rather organize, resist, and advocate for the rights of women who suffer violence. Breaking the silence is key to overcome violence and has been a fundamental step in women's struggle against gender-based violence. The Popular Legal Agents program has, over the years, strengthened the autonomous identity of women, empowering them to make their own decisions. The historical overview above demonstrates the role played by PLPs, which, due to the training they receive, have contributed in helping a significant number of women in the region to overcome violence.

Conclusion

In these dark times we are currently experiencing in Brazil, both the PLPs and CECA continue to be a reference for the formation of women in the struggle for a dignified life in the urban space, and a prophetic voice to the Christian Churches and to those in power. The formation meetings articulate a liberating spirituality that is manifest in the respect for religious, cultural, and social differences and in the strengthening of vulnerable women. It is a formation that insists on "respect for the diversity of life." The formation that PLPs provide is a remarkable example of ecumenical urban Christianity. These women who gather to seek possibilities of education in the fight against violence come from different Christian communities and also from non-Christian communities, becoming one body in the People's Access to Justice Program. CECA has historically been a catalyst for ecumenical urban Christianities and for interreligious dialogue through the richness of its encounters, and the formation and articulation it offers, always emphasizing social justice for women. We affirm that another world is possible, where all violence against women will be overcome. In this sense, CECA's formation of PLPs can be seen as a driving force for an ecumenical urban movement committed to the struggle for the human dignity of all women.

---

[31] Centro Jacobina, Coordenadoria Municipal da Mulher et al., *Guia da rede de enfrentamento da violência contra a Mulher* (São Leopoldo: Centro Jacobina, 2007).

Bibliography

Bourdieu, Pierre. *A dominação masculina.* Translated by, Maria Helena Kühner. 3rd ed. Rio de Janeiro: Bertrand, 2003.

Cavalcante, Ronaldo, and Rudolf Eduard von Sinner. *Teologia Pública em Debate.* TPI. São Leopoldo: Sinodal, Faculdades EST, 2011.

Cavalcante, Alcilene, and Dulce Xavier (Orgs.). *Em defesa da vida: Aborto e direitos Humanos.* São Paulo: Católicas pelo Direito de Decidir, 2006.

Carvalhaes, Claudio and Raimundo Barreto, "A Coalition to Impeach: How Evangelicals Helped Oust Brazil's President," *The Christian Century*, Vol. 33, no. 23. Accessed November, 2016. http://christiancentury.org/article/2016-10/coalition-impeach.

Centro Jacobina, Coordenadoria Municipal da Mulher. *Guia da rede de enfrentamento da violência contra a mulher.* São Leopoldo: Centro Jacobina, 2007.

Centro Feminista de Estudos e Assessoria. *Guia dos Direitos da Mulher.* Brasília: CFEMEA, 1994.

Cornaglia, Graciela Patrícia (Org.). *Prevenção à violência contra as mulheres.* Secretaria municipal de políticas públicas para as mulheres de São Leopoldo. Caderno I. São Leopoldo: CEBI, 2010.

Cornaglia, Graciela Patrícia, and Karine Santos (Orgs.). *Pacto nacional pelo enfrentamento à violência contra as mulheres.* Caderno II. São Leopoldo: CEBI, 2010.

Fundação Luterana de Diaconia. *Projeto Internacional Rua das Rosas, 76.* Porto Alegre: FLD, 2006.

Gebara, Ivone. *Teologia Urbana*: Ensaios sobre ética, gênero, meio ambiente e a condição humana. São Paulo: Fonte, 2014.

Introdução critica ao direito das Mulheres. Organizadores: José Geraldo de Sousa Junior, Bistra Stefanova Apostolova, Livia Gimenes Dias da Fonseca; autores: Adriana Andrade Miranda [et. al.]. Brasilia: CEAD, FUB, 2011.

Lagarde, Marcela. *Cautiverios de las Mujeres: Madresposas, Monjas, Putas, Presas y Locas.* 4th ed. Ciudad de México: UNAM, 2005.

Lei Maria Da Penha e feminicídio. Comissão de cidadania e direitos humanos. Azores, Assembleia Legislativa: RS, 2017.

Núñez de la Paz, Nivia Ivette. "Sólo la Ley no basta! Ley María da Penha: análisis de su aplicación en el contexto brasilero." In *Desigualdade de gênero e as trajetórias Latino-americanas: Reconhecimento, dignidade e esperança.* Amanda Motta Castro, Kathlen Luana de Oliveira (orgs.). São Leopoldo: EST, 2014.

Núñez de la Paz, Nivia Ivette, and Romi Márcia Bencke (Orgs.). *Presidenta Dilma: Em sororidade mulheres resgatam a história*. 1st ed. São Leopoldo: Karywa, 2017.

Núñez de la Paz, Nivia Ivette (Org.) *Da violência de gênero para relações humanizadas*. São Leopoldo: CEBI, 2010.

Perrot, Michelle. *As mulheres ou os silêncios da história*. Florianópolis: Edusc, 2005.

Rocha, Abdruschin Schaeffer, and Claudete Beise Ulrich. "A Dessacralização da Violência contra as Mulheres a partir dos Conceitos Desejo Mimético e Bode Expiatório em René Girard—desafios para a educação teológica latino-americana." *Reflexus—Revista Semestral de Teologia e Ciências das Religiões* XII, no. 19 (2018): 15–38,. Disponível em: accessed November 20, 2018. http://revista.faculdadeunida.com.br/index.php/reflexus/article/view/718.

Stoffel, José Carlos. Centro ecumênico de evangelização, capacitação e assessoria. *Ecumenismo de justiça: reflexão e prática*. São Leopoldo: CECA, Oikos 2006.

12

BETWEEN INDIVIDUALITY AND PUBLICNESS: CHRISTIANITY IN URBAN CHINA SINCE THE 1980s[1]

Zhibin Xie

China's urbanization has significantly developed since the 1980s. The problem of urbanization in China has likewise received increasing attention from scholars representing different disciplines, particularly in connection with issues such as industrialization, rural-urban immigration, urban governance, environment, urban planning, land use etc.[2] This rapid process of urbanization has impacted religious life, including the ways many Christians interact with the city. This essay focuses on the relation between Christianity and urbanization in China, shedding light on the development of Christianity in contemporary China as well as on the understanding of recent changes in contemporary Chinese life.

More specifically, this essay offers a theological examination of the tension between individuality and publicness in urban Christianity, including the shapes it has taken and its impact on Chinese society. While contemporary Christians living in Chinese urban centers continue to associate their faith primarily with the search for meaning in life and the resulting transformation of their values, just as others in the past, many of them today—particularly those under the influence of Reformed theology—have put significant emphasis on certain matters of public concern

---

[1] Some of the cases used in this article were originally in a previous article. See Zhibin Xie, "Religion and State in China: A Theological Appraisal," *Journal of Church and State*, no. csaa005 (February 9, 2020), https://doi.org/10.1093/jcs/csaa005.

[2] See, for example, Ding Lu, ed., *The Great Urbanization of China* (Hackensack, NJ: World Scientific, 2012); Yongnian Zheng, Litao Zhao, and Sarah Y. Tong, eds., *China's Great Urbanization* (Abingdon, Oxon: Routledge, 2017).

such as engaging discourse on constitutionalism and human rights, and theologizing a Christian cultural mandate in the context of an antagonistic state and society. These two emphases have been integrated into the life and theologizing of some Chinese Christians, while others continue to think of their faith in an individualistic fashion. This emerging dynamic in urban Chinese Christianity deserves a deeper analysis, taking into consideration the variety of theologies among different Christian groups of urban centers, while engaging its historical development and context along with the contemporary political-social situation in China.

I will start with a description of the basic church structure in China and then examine social and theological commitments of urban churches, presenting the move from individual pursuit of Christian faith to its public face in various forms, including public disobedience and resistance, and the drive of Reformed theology in publicness. I will then examine how urban Christianity shapes public space in China. As this essay argues that "the public turn" occurring among different expressions of urban Christianity in China has theological roots, it cannot be understood apart from particular sociopolitical circumstances.

From Individuality to Public Face

In Chinese Christianity, there is a general structure of both churches registered with the government under the umbrella of China Christian Council and Three-Self Patriotic Movement and churches without registration with the government in terms of church governance—used to be called "house church"—and of both urban and rural churches in terms of the identity of church members as many urban Christians tend to be more educated and socially engaged while traditional rural Christians consist mostly of women and people with less years of formal education. Both urban and rural churches have involved both registered and non-registered structures. The distinction of urban and rural churches has emerged alongside with urbanization in contemporary China.

The rapid modernization China has experienced since the 1980s has impacted not only Chinese economy, society, and politics, but has also raised new questions about the meaning of life for many people, particularly those living in cities, where significant changes in the pace of life are experienced firsthand and new challenges are raised in a millennial society. Christianity has, on many levels, offered some responses to the spiritual and moral questions raised in that context.

A case study on Christianity and Christian life in Beijing has shown how the Chinese have turned to the Christian faith in that kind of urban context. In her book *Christianity and Christians in Beijing Today*, sociologist of religion Gao Shining describes how urban Christians shape their meaning of life, mentality, moral values, and relationship with others.[3] She focuses on the effects of religious faith on individuals, seeking to understand what she calls "individual religiosity." For the most part, urban Chinese conversion to Christianity derives from inner spiritual concerns such as the pursuit of meaning in life. Accordingly, Christian faith leads to the transformation of moral values, which do not necessarily oppose traditional Chinese values, but instead support them.[4] Therefore, for many Chinese people, Christianity is regarded as a religion with strong moral significance; i.e., one that reinforces the strong connection between faith and morality. In general, "Christian church's participation in Chinese society is limited. Christianity plays a marginal role in Chinese society."[5]

Similarly, Shangyang Sun attributes Beijing college students' turn to the Christian faith to "the scarcity of meaning." Even though Christianity is one of many options in religious belief, the pursuit of "meaning" (such as the understandings of ultimate concerns in matters of life and death, good and evil, happiness and suffering, relationship with others, etc.) plays an important role in their religious decisions.[6] In short, many Chinese people, especially in urban areas, come to the Christian faith motivated mainly by the individual pursuit of meaning in life, and the impact of that experience is primarily individual.

Yet, there is another face to Chinese urban Christianity. In her preface to Zhe He's *The Spiritual Palace in Urban China*, Gao Shining addresses some evolving characteristics in urban churches in China, which include changes from underground existence to being out in the public eyes, matters of institutional development, the shift from a survival mood to a rational defense of rights (based on the Constitution), the improvement of leadership capacity, and the move from a primary concern with the salvation of individual souls to the transformation of society.[7]

These are some of the characteristics of what can be defined as the "public" face of urban Christianity in China. Zhe He also refers to the urban church in China as a "thinking" and "acting" church in his

---

[3] Gao Shining, *Christianity and Christians in Beijing Today: A Case Study in Sociology of Religion* (Hong Kong: Logos and Pneuma Press, 2005), 197–238.
[4] Shining, *Christianity and Christians*, 217.
[5] Shining, *Christianity and Christians*, 297–298.
[6] Sun Shangyang, "Fever of Chinese Culture, The Scarcity of Meaning, and the Orientation of Religious Interest among College Students: An Investigation and Analysis Based in Beijing," accessed January 16, 2018. http://www.pacilution.com/ShowArticle.asp?ArticleID=5918.
[7] Gao Shining, "Preface," in Zhe He, *The Spiritual Palace in Urban China: A Life History of an Intellectual Christian and his Church* (Hong Kong: Ming Feng Press, 2009), vi–ix.

book, *The Spiritual Palace in Urban China*.[8] Many Christians in these growing urban churches have access to higher education. Thinking of themselves in the context of the broader society, they do their theological reflection not only considering the impact of faith on their individual lives, but also taking into account matters pertinent to "church and society."[9] Moving beyond strictly evangelistic motifs and the eagerness to construct new church buildings, these urban Christians have a stronger drive for social participation.

According to Ma Li and Li Jun, the combined processes of marketing and urbanization paved the way for religious activity in the public space in the late 1990s in China.[10] Its public face began to take primarily the form of "openness," in contrast to the traditional understanding of church as "a private space," due to the fear of state control and political pressure. As Deborah A. Brown points out,

> A principal strategy for controlling religious influence is to force religion from the public sphere and to make religious practice a "private matter." Because religion officially can be practiced only at state-approved, registered sites, and because the propagation of theism is forbidden, the spread of religious values in the public sector is frustrated.[11]

Yet, despite the public constraint on religious practice in China, some non-registered churches do not remain confined to private house settings, having moved to more "public" places such as office buildings, thus presenting some level of public appeal. Ma Li and Li Jun use the expression "open religious place" to refer to them.[12] Carsten Vala suggests that the urban church is meant to be public in terms of its emergence over against the background of the official registered church: "Urban church leaders have emerged from TSPM (Three-Self Patriotic Movement) settings to found congregations that violate the red lines circumscribing the public impact of Protestantism by building trust-filled ties with local authorities to assuage fears about Protestant disloyalty."[13] Thus, the public face of the

---

[8] Many traditional Chinese churches are concerned mostly with the salvation of individual souls and missionary work, keeping an otherworldly orientation. See Zhe He, *The Spiritual Palace in Urban China*, 276–277.

[9] Zhe He, *The Spiritual Palace in Urban China*, 277.

[10] Ma Li and Li Jun, "Local Political Culture and State-church Relationships: A Comparison of Urban Unregistered Churches in Two Cities of China," *Logos & Pneuma: Chinese Journal of Theology* no. 44 (2016): 66.

[11] Deborah A. Brown, "The Role of Religion in Promoting Democracy in the People's Republic of China and Hong Kong," in *Church and State Relations in 21st Century Asia*, ed. Beatrice Leung (Hong Kong: Center for Asia Studies, 1996), 86.

[12] Ma Li and Li Jun, "Local Political Culture," 64.

[13] Carsten T. Vala, *The Politics of Protestant Churches and the Party-State in China: God Above Party?* (London: Routledge, 2018), 148.

urban church in contemporary China may be more clearly understood over against the backdrop of the rural Chinese church. Jianbo Huang distinguishes between rural and urban Christians in China as follows:

> The rural Christians seem to be more emotional in church gatherings, and they place more emphasis on prayer, miracles, and personal experiences, while the urban Christians tend to be more intellectual, more text oriented, and their faith is more focused on reading and interpreting the Bible.[14]

This distinction of the urban church sheds light on how the intellectualized character of its faith contributes to its potential and courage to open itself to interactions that are public in nature.

Public disobedience and resistance

One form in which the urban church's public face is manifest is through disobedience and/or resistance. Besides its general resistance to the Three-Self church structure (in which worship and evangelism are only allowed within approved locations), several cases of civil disobedience have been reported among unregistered urban churches. The official form of Christianity in contemporary China emphasizes state authority and church's conformity to society. In principle, this official institution demands the Chinese church's identification with and unwavering loyalty to national political and social institutions, completely avoiding any social criticism. As Fenggang Yang explains, "While the party-state insists that religious believers must accommodate to social and political reality, many religious leaders like to emphasize the importance of mutual accommodation between the CCP and religious believers."[15] The registered TSPM church and its leaders are expected to support this accommodation policy. Nevertheless, there are many cases in which registered churches have also resisted governmental interference in church practice. Thousands of Christians, for instance, protested and engaged in conflict with the police during the demolition of church buildings and crosses in the Zhejiang Province between 2014 and 2016. Among the protestors were a number of registered church leaders.[16] Their disobedience may have originated in their genuine Christian faith in response to the

---

[14] Jianbo Huang, "Being Christians in Urbanizing China," *Current Anthropology* 55, Supplement 10 (2014): 238.

[15] Fenggang Yang, "From Cooperation to Resistance: Christian Responses to Intensified Suppression in China Today," *The Review of Faith & International Affairs* 15, no. 1 (2017): 83. "CCP" means "Chinese Communist Party."

[16] The Zhejiang Christian Council issued an open letter against the campaign of cross removal in July 2015, accessed September 7, 2017, http://www.gospeltimes.cn/index.php/portal/article/index/id/29336.

needs of thousands of suffering Christians. It could thus be seen as a courageous defense of religious freedom and church autonomy in the face of state power.

Fuk-tsang Ying summarizes various statements regarding church officials' reactions to this campaign.

> (1) Forced cross demolitions are acts that violate the Constitution and the law. (2) The principle of separation of church and state, as well as respecting and obeying the government as a principle of biblical truth, is insisted upon; however, if the government refuses to obey God's will, as indicated in the Bible, then churches must be faithful to God. (3) Churches will respond to forced demolitions through nonviolent civil disobedience, will never compromise, and will refuse to take down their own crosses with determination.[17]

Christie Chui-shan Chow, on the other hand, offers an analysis of the "religious dimension of social protest."[18] For example, one elder "drew on the Old Testament to rationalize his calling to defend the church against any hostility" by "imaging himself as a God-chosen watchman."[19] In reality, church leaders face enormous pressure to cooperate with the Communist Party, and some have agreed to voluntarily remove the cross from their building so that the entire building would not be demolished and they would not lose their jobs due to governmental pressure on their employers. In response to that, some church leaders have suggested that the church has faced persecution throughout its history, thus the best thing to do in such circumstances is to pray. After all, when compared to thirty years ago, they now have many more church buildings where to worship.[20] Pragmatic considerations such as these deserve further theological investigation.

Another case of public interaction between the urban church and governmental authorities is exemplified by the case of Beijing's Shouwang Church. After failing to register with the government as a legitimate religious group and facing governmental interference in indoor worship spaces, Shouwang Church began worshiping outdoors in 2009. This strategy resonates with the church's ecclesiology, which emphasizes the image

---

[17] See Fuk-tsang Ying, "The Politics of Cross Demolition: A Religio-Political Analysis of the 'Three Rectifications and One Demolition' Campaign in Zhejiang Province," *Review of Religion and Chinese Society* 5 (2018): 35.

[18] Christie Chui-shan Chow, "Demolition and Defiance: The Stone Ground Church Dispute (2012) in East China," *The Journal of World Christianity* 6, no. 2 (2016): 272.

[19] Chui-shan Chow, "Demolition and Defiance," 270.

[20] See Ian Johnson, "Decapitated Churches in China's Christian Heartland," accessed August 17, 2019, https://tinyurl.com/yxwttglh.

of the "city on a hill." This vision portrays the church as a faith community whose identity and witness motivate its pursuit of registration with the government and their attitude of worshiping outdoors as a form of protest. Their outdoor worship originated in the radical conflict between the ideal of ecclesiology and the political reality of China. Yet, Shouwang sees itself as an apolitical community. Thus, its persistence in worshiping outdoors was aimed, above all, at supporting worship as a basic requirement of Christian life. While Shouwang supports the principle of church-state separation and resists calls to join the official TSPM church,[21] it insists that the church should engage in dialogue and collaborate with the government in discussions about the unregistered churches and the government. The Shouwang Church sees its interaction with the government as part of its social witness and the responsibility of the faith community, grounded in the hope of improving the religion-state relationship in China so as to benefit the whole society.[22] Shouwang's statement on the church highlights its understanding of ecclesiology, which focuses on certain themes: Christ as head of the Church, separation of church-state, respect for governmental authority derived from God and based on the principle of conscience, and church autonomy.[23] This ecclesiology leads to Shouwang's outdoor worship as a form of protest, characterized by its public nature and its peaceful worship, as Hao Yuan argues.[24]

In addition to disagreeing with the official Three-Self church structure, unregistered churches have practiced civil disobedience, and actions such as homeschooling children, organizing unregistered Christian schools as alternatives to atheist education, refusing to wear red ties and sing red songs, or otherwise take part in nationalistic education, publicly renouncing communist party membership, speaking up against social injustice, and defending human rights (especially among Christian lawyers) have been taken up by members of those churches. For these Christians, conversion leads to an ideological shift and a clash with public policies, grounded in theological convictions, according to which Christians serve only one Lord; Christ alone is the head of the Church. Consequently,

---

[21] See Yi Sun, "Why are We Reluctant to Join TSPM?" accessed May 3, 2017, http://www.pacilution.com/ShowArticle.asp?ArticleID=2688.

[22] A fine analysis on the ecclesiology of Shouwang can be found at Yi Le, "Behind Shouwang's Outdoor Worship: A Reflection on Ecclesiology by House Church in China," accessed September 15, 2017, https://t3.shwchurch.org/2012/09/27/守望户外聚会的背后-中国家庭教会对教会论的/.

[23] See Beijing Souwang Church Creeds," accessed April 16, 2018, https://t3.shwchurch.org/2005/07/04/附：基督教北京守望教会信约（全文）.

[24] Hao Yuan, "Chinese Christianity and Their Tradition of Disobedience: Wang Mingdao, Tanghe Church and Shouwang Church as Examples," *Logos & Pneuma: Chinese Journal of Theology*, no. 44 (2016): 114.

children should be brought up according to God's commands and standards as laid down in Scripture, and nationalism and pledging loyalty to a political party through quasi-religious rituals seen as a form of idolatry should be avoided. Underlining those acts of disobedience, there is a belief that God calls Christians to defend the weak and oppressed.[25]

As Li Ma and Jin Li put it,

> Being a member of an unregistered church in itself means challenging the unwritten law of "no assembly" in this country. And being an evangelizing believer makes one even more culpable, for he or she becomes an active diffuser of an alternative ideology. So the Protestant faith with its core concern to spread the message poses a boundary-breaking action against government prohibitions.[26]

Obviously, unregistered churches have a strikingly different conception of the church-state relationship compared to that found in the official church structure and ideology.

A particular example of that is the practice of Christian lawyers in urban China. According to Fuk-tsang Ying's description, one quarter of lawyers in the rights defense (*Weiquan*) movement in contemporary China are Christians. These Christian lawyers dare to speak out and defend the rights of Christians and ordinary people, including other religious believers. In public statements, these lawyers express their Christian faith, not least through actions of civil rights advocacy. Their theology tends to focus on human sinfulness, while their courage and persistence in the face of great pressure and danger is based on their faith and belief in the values of democracy and freedom. For them, rights defense aims not only for a better political and social order, but also for the moral integrity of the human being. They even pray for the people whose actions violate human conscience, and thus for the moral restoration of these people who attack human rights.[27] This movement of Christian lawyers bears far-reaching significance for the future of human rights in China. Today, understanding the role of human rights in China requires a concomitant understanding of the Christian beliefs expressed by this group of Christian lawyers.

---

[25] See Li Ma and Jin Li, "Remaking the Civil Space: The Rise of Unregistered Protestantism and Civil Engagement in Urban China," in *Christianity in Chinese Public Life: Religion, Society, and the Rule of Law*, eds. Joel A. Carpenter and Kevin R. den Dulk (Houndmills, Basingstoke, Hampshire: Palgrave, 2014), 11–28.

[26] Li Ma and Jin Li, "Remaking the Civil Space, 22.

[27] Ying, Fuk-tsang, "Rights Defense Movement and Christian Faith in China," *Newsletter of The Center for Christian Center and Christian Study Center on Chinese Religion & Culture* 21 (March 2014): 1–7.

Furthermore, a growing number of urban house churches in China have challenged the state by courageously advocating for civil and political rights. As Fenggang Yang observes, "Many urban house churches have also adopted avoidance as a resistance strategy. However, since 2000, more and more Christians in the urban house churches have adopted a positive way of resistance—challenging the authorities using the existing law."[28]

The rise of reformed theology in urban church

As we can see, in addition to the social services carried out by Christian groups, there is an emerging interest in matters such as public disobedience and resistance, public discourse on the rule of law, and constitutionalism among Chinese Christians, particularly urban Christians. Those Christians continue to engage in civil rights advocacy, evident most prominently among Calvinist Christians in China.[29] As Alexander Chow suggests, "One group of urban intellectual Christians has drawn on covenantal theology to argue for a stronger understanding of constitutionalism. Another group has relied on the Dutch neo-Calvinist understanding of the cultural mandate to emphasize a stronger engagement with both state and society. Both of these groups have thus placed a higher emphasis on Reformed ecclesiology."[30]

The Chengdu Early Rain Reformed churches in Sichuan, for instance, have drawn heavily on Reformed theology in forming their ecclesiological and sociopolitical views. One example of this is the document "Reaffirming our Stance on the House Churches: 95 Theses."[31] Appealing primarily to the doctrine of the sovereignty of God, biblical authority, and the two kingdoms doctrine, as shown in the statement, the church takes positions on the authority and limitations of government, as well as on ecclesiology, based on the tradition of Reformed theology. It supports the principle of religion-state independence (Zheng Jiao Fen Li, "政教分立") and opposes the official structure of the China Christian Council as well as the "Sinicization of Christianity," according to which Christians may have to sacrifice their genuine faith in its subjection to political

---

[28] Fenggang Yang, "From Cooperation to Resistance: Christian Responses to Intensified Suppression in China Today," *The Review of Faith & International Affairs* 15, no. 1 (2017): 86.

[29] See Alexander Chow, "Calvinist Public Theology in Urban China Today," *International Journal of Public Theology* 8, no. 2 (2014): 158–175.

[30] Sung Bihn Yim et al., "Reformed Theology in Asia and Oceania," in *The Cambridge Companion to Reformed Theology*, eds. Paul T. Nimmo and David A. S. Fergusson (New York: Cambridge University Press, 2016), 314.

[31] The full content of the document is available in Chinese at https://www.cclifefl.org/View/Article/4248, accessed May 30, 2016.

obligations. The document insists that local Christian gathering groups register with the department of civil affairs to obtain their legal status. Beyond this, Christian groups (referred to as house churches or unregistered churches) should show proper respect to governmental authority as the "sword," while practicing non-violent resistance, when necessary, in defense of Christian freedom of conscience and church autonomy.[32] Relying on this theological standpoint, the document calls for a change of policy regarding the regulation of religious groups in China.

Chloë Starr highlights some theological elements embodied in the 95 Theses:

> A Calvinist political community under the lordship of Christ, with both state and church accountable to God; the church as a restored community; a neo-Calvinist belief in the limited role of government and civil protection for religious freedom; a Lutheran call to take up a (metaphorical) sword when the state transgresses into the spiritual realm.[33]

But, this statement leaves little room for the state to negotiate its relationship to the church. As Starr affirms, "The 95 theses document arrogates to the church the right to define relations to the state, based on a biblical view and on a particular reading of theological history, leaving little room for dialogue."[34]

Regarding the problem of church-state relationship, the "95 theses" follows the basic teaching of Calvinism, as summarized by H. Henry Meeter.

> The state is to have authority with respect to the church only insofar as it concerns matters *circa sacra,* not *in sacra,* which means that the state shall have authority with regard to the externalities of the church, its buildings, and other properties, and afford it the same protection under the law as any organization in society within the confines of the country.[35]

The statement represents a typical case regarding the Chinese church's encounter with the state and the wider society in terms of Bible and reformed teaching, which tends to transform the traditional understanding of Christian faith within the church and attach their spiritual quest for "meaning of life" to various spheres of life. As Breton Fulton points out,

---

[32] As one example of resistance in practice, the Early Rain Reformed Church appealed in court when the local bureau of religious affairs intervened in church activities in 2008.

[33] Chloë Starr, "Wang Yi and the 95 Theses of the Chinese Reformed Church," *Religions* 7, no. 12 (2016): 142, accessed July 18, 2018, https://www.mdpi.com/2077-1444/7/12/142.

[34] Starr, "Wang Yi and the 95 Theses," 142.

[35] H. Henry Meeter, *The Basic Ideas of Calvinism,* Rev. Paul A. Marshall, 6th ed. (Grand Rapids, MI: Backer Book House, 1990), 135.

Reformed teaching not only presents a comprehensive systematic approach to the Bible and to issues of faith and church life, but its cultural and political implications also speak to the role of the church at a time when China's urban society is inviting Christian involvement. The concept of cultural mandate provides a biblical rationale for Christian activities outside the walls of the church, including in the realms of commerce, education, and government, where many urban believers conduct their daily lives.[36]

The urban Reformed church tends to change the general picture of Christianity in contemporary China with its strong theological orientation and intellectual character. Here, Fulton continues, "The Reformed emphasis on rational thinking and systematic theology tends to discount the 'emotional' and 'mystical' spirituality of China's traditional, particularly rural, churches."[37]

Concluding remarks: Urban christianity and shaping public space in China

The influence of Christianity is reshaping public space in China. As Gao has observed,

> Although Chinese religions have limited access to social affairs, however, in terms of the number of their followers and organizational structure, religious groups are the largest social organizations in China, who are bound to make contribution to the construction of China's civil society with their striving for their own rights and interests, services for the lower classes of the society, and desires for participation in social activities.[38]

This can be seen in Christianity's contribution in recent decades to the formation of civil society in China. On this point, Haibo Huang and Mark Chuanghang Shan offer strong support. Huang suggests that Christianity in China contains "elements of civil society," emerging through various forms of participation in social services and social work, and institution building. Christian organizations in China have gradually become a positive force for the construction of civil society.[39] In his book *Christianity and Civil Society in China,* Shan proposes that Christianity promotes citizenship rights in China today primarily through "invisible

---

[36] Brent Fulton, *China's Urban Christians: A Light That Cannot Be Hidden* (Eugene, OR: Pickwick Publications, 2015), 38.
[37] Fulton, *China's Urban Christians*, 116.
[38] Gao Shining, "Three Issues in Contemporary Chinese Religions," *Logos & Pneuma: Chinese Journal of Theology* 36 (Spring 2012): 33–34.
[39] Haibo Huang. "Towards Civil Society under Construction: A Reflection on Responsibility of Christianity in China in 2010," In *Blue Book of Religion: A Report on Religions in China (2011),* eds. Jin Ze and Qiu Yonghui (Beijing: Social Sciences Documentation Publishing House, 2011), 128–172.

and unstructured church communities" in their struggle for the right to religious freedom.[40] Christianity's ethical culture, focused on love and justice, contributes to the emergence of a kind of "quasi-political culture." Consequently, Shan contends, "the growth of Christianity of China has already become a crucial element in advancing citizenship rights and the development of a civil society in China."

Yuan Hao's proposal of Shouwang Church (Beijing) as a new type of urban church in China further indicates Christianity's potential to contribute to the strengthening of civil society in its resistance to state power. Hao see the church's civil disobedience as "often intertwined with the awaking of citizen identity and sense of rights."[41] In line with these studies, I would suggest that although the growth of Christianity particularly in urban China results mainly from people's interest in the Christian responses to their pursuit of life's meaning, during such a process, in their seeking for identity as both Christians and Chinese citizens, they have encountered the power of the state and performed their social responsibility in various instances, which in turn has advanced civil participation, community formation, and civil and religious rights.

However, this public face of urban church must be understood in its particular political settings, which sets limits to church's engagement in social and political issues to some extent. In their case study on the urban church in Shanghai and Chengdu, Ma Li and Li Jun attempt to explain the church's public face in terms of the theological and political cultural influence, highlighting the importance of local political culture. For example, comparing to Shanghai, citizens in Chengdu tend to be more open to political issues. With an intellectualized Christian leadership, the public face of the church in Chengdu has been more evident.[42]

While we see the rise and impact of a public urban church in China today, in comparison with more traditional Chinese house churches that tend to emphasize conversion and supernatural acts, we must be aware of and realistic about the limited circumstances of its public expressions due to the political control of social and civil life in China and the limited theological reach of the intellectual elites of many urban Christians in China. As Alexander Chow reminds us, "The risk that arises is that these urban intellectual elite Christians may be a voice mainly to other

---

[40] Mark Chuanhang Shan, "Christianity and Civil Society in China: Christian Ethics is Transforming Citizenship Rights and Church-State Relations in China Through Invisible and Unstructured Church Communities," accessed August 22, 2019, http://www.ccaa2009.org/2013/03/mark-shan-christianity-and-civil.html.
[41] Hao Yuan, "Chinese Christianity," 119–120.
[42] See Ma Li and Li Jun, "Local Political Culture," 83–84.

intellectual elites, and their ability to engage other socioeconomic strata of society may not be as strong."⁴³

In this essay, I have outlined the individual and public dimensions of urban Christianity in China. I employed the distinction between individuality and publicness to describe the transformation of churches in the new urban settings. Based on the discussions and findings already outlined, I have made some claims regarding the nature of urban Christianity in contemporary China.

First, I have claimed that the public face of the urban church in contemporary China has theological roots. While such a public face primarily involves the reorganization of spaces such as the move from "house" to "open" settings, it also typically implies public encounters with the state, which may take different forms, such as dialogue, disobedience, or resistance. This public face is also manifest through certain forms of civil disobedience, defense of human rights, and the promotion of the cultural mandate, involving some sort of public discourse. All these expressions of "publicness" draw heavily on theological perspectives such as the doctrine of God (e.g., sovereignty of God, lordship of Christ), the doctrine of humanity (e.g., human sinfulness, moral integrity of humanity), Christian relationship to God (e.g. the meaning of being faithful to God), ecclesiology (e.g., the "city on the hill"), and the doctrine of the two kingdoms. None of these things happen in isolation. The local political culture is also one factor that exercises influence on the church's public engagement.

Second, the tension between individuality and publicness among Chinese Christians derives from genuine Christian beliefs that Christians must challenge state and society when their religious rights and interests are at risk. In turn, the public face of their Christian practice strengthens their faith. The understanding and practice of Christian faith, as a whole, consist of both the Christian inner/personal pursuit of the meaning of life and the meaning of cultural, social, and political life. As Walter Rauschenbusch declares, "The Kingdom of God is still a collective conception, involving the whole social life of man. It is not a matter of saving human atoms, but of saving the social organism."⁴⁴

I believe that when many Chinese Christians in urban areas struggle for issues that matter for the whole of life itself and practice their Christian faith in a period of great economic-social-political change in China,

---

43 Alexander Chow, *Chinese Public Theology: Generational Shifts and Confucian Imagination in Chinese Christianity* (Oxford: Oxford University Press, 2018), 114.

44 Walter Rauschenbusch, *Christianity and the Social Crisis* (London: Macmillan, 1913), 65.

what challenges them is not only their personal experiences and concerns, but also the surrounding factors with which they have to encounter and in relation to which they interrogate their faith.

Bibliography

Brown, Deborah A. "The Role of Religion in Promoting Democracy in the People's Republic of China and Hong Kong." In *Church and State Relations in 21st Century Asia*, edited by Beatrice Leung. Hong Kong: Center for Asia Studies, 1996.

Chow, Alexander. *Chinese Public Theology: Generational Shifts and Confucian Imagination in Chinese Christianity*. Oxford: Oxford University Press, 2018.

―――. "Calvinist Public Theology in Urban China Today." *International Journal of Public Theology* 8, no. 2 (2014): 158–175.

Chow, Christie Chui-shan. "Demolition and Defiance: The Stone Ground Church Dispute (2012) in East China." *The Journal of World Christianity* 6, no. 2 (2016): 250–276.

Fulton, Brent. *China's Urban Christians: A Light That Cannot Be Hidden*. Eugene, OR: Pickwick Publications, 2015.

He, Zhe. *The Spiritual Palace in Urban China: A Life History of an Intellectual Christian and His Church*. Hong Kong: Ming Feng Press, 2009.

Huang, Haibo. "Towards Civil Society under Construction: A Reflection on Responsibility of Christianity in China in 2010." In *Blue Book of Religion: A Report on Religions in China (2011)*, edited by Jin Ze and Qiu Yonghui, 128–172. Beijing: Social Sciences Documentation Publishing House, 2011.

Huang, Jianbo. "Being Christians in Urbanizing China." *Current Anthropology* 55, Supplement 10 (2014).

Li, Ma, and Li Jun. "Local Political Culture and State-church Relationships: A Comparison of Urban Unregistered Churches in Two Cities of China." *Logos & Pneuma: Chinese Journal of Theology* no. 44 (2016).

Li, Ma, and Li Jin. "Remaking the Civil Space: The Rise of Unregistered Protestantism and Civil Engagement in Urban China." In *Christianity in Chinese Public Life: Religion, Society, and the Rule of Law*, edited by Joel A. Carpenter and Kevin R. den Dulk, 11–28. Houndmills, Basingstoke, Hampshire: Palgrave, 2014.

Lu, Ding, ed. *The Great Urbanization of China*. Hackensack, NJ: World Scientific, 2012.

Rauschenbusch, Walter. *Christianity and the Social Crisis*. London: Macmillan. 1913.

Shining, Gao. *Christianity and Christians in Beijing Today: A Case Study in Sociology of Religion*. Hong Kong: Logos and Pneuma Press, 2005.

―――. "Three Issues in Contemporary Chinese Religions." *Logos & Pneuma: Chinese Journal of Theology* 36 (Spring 2012): 33–34.

———. "Preface." In Zhe He, *The Spiritual Palace in Urban China: A Life History of an Intellectual Christian and his Church*, vi–ix. Hong Kong: Ming Feng Press, 2009.

Starr, Chloë. "Wang Yi and the 95 Theses of the Chinese Reformed Church." *Religions* (2016 /7): 12.

Vala, Carsten T. *The Politics of Protestant Churches and the Party-State in China: God Above Party?* London: Routledge, 2018.

Xie, Zhibin. "Religion and State in China: A Theological Appraisal." *Journal of Church and State*, csaa005 (February 9, 2020). https://doi.org/10.1093/jcs/csaa005.

Yang, Fenggang. "From Cooperation to Resistance: Christian Responses to Intensified Suppression in China Today." *The Review of Faith & International Affairs* 15, no. 1 (2017).

Yim, Sung Bihn, Yasuhiro Sekikawa, Alexander Chow, and Geoff Thompson. "Reformed Theology in Asia and Oceania." In *The Cambridge Companion to Reformed Theology*, edited by Paul T. Nimmo and David A. S. Fergussio, 296–318. New York: Cambridge University Press, 2016.

Ying, Fuk-tsang. "The Politics of Cross Demolition: A Religio-Political Analysis of the 'Three Rectifications and One Demolition' Campaign in Zhejiang Province." *Review of Religion and Chinese Society* 5 (2018).

———. "Rights Defense Movement and Christian Faith in China." *Newsletter of The Center for Christian Center and Christian Study Center on Chinese Religion & Culture* 21 (March 2014): 1–7.

Yuan, Hao. "Chinese Christianity and Their Tradition of Disobedience: Wang Mingdao, Tanghechurch and Shouwang Church as Examples." *Logos & Pneuma: Chinese Journal of Theology*, no. 44 (2016).

Yongnian, Zheng, Zhao Litao, and Sarah Y. Tong, eds. *China's Great Urbanization*. Abingdon, Oxon: Routledge, 2017.

13

CATHOLICISM AND MODERNIZATION: *ACCIÓN CULTURAL POPULAR* AND THE RISE OF A CENTRIST-CATHOLICISM IN COLOMBIA, 1947–1962

Sandra Londono-Ardila

"This is a gigantic work that, in extension, must cover the entire national territory. In intensity, it should reach the very bottom of the human personality to give to the humble, especially to the peasants, a deep and integral education. In tactics, it must seize all resources put on our hands by modern science and technique, to achieve its end."[1]

Modernization was the central and more connecting thread of the twentieth-century world public agenda. The 1950s, in particular, were the years of Developmentalism, the *discovery* of mass poverty and the *making* of the Third World.[2] This decade was crucial in transforming these categories (i.e., Development, Poverty, and Third World) into vanguard knowledge tools for reinterpreting the *social problem*, while also overwriting previously dominant biological interpretations. The Catholic Church was at the center of these social, political, cultural, and

---

[1] Francisco Houtart, and Gustavo Pérez, *Acción Cultural Popular. Sus Principios y Medios de Acción. Consideraciones Teológicas y Sociológicas*. Presentation by F. Jose Felix Restrepo S.J. Bogotá, Editorial Andes, 1960, p. 5. ACPO Archival Collection. Translations of this and all primary sources in this article are done by the author. At the time of evidence acquisition for this research, ACPO's Archive remained uncatalogued at ACPO's *Villa de la Esperanza* building in Sutatenza (Locality in Boyacá-Colombia). This archive was donated to the *Biblioteca Luis Angel Arango-Banco de la República* and moved to Bogota-Colombia in 2008.

[2] I am borrowing the concepts of *making* of the Third World and *discovery* of poverty from Escobar, Arturo. *Encountering Development: The Making and Unmaking of the Third World*. Princeton: Princeton University Press, 1995.

epistemological transformations in Colombian society. This essay devotes its attention to examining the case of the Catholic organization *Acción Cultural Popular* (ACPO) in Colombia during the period 1947–1962. In doing so, it illustrates Catholicism's and the Catholic Church's involvement in Colombian modernization.

This essay claims that ACPO played a critical role in the Colombian Catholic Church's acquiescence to the elites' modernizing consensus, and furthermore, became a vigorous agent of cultural modernization of the Colombian countryside.[3] A central piece of this twofold role was ACPO's agency of Social-Catholic views within the prevalent intransigent Colombian clergy, and concurrently, ACPO's pioneering impulse of a centrist Catholicism in the country.[4]

The period 1947–1962 opened with the return of conservatives to power after seventeen years, and the revitalization of a Catholic Church that had been strongly battled by the secularizing trend of the outgoing liberal governments. ACPO's inauguration in 1947 and its early years of work coincided with two significant national phenomena. One was the outbreak of the partisan political conflict known as *La Violencia*. A series of provincial and local virulent events that peaked from 1948 to 1953, launching the country into a bloody civil war that left a balance of as many as 400,000 casualties.[5] Another simultaneous, if also paradoxical phenomenon, is the modernizing consensus reached among industrialists and a traditional landlord class, along with the so-called take-off of capitalist agriculture in the country. The period of study covered by this study closes with the overthrowing of the military coup that had come to

[3] I will utilize the phrase "modernizing consensus" during this article to refer to the agreement among industrial and traditional landlord elites around modernization and capitalist development that will start consolidating since the end of the 1940s. The problematic relationship between these elites unveiled the contradiction between two different forms of economic exploitation: industrial profits, on the one hand, and land rents, on the other. By the late 1950s, this consensus was to crystallize in the *Frente Nacional*; an elites' pact that limited democracy to the sharing of the power of the state between the two traditional political parties.

[4] The phrase "Social-Catholic" in this essay refers to Social Catholicism; a current of Catholic thought that emerged in Europe during the early 1800s, as a response to capitalist industrialization and its impact upon the working classes. The Catholic Church streamlined a Social-Catholic doctrine through Leo XIII encyclical *Rerum Novarum* (1891). For a broader examination of this subject see: Paul Misner. *Social Catholicism in Europe: From the onset of industrialization to the First World War* (Crossroad Publishing, New York, 1991). Also see: Joe Holland, *Modern Catholic Social Teaching: The Popes Confront the Industrial Age, 1740–1958* (New York: Paulist Press, 2003).

[5] Frank Safford and Marco Palacios, *Colombia: Fragmented Land, Divided Society* (Oxford: Oxford University Press, 2001), 494–502.

power with the elites' support; and the end of *La Violencia*, made possible through a series of elites' agreements that gave rise to what was known as the *Frente Nacional*. This was a bipartisan political pact that assured the alternation in power of traditional elite Liberal and Conservative parties for the following sixteen years, excluding, however, other alternative political forces through the concurrent limitation of common citizens' political rights. The *Frente Nacional* shall also be an expression of the elites' political and economic consensus around a model of modernization and development.[6]

The study begins with a brief description of ACPO; its identity, and the reach and scope of its educative program. It follows by showing ACPO as a vantage point for a renewed appropriation of Social-Catholic views among the Colombian clergy, and therefore, both as an agent of theological renewal and a pioneer of a more conciliatory and politically moderate Catholicism. Next, the essay discusses ACPO's supporting views and attitudes toward the elites' modernizing consensus. I argue that the Colombian episcopacy's embracing of ACPO's enterprise was a sign of the shifting position of the Colombian Catholic church, whose hitherto rejection of modernizing efforts shifted toward committing to back the elites' agreed upon model for capitalist development in the country. The last section illustrates ACPO's ultimate involvement in the cultural modernization of the Colombian countryside and underlines the efficacy of ACPO by portraying its educative program as a disciplining cultural device that acted upon the peasants' time, space, and body. The study concludes by summarizing some of the more relevant statements and outlining future ways of problematization.

ACPO: "Educating for development" from Colombia to the world

An organization of the Colombian Catholic Church, ACPO pioneered in Colombia an ambitious literacy program that simultaneously used different mass communication media for educating ample sectors of adult peasants. Founded in 1947 by the twenty-six-year-old parish priest Jose Joaquin Salcedo, ACPO initiated with one radio transmitter and three receivers, and soon became the largest radio network in Latin America.[7] A country-wide literacy project was possible through ACPO's crafting of a so-called Combined Media System that included the creation of the *Sutatenza* Radio Station and the Radiophonic Schools, various instructional handbooks, a newspaper, and both books' and discs' collections.

[6] For a broader understanding of the social and political complexity that surrounded *La Violencia* and the *Frente Nacional*, see, Gonzalo Sanchez, *Guerra y Política en la Sociedad Colombiana* (El Ancora Editores, 1991).

[7] ACPO, *Reseña Histórica de ACPO* by Lázaro Jiménez, Bogotá 1947–1967. ACPO Archival Collection.

This combined system also included the mailing of letters to follow-up the transformations in radiophonic users' daily life and pioneered in instructing and involving the local laity as agents of the educative work.

Available data for the forty-five years of uninterrupted work (1947–1992) show that ACPO reached 955 of the 1,123 Colombian municipalities at the time. During that period, the Program distributed 6,453,937 instructional handbooks, and 75,749,539 copies of the 1,635 editions of *El Campesino* newspaper. Furthermore, ACPO's institutes instructed a total of 20,039 peasant leaders, and *Radio Sutatenza* ran a total of 1,489,935 hours broadcasting educative programs.[8] Given its broad and enduring impact, ACPO is among the most prominent and ambitious rural educational programs ever developed in Colombia. ACPO's success earned it financial support and technical assistance by international development organizations such as UNESCO, World Bank, and Interamerican Development Bank, and by private corporations such as General Electric, and Phillips.[9] Worldwide acknowledgment of ACPO's methods and success in *educating for development* also made international organizations interested in disseminating ACPO's education model throughout developing countries in Latin America, Africa, and Asia.[10]

ACPO developed an innovative pedagogical approach (the *Educación Fundamental Integral*-EFI) that expressed the program's views and commitments to addressing what, in the eyes of its ideologues, better described the country's *social problem*: the advance of de-Christianization and communism, poverty, and underdevelopment.[11] In light of the international divided Catholicism that penetrated the national arena in a

---

[8] ACPO, Internal documents (n.d.), ACPO Archival Collection.

[9] Hernando Bernal Alarcón, *Radio Sutatenza de la Realidad a la Utopía* (Bogotá, Fundación Cultural Javeriana, 2005), 61–67.

[10] In Latin America, interest by sectors of the national episcopacies in the radio as a means of popular education and development, led to the early functioning of other radiophonic schools starting in the mid-1960s. By the early 1970s, and facilitated by the German Church's organization ADVENIAT, radiophonic schools gathered to create the *Asociación Latinoamericana de Educación Radiofónica*-ALER. By the early 1980s, ALER reunited twenty-three institutions of radiophonic education throughout the region. Alarcón, *Radio Sutatenza*, 68–73. An example of evaluations considering African societies' feasibility of a radiophonic education project is available in Michael y Brauer Young Helen. *Notas sobre las Escuelas Radiofónicas de Colombia,* in Hernando Bernal Alarcón, *Educación Fundamental Integral. Teoría y Aplicación en el Caso de ACPO*. Serie Educación Fundamental Integral, vol. 1 (Bogotá: Editorial Andes, 1978), 91–117. ACPO Archival Collection.

[11] Francisco Houtart and Gustavo Pérez, *Acción Cultural Popular. Sus Principios y Medios de Acción. Consideraciones Teológicas y Sociológicas* (Bogotá, Editorial Andes, 1960). ACPO Archival Collection.

Catholicism and Modernization

predominantly rural country (65% by 1950) whose population lived in barely subsistence conditions, the EFI represented the pioneering effort of one sector of the Colombian clergy to have an impact on those problems.[12] ACPO deemed the educative process *Fundamental* as far as it offered basic knowledge directly related to the peasants' everyday life; and *Integral* as it attempted covering all aspects of life.[13] In this way, the EFI sought to conduct literacy teaching while simultaneously disseminating contents that addressed peasants' spiritual education, health and nutrition, basic math and budget, dwelling and working, leisure and recreation, and various other aspects of family and community affairs.[14]

Upon the belief that transforming culture and individual, family, and community values were the key to progress, ACPO developed ambitious Campaigns that along with the Radiophonic Schools were deemed core components of the EFI for their potentiality in penetrating the peasants' everyday life.[15] Overall, the EFI unfolded as a double-edged cultural *dispositive* to simultaneously Christianize and modernize the Colombian countryside.[16] It assumed the difficult challenge of transforming Colombian peasants' individual and social life toward the realization of a "Christian" ideal of "progress" that entailed "valuing man,"—teaching them to "live with dignity," promoting a "rectified scale of values," and "predisposing peasants' mindsets to Development."[17]

ACPO's push for theological renewal and a centrist Catholicism in Colombia

ACPO acted as an agent of Social-Catholicism within the prevalent Intransigent Colombian Catholic hierarchy.[18] This was a significant role,

[12] Urbanization data available in Safford and Palacios. *Colombia*, 433–437. Also see, Hans Rother, *El proceso de urbanización en Colombia*. Revista de la Universidad Nacional 1944–1992, no. 1 (Bogotá, 1968), 191–223.

[13] ACPO. Hernando Bernal Alarcón, *Educación Fundamental Integral. Teoría y Aplicación en el Caso de ACPO*. Serie Educación Fundamental Integral (Bogotá, Editorial Andes, 1978) ACPO Archival Collection.

[14] Alarcón, *Educación Fundamental Integral*.

[15] Houtart and Perez, *Acción Cultural Popular*.

[16] I am using the concept of *dispositive* in the meaning given by Michel Foucault. Michel Foucault, *Power/knowledge: Selected Interviews and Other Writings, 1972–1977* (New York: Vintage, 1980), 194–228.

[17] Houtart and Perez, *Acción Cultural Popular*, 37–40, 51.

[18] The differentiation made here between intransigent and Social-Catholic matrixes of Catholic thought builds on Emile Poulat's long-reaching understanding of Catholicism in its relation with Modernity. For a broader examination of this subject see, Emile Poulat, and Guy Lafon. *Le catholicisme sous observation: entretiens avec Guy Lafon: du modernisme à aujourd'hui* (Centurion, 1983). Also see, Misner, *Social Catholicism in Europe*. Misner offers an overview of the historical development of Social Catholicism in tension with other currents of

considering that Colombian episcopacy's attempts to address the social question from a Social-Catholic approach, as outlined by the Vatican, had been weak, and that its primary concern during previous decades had been to defend the Concordat and the confessional state from the liberal legislation.[19]

Willing to address historically lagging matters, ACPO was enthusiastic about opening spaces for a national dialogue on the expressions that in Colombia had thorny global issues related to the massification of society and politics. ACPO promoted these dialogues among the episcopate, government, and intellectual elites, following Vatican lines on the Church Social Teaching. Accordingly, ACPO inquired on the presumed challenges and dangers implicit in the relations between capital and labor, poverty, the long-lasting struggles in the country around land distribution, the social situation and mobilization of workers and peasants, and the ongoing tensions on private property.[20] Furthermore, following the Social-Catholic conciliatory tone with modernity, ACPO was also keen about the use of modern sciences for the better understanding of social realities, and technologies for the improvement of living standards.

ACPO's commitment to and agency of the Catholic Church Social Teaching among the predominantly intransigent Colombian clergy, for instance, explains the commonly overlooked fact that ACPO's educative enterprise was, in many ways, a Catholic Action experience in its

---

Catholic thought. For a broader exposition of the clash between these matrixes within Colombian Catholicism, see, Ricardo Arias, *El Episcopado Colombiano, Intransigencia y Laicidad 1850–2000* (Universidad de los Andes, 2003).

[19] While the rupture of the confessional state almost irreversibly stepped forward with the unfolding of religious reform during the liberal governments, the project of secularism in Colombian society continued to be condemned to failure. The ambivalence of liberal elites' behavior between heralding secularizing public positions, and a devout private life, as well as the general interest among the elites (Conservative and Liberal) to preserve Catholic morality and thereby the social and cultural *status quo* of the country, were among the major causes of this corollary. For a broader examination of secularism and the comings and goings of the Concordat in Colombia, see Ana Maria Bidegain, *Concordato, Secularización, Cultura, y Democracia* in *Política Colombiana-Revista de la Contraloría General de la República de Colombia*, vol III, no. 1 (Bogota: 1993) 61–68. Also see, Ricardo Arias, *El Episcopado Colombiano*, 166–171, 187.

[20] ACPO's Department of Sociology as well as *"El Campesino"* newspaper were active in organizing conferences with the explicit aim of facilitating the dialogue on contemporary issues of Colombian reality. Conferences by politicians Carlos Lleras Restrepo, Alvaro Gomez Hurtado, Misael Pastrana Borrero, and F. Pierre Bigó, S.J., published by 1965 under the title *"Revolución Violenta?"*, or three conferences by Professor Lynn Smith published also by 1965 under the title *"La Fisonomía de la Vida Rural"* are examples of the national dialogues promoted by ACPO. ACPO Archival Collection.

traditional (Italian) format.[21] Although ACPO was never explicit in this respect, the dynamics that surrounded the organization of ever-growing radiophonic movements among the peasantry, the gendered-differentiated instruction of leaders, and the groundbreaking appearance among the laity of the Immediate Auxiliaries as the key figures of the educative process and the everyday transformation of peasants' life, contribute to this interpretation.

In light of the often disinterest of the Catholic hierarchy in developing Catholic Action movements, and when formed, the prevalence of an approach that, neglecting the autonomy of the laity, supported those that were limited to be defensive organizations of the Church and the Conservative party, ACPO seemed, eventually, to provide a successful scheme for the apostolate of the lay peasantry that was submissive to the Church's authority. In the long-run, ACPO's educative program seemed to fit the expectations of the hierarchy of unfolding a Catholic Action spirit among the lay peasantry from a conservative approach; one that contributed to channel the loose ends of the past experience of the JOC, dismantled by the Church in 1939, because of its unsubmissive and politicized attitude.[22]

Overall, as ACPO's educative program thrived, taking stock by the early 1960s, it showed it had exponentially expanded throughout the country that was predominantly rural. It had undertaken the enterprise of educating peasant leaders who, in a consistent effort in their family and community life and through the impulse of social organization, were willing to defend Catholicism and the Church, and commit to a *Christian ideal of progress and development*.

---

[21] Promulgated in 1922 by Pope Pius XI in his Encyclical *Ubi Arcano Dei*, the international unfolding of Catholic Action confirmed the relevant role assigned to the laity since Leo XIII *Rerum Novarum*. Two distinct models of Catholic Action arose from the experience of lay Catholic militancy in Europe. One was the Italian Catholic Action (later known as General Catholic Action). The other was the Franco-Belgian model (later known as Specialized Catholic Action). For a broader examination of this subject, see, Gerd-Rainer Horn, *Western European Liberation Theology: The First Wave (1924–1959)* (Oxford University Press on Demand, 2008).

[22] JOC stands for Catholic Workers Youth Movement. The Colombian JOC, founded in 1933, gathered workers and peasants. It developed a mass movement increasingly unsubordinated to the hierarchy and with growing political significance. Because of these reasons, it was dismantled by the church hierarchy in 1939. For a broader exposition of Catholic Action's unfolding in Colombia between 1930 and the 1950s, see, Ana Maria Bidegain, *Iglesia, Pueblo, y Política: Un Estudio de Conflictos de Intereses, Colombia 1930–1955* (Universidad Javeriana, 1985).

ACPO's commitment to Social-Catholic views also created the opportunity for some vanguard Catholic ideologues to participate in envisioning ACPO's principles of action and primary objectives, as well as in outlining institutional standpoints that, later, were to define ACPO's identity within the Church and before other national and international secular actors. Theologians such as Francois Houtart and Gustavo Pérez, recently arrived from Leuven, directly participated in these tasks, while figures like F. Camilo Torres were among the earlier collaborators and sympathizers. Renowned Catholic philosophers such as Jacques Maritain and Emmanuel Mounier, along with theologians such as Gustave Thills, were extensively cited in the endeavor of ideologically founding and structuring ACPO's educative work.

Indeed, ACPO was an attentive listener and interpreter of cutting-edge progressive Catholic views: Integral Humanism, Personalist philosophy, and the *Neuvelle Theologie*. In doing so, it became a vantage point for gathering dissenting voices among the prevalent intransigency and pushing for a theological renovation of a traditional clergy who, in a general sense, had been reluctant to such approaches.

Although highly informed by this progressivism, while ACPO was gradually finding its own identity it had to distance itself from some of its early progressive adherents.[23] In light of more radical ideological appropriations of progressive Catholicism that had been taking place in Latin America, ACPO rather endorsed a developmental path to social change that opposed the "revolutionary way" that was incubating among many Christians in the region.[24]

ACPO's Social-Catholic views, groundbreaking for the Colombian context, put it in the leading position of advancing a politically moderate Catholicism in the country that extended its militant arm in a crusade to re-Christianize society, promote a *rectified* scale of values, fight communism, and foster Development.[25] In this endeavor, ACPO actively committed to using its Combined Media System to intervene in creating

---

[23] Cases such as that of F. Camilo Torres and Monsignor German Guzman portray the increasing ideological ruptures within Colombian clergy in the context of radicalization of sectors of the Latin American church.
ACPO. *Correspondence Archive. Letters involving Father Camilo Torres, Monsignor Monastoque (director of El Campesino newspaper), and Monsignor Salcedo (director of ACPO)*,1962. ACPO Archival Collection.
ACPO. *Memories of the Congreso Cultural de la Habana, Speech by Monsignor German Guzman*, January 1968. ACPO Archival Collection.

[24] Phillip Berryman, "Latin American Liberation Theology," *Theological Studies Journal* 34/3 (1973): 357–395. Also see, Horn, *Western European Liberation Theology*.

[25] Houtart and Perez, *Acción Cultural Popular*.

public opinion and growing a *truly* Christian political culture. From this perspective, ACPO continued to act as a force of modernization within the church as well as a dynamizing agent of Colombian Catholic social and political thought. Ultimately, the standpoints of an emergent politically moderate Catholicism as spearheaded by ACPO were to be central in the Church endorsing of the elites' modernizing consensus.

ACPO and the "modernizing consensus" in mid-twentieth century Colombia

ACPO's frequent clarification about its political neutrality seems to have been a response to the problematic position of the Colombian episcopate in light of the outcomes of *La Violencia*, deemed both "anti-Christian, and even more anti-human."[26] However, it was precisely its non-neutrality that ultimately allowed ACPO's ideologues and precursors to maintain the organization and continue the educational processes in the midst of the political and ideological controversies that characterized the period. ACPO's political stand was critical not only to gain the needed favorability and support among the Catholic hierarchy, but also to fit into the national and international entrenched structures, correlation of forces, and agendas of the period. ACPO successfully navigated two successive conservative agendas, the elites' supported *coup d'état* by General Gustavo Rojas Pinilla, as well as the coalition governments of the *Frente Nacional*. While ACPO thrived during its early years, in part facilitated by a conservative party in power with whom the church had historically established a mutually benefiting and protecting relation, the historical terms of the relationship between church and state also served them well. Colombia was a conservative state which, despite the recent blows by the Liberal Party to undermine its authority and power, continued to rely on the Church's social legitimacy to consolidate its governance.[27]

---

[26] *Pastoral Colectiva del Episcopado,* 1949, in Arias, *El Episcopado Colombiano,* 184. In the pastoral letter of 1953, the episcopate pointed out with concern that, "like a cyclone", violence had passed "with devastating force through the regions." The penetration of international communism, the forgetting of God and Christian principles were the causes attributed. A problematic position arose when although the episcopacy declared its political neutrality and invited to overcome the "partisan divisions and hatreds," it was clear for the public opinion that some priests had been involved in acts of violence or agitation against the liberal party. Arias, *El Episcopado Colombiano.* For an interesting chronicle of *La Violencia*, and a perennial work in Colombian historical sociology, see, Alfredo Molano, *Los años del tropel: relatos de la violencia* (Fondo Editorial CEREC, Bogotá: 1985; 2017).

[27] These are common conclusions by the more general literature on the subject. See, for instance, Fernán E. González, *Poderes enfrentados: Iglesia y estado en Colombia* (Cinep, 1997); Arias, *El Episcopado Colombiano.* Bidegain, *Iglesia,*

Notwithstanding the favorable terms of these relations, ACPO's christianizing, yet also modernizing project, was barely welcomed during the first years of existence, particularly, among conservative sectors of the clergy and the Conservative Party, who saw the project with skepticism. Indeed, only in the early 1950s, with the appointment of Monsignor Crisanto Luque as Archbishop of Bogotá and primate of Colombia, did ACPO receive support from the episcopacy.[28] If contradictory in appearance, the explanation lies in the traditionally intransigent attitude of the Colombian clergy, generally at odds with modernizing views and efforts, and a Conservative Party who had historically represented the interests of the landlord oligarchy. In this position, the Conservative Party had vehemently opposed industrialization during the preceding decades, in an attempt to protect the prevailing model of rentist exploitation of both land and peasants' labor.[29] The 1940s, however, had made clear to both of these skeptical sectors the ineludible path toward modernization.

A series of national and international circumstances favored ACPO's thriving while also transforming the Colombian Church into a critical ally of modernization in the country. Since the 1930s, the consolidation of an industrial bourgeoisie in the country had shaken up the country's structures of power, and the creation by growing industries of a labor market with typical urban characteristics had eroded, profoundly and irreversibly, the base of the agrarian regime.[30] While the contradiction between the young industrial bourgeoisie and the traditional landlord oligarchy had presented itself as insoluble in the short run, the Agrarian Reform of 1936, and, later, the outburst of *La Violencia* in the mid-1940s, ultimately, set the stage for a modernizing consensus among the elites.[31]

  Pueblo, y Politica. Christopher Abel, *Política, Iglesia y partidos en Colombia 1886–1953.* FAES, Universidad Nacional de Colombia, (Bogota: 1987). For an overview of the interplay of political actors in Colombian violence and state legitimacy, see, Palacios, Marco. *Between Legitimacy and Violence* (Duke University Press, 2006).

[28] ACPO, *Sacerdotes y Seglares en la obra educativa popular en Colombia. Informe de la Dirección General de Acción Cultural Popular a la II Asamblea General de la Institución* 1957; ACPO, *Informes a la venerable Conferencia Episcopal de Colombia,* 1955–1964. ACPO Archival Collection.

[29] Salomón Kalmanovitz, and López Enciso López. *La agricultura colombiana en el siglo XX. Fondo De Cultura Económica* (US, 2006: 62–84); Salomón Kalmanovitz, *El Desarrollo de la Agricultura en Colombia.* (C. Valencia Editores, 1982: 16–34).

[30] Kalmanovitz, *Desarrollo de la Agricultura en Colombia,* 273–283. An useful overview of existing interpretations on the development of agriculture in Colombia is available in Absalón Machado, *De la estructura agraria al sistema agroindustrial.* Vol. 2 (Univ. Nacional de Colombia, 2002).

[31] Overcoming the acute partisan violence that had festered in the bases, and menaced national stability, was not possible if not by the bipartisan elites' agreement that led first to the Liberal and Conservative-factional support of the *coup d'état* against the radical Conservative government of Laureano Gomez by

A shared commitment to embracing capitalist development, following a landlord model, paved the way for the take-off of capitalist agriculture in the country.[32]

This consensus also resulted from external pressures. By 1950, Colombia reached an embarrassing tenth position in regional economic growth, and its illiteracy rate continued to be among the highest (38%) in Latin America.[33] The first mission of the World Bank had estimated the majority of Colombian population was rural, lived in subsistence conditions, with high rates of infant mortality, inadequate housing, overcrowding, and lack of public services, credit, and agricultural production techniques. Although the mission acknowledged economic growth, it also warned that only a small parcel of the population benefitted from that growth.[34] During the early stages of the region's Cold War, this situation constituted the backdrop of the Truman doctrine's resonance in the country and transnational organizations' involvement in promoting modernization and development as the means of fighting poverty, considered the primary breeding ground for communism.

In this changing context, ACPO assumed an explicit commitment to fight underdevelopment and back the elites' modernizing consensus that, if fragile, by the early 1950s promised to calm partisan violence and eradicate communism. With the blessing of Monsignor Crisanto Luque, the episcopacy's embracing of ACPO's educative program also represented a Catholic church committed to modernizing views that until recently had been condemned by the national hierarchy. Overall, for liberal and conservative elites, the modernizing consensus meant an alliance that guaranteed the path toward industrialization, keeping unaltered the sources of wealth of the landlord's oligarchy while also advancing a comprehensive effort for strengthening the nation by appeasing the masses and integrating them through limited democratizing measures.[35] For the church,

---

General Gustavo Rojas Pinilla. Three years later, bipartisan elites also convened, this times, to overthrow Rojas Pinilla when he attempted consolidating an autonomous populist third political force. For a broader examination of this subject, see, Marco Palacios, *Between Legitimacy and Violence*.

[32] Kalmanovitz and López, *La agricultura colombiana en el siglo XX*.

[33] Safford and Palacios, *Colombia*, 432. Data on literacy available in M.T. Ramirez and J.P. Tellez, *La educación primaria, y secundaria en Colombia en el siglo XX*. Banco de la Republica (Bogotá, 2006), 40. http://www.banrep.gov.co/docum/ftp/borra379.pdf.

[34] Safford and Palacios, *Colombia*, 432.

[35] The elites reached consensuses on issues such as subsidies and tax exemptions (Palacios, 2006) while they also maintained democratizing measures achieved during previous years. Among those, universal male suffrage, extended to women since 1957, the eight-hour workday, and basic union rights, among others, not committing, however, to a further extension of the citizens' social and political

backing this consensus meant putting aside problems now considered minor–partisan differences—which had caused a "moral crisis" in the country and, instead, join forces to fight the greater evil: communism.[36]

ACPO's contribution to *colombianizing* the countryside, as well as its standpoints on delicate topics such as responsible procreation, popular participation in national development, agrarian reform, private property, and class struggle, were critical in supporting the modernizing consensus of the elites. They were also critical for ACPO's spearheading of a "non-violent revolution" aimed at promoting the much-needed social change through the re-accommodation of the dominant social forces while demobilizing popular masses.

Accordingly, in supporting the elite´s efforts for *colombianizing* the countryside, ACPO dedicated various titles of the *El Campesino* Library to instructing peasants on the biography of the "fathers of the country," national symbols, rhythms, and dances.[37] While this library complemented the work of radio-broadcasted literacy teaching by providing printed materials for peasant audiences and encouraged reading, it also actively promoted a sense of nation-ness by portraying Colombia's national idiosyncrasy. The definition of this idiosyncrasy reflected, nevertheless, the more common positivist and evolutionist logic at the base of conservative nationalist views, according to which it was necessary to *select* and *ennoble* certain traditions to make them representative of the nation, while *vulgarizing* elements of high culture for "increasing the good social taste."[38]

ACPO's overall educative action, notably that accomplished through radio broadcasting, campaigns, and the newspaper was also active in creating public opinion on a thread of interconnected problems that directly concerned the contemporary rural reality and the related historical struggle for land and labor in the country. The agrarian reform contained the conundrum of such a struggle, and ACPO developed significant efforts in educating peasants in the advantages of a non-violent way to

---

rights. For Palacios, "The new plutocracy thought no more highly of social reforms than the old elites did. Social justice was reduced to a matter of minor public spending, rather than the all-permeating issue it represented for Latin American populism." Palacios, *Between Legitimacy and Violence*, 127.

[36] Pastoral Colectiva del Episcopado, 1948, in Arias, *El Episcopado Colombiano*, 182.

[37] ACPO, *El Campesino* Library. The various titles are: Colombian Poetry, Is good to be Colombian, The Farmer Couplet, Sing with the Guitar, Peasants' Pictures, Colombia Our Land, My Name is Simon Bolivar, among many others. ACPO Archival Collection. Some of these titles are now digitized and available at: http://babel.banrepcultural.org/cdm/search/collection/p17054coll24.

[38] ACPO, *Selected Music*. Audio-record. Various materials. (n.d.) Also see: *Sacerdotes y Seglares*, 1957, 29. ACPO Archival Collection.

development. In supporting the elites' consensus on a landlord model of capitalist development, ACPO's Agrarian Reform Campaign chose the way of keeping unaltered the dominant view on land as the primary source of capitalist accumulation in the country and the socioeconomic pattern of concentration of property. ACPO also agreed on the necessity of stimulating a more rational economic exploitation of land in the terms recommended by the World Bank mission, promoting agricultural technification, and the emergence of a middle-class that might become a major tenant of those lands.[39]

Relying on recent Vatican teachings that recognized the conflict between the Christian objectives of promoting the realization of a just, but also a free society, ACPO agreed in asserting that it was the state's obligation to determine the legal tenancy and usufruct of property, as long as it responded to the "true necessities of the common good."[40] In this vein, ACPO aligned with the national hierarchy of the church in emphasizing the difference between "property rights" and "property uses," therefore promoting the embracing of the notion of "distributive justice."[41] This notion envisioned an "internal revolution of the Christian who in choosing to follow God's teachings" abided by the principles of private property that although a natural right was, however, balanced by the common destination of the assets possessed. So that, "the man who possesses the property, possesses it as common in the sense that he easily yields it when the others need it," without affecting the ownership of the land.[42] Therefore, the needed reform was not to be performed "against the [the system of private property], but in accordance with it."[43] In brief, in light of the historical contradiction between a landlords' oligarchy who was heir to the hacienda regime and a mobilized peasantry who continued to claim their right to land, ACPO stuck to the *status quo* on matters of land property. ACPO's Agrarian Reform Campaigns opposed structural transformations, and instead, promoted improving peasants' access to land through tenancy, land market, and extending credit to peasants.[44]

[39] ACPO, *Agrarian Reform Campaign*, Various materials. (n.d.) ACPO Archival Collection.
[40] ACPO, *Declaración de la jerarquía Colombiana sobre el momento social del país*. Reprinted in *Revolución Violenta?* Conference cycle organized by *El Campesino* newspaper, Bogotá, 1965, 10. ACPO Archival Collection.
[41] ACPO, *El Derecho de Propiedad* by F. Pierre Bigo S.J. Reprinted in *Revolución Violenta?* Conference cycle organized by *El Campesino* newspaper *(Bogota*, 1965: 55). ACPO Archival Collection.
[42] ACPO, *El Derecho de Propiedad*, 56.
[43] ACPO, *Declaración de la jerarquía*, Reprinted in *Revolución Violenta?*, 14. ACPO Archival Collection.
[44] ACPO, *Agrarian Reform Campaign*, Various materials. (n.d.) ACPO Archival Collection.

Similarly, ACPO was a hard critic of the notion of "class struggle," and instead advocated the use of "social status" that, rather than signaling a form of social inequality, emphasized the cultural capacity of the individual to achieve progress.[45] In so far as ACPO contended Marxists' interpretations of class and social structures that abounded within the circles of critical Latin American thought and were growing among the mobilized laity and other secular sectors throughout the continent, it strived to gain adherents for understanding the current social problem, i.e., underdevelopment, as a cultural problem. In such an understanding, ACPO coherently articulated the notions that made possible the so-called non-violent revolution; namely, individual development and harmonic integration to social development. Therefore, ACPO insisted that individual values were the key to social mobility. Thus, as far as "[social status is] (…) the position, the social rank attributed to a person (…) [ultimately,] what [the] person is for the whole or part of the individuals who integrate the social universe [,] the social status raises notions of equality and social level in the mind of the one who observes the social reality."[46]

Consistently, ACPO's pedagogical action was openly condemnatory of the advancing of any philosophy that threatened the stability of the social order in both the international structures of the church and the regional and national political life. By 1957, ACPO celebrated their Combined Media System, considering it successful in educating peasants' minds to "obey pastors and priests (…) and abide (…) by the church. [Therefore] it is no longer possible to reach to *Radio Sutatenza's* listeners with messages that threaten the purity of the doctrine or that incite social disorder."[47]

ACPO's fight against communism was vigorous, and seemingly, the *El Campesino* newspaper was instrumental in disseminating interpretations that assessed common popular protests as infiltrated by international communism. F. Camilo Torres denounced in 1962 that the *El Campesino* was advancing a systematic anti-communist campaign by making judgments on individuals and popular movements with no evidence.[48] While

[45] ACPO, Houtart and Perez, *Ideologia y Objetivos*, 18–21. ACPO Archival Collection.
[46] Houtart and Perez, *Ideologia y Objetivos*, 18.
[47] ACPO, *Sacerdotes y Seglares*, 5. ACPO Archival Collection.
[48] Complaints by *El Campesino* such as those published on August 6, 1958: *"the procedures followed by the Communists in their incitement of peasants to class struggle and to the unauthorized seizure of private lands;"* or on July 9, 1961: *"Discovered the communist plot in the strike of the National University;"* and also August 20, 1961 *"the elected board of MOEC directors are almost all the leaders had been appointed of the Liberal Revolutionary Movement (MRL),"* influenced the public climate surrounding the controversy Father Camilo Torres unleashed by denouncing *El Campesino's* anti-communist campaign. The controversy was fueled by quarreling positions portrayed in *El Catolicismo*—the Colombian

F. Torres' claim seems to have been well-founded, it was also evident, through other public statements, that ACPO strongly committed to promoting the *harmonic* integration of individuals and movements to social development, in line with the corporatist approach through which the Catholic church had actively co-opted unions during the previous decades.[49]

To be sure, during the 1950s, some forms of peasants' mobilization responded to partisan ideologies (liberal, communist)—notably, those emerged from the ashes of former peasants and indigenous leagues and unions destroyed by the dynamics of *La Violencia*. Others, however, had no political insurrectional project and did not claim a class identity.[50] These other forms of peasants' mobilization became instead foci of resistance to the terror *of the conflict* or just collective vindications of immediate necessities such as access to credit, subsistence conditions, or demanding control on abuses in regional politics.[51]

Convincingly, ACPO's anti-communist stance, nurtured by its functionalist views on the social role of individuals and its consideration of peasants as naive, almost childish subjects, paralleled, and even more, worked in favor of the official rhetoric of containment emerging at the onset of the region's Cold War. [52]

Eventually, in line with the goal of channeling and straightening peasants' energy and interests in partaking in the definition of their social and political space, ACPO promoted the organization of Community Action Boards among the neighbors. Envisioned as spaces for popular participation, these boards allowed dialogue with the institutions of the state, and were coherently ingrained with the existing regional political-administrative structures. The creation of boards, the instruction of leaders in ACPO's institutes, and the reach of the *El Campesino* newspaper resulted in successful means for disseminating a political culture consistent with ACPO's *rectified* scale of values.

Catholic Church's newspaper since 1849—and the partisan newspapers *El Tiempo* and *El Siglo*.

[49] Sandra Londono, and Javier Mejía, *El Discurso de una Ética Católica Modernizada: El Caso del Programa Acción Cultural Popular 1947–1958*, Editorial Redipe, 2017, 81.

[50] Gonzalo Sánchez, *Guerra y política en la sociedad colombiana* (El Ancora Editores, Bogotá, 1991), 38.

[51] Sánchez, *Guerra y política*, 38.

[52] Greg Grandin, *What was Containment? Short and Long Answers from the Americas*, in T*he Cold War in the Third World*, ed. Robert J. McMahon (New York: Oxford University Press, 2013), 27–47.

ACPO's educative program and Colombian cultural modernization

Undoubtedly, one of the more successful aspects of ACPO's educative program, and a critical piece of its commitment to the modernizing consensus was ACPO's contribution to the cultural modernization of the Colombian countryside. Nationally and internationally praised, the Combined Media System got into the peasants' everyday life and unfolded a powerful cultural dispositive. Using popular language, rhythms, and beliefs, this cultural dispositive achieved the goal of re-signifying traditions, instilling modern habits and behaviors, and promoting a *truly* Christian political culture. In ACPO's words, it was about unfolding a "civilizational" enterprise aimed at "dignifying the peasant" while also fighting ignorance, considered "the major obstacle for progress, and root of underdevelopment."[53] Among its ideological principles, ACPO also stated its objectives of promoting a "Christian-based public consciousness" about the problems of the countryside and the peasants' life, and integrating peasants to the apostolate of the church following an "authentic hierarchical organization."[54]

Consistently with its political and ideological standpoints, ACPO claimed that "economic and social underdevelopment" was in a large extent a "cultural problem" dependent on the individual's mind, attitudes, and behaviors.[55] Accordingly, "underdevelopment [was], not material lack, but rather the inability of people to use their own potential and intelligence, (...) Underdevelopment is in the mind of men, (...) [therefore,] there are not underdeveloped countries, but underdeveloped men."[56] Thus, ACPO envisioned its pedagogical role as a cultural action meant to affect the country's traits of "backwardness": illiteracy, ill health, low productivity, and overpopulation.

As I have claimed elsewhere, ACPO's significant transformations in the peasant's everyday life might be referred to as a disciplining process on the peasants' subjectivities that involved their experience of time, space, and the body.[57] ACPO's regulation of these three realms of human experience entailed the production of an abstract framework of

[53] ACPO, *Sacerdotes y Seglares*, 4. Also see, ACPO *Las Pequeñas—Grandes Campañas de Acción Cultural Popular*. Documento elaborado por Pbro. José Ramón Sabogal como Ponencia para el Seminario sobre la Obra Diocesana y Parroquial de ACPO (Sutatenza, 1966). ACPO Archival Collection.
[54] Houtart and Pérez, *Ideología y Objetivos*, 1960, 40–B. ACPO Archival Collection.
[55] Houtart and Pérez, *Ideología y Objetivos*, 37.
[56] Jose Joaquín Salcedo, *Mensaje de la Dirección General a los colaboradores de la Institución*, 1973, 66, ACPO Archival Collection.
[57] Sandra Londono, and Javier Mejía, *Ocupación simbólica y subjetivación en el caso del programa Acción Cultural Popular, 1947–1958, Revista Magistro*, 5 (10), (Bogota, 2011), 59–72.

interpretation that, articulating subtle relations of knowledge and power, instituted "legitimate" and "virtuous manners" of being, using time, behaving in the social group, constructing family relations, and fulfilling their religious duties. Therefore, ACPO's cultural dispositive managed to organize both the individual and the collective social experience of a considerable number of peasants in both the symbolic and material realms.

The disciplining of time in ACPO's education was critical for breaking the traditional unitarian time of peasants' life. ACPO's Combined Media System emphasized the introduction of modern chronosystems with productive criteria and looked at reinforcing an ideal of the future. Reading tasks disseminated within literacy handbooks insisted on partitioning and organizing the day, the week, and the month.[58] Notions of efficiency, efficacy, need for achievement, and empathy for saving and planning filled the contents of reading tasks, anecdotes, and jokes while math handbooks taught basic arithmetic operations and recommended the household's head to envision monthly incomes, save money, and create a "family budget."[59]

Similarly, recreation campaigns contributed to the disciplining of time by promoting appropriate uses of leisure time. ACPO's recreation campaigns encouraged the practice of chess and basketball, animated peasants to listen to *Radio Sutatenza's* selected music sections, and reading the newspaper sections dedicated to disseminating selected couplets, verses, songs, and jokes. In all cases, recreation campaigns' contents responded to the presumed necessity of combating laziness and addictions, promoting a healthy and productive body, and discouraging revolution-driven community gatherings.

ACPO's disciplining of peasants' spatiality sought to reorganize both family and communitarian social life and relations. Housing campaigns were groundbreaking, as they disseminated models for building "the house," "the sports field," "the village," "the market," "the town."[60] These campaigns connected the promotion of health and sanitation with ideals of productivity and domesticity, and with envisioned social networks for channeling popular participation.

Individual bodies and individual identities were also a central part of the program's intervention. The objectives of "raising peasant's dignity," increasing levels of individualization, and reinforcing "the sense of decency"

---

[58] ACPO, *Cartilla Alfabeto* by Numa Pompilio Mesa (Bogotá, 1962), 86–102. ACPO Archival Collection.

[59] ACPO, *Cartilla del Numero* by Luis Francisco Munevar, 139–145. ACPO Archival Collection.

[60] ACPO, *Las Pequeñas—Grandes Campañas de Acción Cultural Popular*. Also see, ACPO, *Sacerdotes y Seglares*, 26–31. ACPO Archival Collection.

in regards to sexuality, remained a cross-cutting objective throughout the Combined Media System.[61] Controlling individuals' emotions and sexuality, reinforcing individual roles with gendered criteria, educating on the "natural definition" of social relations, and teaching mechanisms of solving conflict among family, couples, and peers were among the more common topics of instruction. In this regard, ACPO received generalized high appraisement by the public opinion for achieving to organize the family that was, in turn, considered as the base for organizing the nation. Cultural predisposition to Development and advancing the idea of change without revolution were the more cherished outcomes.[62]

Hygiene campaigns complemented ACPO's efforts for intervening on structural Colombian rural problems such as overpopulation, mortality rates, poverty, and violence. Campaigns of Responsible Procreation matched recommendations by the World Bank mission as well as concerns by the more recent Mission of Economy and Humanism conducted by a French priest Louis-Joseph Lebret, even though this represented a thorny issue and encountered detractors within the church hierarchy.[63]

In every case, the disciplining of bodies and identities followed gender-differentiated approaches that explained and justified "the natural differences between feminine and masculine temper and sexuality."[64] Therefore, in addressing overpopulation and emotional control, for instance, ACPO extended the male-vs-female matrix for differentially educating in "responsible procreation" vs. "sexual modesty," and in "anger management" vs. "how to be a good wife."[65]

Overall, ACPO's involvement in the peasants' everyday life was the central piece of its agency in Colombian cultural modernization. The EFI achieved the dissemination of an abstract framework of interpretation for *disciplining/governing* the peasants' everyday life. Self and social regulation mechanisms were active in defining the contours of peasants' subjectivities. In that vein, the possible, the imaginable, the feasible, the "nature" of social relations, the social organization, and peasants' participation in political matters, were all objects of normalization. Ultimately, the connection between the everyday life and the social and political organization

---

[61] ACPO, *Las Pequeñas. El Campesino* newspaper and radio broadcasting were crucial means of dissemination of ACPO's campaigns. By editorial decision, in both cases, it was common that entire sections of daily editions were dedicated to permanent or occasional campaigns.
[62] ACPO, *Sacerdotes y Seglares*, 1957. ACPO Archival Collection.
[63] Louis Joseph Lebret, *Misión Economía y Humanismo. Estudios sobre el Desarrollo Económico de Colombia (*Bogotá, Aedita Editores, Cromos, 1958).
[64] *El Campesino* newspaper, Section: *Como llegar a ser bella*, August 28, 1962.
[65] *El Campesino* newspaper.

of peasants was the method to crystallize the envisioned "non-violent revolution" toward a Christian realization of Development.

CONCLUSION

ACPO was a strong agent of cultural modernization both inside and outside the church. In so far as an active promoter of Social-Catholic views and a pioneer of a politically moderate Catholicism in the country, ACPO contributed significantly to advance a process of theological renewal among the Colombian clergy, and more broadly, to dynamizing Colombian Catholic, social, and political thought. Moreover, ACPO's vast and encompassing educative program managed to penetrate the peasants' everyday life, promoting modern values, and cultivating both public opinion and a political culture that matched the broad objectives of promoting a "rectified scale of [Christian] values," and advancing a "non-violent revolution" towards Development.

The Catholic hierarchy's embracing of ACPO's developmental path to social change reflected the shifting position of the Church toward modernization. Eventually, this shift was decisive for the Church endorsement of the elite's modernizing consensus, and the latter, indispensable to Colombian development. That is, in so far as the state's governance continued to rely on the Church social legitimacy, the Church ended up being a central actor in the crystallization of the bipartisan coalition sealed at the onset of the *Frente Nacional*. While economically committing to a landlord way of capitalist development of the Colombian countryside, the elites' coalition politically aimed at excluding third political forces, limiting the upsurge of popular nationalisms, and halting communism. For the Church, the modernizing consensus meant not only joining forces to fight the greater evil of communism. It also meant—what was to be an ephemeral achievement—the bipartisan acquiescence to the triumph of a state model that by the late 1950s, having truncated much of the projects of secularization, still retained many characteristics of the much-cherished confessional-state.[66] In middling this tangled network of relations and interests, ACPO's work and impetus were decisive.

---

[66] While by the end of the 1950s, the bipartisan consensus appeared favorable for the church position in Colombian society, the years to come were to confirm the growing and irreversible trend toward the rupture of the confessional state in Colombia. During the 16 years of *Frente Nacional* governments, political and structural transformations were to lead to the relative withdrawal of the church intervention in politics. According to Arias and Gonzalez (2005), in so far as the church became an integral part of the bipartisan regime, electoral activity in favor of the Conservative party disappeared. Also, these years were at the onset of a most profound "crisis of the Catholic Church model in Colombian society" caused by the loss of control upon the family and the scholar system. Ricardo

In connection to the broader discussion of this book, ACPO's remarkable experience has provided a valuable entry for the scholarly discussion of Catholicism's role in Colombian—more broadly, Latin American—public life and agendas. Colombia's case adds evidence to the historiographical record that shows that in contrast to the presumed "privatization of religion" as the backdrop of nation-state formation processes, in Latin America, Catholicism remained influential, and the church prevailed as a critical agent in its crafting.[67] In transnational scope also, ACPO's case allows recognizing the myriad maneuverings and differential outcomes of Catholicism's confrontation with modernity. Therefore, it contributed to the already thick problematization of the ambiguous unfolding of both liberalism and modernization in the region.

Finally, ACPO's case has also contributed to unveil the minutia of religious mechanisms of social regulation at work in the interconnection between daily life, social organization, the construction of political culture, and the broader exercise of citizenship. In this perspective, a whole discussion remains awaiting, to further our understanding of the interaction of subjective and structural dimensions of religion implied in the production of social and political life.

Arias, and Fernán González, *Búsqueda de la paz y defensa del "orden cristiano": el episcopado ante los grandes debates de Colombia (1998–2005)* in Francisco Leal Buitrago, ed. *En la encrucijada: Colombia en el siglo XXI* (Editorial Norma, 2006).

[67] Raimundo Barreto, Ronaldo Cavalcante, and Wanderley Pereira da Rosa (eds.), *World Christianity as Public Religion* (Minneapolis, MN: Fortress Press, 2017).

Bibliography

Abel, Christopher. *Política, Iglesia y partidos en Colombia, 1886-1953.* FAES Bogota: Universidad Nacional de Colombia, 1987.

Arias, Ricardo. *El Episcopado Colombiano, Intransigencia y Laicidad 1850-2000.* Bogota: Universidad de los Andes, 2003.

Arias, Ricardo, and Fernán González. *Búsqueda de la paz y defensa del "orden cristiano": el episcopado ante los grandes debates de Colombia (1998-2005).* In *En la encrucijada: Colombia en el siglo XXI*, edited by Francisco Leal Buitrago. Bogota: Editorial Norma, 2006.

Barreto, Raimundo Jr., Ronaldo Cavalcante, Wanderley Pereira da Rosa. *World Christianity as Public Religion.* Minneapolis, MN: Fortress Press, 2017.

Bernal Alarcón, Hernando. *Radio sutatenza de la realidad a la utopía.* Bogotá, Fundación Cultural Javeriana, 2005.

Berryman, Phillip. "Latin American Liberation Theology." *Theological Studies Journal* 34, no. 3 (1973): 357-395.

Bidegain, Ana Maria. *Iglesia, pueblo, y politica: Un estudio de conflictos de intereses, Colombia 1930-1955.* Bogota: Universidad Javeriana, 1985.

———. *Concordato, secularización, cultura, y democracia* in *política Colombiana—Revista de la Contraloría General de la República de Colombia*, vol III, no. 1, 61-68. Bogota: n.p., 1993.

Escobar, Arturo. *Encountering Development: The Making and Unmaking of the Third World.* Princeton, NJ: Princeton University Press, 1995.

Foucault, Michel. Power/Knowledge: Selected Interviews and Other Writings, 1972-1977. Vintage, 1980.

González, Fernán E. *Poderes enfrentados: Iglesia y estado en Colombia.* Bogota: Cinep, 1997.

Grandin, Greg. "What Was Containment? Short and Long Answers from the Americas." In *The Cold War in the Third World*, edited by Robert J. McMahon, 27-47. Reinterpreting History. Oxford: Oxford University Press, 2013.

Holland, Joe. *Modern Catholic Social Teaching: The Popes Confront the Industrial Age, 1740-1958.* New York: Paulist Press, 2003.

Horn, Gerd-Rainer. *Western European Liberation Theology: The First Wave (1924-1959).* Oxford: Oxford University Press on Demand, 2008.

Kalmanovitz, Salomón. *Las instituciones y el desarrollo económico en Colombia.* Bogota: Grupo Editorial Norma, 2001.

Kalmanovitz, Salomón. *El Desarrollo de la agricultura en Colombia.* C. Valencia Editores, 1982.

Kalmanovitz, Salomón, and López Enciso López. *La agricultura colombiana en el siglo XX*. Bogota: Fondo De Cultura Económica, 2006.

Lebret, Louis Joseph. *Misión economía y humanismo. Estudios sobre el desarrollo económico de Colombia*, 1958.

Londono, Sandra, and Javier Mejía. *Ocupación simbólica y subjetivación en el caso del programa Acción Cultural Popular, 1947-1958*. Revista Magistro 5, no. 10 (2011): 59-72.

Londono, Sandra, and Javier Mejia. *El discurso de una etica catolica modernizada: El caso del programa Accion Cultural Popular 1947-1958*. Colombia: Editorial Redipe, 2017.

Machado, Absalón. *De la estructura agraria al sistema agroindustrial*. Vol. 2. Sede Bogota: Univ. Nacional de Colombia, 2002.

Misner, Paul. *Social Catholicism in Europe: From the Onset of Industrialization to the First World War*. New York: Crossroad Publishing, 1991.

Molano, Alfredo. *Los años del tropel: relatos de la violencia*. Bogota: Fondo Editorial CEREC, 2017.

Palacios, Marco. *Between Legitimacy and Violence*. Durham, NC: Duke University Press, 2006.

Poulat, Emile, and Guy Lafon. *Le catholicisme sous observation: entretiens avec Guy Lafon: du modernisme à aujourd'hui*. N.p.: Centurion, 1983.

Ramirez, M.T., and J.P. Tellez. *La educación primaria y secundaria en Colombia en el siglo XX*. Banco de la Republica. Bogota, 2006. http://www.banrep.gov.co/docum/ftp/borra379.pdf.

Rother, Hans. *El proceso de urbanización en Colombia*. Revista de la Universidad Nacional 1944-1992, no. 1. Bogotá, 1968.

Sanchez, Gonzalo. *Guerra y politica en la sociedad colombiana*. Bogota: El Ancora Editores, 1991.

Safford, Frank, and Marco Palacios. *Colombia: Fragmented Land, Divided Society*. Oxford: Oxford University Press, 2001.

Primary Sources (ACPO Archival Collection)

ACPO. *Reseña Histórica de ACPO* by Lázaro Jiménez, Bogotá, 1947-1967.

ACPO. *Sacerdotes y Seglares en la obra educativa popular en Colombia. Informe de la Dirección General de Acción Cultural Popular a la II Asamblea General de la Institución*, 1957.

ACPO. *Informes a la venerable Conferencia Episcopal de Colombia*, 1955-1964. ACPO Archival Collection.

ACPO. Newspaper *El Campesino*, 1958-1962.

ACPO. *Cartilla Alfabeto* by Numa Pompilio Mesa, Bogotá, 1962.

ACPO. *Cartilla del Numero* by Luis Francisco Munevar, Bogota, 1962.

ACPO. *Correspondence Archive. Letters involving Father Camilo Torres, Mons. Monastoque (director of El Campesino newspaper), and Mons. Salcedo (director of ACPO)*, 1962.

ACPO. *"Revolución Violenta?"* Cycle of Conferences organized by the El Campesino newspaper. Editorial Andes, Bogota, 1965.

ACPO. *"La Fisonomía de la Vida Rural,"* three conferences by Professor Lynn Smith. Department of Sociology, Bogota, 1965.

ACPO. *Las Pequeñas—Grandes Campañas de Acción Cultural Popular*. Documento elaborado por Pbro. José Ramón Sabogal como Ponencia para el Seminario sobre la Obra Diocesana y Parroquial de ACPO. Sutatenza, 1966.

ACPO. Memories of the *Congreso Cultural de la Habana, Speech by Monsignor German Guzman*, January, 1968.

ACPO. *El Campesino* Library, various years.

ACPO. *Selected Music*. Audio-record, various materials. (n.d.)

ACPO. Internal documents (n.d.), ACPO Archival Collection.

ACPO. *Agrarian Reform Campaign*, various materials. (n.d.)

Bernal Alarcón, Hernando. *Educación Fundamental Integral. Teoría y Aplicación en el Caso de ACPO. Serie Educación Fundamental Integral*. Bogotá, Editorial Andes, 1978.

Houtart, Francisco, and Gustavo Pérez. *Acción Cultural Popular. Sus Principios y Medios de Acción. Consideraciones Teológicas y Sociológicas*. Bogotá, Editorial Andes, 1960. ACPO Archival Collection.

Salcedo, Jose Joaquín. *Mensaje de la Dirección General a los colaboradores de la Institución*, 1973.

Young, Michael, and Helen Brauer. *Notas sobre las Escuelas Radiofónicas de Colombia*. In *Educación Fundamental Integral. Teoría y Aplicación en el Caso de ACPO*. Hernando Bernal Alarcón. Serie Educación Fundamental Integral, vol. 1. Bogotá: Editorial Andes, 1978: 91–117. ACPO Archival Collection.

GENERAL CONCLUSION

Moses O. Biney, Kenneth N. Ngwa, and Raimundo C. Barreto

This collection of essays offers a hermeneutical approach to the study of religion in relation to place, time, ideology, and community. A confluence of globalization, technological transformations, human migrations within and across national borders, and persistent colonial and postcolonial ideologies of extraction, marginalization, and even death has produced multiple "crisis" moments and places for the world, as well as creative responses.

In an often-cited essay about the historical origins of the ecological crisis published in 1967,[1] Lynn White Jr. developed a religious and theological theory for the crisis. The main question driving the work was hermeneutical: "What did Christianity tell people about their relations with the environment?" To answer this question, White examined the teleological (non-repetitive and linear) concept of time that Western Christianity had inherited from Judaism, and a particular conceptualization of creation in which the Genesis story depicts an apparently loving deity gradually bringing creation into existence, starting with non-human life and ultimately culminating with the human (male) placed in a garden—perhaps an urbanized view of space. As White saw it, "God planned all of this for man's benefit and rule: no item in the physical creation had any purpose save to serve man's purposes."[2] Such theological and urban "planning" however produced a Manichean split between humans and the earth, and would manifest itself in what White describes as Christianity's destruction of pagan animism as the first step toward the exploitation of nature "in a mood of indifference to the feelings of natural objects."[3] This split, which White also explored in terms of social class, had devastating effects on nature:

---

[1] Lynn White Jr., "The Historical Roots of our Ecological Crisis," *Science: New Series* 155, no. 3767 (1967): 1203–1207.
[2] White, "Historical Roots," 1205.
[3] White, "Historical Roots," 1205.

At the level of the common people, this worked out in an interesting way. In Antiquity every tree, every spring, every stream, every hill had its own genius loci, its guardian spirit. These spirits were accessible to men, but were very unlike men; centaurs, fauns, and mermaids show their ambivalence. Before one cut a tree, mined a mountain, or dammed a brook, it was important to placate the spirit in charge of that particular situation, and to keep it placated. By destroying pagan animism, Christianity made it possible to exploit nature in a mood of indifference to the feelings of natural objects.

White then addressed the apparent attempt to remake or substitute for the lost spirituality:

It is often said that for animism the Church substituted the cult of saints. True; but the cult of saints is functionally quite different from animism. The saint is not in natural objects; he may have special shrines, but his citizenship is in heaven. Moreover, a saint is entirely a man; he can be approached in human terms. In addition to saints, Christianity of course also had angels and demons inherited from Judaism and perhaps, at one remove, from Zoroastrianism. But, these were all as mobile as the saints themselves. The spirits in natural objects, which formerly had protected nature from man, evaporated. Man's effective monopoly on spirit in this world was confirmed, and the old inhibitions to the exploitation of nature crumbled.[4]

White was sensitive to the generalizing claims in his essay, arguing for contextual and theological variety in assessing the history of the world, its technological developments, its theological credos and cultural meaning-making processes, and its biblical interpretations. Nevertheless, White was forceful in his claims about Christianity's role in providing the critical framework for the ecological crisis; he talked about Christian missionaries "chopping down sacred groves, which are idolatrous because they assume spirit in nature," and openly claimed that "more science and more technology are not going to get us out of the present ecologic crisis until we find a new religion, or rethink our old one."[5] Although White considered the religious tradition of Zen Buddhism as constituting a potential antidote to the ecological crisis, he ultimately considered the tradition too alien to his Western audience to have lasting impact. So, he turned to the work of Saint Francis of Assisi who "tried to depose man from his monarchy over creation and set up a democracy of all God's creatures. With him the ant is no longer simply a homily for the lazy, flames a sign of the thrust of the soul toward union with God; now they are Brother Ant and Sister Fire, praising the Creator in their own ways as Brother Man does in his."[6]

---

4   White, "Historical Root," 1205.
5   White, "Historical Roots," 1206.
6   White, "Historical Roots," 1206.

General Conclusion

The language of "democracy of all God's creatures" puts the theological task right in the middle of the modern Western discourse about individual autonomies within specific governing ideologies and processes. What the language does not do, though, is to explain the traumas inflicted on non-Western epistemologies and political systems through processes that upscale privileged individual autonomies into the production and regulation of nation-states (e.g., colonialism, racism) and their extracting economies. The question is not simply about the extreme focus on anthropocene ideology to the detriment of the non-human life; it is not simply that humans ought to allow the ants and fires to sing their own songs in their own ways. The central issue—one made particularly acute for postcolonies and their subjects—is what to do with the traumas that have been unleashed at the violent intersections of politics, religion, race, urbanization, identity, and ecology. The postcolonial urban Christian subject and community—very much like the rural Christian subject—does not really have the privilege of theorizing individual autonomy, much less implementing it. The monotony of mono-thinking (and mono-autonomy) is the foundational origin of the current stressors of World Christianity.

The proper response to the theological, historical, biblical, and sociological challenges of humankind's religious, spatial, and even ontological processes of self-definition and existence is not to retreat into the enclaves of nativism and individualism. The solution lies in developing communitarian theories and hermeneutics infused with ideological and ethical commitments to human and non-human flourishing. This commitment may manifest in the form of sustainability of holistic living; it may also manifest in the form of resistance against oppressive and extracting machineries. What hermeneutics offers as a method of being and belonging is an epistemological mode of communal belonging that infuses accountability into the social contracts and processes that hold together World Christianity, Urbanization, and Identity.

The rise of nationalist and ethnonationalist movements around borders represents a real threat to human and non-human flourishing. And the decline in nineteenth and early twentieth century forms of religious expression and belonging in the West cannot be analyzed simply in contrast to the rapid expansion of Christianity in the majority world. Such binary modes of engaging and theorizing World Christianity, Urbanization, and Identity cannot and do not adequately capture the multiplicity, the contextual nuances, the cultural dynamics, and institutional apparatuses that make religion travel and settle and take new forms. Colonial and postcolonial rural-to-urban migrations and growth are not totalizing, nor do they completely rupture the social, emotional, spiritual, and political affinity to the rural space. Because of the anxieties associated with urbanization and globalization, we have also signaled that there is no need to commit the opposite error and retract into rural enclaves or to create unnecessary nostalgias about the rural place, in opposition to the urban space.

This book, therefore, without exhaustive ambitions, advances a number of creative hermeneutical tools to engage multifaceted urban-rural relations informing the complex processes of identity formation in the city and beyond. It is a book about reimagining urban spaces and relations, particularly in postcolonial contexts. There are aspects of such reimagination that are not covered in this volume or which only appear in passing. Some of those emphases will be more fully addressed in the three final volumes of this series. The religious-plurality particularly characteristic of urban environments and the interreligious relations imperative that derivates from it will be addressed in volume 4. The impact of urbanization on the environment and the discussion of sustainable ways of life will be the central concern of volume 5. Finally, the racialization of contemporary societies—especially visible in urban spaces—and matters related to gender and sexual difference in World Christianity scholarship will be the focus of the sixth and final volume of this series.

Although the book does not address every issue related to urbanization and World Christianity, Urbanization, and Identity—as no single book of this size is capable of doing— it challenges religious practitioners and scholars to re-envision and re-think how they do practical ministry in the urban context as well as how they write about it. Coincidentally, many of the authors of this volume, including all its three editors, teach in seminaries. In these and many Christian seminaries, particularly those located in and near cities, courses and practicums that focus on ministry in the urban context are offered. Additionally, many of the students who are trained here serve as ministers and teachers in urban centers. For this reason, theological education cannot be oblivious to the changes and challenges of urban life. It is our hope that this book will sensitize theological educators to address the key question, "What kind of theological education is necessary to adequately engage urbanization, and its prospect of increase?" In other words, "What challenges and opportunities does urbanization present for theological education?" and, "What responses must theological/religious educators offer for now and the future?"

Our work has attempted to address these issues around four major categories. First, conceptually, we have refrained from examining the relation between Christianity, Urbanization, and Identity as distinct "fields" of study. It is an approach that transgresses disciplinary modes of knowledge production and circulation, top-down social organization and regulation, and a privileging of nation-state or denominational citizenship.

Our work is conceptualized as inherently communal, not singular; power and theory are communal and contextual, not privatized and alien; and knowledge is intersectional and elastic, not binary, bloated, or brittle.

Second, contestation (not conflict) defines the study and material expression of World Christianity, Urbanization, and Identity. This contestation brings Christianity into conversation with other (indigenous) religious traditions; puts urban spaces in relation with rural and virtual spaces; and explores identity as an unsettled subject of being and belonging.

Third, we point to convergences. The excellence that has defined disciplinary studies in church history, theology, biblical interpretation, and anthropology is deployed for theorizing and conceptualizing an interdisciplinary approach to World Christianity, Urbanization, and Identity.

Finally, this work offers creative responses to ideologies, structures, and processes of oppression and marginalization. The multiple forms of Christianity in urban and rural spaces, as well as Christianity's interactions with indigenous knowledge traditions require attention to the creative agency of Christians in responding to the dynamics of a rapidly changing world.

BIBLIOGRAPHY

White, Lynn, Jr. "The Historical Roots of Our Ecological Crisis." *Science: New Series* 155, no. 3767 (March 10, 1967): 1203–1207.

INDEX

A

Acción Cultural Popular (ACPO) in Colombia 9, 257, 258, 260, 261, 264, 266, 271, 272, 273, 278, 279
Adogame, Afe 10, 11, 44, 58, 162, 164, 166, 167, 168, 169, 171, 177, 184, 198
African Christianity xvi, 108, 121, 161, 177, 201, 213, 214, 218
  non-missionary African Christianity 214
African churches in New York 161
African Independent churches 161
African Initiated Churches 167, 213
African Traditional Religion 7, 103, 107, 112, 113, 114
Agrarian Reform of 1936, the 266
Aihiokhai, SimonMary Asese 114, 119
Aitken, James 27, 28, 38
Albright, William 66, 78
alterity 48, 56, 57, 191
alternative reality 191, 192
Andalzúa, Gloria 57
anti-blackness 146, 147, 148, 149
anti-Judaism 36
Arabia 67, 69
Arab Protestant immigrants 148
Arendt, Hannah 50, 58

Armange, Marcos 129, 135, 140
Asian Americans 151, 152, 154, 156
assimilation 69, 112, 169, 171
Assmann, Hugo 55, 58
Augmented Reality 82, 87, 88, 89, 95, 97, 98
Augustine 5, 20, 21, 32, 38

B

Baker, Albert Weir 211, 212, 219
Baptist(s) xv, xvii, xviii, xxii, 34, 153, 171, 173, 174, 212, 216
Barreto Jr., Raimundo vii, viii, 1, 10, 11, 44, 186, 195, 235, 276, 281
Base Ecclesial Communities (CEBs) 228
Basel Missionaries 189
Bauman, Zygmunt 81, 82, 83, 84, 90, 92, 97
Baum, Robert M. 102, 104
Beck, Ulrich 46, 81, 83, 84
Berghen, Constan Vanden 102, 109, 115, 119
Bhabha, Homi K. 54
Bible xvi, xvii, xix, 5, 6, 7, 27, 28, 34, 38, 61, 62, 68, 75, 92, 111, 113, 123, 124, 125, 126, 133, 141, 167, 168, 217, 233, 245, 246, 250, 251
  popular reading of the 7, 123
Bobo, Lawrence 150, 151

Bonilla-Silva, Eduardo 150
border(s) x, 44, 50, 51, 52, 53, 56, 57, 86
  dynamics 51
  spatiality 51
  studies 49, 51
  the concept of 51
  the meaning of 51
Brazil xi, xii, xv, xvii, xviii, xix, 9, 16, 24, 25, 44, 91, 130, 131, 134, 138, 195, 223, 226, 227, 228, 229, 230, 232, 233, 235, 236
Brown, Deborah A. 244

C

Cain 28, 61
Canada xxi, 8, 44, 161, 164, 165, 166, 167, 168, 169, 170, 171, 172, 173, 177
  Manitoba viii, xxi, 161, 164, 168
  Winnipeg viii, xxi, 8, 161, 164, 165, 166, 167, 168, 169, 170, 171, 172, 173, 174, 175, 177
Canclini, Néstor García 45, 58
capitalism 17, 82, 83, 84, 85, 86, 87, 88, 95
Cardoso de Oliveira, Roberto 50, 58
Catholic xvii, xxi, 9, 66, 79, 101, 108, 109, 111, 113, 114, 118, 119, 165, 166, 232, 257, 258, 259, 261, 262, 263, 264, 265, 267, 271, 275, 276, 277
  action experience 262
  action experience/ movements 262, 263
  mission 109
  the Catholic church 271
  the Colombian Catholic Church 258, 259, 271

Catholicism viii, xxi, 257, 258, 259, 260, 261, 262, 263, 264, 265, 275, 276, 278
  a centrist 258, 261
  social Catholicism 258, 261, 278
Centro Ecumênico de Evangelização, Capacitação e Assessoria (CECA) viii, xx, 9, 223, 224, 227, 228, 229, 230, 232, 233, 237, 239
  Awareness-raising Project, the 232
  Ecumenical Training and Advisory Center 223, 227, 228
  Not So Sweet Home Project 232
  Popular Legal Agents (PLPs) viii, 9, 223, 224, 229, 230, 231, 232, 233, 234, 236, 237
  Youth Working against Gender-based Violence Project 232
China viii, xxii, 9, 16, 40, 166, 167, 205, 241, 242, 243, 244, 245, 246, 247, 248, 249, 250, 251, 252, 253, 254, 255, 256
  Chengdu Early Rain Reformed churches in Sichuan 249
  Shouwang Church 246, 247, 252, 256
  urban Christians 9, 196, 242, 243, 244, 245, 249, 252
  urban church 243, 244, 245, 246, 249, 252, 253
Chirico, Joann 47, 59
Choi, Ki Joo (KC) 151
Chow, Alexander 249, 252, 253, 256
Chow, Christie Chui-shan 246
Christian church(es) 243
Christian faith 81, 96, 189, 223, 242, 243, 245, 248, 250, 253

Christianity i, iii, v, vi, vii, viii, ix, x, xi, xii, xv, xvi, xvii, xviii, xix, xxi, xxii, 1, 2, 4, 5, 7, 8, 9, 10, 11, 29, 41, 44, 56, 58, 81, 82, 85, 87, 92, 94, 96, 101, 102, 103, 106, 107, 108, 109, 110, 111, 112, 113, 114, 115, 117, 118, 119, 120, 121, 145, 147, 148, 156, 157, 161, 163, 164, 165, 166, 167, 168, 169, 170, 171, 172, 173, 174, 175, 176, 177, 180, 182, 183, 184, 185, 186, 187, 189, 190, 191, 194, 195, 196, 197, 198, 199, 200, 201, 211, 212, 213, 214, 215, 216, 217, 218, 219, 223, 224, 229, 237, 241, 242, 243, 245, 246, 247, 248, 249, 251, 252, 253, 255, 256, 276, 277, 281, 282, 283, 284, 285

    polycentric 165, 166, 169, 173, 174

    Senegalese 117

    the Sinicization of 249

    urban Christianity in China 9, 242, 243, 253

    Western 85, 167, 185, 281

Christian mission(s) 183, 194, 199, 200

Christians ix, x, xi, xvii, xxi, 1, 8, 9, 20, 27, 29, 30, 31, 35, 36, 40, 41, 81, 82, 88, 91, 92, 93, 94, 95, 96, 101, 109, 111, 112, 114, 115, 118, 145, 146, 151, 153, 163, 167, 168, 174, 175, 180, 183, 189, 194, 196, 217, 241, 242, 243, 244, 245, 246, 247, 248, 249, 251, 252, 253, 255, 264, 285

    rural Christians 242, 245

    urban Christians in China 9, 245, 252

church-state relationship 248, 250

citizenship xi, 9, 20, 30, 31, 48, 53, 54, 76, 223, 227, 229, 231, 251, 252, 276, 282, 284

city 1, 2, 3, 5, 6, 8, 9, 10, 15, 16, 17, 19, 20, 21, 22, 23, 24, 25, 26, 27, 28, 29, 30, 31, 32, 33, 34, 35, 36, 37, 45, 61, 62, 63, 64, 65, 66, 72, 73, 75, 76, 77, 109, 110, 115, 116, 130, 138, 161, 164, 165, 166, 167, 168, 171, 176, 180, 182, 201, 207, 232, 233, 241, 247, 253, 284

    global cities 17, 180, 181, 182, 192, 194

    megacities 16, 72

    the right to the city 5, 26, 27, 31, 33, 34, 35, 36, 37

civil disobedience 245, 246, 247, 252, 253

civitas 15, 34

Colombia viii, 9, 74, 257, 258, 259, 260, 261, 262, 263, 265, 266, 267, 268, 274, 275, 276, 277, 278, 279

Colombian Catholic Church, the 258, 259, 271

colonialism 17, 46, 50, 53, 101, 148, 151, 215, 283

communism 260, 264, 265, 267, 268, 270, 275

Congo/ Democratic Republic of Congo, the 25, 104, 122, 166, 170, 204

    Kinshasa 25

constitutionalism 9, 242, 249

consumption 16, 86, 90, 93, 112, 181, 207

contestation(s) 7, 285

contingent dialectics 52

convergence(s) 2, 182, 183, 192, 194, 196

conversion 25, 114, 125, 126, 127, 135, 138, 168, 184, 185, 189, 243, 247, 252
Coptic Christians 167
Cormier, Marie-Christine 117, 119
Cosmopolis 18
Costa, Lúcio 24

D

De Boek, Filip 25
decolonial turn 49
deity 65, 67, 68, 106, 107, 113, 114, 281
   Almaqah 68
   Amm en Qataban 68
   Émit (Ala Émit) 106, 107
   Shams 68
   Sin 68
   Wadd 68
Developmentalism 257
diasporic studies 49
Diatta, Nazaire N. 101, 107, 111, 112, 113, 114, 117, 119
digitalization 6, 81, 82, 83, 85, 87, 90, 92, 95
Diola vii, xvii, 7, 101, 102, 104, 105, 106, 107, 108, 109, 110, 111, 112, 113, 114, 115, 116, 117, 118, 119, 121, 122
   Christianity vii, 7, 101, 102, 108, 111, 112, 118, 119
   customs 105
   migrants 110, 116
   people 7, 101, 105, 106, 107, 110, 111, 112, 113, 114, 115, 118
   religious practices 108
   (religious) thought and life 110
   Senegalese 101

(traditional) religion 102, 106, 107, 109, 111, 112
diversity xvii, 6, 23, 43, 45, 46, 47, 50, 56, 61, 123, 124, 126, 133, 136, 137, 138, 145, 146, 150, 164, 175, 182, 184, 186, 187, 189, 192, 228, 232, 237
   gender and sexual diversity xvii, 123, 124, 126, 133, 136, 137, 138
Dominican Republic 44, 148
Doniger, Wendy 190, 198
Dussel, Enrique 49

E

ecclesiology 33, 246, 247, 249, 253
ecumenism 9, 223, 228
El Campesino, the 260, 262, 264, 268, 269, 270, 271, 272, 274, 278, 279
Escobar, Arturo 49, 58, 257, 277
E.S. Grogan 205, 219
Essex, Barbara 140
Ethiopia 63
   Ethiopian Church 66, 213, 214, 216
   Ethiopianism viii, 201, 213, 215, 216, 217, 218
   Ethiopian Movement 213
exile(s) 50, 53, 54, 56

F

femicide 227, 235
Forman, Tyrone A. 150, 151, 156
Francis of Assisi, Saint 282
Frente Nacional, the 258, 259, 265, 275
Fulton, Breton 250, 251, 255

G

Gebara, Ivone 130, 131, 140, 225, 238
gender and sexuality 7, 124, 125, 127, 136
Gibeon 6, 62, 63, 64, 66, 72
Giddens, Anthony 81, 83, 84, 85, 97
globalization/ globalisation xi, 2, 4, 6, 37, 43, 44, 45, 46, 47, 49, 50, 56, 84, 181, 182, 187, 281, 284
Global North, the x, 181, 183
god/ goddess
    Astarte 69
    Athar 67
    Baal 70, 71
    Hadramaut 68
    Hathor 71
    Ishtar/ Isis 67, 71
    Qataban 68
    Shayba 68
    Sheba (Sabea) 66, 67, 68, 69, 71, 75, 78, 80
God/ God's xvii, 1, 6, 15, 20, 21, 24, 28, 31, 32, 33, 34, 36, 37, 38, 55, 56, 57, 59, 62, 63, 65, 69, 70, 71, 72, 74, 76, 95, 106, 114, 115, 118, 119, 125, 126, 127, 128, 133, 134, 136, 139, 140, 168, 182, 185, 189, 190, 191, 192, 193, 196, 197, 226, 244, 246, 247, 248, 249, 250, 253, 256, 265, 269, 281, 282, 283
    a colonizing vision of God 55
    presence 197
    purpose 192
    reign 192
    the image of 34, 55
    the kingdom of 34, 127
    the Triune 196
    will 226, 246
gold rush 202
Gómez, Liliana 23, 24, 25, 32, 39
Gornik, Mark R. 161, 177, 179, 196, 198
Goss, Robert 124, 125, 128, 133, 136, 140
Gottwald, Norman K. 29, 39
Griffin, David 47, 58
Grimes, Katie Walker 145, 147, 149, 156
Grimson, Alejandro 51, 52, 58

H

harem 63, 69, 71
Harvey, David 81, 84, 85, 86, 97
Heidorn, Lisa 63, 78
Hendricks Jr., Obery M. 36, 39
Hervieu-Léger, Danièle 83, 85, 92, 93
heterogeneity 7, 47, 49, 52, 53, 143, 144, 147, 149, 150, 152, 153, 154, 155, 190
He, Zhe 243, 244, 256
Hoffmann, Arzemiro 132, 133, 140
Holy Ghost Fathers, the 7, 101, 108, 110, 111, 112, 113
Holy Spirit, the 24, 33, 38, 40, 75, 193, 196
Hordge-Freeman, Elizabeth 148, 149, 156
house churches in China 249
Houtart, Francois 257, 260, 261, 264, 270, 272, 279
Huang, Haibo 251
Huang, Jianbo 245
human rights xix, xxi, 9, 223, 228, 229, 230, 231, 236, 242, 247, 248, 253

Hüyük, Çatal 22

I

identity(ies) x, xii, xvi, xix, 1, 2, 3, 4, 5, 6, 7, 8, 17, 31, 34, 37, 43, 45, 46, 47, 48, 49, 50, 51, 52, 53, 54, 81, 82, 83, 87, 89, 90, 91, 92, 93, 94, 95, 96, 104, 118, 123, 124, 125, 133, 134, 135, 137, 138, 139, 143, 144, 145, 146, 147, 149, 152, 153, 155, 162, 174, 183, 188, 190, 194, 195, 196, 237, 242, 247, 252, 259, 264, 271, 274, 283, 284, 285

    alternative identities 138

    formation(s) 3, 4, 7, 8, 43, 49, 50, 53, 83, 284

    regressive reifications of 143, 149

    transformation 155

    Western Christian religious identities 7, 87

imperialism 48, 148, 188

inculturation 101, 121

India viii, xviii, 145, 146, 179, 181, 182, 183, 185, 187, 188, 189, 190, 199, 200, 205

    the cities in 188

Indian American Christians 145

Indian American church 146

Indian American(s) 145, 146, 156

individualism 83, 85, 93, 95, 283

industrialization 8, 130, 201, 241, 258, 266, 267

Information and communication technologies (ICTs) 81, 82, 84, 86, 87, 88, 90, 91, 92, 93, 94, 95, 96

intercultural dialogue 54

intercultural leadership 182, 189, 190, 191, 192, 195

Ioanide, Paula 144, 146, 147, 150, 152, 153, 154, 156

Irvin, Dale T. vii, xix, 5, 15, 17, 39, 180, 181, 182, 184, 185, 192, 199

J

Jeroboam, King 63, 64

Jerusalem 6, 29, 30, 31, 32, 33, 34, 35, 36, 40, 41, 61, 62, 63, 64, 65, 66, 70, 75, 126

    the New Jerusalem 32, 33

Jesus/ Jesus Christ 5, 27, 29, 30, 31, 33, 34, 35, 36, 37, 38, 39, 41, 55, 56, 74, 82, 91, 95, 101, 110, 112, 113, 115, 121, 126, 127, 133, 136, 140, 153, 154, 174, 190, 193, 196

    lament over Jerusalem 35

    Roman Citizenship 30, 38

    the risen Christ 33, 34

John 2:16 36

John 18:37 193

John 20:21 196

John the Baptist 34

Josephus 31

Jun, Li 244, 252, 255

K

Keller, Catherine 56

Kim, Nadia Y. 147, 157

Kirk, J. Andrew 191

Korean immigrants 148

Kuandiya, (Hermann) Anandarao 189

Kuo, Henry 153, 154

Kurien, Prema 145

L

labor migration 204, 216
Lampard, Eric E. 21, 22, 39
Laurier, Wilfrid, Prime Minister, Canada 165
La Violencia 258, 259, 265, 266, 271
Lebret, Louis-Joseph 274, 278
Lefebvre, Henri 5, 17, 18, 26, 31, 37, 39
LGBTIQ(+) xix, 124, 133, 134, 135, 137, 138
liberation theology xviii, 123, 140, 263, 264, 277
Li, Ma 244, 252
Liu Wong, Maria 179, 196, 198
Lupton, Robert 196, 197, 199
Lutheran(s) 215, 216, 232, 250

M

Manga, Adrien 102, 109, 115, 119
Maritain, Jacques 264
Mark, Peter 103
Mar Thoma Church, the 145
Matsuda, Mari J. 154
Meeter, H. Henry 250
megachurch(es) 145, 156
Mennonite(s) 161, 165, 171
Methodist(s) xix, 1, 213, 216, 219
methodological nationalism 51
metropoles, the rise of 181
Metz, Johannes Baptist 153
Meyer, Cassie 192, 193, 199
Mignolo, Walter 49, 51, 53, 59
migrant communities 147, 149, 151, 164
migration(s) vii, viii, xv, 8, 10, 11, 17, 39, 44, 58, 111, 123, 147, 157, 159, 161, 162, 171, 177, 179, 181, 182, 183, 187, 188, 195, 198, 199, 201
  African 161, 177, 183, 198
  feminization 236
  global migration 2, 187
  labor migration 204, 216
  mass migration 4, 181, 182, 216
  sexual 7, 123, 125, 126, 127, 136, 138, 139
mimesis 53
missionary(ies) xi, xviii, 7, 8, 101, 102, 108, 109, 110, 111, 112, 114, 118, 162, 163, 172, 188, 196, 201, 202, 206, 211, 212, 213, 214, 215, 216, 217, 244, 282
  paternalism 212, 215
mission(s) xviii, 55, 58, 165, 171, 177, 180, 183, 189, 190, 191, 192, 194, 199, 200, 211, 212, 214, 215, 217, 274
modernity 49, 81, 82, 83, 84, 85, 87, 90, 92, 93, 95, 97, 98, 104, 119, 181, 261
modernization 242, 258, 259, 265, 266, 267, 272, 274, 275, 276
monotheism 6, 66, 76
Monsignor, Crisanto Luque, Archbishop of Bogotá, Colombia 264, 266, 267, 279
Mounier, Emmanuel 264
multicultural encounters 187, 188
multicultural leadership viii, 179
multilingualism 3
Mumford, Lewis 21, 22, 40
Myers, Garth 4, 5

N

National Pact for Combating Violence against Women 230, 236

Native Urban Area Act, the 207
North America xi, xii, 2, 16, 28, 161, 162, 163, 167, 168, 172, 173, 183
North, Frank Mason 1

P

Pachuau, Lalsangkima 185, 186, 199
Palmeri, Paulo 102, 107, 121
Parker, Richard 130, 131, 138
Patel, Eboo 192, 193
Paul, the Apostle 27, 29, 40, 101
people of color 151, 154, 155
Pérez, Gustavo 257, 260, 264, 272, 279
Plaskow, Judith 72, 79
plurality 45, 47, 48, 96, 182, 183, 189, 190, 284
Pontifical Council for Interreligious Dialogue and the World Evangelical
Alliance, the
193
postcolonial approaches 45, 49
postcolonialism 5, 48
postcolonial theory 49
Presbyterian(s)/ Presbytery, the xii, xv, xvi, xxi, 165, 167, 168, 171, 172, 177, 216
Prodigal Son, the vii, 7, 123, 126, 132, 140
prophecies 34, 65, 68, 75
prophetic message 191, 192
prophets 66, 191, 192
public discourse 249, 253
public disobedience and resistance 242, 249
publicness 9, 241, 242, 253
public theology vii, xviii, xxii, 43, 249, 253, 255

Q

Quijano, Anibal 46, 48, 49, 59

R

race 1, 103, 120, 144, 148, 150, 154, 156
  racial segregation 206, 215
  racial socialization 149
  racism 44, 144, 145, 150, 151, 152, 153, 154, 283
Radiophonic Schools 259, 261
Radio Sutatenza 260, 270, 273
Ras Shamra 70
Rauschenbusch, Walter 253, 255
Reformed church xv, 165, 214, 250, 256
Reformed theology 241, 242, 249
religious pluralism 55
Rieger, Joerg 56, 59
Rius-Caps, Josep 137
Rivera-Pagan, Luis 10, 53
Robertson, Roland 47
Roman Catholic(s) 165
Rome 20, 29, 30, 31, 38, 40
Roth, Wendy 147
Rousseff, Dilma Vana, President 227, 234, 235

S

Said, Edward 48, 50, 53
salvation, the Christian doctrine of 37
Sanneh, Lamin 108, 183
Sassen, Saskia 17, 19, 181
Schulte, Hannelis 62, 63
Scott, Allen J. 15, 18
Sebastian, Mrinalini 189
secularism 55, 143, 262

segregation 206, 215. *See also* race: racial segregation
Segundo, Juan Luis 56, 59, 126, 141
Senegal, West Africa xvii, 7, 101, 104, 107, 108, 109, 116, 117, 119, 121
Shining, Gao 243, 251
Sibilia, Paula 91, 97
Sifton, Clifford, Minister of the Interior, Canada 165
Soja, Edward J. 5, 11, 18, 22, 26, 27, 28, 34, 37, 40
solidarities 152
Solomon, King 69
South Africa viii, 8, 185, 201, 203, 204, 205, 206, 211, 212, 213, 214, 215, 216, 217, 218, 219
   Compounds 211, 212
   Johannesburg 201, 202, 203, 206, 208, 209, 212, 214
Spickard, James V. 162, 163, 164, 166, 167, 168, 169, 171, 177
Starr, Chloë 250, 256
Stöger, Alois 126, 127, 129, 135, 141
Storper, Michael 15, 18, 40
subjectivity(ies) 7, 46, 53, 54, 56, 82, 90, 91, 93, 95, 272, 275
   fetishism of subjectivity 90
Sun, Shangyang 243
synekism (synoecism) 18, 23

T

Temple (*hêkal*) 31, 36, 37, 38, 41, 62, 64, 65, 66, 76, 79, 80, 170, 171
   of Yahweh 66
   Solomonic 76
   Solomon's 6, 62, 63, 64, 65, 66, 70, 79, 80
Temple, William, Archbishop 37

Theology vii, xii, xv, xvi, xvii, xviii, xix, xx, xxii, 17, 24, 38, 39, 40, 43, 56, 57, 59, 123, 140, 151, 154, 156, 173, 179, 181, 198, 244, 247, 249, 251, 253, 255, 256, 263, 264, 277
   liberation theology xviii, 123, 140, 263, 264, 277
   public theology xxii, 224, 229
   reformed theology 241, 242, 249
Thills, Gustave 264
Thomas, Louis-Vincent 102, 109, 110, 116
Three-Self church structure 245, 247
Three-Self Patriotic Movement (TSPM) 242, 244, 245, 247
Tiede, David L. 127, 128, 129, 130, 132, 141
Torres, Camilo F. 79, 264, 270, 271, 279
Trinity, the doctrine of the 33

U

Ukrainian Orthodox 165
Urbanism viii, 21, 23, 38, 223
urbanization/ urbanisation xii, 1, 2, 3, 4, 5, 6, 8, 16, 18, 27, 37, 61, 130, 143, 145, 147, 153, 180, 182, 183, 186, 187, 188, 189, 190, 191, 192, 194, 195, 196, 197, 241, 242, 244, 283, 284
   global urbanization 16
   process 18
   the intensity of urbanisation 191
Usarski, Frank 24, 25, 41

V

Vala, Carsten 244

Van Herck, Walter 23, 24, 25, 32, 39, 41
Vansina, Jan 103, 104, 122
virtual/ virtuality 82, 87, 88, 89, 92, 94, 95, 96, 127, 285
   virtual spaces 82, 88, 92, 95, 285

W

Walsh, Catherine 49
Wenzel, João Inácio 126, 128, 141
Wesley, Charles 36
White Jr., Lynn 10, 281
Witwatersrand Native Labour Association, the (WNLA) 204
Womack, Deanna Ferree 147, 148, 157
women xvi, xix, xxi, 9, 35, 62, 66, 68, 69, 70, 71, 72, 74, 75, 76, 117, 127, 130, 173, 184, 185, 186, 187, 195, 223, 224, 225, 226, 227, 229, 230, 231, 233, 234, 235, 236, 237, 238, 242, 268
   female evangelical politicians 74
   female leaders 74
   female ordination 226
   the denial of 76
   the recognition of 74
   violence against women xxi, 9, 224, 225, 227, 229, 233, 235, 237
World Christianity i, iii, v, vi, vii, viii, ix, x, xi, xii, xv, xviii, xix, xxii, 1, 2, 4, 5, 8, 10, 11, 44, 58, 161, 163, 164, 167, 170, 171, 172, 173, 175, 180, 182, 183, 184, 185, 186, 187, 189, 190, 191, 195, 196, 198, 199, 200, 246, 255, 276, 277, 283, 284, 285
   polycentric 8
   salient features of 185
   the necessity for World Christianity 185
   the study of World Christianity 183, 186
World Council of Churches, the 193, 194, 195, 232

Y

Yahweh 29, 39, 64, 65, 66, 69, 70, 72
Yang, Fenggang 245, 249
Ying, Fuk-tsang 246, 248
Yuan, Hao 247, 252

Z

zonah, zonoth 62

Symbols

95 Theses, the 249, 250, 256

Old Testament

Genesis 2:8 28
Genesis 2:15 28
Genesis 3:8 28
Genesis 4:16 28
Exodus 15 70
Exodus 15:20 65
Joshua 10:5 62
Joshua 10:12 62
1 Samuel 10:5 65
1 Samuel 10:10; 19:20–23 65
2 Samuel 7:1 64
2 Samuel 7:5–7 64
1 Kings 3:1–3 62
1 Kings 3:4–15 62
1 Kings 3:5 62
1 Kings 3:16–28 62
1 Kings 4 62
1 Kings 5 62, 63
1 Kings 6–8 62
1 Kings 6:26 65
1 Kings 6:31–36 64
1 Kings 6:33–34 65
1 Kings 6:37 64
1 Kings 7:1 64
1 Kings 7:17–20 67
1 Kings 9:2 62
1 Kings 10:1–13 67
1 Kings 11:1–8 70
1 Kings 11:14–25 64
1 Kings 11:26–40 64
2 Kings 3:15 65
2 Kings 4:1–7 66
2 Kings 5 65
2 Kings 8:20 64
1 Chronicles 17:3–7 64
Isaiah 56:6–7 36
Jeremiah 29:5 28
Jeremiah 44 66, 75
Jeremiah 44:15 66

New Testament

Matthew 3:2 34
Matthew 3:5 34
Matthew 22:1–14 35
Matthew 22:15–22 30
Matthew 23:37–39 35
Mark 5:9 30
Mark 11:17 36
Luke 2:22–38 34
Luke 4:18–19 37
Luke 8:19–21 137
Luke 9:51–19:28 126
Luke 13:33–35 35
Luke 14:15–23 35
Luke 14:21 35
Luke 15:11–32 124, 125, 126, 127, 136, 137, 140
Luke 23:43 36
Acts 10–11 114
Acts 10:34–35 114
Galatians 3:13 33
Ephesians 5:23 74
Philippians 3:20a 31
Colossians 1:15 34
Hebrews 11:10 15, 37
Revelation 7:9 32
Revelation 11 32
Revelation 21:22 31, 32
Revelation 21:24 32
Revelation 21:25 32
Revelation 22:2 32
Revelation 22:3 32